Behind
the
Factory Walls

Behind
the
Factory Walls

DECISION MAKING

IN SOVIET AND US ENTERPRISES

by
Paul R. Lawrence
Charalambos A. Vlachoutsicos

Igor Faminsky
Eugene Brakov

Sheila Puffer   Alexander Naumov
Elise Walton   Vitale Ozira

Editors, US Edition
Paul R. Lawrence
Charalambos A. Vlachoutsicos

Foreword by Adam B. Ulam

Harvard Business School Press
Boston, Massachusetts

94   93   92   91   90   5   4   3   2   1

The recycled paper used in this publication meets the
requirements of the American National Standard for
Permanence of Paper for Printed Library Materials Z39.49-1984.

Library of Congress Cataloging-in-Publication Data

Behind the factory walls : decision making in Soviet and US
    enterprises / Paul R. Lawrence . . . [et al.]. — US ed. / editors,
    Paul Lawrence, Charalambos A. Vlachoutsicos.
        p.   cm.
    Includes bibliographical references.
    ISBN 0-87584-224-0 (alk. paper)
    1. Industrial management—Soviet Union—Decision making.
    2. Industrial management—United States—Decision making.
    3. Comparative management.   I. Lawrence, Paul R.
    II. Vlachoutsicos, Charalambos A., 1931-
    HD70.S63B395   1990
    658.4'03'0947—dc20   89-71723
                                                          CIP

Contents

PART I
Theory and Context

PART II

Field Research on Decision Making

PART III

Comparative Decision-Making Patterns

PART IV
Appendices

Foreword

by Adam B. Ulam
Director of Russian Research Center
Harvard University

There was a time when the reputation of the Soviet economy stood high in the West, and not only among left-wing sectors of public opinion. Unlike Europe of the 1930s, mired in the Great Depression, the USSR was one country not suffering from mass unemployment. The Russian peasant, unlike the American farmer, was not paid to curtail crops but given every incentive to produce as much as possible. Few in the West had an inkling of the real state of affairs under communism and of the frightful price the Soviet people were paying for Stalin's "great leap forward." Even after 1945 and the coming of the Cold War, outside observers with little or no sympathy for Moscow's ideology could still speak with respect about the Soviets' achievements in constructing a planned economy and thus avoiding what was then referred to as the "anarchy of the free market," which after a brief postwar boom was bound to plunge capitalism into another major depression. Nor do we forget those, again not left wing, but dispassionate analysts of the Soviet scene who professed to see the USSR of the 1930s and 1940s as undergoing a "managerial revolution," with its economic life increasingly run by pragmatists rather than ideologues. The rapid recovery of Soviet industry from the devastation of the war, the attraction of the "Soviet model" of modernization for the new nation, and the undeniably steady—if not spectacular—rise in the living standard during the two post-Stalin decades all seemed to attest to the essential soundness of the Soviet economy.

Today not only Western analysts, but also the great majority of Soviet economists have recognized that such appraisals, if not actually the products of misperception, were at least greatly oversimplified. The stagnation of the latter Brezhnev period and the present parlous state of the Soviet economy are now recognized to have been caused by the inherent flaws of the entire socioeconomic system. Glasnost has revealed to the Soviet people the enormous and incommensurate human costs of such feats of social engineering as forced collectivization and the hurried industrialization of the Stalin era. But quite apart from the moral consideration, the methods that secured rapid industrial growth in those years—a blend of coercion and ideological indoctrination—are simply ineffective when applied to the requirements of modern technology and industrial development, and unthinkable in a society that is trying to emancipate itself from authoritarianism.

Thus perestroika, from one point of view, is a reaffirmation of common sense. Nowhere else is this reaffirmation more necessary yet more difficult than in the sphere of economics. For some sixty years now, platitudinous propaganda slogans and ideological superstitions both obscured and contributed to the debilitating ailments of the Soviet economy. And now the regime faces the hard task of providing material incentives and resuscitating the farming skills of the peasantry and of importing fresh dynamism to the industrial sector, where the dead hand of bureaucracy has for long weighed heavily on manager and worker alike.

Of course, a change for the better depends heavily on the policies determined at the national level and on the pace of the political reform. But what happens at the industry and factory level is also of great importance in determining to what extent the industrial cadres can become imbued with the entrepreneurial spirit as they discard old and bad bureaucratic habits and inhibitions. It is on this count that a study such as this one is both important and interesting. In this book we have an account not merely of decision making, but of the dilemmas of modern industrial life in general, drawn from the experience of the management of select Soviet and American enterprises. Here we see the problems of factory management and labor relations not through the prism of abstract theories and competing philosophies, but through the open window of everyday concrete experience. As such, the project and the book should be of great help to Soviet economic planners and administrators, but I believe it will be equally instructive to American business people and entrepreneurs. And the general reader should be grateful for this close look at an important segment of Soviet reality during a time of great change. The editors and researchers of the project are to be congratulated for this painstaking and illuminating joint venture.

Acknowledgments

We want to express deep appreciation to the four enterprises that were the subjects of our study and that must remain anonymous. In every instance cooperation was undertaken in a spirit of friendship and warm hospitality. Their participation required the commitment of significant amounts of time from personnel at all organizational levels. It meant tolerating and responding to probing questions and reviewing the manuscript to catch errors and add clarifying facts. All the people involved made a significant contribution to increasing our knowledge of systems of management and to building bridges of human understanding. We gratefully acknowledge their public service.

We want to thank our families for their dedicated support of this project. Special recognition goes to the field researchers' families, who not only tolerated their long absences during field trips but also, in each case, assumed extra and demanding parental responsibilities.

We benefited from the expert criticism and counsel of three distinguished Soviet scholars: Joseph Berliner, who reviewed the sections on Soviet theory and context; Loren Graham, who reviewed the section on Soviet theory; and Edward Keenan, who reviewed the section on Soviet culture. Furthermore, we are particularly grateful to Adam Ulam for writing the foreword.

The work of the Soviet team was supported at numerous points by fellow staff members at the Institute of External Economic Affairs. Alexei Maximov was especially helpful in arranging for site visits in the Soviet Union; he participated in some of the field work and provided helpful assistance in translation. Anatole Zhuplev did background research and the initial draft of the Soviet sections of Chapters 2 and 3. Tatiana Artemova did background research and contributed to the initial draft of Appendix

A. Galina Petrova performed similar services for the Soviet section on legal requirements. Larissa Korshanova helped with site visits and translations.

We wish to thank Chryssi Inglessi and Martha Lawrence for their valuable ideas and critical suggestions.

We appreciate the help of gifted professionals who assisted in guiding the US edition through the involved processes of editing, production, and marketing. We particularly want to thank Eliza Collins, Marilyn Shepherd, Carol Beckwith, Carol Franco, Natalie Greenberg, and Paula Duffy.

We owe a special debt of gratitude to Rita Perloff. Her role as administrative assistant to the US editors was vital. She handled complicated arrangements for travel and working sessions, oversaw preparation of the manuscript, and acted as communication coordinator for the entire project.

The sponsoring institutions were consistently generous in support of this project. At the Harvard Business School Dean John McArthur and Professor Jay Lorsch, Senior Associate Dean for Research, offered encouragement and financial assistance at every stage of the work. Ivan Ivanov, Vice Chairman of the State Foreign Economic Commission, which has responsibility for IEEA, was equally supportive of the research.

While all these considerable contributions are gratefully acknowledged, the authors take full responsibility for the work.

P.R.L.   C.A.V.

I.F.   E.B.

S.F.   E.W.

A.N.   V.O.

PART
I

Theory and Context

Chapter 1

A Comparative Study of Soviet and American Management Systems

This book is about the ways that managers make decisions in two very different countries, the Soviet Union and the United States. It is based on a pioneering 1988 study in which researchers from both countries, working together as a team, studied managerial work patterns in roughly comparable enterprises in each nation. The study was undertaken in the belief that a better understanding of the ways of work could increase the chances of success for joint business ventures between US and USSR enterprises, and that such successful ventures would contribute significantly to an improved overall relationship between the two nations.

By 1987 the political mood in the USSR was changing dramatically. General Secretary Mikhail Gorbachev had initiated a policy called glasnost (openness), which led to multiple exchanges of many kinds with the West; for the first time in decades, Soviet citizens could speak openly about issues facing the nation. The second, more difficult and ambitious, arm of Gorbachev's domestic reform movement was perestroika (restructuring). Perestroika entailed nothing less than a sweeping revision of the Soviet Union's political and economic systems.

Glasnost and perestroika were complemented by dramatic moves in foreign affairs. The United States and the USSR began to ameliorate their intense adversarial relationship, the cold war of the past 45 years. While maintaining their national security concerns, both countries are now committed to acting jointly and cooperatively in as many areas as possible. Joint activities for mutual benefit have emerged as a practical response to the imperatives of global survival. Doing things together increases understanding of each other's systems and values and in itself becomes an effective way of reducing tension. Business ventures are a principal form of joint activity.

Joint business ventures between our two countries offer an opportunity for long-term cooperation with significant mutual benefits. Both nations

3

know that in the emerging era of the global marketplace, joint ventures and other forms of business alliance can help firms build their competitive strength and market share. On the one hand, the Soviet Union is too big a part of the globe for any US firm engaged in international activities to ignore for long. On the other hand, given its concern with modernization and improved living standards, the Soviet Union cannot ignore the technical and managerial sophistication of the United States. The success or failure of US–USSR joint ventures is of vital interest to both government and industry. In fact, these ventures may be the crucial test of whether the two systems and cultures can cooperate effectively at this stage of history. For these reasons it is important that joint ventures be given the best possible chance to succeed.

Until recently, both sides have focused the greatest attention on working out mutually acceptable agreements for the startup of joint ventures. But now that joint ventures are actually forming in significant numbers,[1] the need to address *operating issues* becomes more and more pressing.

Operating issues in any joint venture are difficult to manage, even for partners with a common cultural background. US-Soviet joint ventures will be more difficult because the partners have no shared cultural heritage and little shared management knowledge. Because few American and Soviet managers have experience with each other's systems, they are likely to hold distorted views of each other. Accurate information about each country's customary management practices and expectations is essential.

Given the need for information on comparative management practices, Paul Lawrence and Charalambos Vlachoutsicos developed the basic ideas for this research project and proposed it to the Soviets. A fortuitous partnership resulted in late 1987 between researchers from the Harvard Business School and the Institute of External Economic Affairs (IEEA), the research arm of the Foreign Economic Commission. Because perestroika had created the Foreign Economic Commission to coordinate all forms of foreign economic activity in the USSR, the IEEA had both the responsibility and the resources to conduct research in support of joint ventures. Early in 1988, these partners reached a detailed agreement to conduct the proposed joint research project. Every aspect of the project was to be shared on a balanced, fifty-fifty basis. Both sides were to provide equal financing for the research, and both were to be involved at all stages of collection, analysis, and presentation of research data. Leaders from each side were to have parallel roles.

A research team was formed to carry out the project. Professor Igor Faminsky, head of the IEEA, and Professor Paul Lawrence of the Harvard

1. In late 1989, 1,106 joint ventures with Western companies had been officially registered in the Soviet Union.

Business School were named academic directors. Eugene Brakov, director general of Zil Motors and a member of the USSR Economic Commission, and Charalambos Vlachoutsicos, a Greek businessman and Harvard research fellow long engaged in trade with the USSR, became practitioner directors. These directors, in turn, recruited a four-person field research team from management scholars with special training in both cultures. The Soviet scholars, Alexander Naumov and Vitale Ozira, each had spent a year in the United States doing management graduate work, Naumov at the MIT Sloan School and Ozira at the Harvard Business School. The two US organizational behavior scholars, Sheila Puffer and Elise Walton, had worked and studied in socialist countries, Puffer in the USSR and Walton in Yugoslavia.

With our team in place, we faced some key research decisions. We were clear about the purpose and framework of our study: we wanted to develop a better understanding of managerial decision-making behavior in each country. By doing that, we hoped to shed light on some important questions. Would it actually be possible for Soviet and US managers to cooperate effectively in the management of joint ventures in the USSR? What kinds of accommodations would have to be made? What attitudes would need to be brought to bear? Whereas technical know-how is directly transferable, we knew that managerial systems are not. For a joint venture to succeed, it would have to create an amalgam of US and Soviet managerial systems; recognition of important differences and similarities would be essential. Only then could the very intricate process of adjustment and integration take place, allowing the features of both systems and cultures to work in harmony. Only then would managers of joint ventures be able to reach decisions that would be realistic in both the cultural and the economic environments of the Soviet Union.

To pursue our purpose we decided to do a qualitative, in-depth study of two enterprises in each country and two factory sites at each enterprise. This would make a total of four sites in each country. The aim was to study roughly comparable industries. As matters developed, we were able to gain access to study truck engine and electrical equipment enterprises in each country. The USSR sites were in the Great Russian and the Ukrainian republics; the US sites were in midwestern, southern, and eastern states. We initiated our research in the United States. The four field researchers worked together for approximately two weeks at each of the eight sites. It will be apparent to readers that these sites represent but a small sample of the regional and industrial diversity of each country.

We focused our field questions and observations on four decision issues: the formation and implementation of an annual business plan, the hiring and firing of managers, the acquisition of capital equipment, and the introduction of new products. These issues gave us the opportunity to inquire about such central functions as finance, procurement, marketing, human resource management, manufacturing, and overall planning. Because the issues crossed functional lines, we believed they would be particularly revealing of underlying decision patterns.

We explored the four issues by tracking specific decision situations. For each decision studied, we examined not only the moment of choice, but also all available facts about predecision activity and the action (or inaction) of implementation. Since many of the decision episodes we studied were in the implementation phase, we reconstructed earlier events by interviewing key players. We observed where the decision sequence was initiated; how the action cycled and recycled from role to role, group to group, and level to level; who made the key choice; who influenced that choice; and what were the dominant arguments in the choice.

These basic decisions about our research design were predicated on the working assumption that underneath the variations created by type of industry, company culture, and decision, there would be certain patterns characteristic of each system. We believed that both parties in a joint venture would need to take these persistent patterns and customs into account for a working relationship to be effective.

We explored these decision patterns at the level of theory as well as of practice. In terms of theory we examined relevant ideas, values, and norms, as publicly articulated in each society. Our theoretical examination also included the cultural context, the historical evolution of economic institutions, and relevant external constraints.

We discovered that openness or glasnost was a reality in both countries. With only minor exceptions, all the enterprises were open and responsive to our requests and questions. We had the opportunity to interview personnel at all levels and to attend regular management meetings. We routinely audiotaped all these sessions. A videographer accompanied us for a portion of our stay in each enterprise to record some meetings and interviews. We observed managers going about their daily activities and were granted access to relevant documents. In fact, given the history of caution with which Soviets in particular have regarded Western contacts until the recent past, we were especially gratified by the candor at all levels.

To the best of our knowledge, our study represents the first time US scholars have been able to conduct in-depth, on-the-spot research in Soviet factories, or that Soviet scholars have had such access to US factories.

As the reader may recognize, we faced some unusual issues in the final presentation of our research material. For example, we decided that in keeping with the completely shared nature of the project, we would prepare a single book, even though this meant that it would have to address two distinctly different audiences.[2] A by-product of this decision was that some chapters cover both US and USSR material, with roughly half being more familiar to one audience than to the other. Nonetheless, we believe a reader will find the more familiar sections valuable as summaries and points of comparison. It is important, moreover, to bear in mind that the material about context and theory has been written in the way each side sees itself. In some instances this may be different from the way the other side would have portrayed it.

It is equally important to bear in mind that the study underlying this book was a first-time event and can offer only a limited mapping of a largely unknown and diverse territory. For this reason we have chosen to present full and detailed descriptions of what we observed. Our interpretations focus on the implications for joint ventures. We hope our descriptive material lends itself to drawing out other conclusions for other purposes. For example, the material may be of use to trading partners or even in government-to-government relations.

Finally, we want to remind the reader that managerial systems are not static in either country; they are in a state of flux. This is true in the United States, where we found more rapid change and more diversity than we had anticipated, and it is certainly true in the Soviet Union. We were fortunate to be able to observe close-up the early evidence of perestroika reforms being implemented in Soviet factories, but in reporting these observations we recognize that any substantive conclusions about their effect would be premature.

For those readers who have a focused interest in creating and operating joint ventures in the USSR, we must explain that we studied state enterprises instead of joint ventures because existing joint ventures are still too few and too new to teach us much of value about operating issues. With the recent small-scale exception of cooperatives, all Soviet enterprises are state enterprises, and they are the logical partners for joint ventures with Western firms. State enterprises operate under a different set of laws and regulations than do joint ventures, and the rules governing joint ventures are themselves changing.[3] Regardless of the laws and regulations, however, we are convinced that any joint venture in the USSR must come to terms with the customary thought processes and behavior of Soviet managers and the Soviet government. It is at this more basic and persistent level that our findings can be of use to American managers of joint ventures.

Our book is organized into four parts. Part I presents some traditional

2. The Soviet edition will be the same as the US one, except that it will be printed in Russian with editorial notes by the Soviet authors. Plans call for it to be published at the same time as the US edition and made widely available throughout the Soviet Union.
3. See Appendices A and B for a summary of the current Soviet joint venture rules.

cultural characteristics of each society, historical reviews of each nation's economic institutions, and reviews of contemporary theory on managerial decision making in each system. Part II presents background on the research process and on the field study sites. It also contains the detailed descriptions of actual decision episodes organized around the four decision issues. As the reader will see in Chapter 5, we have followed the convention of disguising the names of the companies, locations, and individuals. In Part III we state our observations, emphasizing those relevant to the operation of joint ventures. For example, we offer insights on influence patterns, basic assumptions about hierarchical systems, and phases of the decision process. With such insights we pinpoint the elements of US management theory and practice that we believe can be absorbed usefully by the Soviet environment to help joint ventures function effectively. We also select aspects of the Soviet management system that we believe would be wise and probably essential to incorporate in any joint venture. We hope that the double collaborative nature of all phases of the project (Soviet-American and academic-practitioner) constitutes a firm ground for generating realistic and useful observations. These elements, diagrammed in Exhibit 1.1, have provided the framework for all phases of the study. Part IV summarizes current Soviet laws and regulations covering joint ventures in the USSR; there we offer suggestions for arranging and negotiating joint ventures.

We hope the reader will develop an appreciation for the ways joint ventures between US and USSR partners can be operated successfully. We believe that an imperative ingredient of success is an understanding of the distinctive aspects of each other's management systems. Operating guidelines based on this understanding can go a long way toward resolving differences and building on complementary strengths. Our book is intended as a contribution toward creating such an understanding.

EXHIBIT 1.1   Research Model

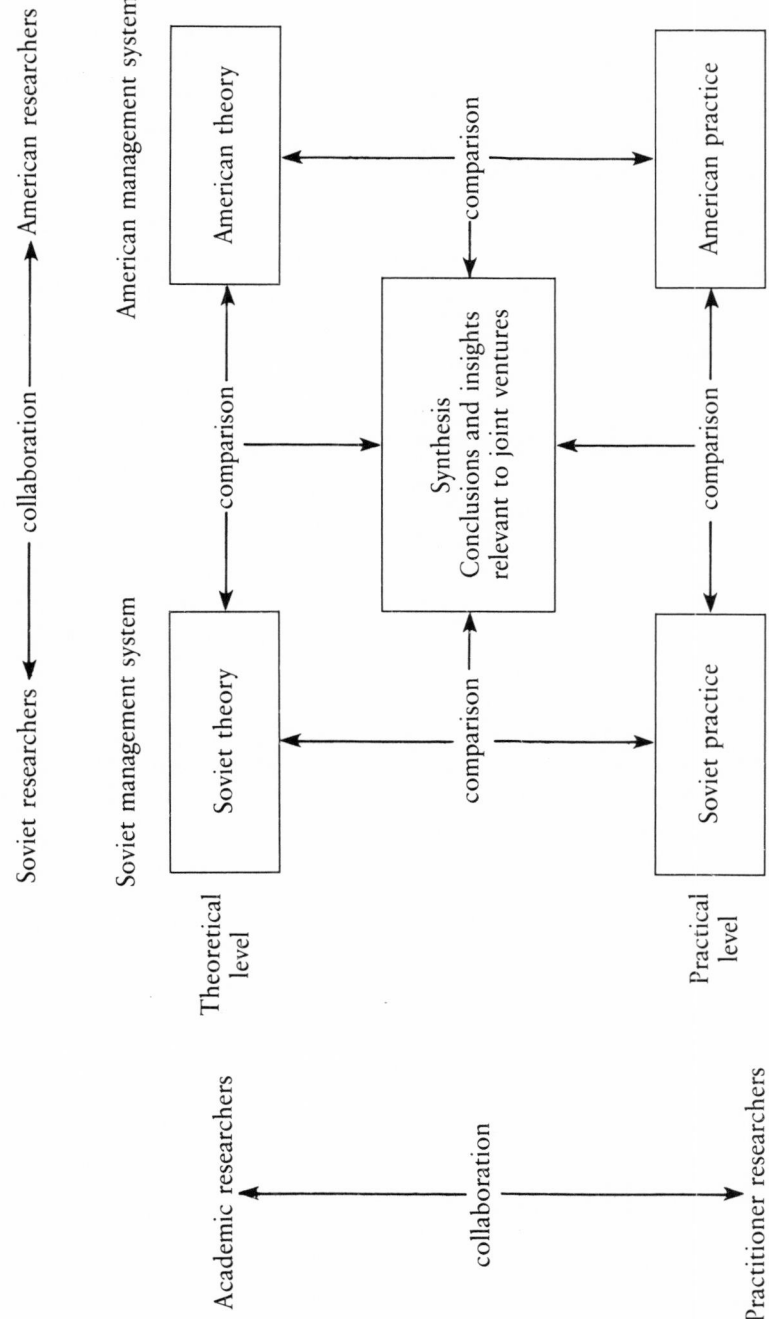

Chapter 2

US and USSR Cultural Characteristics

Management of economic enterprise in the United States and the USSR has evolved from two very different theoretical and ideological starting points, which need to be understood. These theories or ideologies are based on answers to three fundamental questions that any economic system must address: (1) How do we arrange for property rights (ownership) and associated rewards? (2) How do we arrange for resource allocation and coordination? (3) What human motivations are relied on?

Let us see how each nation addresses question one. Under socialism, as interpreted by the USSR constitution, productive assets are owned by the state on behalf of the people, and the state distributes the rewards of those assets. Under capitalism, as developed under US law, productive assets are owned largely by individual citizens who can directly claim the rewards thereof.

To the second question, USSR theory responds that resources can best be allocated and coordinated by the central planning agencies of the state. US theory asserts that resources can best be allocated and coordinated by market transactions among independent buyers and sellers. The Soviet theory assumes that a centralized political hierarchy can know best what the priority needs of a people and nation are and how the component elements can be gathered most efficiently into final products and distributed. The US theory assumes that the multiple market transactions among organizations and individuals in competition with one another will, as if manipulated by an invisible hand, reflect the aggregated priorities and preferences of a people and drive the assembly of components and the distribution of final goods and services without central guidance.

In answer to the third question, Soviet theory assumes that people can be motivated to work for the collective good and that consequently both productivity and economic justice will best be served. Behind the US theory is

11

the assumption that people will be more productive if there is a direct connection between their effort and their individual reward and that this will result in a just distribution.

Clearly, these two ideologies hinge on very different assumptions about human behavior and human needs. And while the theories can be elaborated in far greater detail, our simple version is not a serious distortion of the concepts held by many managers in both countries. This seems true even though managers know that the practice of these ideologies in each country is much more complex and, as we shall see, has evolved and continues to evolve well beyond the starting premises. (The two theories are summarized in Exhibit 2.1.)

EXHIBIT 2.1   Historical Premises

	Ownership	Resource allocation and coordination	Motivation
US	Private	Market	Self-interest
USSR	State	Central planning	Collective interest

In addition to their different ideological foundations, the two nations have vastly different histories, and those histories have produced disparate cultures and economic institutions. Because they provide the context for our treatment of contemporary management decision practices, an awareness of these historical/cultural differences is essential.

Cultural Characteristics of the United States

[*Editors' note:* The following section was prepared primarily to assist Soviet readers by summarizing some aspects of traditional American culture. Much of it will be familiar to American readers.]

Most informed commentators on the United States have highlighted some combination of five themes to characterize its culture: (1) individualism and competitive behavior, (2) voluntary association and cooperative behavior, (3) innovation and change, (4) choice and democratic behavior, and (5) individual ownership and self-reliance. The emergence of these traits has been explained in many ways, but the most persistent and persuasive explanations cite the frontier experience, the motives for immigration to America, the inherited traditions of English law and government, and the influence of religion and abstract ideas (i.e., John Locke and Adam Smith).

A reference to the American frontier typically evokes an image of the Far West, of cowboys and Indians. But this imagery misses a profound point about America: From its earliest days it has continuously had a frontier. The original American frontier was the English settlements along the eastern seaboard in Virginia and Massachusetts. The frontier moved westward generation by generation, into the upland South, across the Alleghenies, into the Ohio valley, the upper Midwest, the Mississippi valley, and on across the prairie states and the Rocky Mountains. This continuous advance made the living conditions of the frontier a constant influence on the national character. The best-known historian of this influence was Frederick Turner, whose famous 1893 essay, "The Significance of the Frontier in American History," begins with this theme: "Up to our own day American history has been in a large degree the history of the colonization of the Great West. The existence of an area of free land in continuous recession and the advance of American settlement westward, explain American development."[1]

Turner spoke to every one of the five aspects of American culture.

1. Individualism:

That coarseness and strength combined with acuteness and inquisitiveness; that practical, inventive turn of mind, quick to find expedients; that masterful grasp of material things, lacking in the artistic but powerful to effect great ends; that restless, nervous energy; that dominant individualism, working for good and for evil, and withal that buoyancy and exuberance which comes with freedom—these are traits of the frontier.[2]

2. Cooperation:

From the first, it became evident that these men had means of supplementing their individual activity by informal combinations. One of the things that impressed all early travelers in the United States was the capacity for extra-legal, voluntary association. This was natural enough; in all America we can study the process by which in a new land social customs form and crystallize into law. This power of the newly arrived pioneers to join together for a common end without the intervention of governmental institutions was one of their marked characteristics. The log rolling, the house-raising, the husking bee, the apple paring, and the squatters' associations whereby they protected themselves against the speculators in securing title to their clearings on the public domain, the camp meeting, the mining camp, the vigilantes, the cattle-raisers' associations, the "gentlemen's agreements," are a few of the indi-

1. Turner, Frederick Jackson, *The Frontier in American History* (Huntington, NY: Kreiger, 1976, reprint of original ed., 1920), p. 1.
2. Ibid., p. 2.

cations of this attitude. It is well to emphasize this American trait, because in a modified way it has come to be one of the most characteristic and important features of the United States today.[3]

3. Innovation:

First of all, there was the ideal of discovery, the courageous determination to break new paths, indifference to the dogma that because an institution or a condition exists, it must remain. All American experience has gone to the making of the spirit of innovation; it is in the blood and will not be repressed.[4]

4. Democracy:

Then, there was the ideal of democracy, the ideal of a free self-directing people, responsive to leadership in the forming of programs and their execution, but insistent that the procedure should be that of free choice, not of compulsion.[5]

5. Individual ownership:

The American belief in individual ownership of property was strongly rooted in the frontier experience. Land was the primary object of ownership, and the land free-for-the-taking on the frontier steadily reinforced individual ownership. As Turner argued,

> When we consider the public domain from the point of view of the sale and disposal of public land we are again brought face to face with the frontier. The policy of the United States in dealing with its lands is in sharp contrast with the European system. . . . Efforts to make this domain a source of revenue . . . were in vain. . . . The reason is obvious . . . the West demanded . . . land.[6]

For Turner, one of the principal American ideals "was that of individual freedom to compete unrestrictedly for the [land] resources of a continent."[7] And individual ownership of the land and self-reliance went hand in hand. Americans have always expected to be self-sufficient in their economic activity and to take responsibility for their personal finances and household budgeting. In general they expect to find opportunities for self-improvement and to take charge of their work careers.

Turner highlighted the positive aspects of the frontier's influence on American culture, but he also saw the negative side of individual ownership and frontier democracy: "The democracy born of free land, strong in selfishness and individualism, intolerant of administrative experience and education, and pressing individual liberty beyond its proper bounds, has its dangers as well as its benefits."[8] Others also pointed out the darker side of self-sufficiency. Individualism and competition periodically have erupted

3. Ibid., p. 34.
4. Ibid., p. 306.
5. Ibid.
6. Ibid., pp. 25–26.
7. Ibid., p. 320.
8. Ibid., p. 32.

into violence. Tension between competitive and cooperative tendencies continues. Moreover, the urge toward innovation and change has at times fostered chauvinistic nationalism and adventurism. Private ownership can turn into excessive materialism, and democracy can devolve into factionalism and separatism.

Though Turner saw the frontier influence as a rejection of European mores, other historians have traced the influence of Old World laws and customs in the developing America. America's founders clearly patterned its law and government after the English system. America's formative settlement years coincided with the revolution that established the English Parliament and temporarily set aside the monarchy. Furthermore, the influence continued. As England moved away from feudalism and toward industrialization, the New World did too. However, the broad Atlantic gave America scope to develop such local democratic institutions as town meetings and county and state government even during its colonial years under the British crown. And after the Revolution, America's leaders established a federal democratic system that has remained essentially unchanged for 200 years. Beyond the English, other immigrants soon affected American culture. The slave trade brought the African influence early on. One can still find evidence of French influence on American law and customs in the Mississippi valley, Spanish and Mexican influence in California and the Southwest, and Russian influence in the Northwest. Later waves of immigration from other European countries and the Far East have left their obvious marks. Ultimately, though, in spite of all these influences, one principle from the frontier experience tends to prevail: *the least government is the best government.*

No overview of American cultural development is complete without citing the influence of religion. The Pilgrims came to the New World seeking freedom to observe their own form of Protestantism. They accepted the dangers of immigration to a distant, hostile land because they wanted to escape the Old World restrictions on their religious and political beliefs. Other sects, mostly variations of Calvinism, soon followed. Their leaders stressed individual redemption through divine grace and believed that material well-being was evidence of godliness. Max Weber observed the strong connection between the Protestant ethic and the rise of capitalism worldwide. Clearly, the United States can be cited as a prime example.

Turner's tracking of the frontier influence emphasized the settling of the land and farming. At the time he wrote, the frontier of free land was rapidly closing, and he recognized that the new frontier was the rapid industrial development of his day. For a richer understanding of industry, we must turn to other historical analysts and shift our focus from culture to institutional development—in particular, to the rise of the modern American business corporation. But first we will examine Russian cultural development and compare it with the formation of America's culture.

Cultural Characteristics of the Soviet Union

[*Editors' note:* This section was prepared primarily to assist American readers with a summary of some aspects of traditional Russian culture. Our editing has been limited to the clarification of what our Soviet colleagues have chosen and interpreted.]

A popular point of view holds that culture is an adaptation of the people and everything they have created that extends beyond their lives and their history. When we examine national peculiarities in connection with economic management, it is important to review the customs and habits that have grown out of the encounter of people with their natural surroundings. A number of Russian pre-revolutionary historians have tried to define a few features of the Russian national character.

1. Cautiousness: Vasily Klyuchevskiy is one who has noted the alert cautiousness of the Russian character. Speaking about the circumspection of the Great Russians, he writes,

> Great Russia of the thirteenth to the fifteenth centuries, with all of its forests, marshes, and bogs at every step, presented to settlers thousands of minor dangers, unforeseen difficulties and unpleasant things, with which it was constantly necessary to cope and struggle. This trained the Great Russians to follow nature vigilantly, *to look both ways,* as their phrase had it, to walk, mindful of the surroundings and feeling the soil beneath, not falling into the water, not having found a ford. Resourcefulness was developed in the settler through the minor difficulties and dangers, as well as a habit towards patient struggle with adversity and hardship.[9]
>
> In conditions of severe and willful nature, the impossibility to calculate in advance, to think out beforehand a plan of action and directly advance to the projected goal, was noticeably reflected in the mindset of the Great Russian and in the manner of his thinking. Everyday difficulties and chance occurrences accustomed him more to discuss the path already trodden than to imagine the future, more to look behind him than to look forward. In the battle with unexpected blizzards and thaws, with unforeseen August frosts and January sleet, he began to be more circumspect than farsighted; he learned to think more of consequences than to make goals; he nurtured in himself the ability to sum up things concerning craftsmanship and to make estimates.[10]

2. Unpredictability: On the other hand, Klyuchevskiy observes,

9. Klyuchevskiy, Vasily O. *Works in 9 Volumes,* vol. I (Moscow: Mysl, 1987), p. 312.
10. Ibid., p. 316.

[nature] often laughs at the careful calculations of the Great Russian; the willfulness of the climate and the soil deceive his most humble expectations, and having become accustomed to these deceptions, the thrifty Great Russian at times loves, thoughtlessly, to choose the most hopeless and least careful decision, contrasting the caprice of nature with the caprice of his own courage. This inclination teases with chance, plays with good fortune, and this is the Great Russian "*avos*" (somehow).[11]

In summary, he explains,

By his habit of hesitating and avoiding the unevenness and the chance occurrences of life, the Great Russian often seems to be indirect and insincere. The Great Russian often thinks ambiguously, and this seems like duplicity. He always goes straight to his goal, even though it is often not carefully considered; he goes, looking about him, and for this reason, his gait seems evasive and hesitant. Nature and fate led the Great Russian so that he learned to go out onto the straight road by roundabout ways. The Great Russian thinks and acts as he walks. What thing more crooked and winding could one devise than a Great Russian country road? Such a road looks just like the slithering track of a snake. And just try to find a more direct path; you will end up wandering about and will come out onto the same winding path.[12]

3. Intensive work and rest: The Russian historians noticed also the capability of the Great Russian to do "storming" work. Klyuchevskiy explains:

The Great Russian is sure of one thing—that he must value the clear summer day; he must appreciate that nature allows him little suitable time for working the land and that the short Great Russian summer can turn out to be still shorter, by means of premature, unexpected inclement weather. This forces the Great Russian peasant to hurry, to work hard in order to accomplish much in a short time and just at the right time to collect his yield from the field and then to be idle in the fall and winter. Thus the Great Russian became accustomed to an extreme, short-term exertion of his strength; he became accustomed to work quickly and feverishly, and then to rest during the time of forced idleness in the fall and winter. Not one people in Europe was capable of such exertion of labor for a short time as the Great Russian developed; but also, nowhere in Europe, apparently, do we find such lack of habit for regular, moderate, measured and constant labor as in Great Russia.[13]

A. N. Engelgardt noted these traits as well, but gave them a different emphasis:

It is very difficult to find Russians who work like Germans. But at the same time it is very difficult to find German workers who are as capable of working so very hard at harvest time as the Russians. When the peasant works for himself at mowing time, he produces a tremendous volume of work. You

11. Ibid., p. 315.
12. Ibid., pp. 316–317.
13. Ibid., p. 315.

should see how he does it, how he concentrates his efforts. However, in the fall, after the harvest, you cannot recognize him. Then he has his rest. Nobody can rest as he does it.[14]

4. Communal work: The inclination to work together in groups developed gradually in the Russian character. Sociologists connect this proclivity with the transformation from the cultivation of small pieces of land inside the forest to the work on vast open lands that required collective efforts. According to Engelgardt, "Some people even think that to do something together is contrary to the spirit of peasantry. When it is possible to estimate concrete results from each one's work and award him accordingly, the peasants will work together easily and with great hope."

The Soviet writer V. Lichutin, who has studied the Russian character in depth, believes that

> sociability and the qualities of the noisy crowd (*vatazhnost*) are characteristic of Russians; from this combination, from the support of a neighbor's shoulder, was later born the Russian commonality, that same serf community, among the flat forest fields, which was constantly being annoyed by thieves stealing timber, by the treacherous Tatar and by the evil highwayman. The very expanses, full of good and evil elements, with time fostered that self-defense, that communal world.[15]

Because the medieval Russian commune developed under conditions where land was relatively plentiful, rules limiting individual land use seemed unnecessary. Moreover, the small dimensions of the settlements made elaborate rules superfluous. In terms of self-management, the peasant commune (*prichnina-volost*) had extensive jurisdiction. It managed the distribution of lands and the regulation of their use, the allotment of *tiaglo* (a tax levied on the peasants of medieval Russia), the selection of village authorities, the collection of resources to defray commune expenses, the organization of mutual aid, and the resolution of civil and minor court affairs.

By the end of the nineteenth century, however, the peasant commune had developed characteristics of cliquishness and rigidity that tended to tie peasants to the land and block the growth of the whole Russian market and capitalism. This inflexibility led the government to foster breakup of the commune with an eye toward expanding Russian capitalism and supporting the agrarian reform of Stolypin (minister of the interior, 1906–1911). But in the process of equalizing land distribution after the revolution of October 1917, the Soviet government revived the peasant commune. During their first years of power, the Soviets encouraged and supported the traditions of mutual aid and collectivism in the commune. Later, during the period of complete collectivization of agriculture and submission of the commune to rural councils, the Soviets converted the commune into an association of neighboring individual peasants who used the land jointly. Moreover, beyond the agricultural sector, the government widely applied the forms, traditions, and habits of collective labor—consumption and mutual aid, as well as the organizational and managerial elements of collectives—in building socialism in

14. Engelgardt, A. N., *From the Village: 12 letters. 1872–1887* (Moscow: Mysl, 1987), pp. 153–154.
15. Lichutin, V., "On ill-starred grief," *Oktiabr*, no. 10, 1987, p. 145.

the USSR (for example, the collective contract in industry and self-management in the labor brigades).

5. Centralism and decentralism: Geography was a primary force behind the development of unity and centralism in the Russian character. The closeness of main river basins and the uniform surface of the plain prevented settlements from becoming isolated. Rivers promoted communication among Russian people, preparing them for national unity. Solovev explains how the river system helped the state to unite the people:

> The state had its roots in the sources of the main rivers on the plain, and moved to enlarge its sphere and provide for defense by moving population toward the mouth of the rivers. So the center of government was determined by the upper river places and further settlement by the river basins. This radial, or "fan," system of settlement found its reflection even in the planning of big Russian cities. We may, therefore, say that nature to a degree predetermined the centralized character of the Russian state.[16]

Centralization had deep historical roots. Born in the struggle against the Mongol-Tatar yoke, it continued to strengthen through the creation of the Russian state. Dispersion of the population throughout huge territories, poor roads, illiteracy, and an undeveloped political life provided the base for centralization of power. Despite its negative aspects, people understood that centralization was a necessary guarantee against enemy attack and the arbitrary rule of local officials.[17] On the other hand, self-management of the rural village—for example, the Kazak settlements and the Siberian communities—infused in some people the idea of government decentralization, but bureaucracy did not give them the chance to develop it in full scale.

To understand the dual nature of the pre-revolutionary state government, it is important to consider its historical roots carefully. The state government bonded Asian "relational bureaucracy," which was brought into the Russian feudal aristocracy by the Mongol-Tatars, with a Western "functional bureaucracy," which was Peter the Great's contribution to state management. The first type of bureaucracy brought a belief in the power of the top authorities and their fairness in making independent decisions. The high degree of state involvement in the country's societal and economic life made possible some very predictable approaches to management. Even the introduction of the best foreign experience about management was accomplished by the orders of the Czar. Thus even industrial relationships have had a feudal character for a long time.

These strong centralist tendencies, however, could not stop the development of new, nonstandard, more decentralized approaches to organizing state government. Russian history abounds with examples of such approaches. First, there was the colonization of Siberia in the seventeenth century; then came Peter the Great's program to build the Russian fleet, followed by his collegial management of state administration; the nineteenth-century organization and methods of provincial and countryside administration; and the building of the great Siberian railroad. The Russian version of the early

---

16. Solovev, S. M. *Works in 18 Books* (Moscow: Mysl, 1988).
17. Piskotin, Mikhail, I., *Socialism and State Management* (historical lessons and perestroika), 2d ed. 1988, pp. 275–276.

European workshops that appeared in the old Russian cities was frequently organized by peasant handcrafters. As in other Western countries, some of these workshops evolved into factories.

Historically, the Russian people have passed through wave after wave of turbulence and crisis. They have experienced the internal wars of the princes, the Mongol-Tatar yoke, collectivization of lands, *oprichnina* (the terrorism of Ivan the Terrible), the time of troubles, the Petrine reforms, centuries of serfdom, autocratic-bureaucratic despotism, the newly arisen capitalism, and three revolutions. Crisis and turbulence have been the norm in Russian history. Later in this text we will attempt to show how socioeconomic conditions since the Revolution have affected the culture, in particular the Soviet economic institutions.

Cultural Comparison

Great Russians have been conditioned by adversity, crisis, and uncertainty. They have learned to be cautious and to move in response to unpredictable and uncontrollable events by alternating intense work and rest. They have developed a special capacity for communal work and have struggled to reconcile centralization and decentralization.

In contrast, Americans have been conditioned by a more plentiful environment and have learned to expect that as individuals they will be able to influence their environment and achieve their goals. They have drawn on the plentiful land of the frontier in developing traits of individualism and voluntary association. Local government and democratic institutions have dominated centralized government.

Great Russians have been buffeted by recurrent revolutions and external invasions. Change has come in abrupt shifts and violent episodes. Americans have developed more by evolution, with little exposure to external enemies. Change in the United States has been gradual, with one developmental stage blending into the next. These historical differences are reflected in national character and culture.

Chapter 3

History of US and Soviet Economic Institutions

Historical Review of US Economic Institutions

[*Editors' note:* This section was prepared primarily to assist Soviet readers with a summary of some aspects of US industrial history. Much of it will be familiar to American readers.]

An historical review of American enterprise can enrich one's understanding of contemporary management practice. We find it convenient, if somewhat arbitrary, to break the review into four periods: workshop/craft enterprises (dominant from 1620 to 1820); functional/market enterprises (dominant from 1830 to 1925); multidivisional/technocratic enterprises (dominant from 1925 to the present); and network/career enterprises (currently becoming dominant). In this section we will discuss the nature of the four forms and the historical forces that have driven them.[1] Chapter 4 will examine in more detail the theoretical foundations of the forms that are widely used today.

THE WORKSHOP/CRAFT ENTERPRISE SYSTEM

Most Americans have a general understanding of the workshop/craft enterprise system,[2] but few realize that this was the system that dominated American industrial life for nearly 200 years—until the 1820s. Small work-

---

1. This historical review will draw primarily on Lawrence, Paul, "The History of Human Resource Management in American Industry" in *HRM: Trends and Challenges,* Lawrence, P. and R. Walton, eds. (Boston: Harvard Business School Press, 1985), pp. 15–35; and on Chandler, Alfred, *The Visible Hand: The Managerial Revolution in American Business.* Cambridge, MA: Harvard University Press, 1977).

2. *Workshop* refers to the type of organizational structure employed, while *craft* refers to the type of human resource system used. This compound convention will also be used in labeling subsequent historical systems.

shops carried out most of the production of industrial goods and services in colonial America. These shops organized to supply, on a custom-order basis, the basic needs of the local market. The shop owner was typically a master craftsman—shoemaker, cabinetmaker, blacksmith—who was assisted by apprentices and journeymen, usually one or two of each, although there were larger shops in the cities. The technology consisted almost entirely of hand tools and simple human-powered machines. When apprentices joined a given trade, they could reasonably expect to spend a lifetime in it, hoping to move through the customary career sequence from apprentice to journeyman to master. In the small shops a single team, directed by the master, shared an entire task. Although the master had complete control of the shop, tradition and law restricted his right to dismiss journeymen and apprentices, and governed wages, mutual rights, and obligations. Disputes were usually handled directly in the shop, although a case could, of course, be taken to court. Associations of journeymen and masters were the beginnings of craft and trade unions.

Historians generally agree that the workshop/craft system was essentially harmonious. Skilled labor was relatively scarce, and masters rarely exploited apprentices. Journeymen could earn wage rates that permitted a relatively good living standard. Turnover was low, layoffs and strikes infrequent. The owner-master undoubtedly made the decisions but customarily consulted with and informed the journeymen. The system provided a well-institutionalized balance of power between employer and employees. In the 1820s, however, the workshop/craft system rapidly lost its dominant place in the American industrial scene. Today it is found only in a limited number of small enterprises, such as tool and die shops.

Two developments triggered the eventual change from the workshop/craft system to the functional/market system of management. The first, improvement of transportation and communication facilities, made possible the expeditious movement of manufactured goods from city to city and from cities to outlying towns. This expanded the competitive domain of many firms from local to regional.

The second factor had an ironic twist. In the interest of journeymen, masters tried to stabilize employment in slack times by producing goods to be inventoried for ready-made sales. But the master craftsmen were poorly equipped to handle large inventories, to ship between cities, to extend credit, or to predict demand. This created the opportunity for established wholesale merchant capitalists, particularly from shipping and real estate, to apply their expertise to the realm of manufacturing. After 1800, these merchants began placing large orders with the owners of the workshops. Soon the shop owners came to depend on the wholesale orders, thereby giving the merchants the power to press for lower prices. By 1830, the merchants dominated the industrial economy. The pressure on workshop owners for lower prices forced them to look for ways to cut labor costs. At the same time, with immigration increasing, a labor shortage turned into a surplus. The hard-pressed workshop owner could—and did—use unskilled instead of skilled labor, and reduced wages. With these new pressures, the employment relationship in the workshops changed dramatically. The craft system evolved into the market system of human resource management, with higher turnover and less mutual obligation between owners and workers. Eventually, as the number of workers in each enterprise gradually increased, the craft workshops gave way to factories, and a functional management system came into prominence. The emerging system was to dominate American industry for nearly a century and still characterizes many organizations in the United States today.

THE FUNCTIONAL/MARKET ENTERPRISE SYSTEM

As the small workshops gave way to factories, organizational forms and human resource management systems began to change. The textile mills constructed at the sources of water power in New England led this process of change. Either a mill agent or a superintendent managed each mill and usually reported to a company treasurer located in a major commercial center. The superintendent supervised the work of foremen, each of whom oversaw a single step in the manufacture of cotton cloth. Superintendents permitted their foremen a free hand in dealing with employees, even in hiring, firing, and processing payrolls. The superintendent understood the technology and was the primary decision maker regarding maintenance and replacement of machinery as well as the mix of yarns and fabrics to be scheduled. Purchasing, finance, and marketing emerged as separate functions, managed by specialists who rarely worked at the mill site and at times were in different enterprises. Thus began the functional decision-making system that became the dominant pattern in this country well into the twentieth century: decision issues were handed from one functional department to the next in sequence.

By the time of World War I, the leading functional enterprises had grown enormously in scale and scope. Functional departments such as production, sales, and engineering managed these corporations centrally. Other specialized staff departments such as personnel, finance, and purchasing supported the functional (or line) departments that carried out the main work of the firm (see Exhibit 3.1).

EXHIBIT 3.1   Functional/Market Enterprise Structure

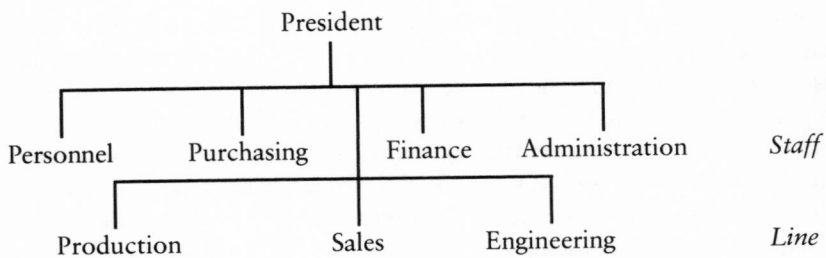

Many of the large firms were built up by merger to create vertically integrated organizations that moved raw materials to finished products in fields such as steel, oil, machinery, and electrical equipment. These firms expanded at enormous rates. For example, by 1907, the United States had surpassed Great Britain, Germany, and France *combined* in the production of iron and steel; a single firm, U.S. Steel, accounted for over two-thirds of this output.

By the 1920s, most of these large corporations were owned by considerable numbers of stockholders. Stockholders elected boards of directors, who in turn selected executive officers. Professional managers rather than owners gradually began to head these firms. Schools instituted specialized training for professional managers. Although corporations required multiple echelons of managers, the decision process remained centralized and functional. General Electric, Standard Oil (now Exxon), and Du Pont probably developed the functional form in its most refined state.

In large functional organizations the market system managed rank-and-file employees. Management increasingly considered both skilled and unskilled labor to be variable costs, with hiring and firing a response to fluctuation in the demand for output. This created a very high turnover rate. Management consistently fought the formation of unions, and with the help of the courts largely succeeded. Only among skilled craftspeople were unions able to survive, and even these unions represented only 6% of the labor force by the turn of the century.

Without strong unions or legal recourse, each worker had to settle any disputes directly with a foreman, as best he or she could. The free market value of the work performed determined wage rates, as managers compared outside contracting prices with inside piece rates. The availability of replacement labor affected these rates, of course, and chronic unemployment strengthened the employers' position. Long hours and adverse working conditions were normal, and intense conflict was pervasive throughout this period. Strikes went hand in hand with every major fluctuation in the economy. And on the factory floor, continuous covert conflicts flared between workers and foremen over working conditions and rates of output.

Nevertheless, much was accomplished under the functional/market management system in terms of creating industrial plants and an infrastructure. The textile industry had set the pace, and other large-scale industries soon copied it. In some firms established during this period, the system still exists. Although the distribution of hardship or resulting wealth was hardly equitable, the functional/market system was central to bringing about the decisive shift in the United States from an agrarian to an industrial society.

THE MULTIDIVISIONAL/TECHNOCRATIC ENTERPRISE SYSTEM

Between 1914 and 1924, American industry witnessed two closely related changes: the switch from the market to the technocratic system of managing human resources and, shortly thereafter, the emergence of the multidivisional organizational form.

Technocratic enterprise.   The basically technocratic system that replaced the market system of human resource management in America began, in fact, as an attempt to address the problems of hardship and escalating conflict with workers. During the wave of strikes in coal mines and steel plants at the turn of the century, writers drew national attention to the appalling working conditions in both industries. Violence became more frequent and more severe. Clearly, the pendulum had swung too far; key leaders of labor and industry knew that a solution would have to be found.

Important technological and economic changes coincided with the changing social climate and further nudged the technocratic system into place. Improvements in transportation (the intercontinental railroad network, followed by trucks) and communications (the intercity telephone) enabled competition in many industries to expand from regional to national. The development of the electric motor allowed new factory layouts. The time and motion studies of industrial engineer Frederick Taylor inspired ideas for using technical advances to increase productivity.

These forces for change did not coalesce into a new system of human resource management until about 1914, when automaker Henry Ford finally got the assembly line in his big Dearborn plant to run smoothly. Ford's genius was to combine a fine-grain division of labor with the automatically paced assembly line and high wages—his famous five dollars a day. Before this innovation, the labor turnover at Ford had exceeded 400% per year, registering 48% in the single month of December 1912. With Ford's new approach to labor, turnover and unit costs dropped, volume increased, and

profits soared. Widespread imitation of Ford came quickly. The technocratic system was established.

The key feature of the technocratic system—its dependence on a fine-
grain division of labor and machine pacing—affected every aspect of a
firm's management of human resources: work organization, rewards,
flows, and eventual employee representation. The supervisor no longer
needed to push and drive employees to work fast; that role was built into
the moving components of machines and assembly lines timed by motion
studies. Once pace was determined, pay could be set at an hourly rate; employers could avoid piece-rate disputes and even afford to be generous with
workers who accepted the discipline of machine pacing. Improved wages
reduced turnover, and the remaining turnover was less costly because the
fine-grain division of labor permitted workers to acquire the necessary
knowledge and dexterity quickly. As business fluctuated, employees were
laid off but with less frequency.

In the 1920s, for the first time in a century, an economic boom did not
trigger an increase in union membership. A major effort of many employers
to institute "welfare capitalism" thwarted unionization. Companies set up
extensive programs to improve the lot of both blue- and white-collar workers. Policies began to include limited benefits for accident compensation,
pensions, stock purchases, and the beginnings of medical insurance. Sophisticated personnel departments developed and administered these plans.

Given these refinements, it is not surprising that the Great Depression of
the 1930s proved particularly disillusioning and embittering. At the depth
of the depression, one-third of the American labor force was unemployed.
Vivid memories of the suffering and anger of those days fueled the organizing drive that the unions began at the first flicker of economic recovery in
the mid-1930s. With support of the federal government, unions organized
all major industries, and collective bargaining became the customary vehicle for employee representation in the technocratic system.

From the perspective of the 1980s, we can see that the technocratic system had from its inception two main strengths and eventually four serious
weaknesses. Its chief strength was that it made possible the production of
large volumes of standardized goods at low cost. In addition, even though
adversarial worker-employer relations persisted, the technocratic system
reduced the level of conflict from the extremes of the market system.

The weaknesses in human resource management became apparent in
heavy industry during the 1970s. First, the technocratic system has built-in
rigidity that makes it difficult to track changing market demands for more
customized and higher-quality products. Second, as time passed, workers
came to question the attractiveness of bargaining high pay for boring jobs
with little opportunity for promotion. Third, industrywide contract settle-

ments frequently escalated labor costs faster than productivity gains, leaving American industry extremely vulnerable to foreign competition. Fourth, the resources and time consumed by ongoing shop-floor disputes became less tolerable. Although some variation of the technocratic system still manages approximately one-third of the work force in the United States, that system has waned steadily in favor of the network/career system, which we will discuss shortly.

Multidivisional enterprise. Multidivisional organization evolved roughly in parallel with the technocratic system and took form initially at General Motors, the automobile company that was shortly to wrest leadership from Ford. The new form grew out of a crisis at General Motors precipitated by a sudden drop in the demand for cars in late 1920. William Durant, GM's founder and president, had recently merged a diverse group of car and parts manufacturers. In the credit crunch of 1920, Durant lost control of his firm to a major investor, Pierre Du Pont, who also headed Du Pont Chemical. With the help of newly appointed GM president, Alfred Sloan, Du Pont moved quickly to gain control over the chaotic conditions. They inventoried cars and parts every ten days and monitored the sales of both General Motors and its competitors. They regularized market forecasting and began reviewing divisional plans for purchasing supplies and scheduling output on a month-to-month basis to gear the flow of product to market fluctuations. All this required the creation of a central planning staff. At the same time, however, Du Pont recognized that headquarters could not handle all the detailed operating decisions for GM's multiple car lines. So GM defined a market niche for each car division and asked each divisional general manager to develop plans for profitable operations: to become, in fact, a profit center.

Over time, the establishment of profit centers led to the creation of more sophisticated accounting systems that often allocated corporate overhead to the operating divisions as a percentage of sales. The functional departments within the new divisions were treated as cost centers for accounting purposes. Managers learned that the decentralization of decision making could only follow the institution of good accounting systems. It was this combination of centralized planning and decentralized operations that evolved into the multidivisional organizational form. Historian Alfred Chandler summarized the new structure:

> A general office plans, coordinates, and appraises the work of a number of operating divisions and allocates to them the necessary personnel, facilities, funds, and other resources. The executives in charge of these divisions, in turn, have under their command most of the functions necessary for handling one major line of products or set of services over a wide geographical area,

and each of these executives is responsible for the financial results of his division and for its success in the marketplace.[3]

Alfred Sloan, the GM president who worked with Du Pont to design the system, referred to it as *coordinated decentralization,* expressing a paradox somewhat similar to the important Soviet concept of democratic centralism currently emphasized by Chairman Gorbachev. The top managers, or executive committee, focused attention on planning and resource allocation and strategic decisions, while the divisions operated as profit centers and focused on operational decisions. A central corporate staff advised divisional officers in areas such as manufacturing, purchasing, advertising, engineering, and design (see Exhibit 3.2).

EXHIBIT 3.2   Multidivisional Enterprise Structure

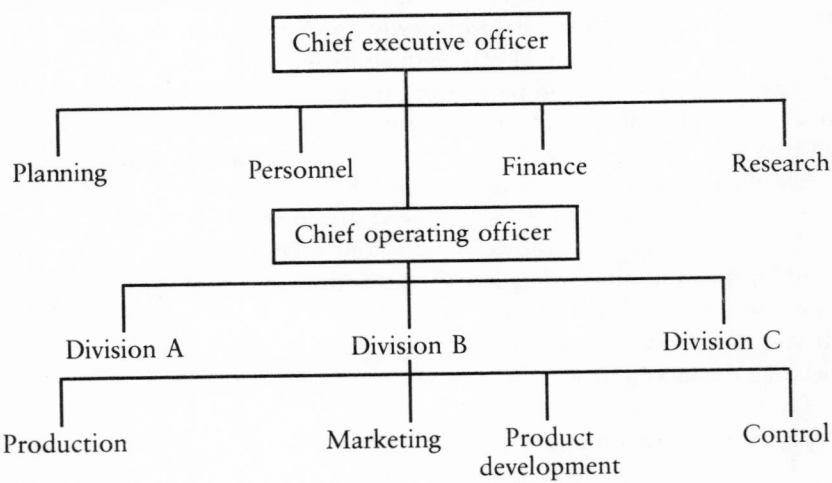

To deal with incipient tensions between central staff and divisional executives, "interdivisional relations committees" brought line and staff officers together around problems of common interest on a function-by-function basis. For example, purchasing officers of each division would meet as a committee with planning and finance officers from headquarters. The central finance staff took on an important negotiating role by assuming responsibility for auditing divisional affairs.

These were the basic elements of the new organizational form, which quickly demonstrated its superiority by 1927 as it helped boost the sales

3. Chandler, *The Visible Hand,* p. 2.

and profits of General Motors past those of Ford. Throughout the 1920s and 1930s, the new model spread to other US companies such as Allied Chemical and Union Carbide.

The multidivisional system has demonstrated lasting advantage in many industries, proving especially effective in those industries where change in the marketplace and the relevant technology is moderate. In cases where change has been rapid and uncertainty great, however, the form has shown some competitive weaknesses. Like its labor correlate, the technocratic system, it innovates slowly in terms of new products and new services. It responds sluggishly to rapid market shifts and can be slow to take advantage of new technologies. Under more dynamic conditions, newer network forms of organization are emerging.

The Network/Career Enterprise System

The network/career system began in electronics and other high-technology fields because it met their special needs for innovation and flexibility (Burns and Stalker). During the post–World War II period, the technologies of jet airplanes, satellite communications, and computers facilitated a rapid shift to global competition in industry. The resulting growth opened unprecedented opportunities for American companies, opportunities that meshed with the rising career expectations of unparalleled numbers of college-educated workers. The bulk of the new jobs were white-collar—that is, they were geared to workers with a professional or semiprofessional level of knowledge. People had to devise the organizational form and the human resource management system that could cope with these opportunities for rapid market growth and accelerated technological change. Just as General Motors and the auto industry were pacesetters for the multidivisional/technocratic system, IBM and the computer industry took the lead in establishing the network/career system.

The network organizational form that emerged from these challenging circumstances could handle a much heavier load of information processing and decision making than could the classical hierarchical systems, with or without the multidivisional feature. More channels of communication opened, and more decision centers were created to handle the rate of change. The result was a cluster of new structures and systems that combined in many different ways to create the network form. All these structures and systems centered around the enormous task of integrating the highly diverse activities of the firms. A simple listing of some of the relevant organizational techniques helps make the point: liaison roles, interfunctional task forces, product managers, project managers, variable budg-

EXHIBIT 3.3   Matrix Structure

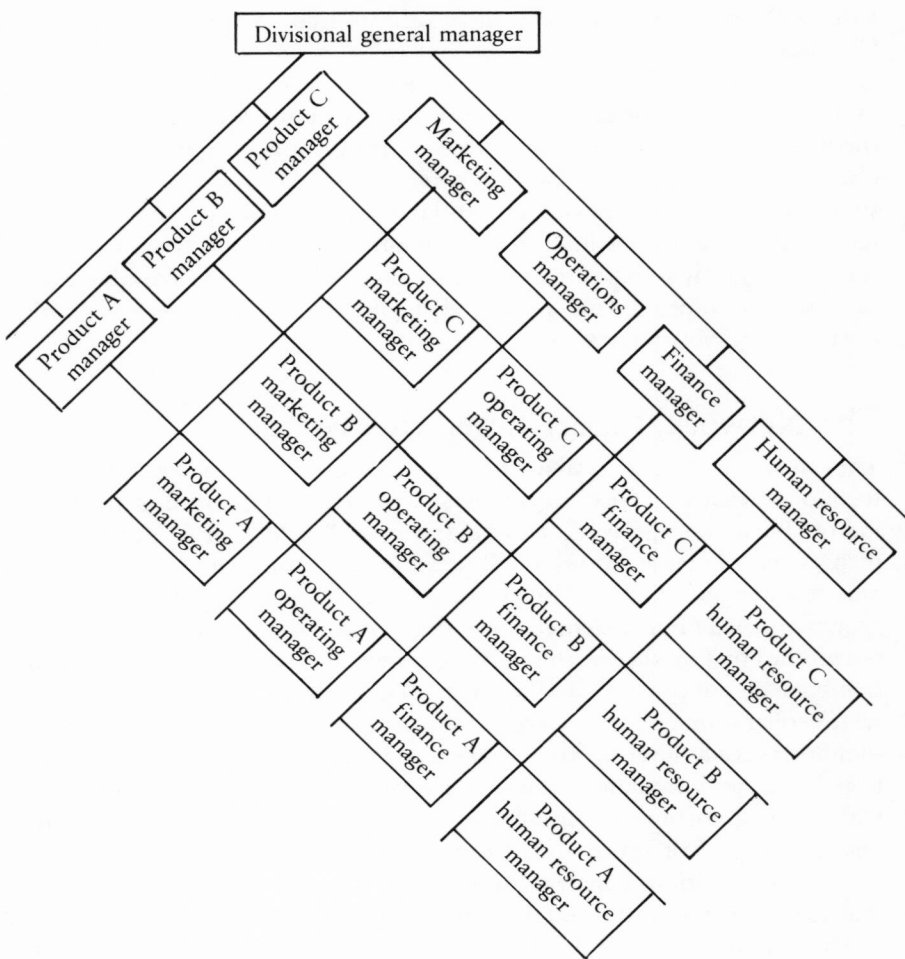

EXHIBIT 3.4   Cross-Functional Product Structure

ets, computer networks, computer-aided design, and intrapreneurial teams. More will be said about these mechanisms later.

Some firms combined sets of these devices to form a matrix structure with both a functional and a product chain of command. (See Exhibit 3.3.) Some matrix structures required middle managers to report to two line authorities, thus violating the traditional hierarchical rule of "one person, one boss." In others, the cross-cutting channels did not carry line authority but depended instead on expert authority to influence decisions (Exhibit 3.4).

Although difficult to develop and manage, network forms have the potential to generate faster, more innovative responses to environmental challenge and opportunity.

Network forms have grown up hand in glove with career systems as vehicles for managing human resources. The hallmark of the career system is its delicate handling of the flow of people in, through, and out of the organization. The firm recruits people for positions that are spelled out with explicit, detailed attention to duties and rights. Every position links to other positions offering promotion opportunities that form a career ladder. The firm publicly posts job openings so that every employee has the opportunity to apply for upward or lateral mobility. Thus the firm in effect offers an employee not only a job, but also a career. Management encourages longer-term employment and uses layoff only as a last resort. If layoffs become necessary, both seniority and merit commonly are considered in an orderly fashion.

Career-system firms typically pay employees on a salary basis, implementing a continuum of salary grades and subgrades with explicit provision for raises on the basis of both merit and seniority. Every worker's right to air individual grievances is protected; all employees have the right to a second or even a third hearing on their own situation or in other company matters.

The career system is notable for its capacity to create a single homogeneous work culture throughout a firm, thus reducing the traditional barrier between blue-collar and managerial employees that characterized the technocratic system. This kind of culture reduces adversarialism and its associated costs, and increases flexibility and innovation. From the viewpoint of both the firm and the employee who wants upward mobility, the career system is more responsive than the technocratic system.

A recent extension of the career system in terms of work organization and employee representation has led to a stronger mutual employer-employee commitment. The distinctive element of this evolving system is the semiautonomous work group. Semiautonomous work groups (which have some interesting parallels with the Soviet brigades) are free to organize their division of labor for the performance of a complete task—for example, the production of a component or the assembly of a final product. The firm provides the necessary resources; the work group assumes responsibility not only for the volume of work, but also for quality control, equipment maintenance, work scheduling, process improvements, training, hiring, and—occasionally—worker discipline and leader selection. Use of semiautonomous groups makes it possible to reduce the number of staff support positions and often enables a firm to eliminate one or more levels of the hierarchy, thus reducing costs and tightening lines of communication. Consistent high performance will require further experimentation, but already most of the new work arrangements clearly outperform the methods they replace. Procter & Gamble is one of the pioneers in these developments.

Some firms are extending individual appeal rights into mechanisms that provide for collective representation on business decisions. For example, GM and Ford are testing new employee-representation methods that utilize worker councils to engage in joint union-management consultation at plant, divisional, and corporate levels. For example, management consults employee groups about annual business plans, product plans, and technology changes. American Telephone & Telegraph is trying a similar approach with the Communication Workers of America. Polaroid and Cummins Engine too are learning from multilevel consultation in their nonunion plants. But we must look overseas to see the most fully developed representation arrangements functioning as a key part of the career system.

German and Japanese managers usually agree that they could not run their businesses effectively without the help of shop-level joint union-management consultation. The low strike rate of these nations is no coincidence. America's strongest foreign competition comes from Japan and Germany, where workers are well known for their high level of commitment to and involvement in their enterprises. Today more companies are developing reward systems that share with employees the firm's productivity gains as well as the sacrifices associated with poor economic performance. The Scanlon Plan, with its plantwide monthly bonus, is one example of a gainsharing system.

The value-adding partnership, an additional element of the network structure, is under current development (Johnston and Lawrence). This kind of partnership involves more intense, long-term relationships between vendor firms and industrial customers along the links of the value-added chain from raw material to finished consumer product. Partners exchange all kinds of knowledge that can help each be an efficient and innovative contributor to its specialized place in the chain; they share sensitive information about costs, new production techniques, and long-term product and market plans. Direct computer linkage usually facilitates the process. It helps achieve high performance in areas of quality, delivery, cost control, and speed of product innovation. In a sense the new supply relationships are a lateral extension of the decision-making network organization. McKesson, a pharmaceutical distributor, and Ford have provided examples of different ways to build such value-adding relationships. All these extensions of the network organization represent a response to the competitive challenge that much of US industry currently faces from both the Far East and Western Europe.

Overview of the US Economic System

A description of the context of managerial decision making in the United States would be incomplete without a summary of the broader institutional framework within which US firms and markets have evolved.

The US economic system is known as a *free enterprise system,* but this term may convey to Soviet readers an image of anarchy that is by no means accurate. A more accurate label might be *guided enterprise system.* At the level of the industry and the firm, each enterprise is free to select and develop its own products and services, to seek its own customers, to obtain resources of capital and material from its own sources, and to employ people of its own choosing. However, this free-choice behavior is done within a complex framework of governmental institutions that both constrain and support the action of the enterprise.

Government regulatory agencies exert authority at three levels: local, state, and federal. Some regulatory agencies monitor a single industry. The Securities and Exchange Commission, for example, regulates the financial investment industry, and the Nuclear Regulatory Commission oversees the nuclear power industry. To cite a different kind of example, each of the 50 states has its own regulations for the insurance industry. And authorities such as the US Environmental Protection Agency regulate one aspect of all industries.

The primary mission of another set of governmental agencies is to support and facilitate enterprise. The US Department of Agriculture finds hundreds of ways of helping farmers and agribusiness. The US Department of Labor is dedicated to assisting the working population, in particular the unions. In the United States, the employees of every enterprise have the right by majority vote to join together in a union and be recognized for collective bargaining with their employer. The US Commerce Department supports the business community in a variety of ways, including the collection of helpful statistics, research of problem areas, and special assistance in developing foreign trade and overseas investments. The US Department of Education is the federal agency that cooperates with state and local authorities to administer an extensive public education system, which in turn supports the economy.

Many private organizations provide important support for enterprise in the United States. Most industries form trade associations that perform a variety of functions: representing the particular industry with the government, for example, or establishing product standards that help coordinate industry affairs. Business people organize chambers of commerce and industrial associations to support economic activity on a local and regional level.

Within the US economy it is also possible for a variety of people who are affected by the actions of enterprises to have real influence on them. These constituent or *stakeholder* groups include organizations of consumers, environmentalists, minorities, women, local citizens, and others who join forces to communicate their concerns to the relevant enterprise. Their effect is to balance the claims of these interest groups with those of the shareholders in the considerations of senior management and the boards of directors.

Markets in the United States can be viewed as falling into three general types: wholesale, retail, and commodity. Wholesale markets channel direct, bilateral exchanges between two enterprises with the terms of sale negotiated between the two parties. Retail markets sell all kinds of merchandise to the general public through hundreds of thousands of private stores and shops. In the commodity markets, buyers and sellers meet at set locations to negotiate and execute by auction the sale of a specific commodity. Commodity markets channel not only material commodities such as grain, cattle, fruits, and flowers, but also intangibles such as shares of stock, currencies, bonds, mortgages, and future options. As a source of capital funding, the financial market provides business and industry an important alternative to banks.

The banking system in the United States is another important contextual factor whose complexity makes it difficult to summarize. In brief, thousands of separate banks across the country are privately owned. They can be commercial, investment, or savings banks, and they can be chartered at either the national or the state level. In general, each type of bank has its own regulatory agency. However, all are linked as members of the Federal Reserve, a government banking agency that provides credit reserves, exchanges commercial paper, and exercises two types of monetary controls: fixing the rate of interest on loans to member banks and trading in currencies.

Together the agencies of government and the private sector supply a system of checks and balances that helps the United States address the basic problems with which every national economy struggles—inflation and deflation, swings of the business cycle, employment levels, balance of foreign trade, and growth of the standard of living. Because these government agencies are coordinated only loosely, their actions at times can contradict one another. Nonetheless, they serve to guide the economy and provide a critical context for the independent decisions made by enterprises.

To take our description one step farther, consider the multiple ways the US federal government can oversee a healthy degree of competitive pressure among commercial enterprises, yet avoid the hazards of monopoly or the extremes of cutthroat competition. Antitrust action to break up or block monopolistic combinations heads the list of tools at the government's disposal to affect competition, but it is not the only one. Federal tax policies affect competitive conditions in multiple ways, from direct tax credits for research and development, to depreciation and depletion regulations, to the impact of capital gains taxes on mergers. Historically, trade policies have been a favorite to influence competitive pressure. Price supports and price regulation have been used in limited ways. Direct government loans or loan guarantees, direct subsidies, and research grants are available. The list could be extended, but the point is already clear: the US government can and does influence US enterprise in vital ways through its network of agencies.

US LAWS AND REGULATIONS CONCERNING ENTERPRISE*

An important point in reviewing US laws for business is the fact that there is no national law for corporations except in specialized areas such as finance and securities regulation. The US government does not issue corporate charters. Each state has a corporate law and is authorized to issue corporate charters under that law. The founders of a corporation can choose in which state they wish to file for a charter—regardless of the location of their headquarters. It is incumbent on them, however, to register the corporation in every state in which they expect to do business so as to establish their standing in the state courts. Often they must also register with the cities or towns where they are to do business.

The multiple levels of government in the United States affect not only the chartering and registration procedures, but also many other facets of enterprise. For example, in the area of environmental pollution, firms must expect to comply with federal, state, and often city or township regulations. The same thing applies to tax regulations and national and state antitrust laws. One way to further clarify the number and complexity of US

*This section was written with the help of Joseph Auerbach, Esq., Professor Emeritus, Harvard Business School.

laws and regulations is to summarize the more obvious ones that are relevant to our four decision issues: planning, human resource management, acquisition of capital equipment, and new product development.

Suppose an annual business plan suggests introducing products to a new region. This triggers the need not only to register for business in those states and cities, but also to acquaint management with the unique laws that will govern business there, including zoning laws that control where particular enterprises may be conducted. Further, each new state to be entered has tax regulations that must be understood and complied with. As we noted in Chapter 2, law in some states has evolved from French or Spanish law as well as from English common law. When entering new types of business or raising capital for expansion, managers must also be aware of the complex security regulations and required disclosures.

In the hiring and firing aspect of human resource management, a number of laws and regulations must be understood. Federal and state regulations prohibit discrimination as to gender, age, race, religion, and handicaps. If they break the law, firms can be subject to suits and expensive damage claims. There are extensive regulations concerning pension plans and others delineating a firm's responsibility for workers injured on the job. There are regulations as to the hours of work and overtime. Special regulations govern the employment of women and children. There are minimum wage laws. There are laws concerning the rights of workers to unionize and bargain collectively for better wages and working conditions. There are rules concerning unemployment insurance and social security taxes. And there are many more laws affecting employment.

When it comes to the purchase of capital equipment, additional laws come into play. We have mentioned the environmental regulations that may apply. In addition there are numerous federal and state regulations concerning the safe operation of equipment, which often must undergo mandatory inspection for adequate guards and switches, noxious fumes, noise, vibration, and so on. Some federal and state tax regulations may provide the benefits of rapid depreciation of capital equipment.

In developing new products, firms must be aware of the many consumer health and safety regulations at all three levels of government in the United States. Regulations abound in the area of food and drug products. Regulations govern how products are packaged and labeled. Regulations control fair advertising and promotion and prohibit discriminatory pricing. Special rules govern the manufacture and distribution of products intended for children. And beyond the specific statutes, firms are responsible for any damage their products might cause under the "common law" of each state, which has been established by the precedent of earlier court cases.

One of the stereotypes many foreign business people assign to the

United States is that the country is relatively free of governmental regulation of business. Perhaps the foregoing outline of relevant laws will dispel that notion. But foreign firms may take comfort in knowing that if they enter a joint venture with an American firm, their partner's compliance with US law will ensure that they are in compliance also. The United States has no laws specific to joint ventures with foreign partners.

Joint ventures must abide by exactly the same laws as every other business firm in the country does, with two principal exceptions. One relates to security-sensitive enterprises, including ownership of certain communications media. Another occurs when the US government and the particular foreign nation have a bilateral economic treaty specifying reciprocal economic rights of firms in each other's country. However, the general effect of these treaty rights is to free the foreign business from some US business regulations rather than to make the rules more restrictive.

Historical Review of USSR Economic Institutions Since the Revolution

[*Editors' note:* This section was prepared primarily to assist American readers with a summary of some aspects of the history of USSR economic institutions since the revolution. Our editing has been limited to a clarification for American readers of what our Soviet colleagues have chosen and interpreted.]

To put the contemporary USSR enterprise into context, we begin with an overview of the evolving Soviet economic system. Our focus will be on the following sequence of structures: the system developed under Lenin, the system developed under Stalin, the system at the start of perestroika, and the nature of the reforms instituted by perestroika.

FIRST STEPS TOWARD BUILDING A MANAGEMENT SYSTEM UNDER SOVIET POWER

The Soviets were in power for only a few months between the victory of the revolution in 1917 and the beginning of the civil war, in the so-called time of the peaceful breath. During that period, the government attempted to convert the system from a war economy to a peace economy. They used the following mechanisms: economic intervention to regulate production and distribution; nationalization of the banks and a number of the larger syndicated enterprises; organization of an exchange of products between the cities and the villages built on cooperatives; and establishment of workers' control of enterprises. To implement this program, it was necessary to create a new management system. The Supreme Council of the National Economy (SCNE) was created to provide centralized management of the economy through its territorial organs or bodies. Because there was no plan for a universal nationalization of production, administrative guidance needed the support of financial regulations. Consequently, the government nationalized and united all the banks into a state bank. Owners of private enterprise were directed to reform their business and introduce workers' control by teaching workers how to manage.

Managing the nationalized enterprises was a more complicated problem. Here bourgeois specialists formed one-third of the management team, and either the state or unions and workers' collectives designated the other two-thirds.

Interindustrial connections continued on a market basis except for workers' control of the distribution of products and government control of the finance and credit. The system of workers' control existed independently of executive state power and had its own internal hierarchy from plant committees to the all-union council represented on the SCNE.

However, sharp political and economic changes in mid-1918 forced the government to speed up the process of nationalization of enterprise. This enlargement of the state sector of the economy strained the very weak state apparatus. Moreover, the absence at that time of the required economic mechanisms and trained personnel highlighted the problem of how to develop administrative and command methods to strengthen centralized management.

WAR COMMUNISM AS A SYSTEM OF MANAGEMENT

In September 1918, as the government was modernizing the system of management, the civil war and foreign intervention forced the Bolshevik party to move to a war economy. It had to provide everything necessary for the Red Army to win the civil war, so it distributed all resources and products to those who needed them. The basic features of war communism were the nonmonetary character of production and exchange, with the state forcing the laborer to work under very tight centralized management. The influence of money was nil. Trade was unlawful, and the government introduced a controlled exchange in the form of centralized supply and distribution. The Bolsheviks mobilized labor armies, using the principle that one who does not work does not eat. Centralization of management was so high that it became known as *vertical centralism,* in contrast to the principle of *democratic centralism.* Commanding became the only management method. The logical explanation for this system of management was that it systematically organized and finally delivered the desired result: winning the civil war. In terms of economic development, however, it was a disaster. In 1920, industrial production amounted to about 20% of what it was in 1913.

New Economic Policy

After the civil war it was clear that war communism could no longer serve the development of the socialist economy. Therefore Lenin formulated a new approach to the building of socialism in Soviet Russia that became known in 1921 as the *new economic policy* (NEP). The main focus of NEP was to create a base for industrialization by building channels for product exchange between cities and villages and by developing industrial capacity and effectiveness. In contrast to the policy of war communism, NEP allowed more market influence—with monetary regulations guiding production and exchange but with decentralized economic management. The most important political and economic task was to take into account the market, run it, and regulate market and monetary exchanges. The government began to tax production instead of expropriating it. This approach made for a lively exchange of commodities between a city and its surrounding villages at a time when the Soviet economy was 80% agricultural. State management became the way to manage only the big and profitable enterprises. All other enterprises had been either closed or moved into the private sector. Handcrafters were free to sell their products. The operating principle within the system during that period of time was decentralization of economic management within the context of centralized regulation by the government.

Two major groups of industrial enterprises emerged: the so-called state-budgeted enterprises, which produced to state orders under the principle of self-financing; and those enterprises that were not state budgeted, which had the right to sell their product at market prices with profits subject to taxation. During this period, there was no overall system of planning throughout the country. Enterprises developed horizontal market links between themselves. Thus NEP and its methods led from bureaucratic centralism to economic management through the use of prices, credit, and other market methods.

NEP also brought changes in personnel policy, reducing administrative and managerial staff in the central and local government. Under NEP, the government finally effected the principle of "one-man leadership" in all enterprises on a full scale. Under this plan, the manager was required to be not only a communist, but also an effective manager. The manager's status increased, and the government invited more bourgeois specialists to help manage the economy. There was also more party participation in the management of production; many of the best party personnel received management training and moved into management positions. Economic management under NEP brought high productivity and effective work.

During the short period of the NEP, when taxation of farm products replaced confiscation, agriculture improved and starvation was eliminated. Industry and transportation also began to improve. Large numbers of stock exchanges, fairs, and trading enterprises developed strong market links between cities and the peasants. Inflation became less dangerous, and the monetary system grew stronger with more banks, a new currency, and increased trade. The NEP system significantly improved the economic situation in the country, but the economy was still primarily agrarian. A weak industrial sector could not provide peasants with all the commodities they needed, and these shortages in turn limited agricultural development and that of the economy as a whole. There was a widely perceived need to speed up industrialization.

ADMINISTRATIVE SYSTEM OF MANAGEMENT*

A governmental commitment was made to speed up industrialization across the country through the mechanization of industry, agriculture, construction, and transportation. However, both the internal and the external economic environment limited the choices of how to industrialize in a very short period of time. Only internal resources were available, and because of the civil war destruction they were very limited. It became necessary to concentrate all available resources on the basic task of reconstructing industry. While no one in either the party or the country opposed industrialization, there were different points of view concerning the pace and the methods to be used.

One proposal was to use the experience of the NEP. This approach required more time and was based on objective economic laws. In contrast, key party members, including Stalin, wanted to use the command methods of management developed during the civil war. Because of specific internal and external factors, power finally went to those who ignored the objective laws of societal development and who rigidly applied war communist methods to building a new society. Stalin and his lieutenants rejected Lenin's policies of political and economic reform, improving party and state leadership, and democracy for the society. They opposed the idea of making

*The Russian word *administration* means management from the central government.

peasants and workers equal partners in building socialism. They saw private ownership of industry as well as market and monetary relations as a temporary evil. The great turnaround initiated by Stalin was a direct reflection of his belief in resolving all internal contradictions in social and economic areas on the basis of power and administrative methods. The government presented this system as the only possible way. Even though the model had a lot in common with war communism, it had its own logic and can be considered as an independent historical system of management in the USSR.

Management from 1926 to 1940

The intense industrialization during this period focused particularly on the development of heavy industry.[4] This was done to create a technological base for Soviet society. The work of industrialization gave preeminence to management by directives and to the use of administrative command methods such that the achievement of goals depended on the power of formal authority. Within the enterprise, the authority was held by the manager; above that, it was held by the government and the party. By virtue of their essence, these methods can be used only when they encompass all sectors, all factors of production, and all participants. The tasks, resources for their fulfillment, and forms of remuneration for labor became the object of direct centralized regulations. These administrative methods were intended to regulate all aspects of work life.

A central feature of management during this period was that success was measured almost exclusively by the fulfillment of physical output quotas. Directives could call attention to financial or efficiency indicators, but the main indicator was always fulfillment of the plan and growth of output. It followed that the evaluation of the worker was based primarily on output. Rates of pay were centrally regulated, and management offered bonus incentives for fulfilling or exceeding quotas. However, over time the bonuses became a significant and expected part of the workers' and managers' pay, thereby losing their intended motivational effect.

The positive side of management by centralized directive was rapid decision making, clear definition of tasks, and controlled resource allocation between sectors of the production system. Because of time pressures, all these advantages were important during the industrialization period.

The government's main problem was the accumulation of resources for industrialization. Resources were scarce, so their allotment was centralized at the state level. The state also assigned all production output quotas. And

4. Here and elsewhere, selections are taken from Popov, G. Kh., *Effective Management*, 2d ed. (Moscow: Ekonomika, 1985), pp. 17–22.

although part of the output might later return in the form of capital invest-ments to the same enterprise that produced them, return was in no way connected with the contribution of the enterprise to the state pool of resources.

Enterprises dating from the pre-industrialization period were seen as antiquated and of secondary importance. This had a negative effect on light industry and agriculture, which were allocated no money to develop new products and therefore essentially subsidized heavy industry. More-over, the criterion of profit had almost no significance during the period of industrialization, and production efficiency had only secondary im-portance to physical output. Prices were centrally set on the basis of na-tional priorities that bore little relation to costs or supply and demand. This resulted in a generation of managers with an underdeveloped aware-ness of either profit and efficiency, or how to measure those qualities. The enterprise had few rights or choices. Whole industries could survive even as they lost money.

As the system of managing society through the state's apparatus became more pervasive and powerful, the role of employee participation, em-bedded in the traditional Soviet concept of democratic centralism, was lost. There was a growing drive to nationalize everything. Management practice was essentially paternalistic and directive, demanding the punc-tual, absolute, selfless execution of each directive. Sparing no effort, work-ing all the harder, the director kept the whole operation on its toes. But such a system discouraged innovation and creativity. Even in the best-run enterprise, detailed and petty rules from above made the manager merely an implementer.

As the system proceeded, the conventional conflict between workers and managers reemerged, and the feeling of solidarity between the director and his subordinates as fellow members of a socialist society weakened. In time, though, another type of solidarity appeared and grew—the common interest of worker and manager in reducing production goals. Thus a spe-cial feature of managerial activity turned out to be the skill of negotiating easily fulfilled plans and reserves for supplies and investments. This resulted not so much in a decrease in the volume of output, as in simplifying it. A modest increase in the volume of repetitive operations was found to be the easiest way to simplify the tasks and concomitantly avoid the need to inno-vate and address long-term issues. Above all, it averted the danger of under-fulfilling quotas.

After Stalin's regime, a number of different reforms of the administrative management system were undertaken. In 1957, there was a shift from the so-called ministerial management to regional management. The branch ministries were abolished and the economy was managed through so-called regional councils of the people's economy. In 1965, there was an attempt to radically reform the management system by widely introducing monetary and market mechanisms such as price and profit. Enterprises obtained increased flexibility in making economic decisions. However, these reforms did not succeed.

CENTRALIZED MANAGEMENT ON THE EVE OF PERESTROIKA

State management of the economy. The socialist state acts as a powerful regulator of socioeconomic processes. According to the USSR constitution, the basic law of the country, the state is the sole owner of land, its resources, water, and forests. The primary means of production belong to the state: industry, construction, agriculture, transportation and communications, banks, stores, and most housing. Only the state possesses the organs and means of enforcement. Moreover, the state has at its disposal powerful means of ideological influence. Armed with the prerogatives of political power, authority, and the tools to influence people, the state plays a large role in the management of Soviet society. It is the main executor of party policy, the organizer for fulfilling party decisions.

State management includes levels corresponding to the levels of organization found in society and reflects both economic sectors and territorial regions. The highest organ of the state is the Congress of the People's Deputies of the USSR, which formats the government structure, which in turn oversees many ministries and departments both within and straddling sectors of the economy. The hierarchical structure of management in an area or sector of the economy is uniformly multileveled—from ministry and department to enterprise and organization. It may help Americans to think analogously of the Soviet economy as an enormous corporation with tens of thousands of subsidiaries and divisions. Legal acts regulate all the basic functions of management with laws, resolutions, orders, and instructions. Each participant in management is expected to know the laws and act on the basis of them. The observance of laws makes management stable and strong.

The scale of industrial activity in a particular region predetermines the relative weight of territorial approaches and industrial approaches to management. The two strategies are very different. First, while the industrial sector structure is organized by the type of finished product, technology, or raw material used, the territorial structure is broken out by republics, regions, and so on. More important, whereas the industrial sector and the territorial sector have the same objective—production—they differ widely in approach. Overdoing the territorial approach often leads to local interests dominating state interests and weakening the centralized management by industries. But an equally slavish devotion to absolute measures in the industrial approach leads individual industry to put its own interests ahead of society's needs and the development of the territory. In either case, society and the economy of the whole country suffer. Reconciling the two approaches is a contradictory and complex task, which is why there is a constant search for the optimal combination of industrial and territorial management of production.

Party role in the development of the economy.   The constitution of the USSR guarantees a leading role to the Communist party. The party is central to all aspects of political, social, and cultural, as well as economic life in Soviet society. The party role in economic development is determined by the following mechanisms: congresses, conferences, plenums of the Central Committee of the party and analogous organs of the Communist parties of the union republics, and territorial and local party organs. Territorial and local party organs control and help fulfill development targets by doing ideological, political, and educational work, selecting and assigning executives.

Much of the work of territorial party organs concerns the daily life and leisure time of workers, their housing, education, retail trade, public health, and so on. In addition, the local party organs assume large responsibilities in organizing the workers to solve the problems of economic development, raise productivity and quality, and use material resources rationally and economically. The party is also expected, by means of self-criticism, to lead the struggle against red tape, petty bureaucratic attitudes, and violation of state laws, as well as enforce labor and production discipline, forestall attempts to cheat the state, and strive for a sober lifestyle.

While the party is called on to monitor the economic development, it is not expected to substitute for management, the people directly responsible for an enterprise. Such substitution discourages a sense of responsibility among managers and allows them to hide behind party authority. But at times, party organs interfere without justification in the functions of management. Managers may be invited in by party organs, for example, dressed down, and given all manner of instructions and orders. The party leader may even shove the manager aside and assume his or her functions. It is necessary to understand that the party's role in the economy is different from that of economic management in both form and content. The party's role is to work with political and ideological management issues rather than to perform operational functions.

Planning economic activity.   Planning is organically inherent in the management of production; it covers all aspects of production and affects the whole economy. Economic plans differ along the following parameters:

- Termination dates—long-term (5–20 years); mid-term (2–5 years); current (annual, quarterly, monthly).
- Planning level—plans at the level of the whole state, sector of the economy, the union republics and the administrative and territorial units under their jurisdiction, industrial and agricultural complexes, consortia, enterprises, and organizations.
- Planning elements—plans for the development of industry and science and technology; a plan for social development; one for capital investment, labor, and finances, and so forth. The plans are not independent and unconnected to one another but are part of the plans of the overseeing level and serve as vehicles for integration and coordination throughout the economy.

Until now, draft plans were worked out and, after discussions at party congresses, they were sent for approval to the higher organs of state power. When worked out and approved at higher levels, these centralized plans have the force of law. The main criterion for evaluating the activity of an enterprise has consistently been to fulfill the plan according to all indicators.

Share with us the observation of academician N. N. Moiseev:

On more than one occasion, I have put this very question to managers of different ranks, both economic managers and party ones: What daily activity causes you the most problems? And, as a rule, I always got the same answer: the plan, to need to meet the plan. I think that this question illuminates one of the mistakes of our bureaucratic system of management, the fact of substituting a basic goal with an interim one.[5]

PERESTROIKA: RADICAL MANAGEMENT REFORM

In terms of the development of the Soviet enterprise, perestroika represents radical economic reform. Initiated in the second half of the 1980s in combination with democratization and glasnost in the political sphere, perestroika was designed to create a qualitatively new situation.

The Soviet economy, immense and intricately complex, cannot be reformed on a sector-by-sector basis. Reform of such a highly centralized system of management affects not only the activity of enterprises, but also the vital functioning of every centralized economic department and ministry.

A key idea of perestroika is to have enterprise management reform as the

5. Moiseev, N. N., "Portrait of a Manager," *Novyi Mir,* No. 4, 1988, p. 184.

core of the overall economic reform. A radical change in enterprise status and management in the beginning of perestroika will then require corresponding change in the larger socio-economic environment.

The impetus for reform.   Soviet economic reform of the 1980s sprang from a sheer necessity for radical change in the society. It should be noted that this was not the country's first attempt to set in motion serious, large-scale social and economic transformations with the goal of providing new impulses for its development. For all management reforms in the USSR, the key question has been the relationship between centralization and decentralization of economic and administrative power, and, consequently, the extent of the independent status of the enterprise in managerial decision making. The reform now being instituted in the Soviet economy is no exception.

What problems arose in the late 1970s and early 1980s and confronted Russian leaders with the need for serious change in the economic and social life of the USSR? Here we identify seven basic domestic, social, and economic reasons for economic reform:

1. *A falloff in the rate of economic growth.* Beginning in the 1970s and accelerating in the 1980s, the growth rate of the principal macroeconomic indicators of the USSR declined. Before reform was instituted, central government and industrial-sector ministerial bodies attempted to improve economic growth rates by means of administrative decrees for enterprises, setting percentages by which economic indicators should grow in a given year. Enterprises, having no serious incentives and even counterproductive ones, were fearful that inflexible plans would be foisted on them from above. Consequently, as upper management tried to impose plans with high growth rates, the enterprises used various pretexts to hold out for plans with lower growth rates.

Reform proposes to alleviate the administrative pressure ministries put on enterprises by introducing legal guarantees of the rights of enterprises, new planning procedures, and stable economic guidelines over the long term to replace subjective and willful directives from above.

2. *The low level of effectiveness of the Soviet economy.* The effectiveness of the Soviet economy from 1981–1985 declined in comparison with the growth from 1971 to 1975. At the beginning of 1988, many money-losing enterprises were recipients of annual subsidies from the state. In order to turn the money-losing enterprises around and increase labor productivity, reform proposes a complete system of measures, starting with the total technological modernization of the Soviet economy and ending with the financial self-sufficiency of enterprises as foreseen by the new Law on the Soviet State Enterprise.

It must be said, however, that in addition to the problems associated with economic reform itself, the measures for raising labor productivity may clash with the well-entrenched system of low social, ethnic, and geographical rates of population mobility in the USSR, as well as with the multitude of barriers to transfer capital and labor from one sector of the economy to another, and with wage leveling. A major challenge of reform is to ensure full labor utilization and avoid unemployment. Managerial mechanisms that would enable these needs to be met with a simultaneous increase in productivity are yet to be found.

3. *The need to bring about technological modernization.* One can appreciate the scale and depth of the problems confronting the Soviet economy by considering the fact that the proportion of equipment in industry that is fully depreciated but still in use rose from 36% in 1980 to 43% in 1987, and that the number of types of new technology created annually in the entire country has fallen in the last quarter century. On the enterprise level, the solution to these problems will require long-term efforts, possibly as long as several generations, to train and retrain executives, create a new type of economic and social thinking, and develop an appropriate organizational culture plus a new set of values among members of the enterprise.

4. *Thorny problems connected with the improvement of everyday life.* The most important of these are improving the food supply, improving the manufacturing and distribution system for consumer goods and services; solving the housing problem; guaranteeing public health services for the population; restructuring the cultural and educational development of society; and solving environmental problems. These issues must be addressed at the level of the enterprise as well as at the state level.

5. *Societal problems brought into the open by glasnost.* In general, these can be categorized as personal and social morality, the abuse of power, corruption, lawlessness, padding official statistics, and alcoholism, to name a few examples. While the eradication of these problems is, of course, beyond pure economic reform, the enterprise has a significant contribution to make.

6. *The rigidities of centralized price determination.* Until recently, pricing in the Soviet Union was done by the central government through an essentially paternalistic system dating back to the 1930s. The role of prices as an active economic lever in managing the economy was minimal. In practice, prices performed an accounting function and did not create the conditions for improving the efficiency of production and resource conservation. Fixed prices permitted enterprises to make profits regardless of their economic efficiency. The resulting imbalances were felt at the wholesale and the retail price level for industrial goods and foodstuffs, leading to a lack of balance between supply and demand, creating a shortage of some goods, limiting the demand for others, and producing a whole series of goods at excessively high prices. The black market grew, and other negative phenomena appeared in the economy. This was one of the reasons the purchasing power of the ruble fell.

7. *Centralized allocation of resources and products.* Before the reform period, the organization of material supply was characterized by a lack of free-market trade. Central authorities distributed the overwhelming majority of resources and products produced. The lack of market forms of trade, combined with the inflexibility of credit mechanisms and chronic shortages, spurred enterprises to hoard resources for "a rainy day." The accumulation of surplus supplies permitted the enterprises to avert a break in the rhythm of production for want of raw materials and supplies, but it often intensified shortages. Another aspect of the problem was the existence of an illegal black market, where various enterprises exchanged surplus resources for those in short supply in such a way that resources became almost a form of currency. Even with relatively stable wholesale prices, the shortages only strengthened the need for hoarding and bartering for resources.

To implement the USSR enterprise law requires the reform of macro-economic and state management policy regarding the following fields of enterprise activity: planning, investment, supply, technology, pricing, credit, compensation and motivation, external economics, property, management, and law.

Ownership.   Like previous reforms of the 1960s and 1970s, perestroika treats management reform as an important part of overall economic changes. But it is now understood that there cannot be a real management improvement without solving the property issue. The formula "he who owns should also manage" really works. To the Soviets this means moving the sense of ownership close to the people who actually manage the enterprise. In other words, perestroika intends to increase the role of managers in decision making and to reinstate such forms of ownership as will make this idea a practical reality.

The supply of enterprises under the new reforms.   Economic reform aims to initiate the transition from centralized funding of material resources to direct negotiated wholesale trade among industrial suppliers and customers. The new reforms stipulate that only those products that are particularly significant for the pace and scale of production will be distributed in a centralized manner. There are two stages to the development of supply reform. In the first stage state orders for goods will still constitute the lion's share of production, but direct wholesale trade will increase in proportion. During the second stage the scale of wholesale trade will dominate, and the enterprise will have the right to determine the resources it needs and acquire them by means of direct wholesale trade without limit.

The new financial and credit system.   Before reform, in accordance with the tradition of strict central planning, the work of the financial and credit system both outside and within the enterprise was controlled by the Ministry of Finance of the USSR and other agencies of the country's banking system. Fundamental problems of the Soviet financial and credit system prior to economic reform included an overall underestimation of the role of the credit system in managing the country's economy, the weakening influence of trade and monetary relations on the activity of enterprises, the practice of granting credit without proper economic justification, using credit to cover losses and long-term insolvency, a worsening record of meeting payments, and a considerable increase of the country's money supply without a corresponding increase of products to absorb it.

Under reform, existing banks will be reorganized as specialized banks, taking into consideration the needs of the population for credit and accounting services. The new interrelation between the enterprise and the financial and credit system is regulated by Articles 17 and 18 of the Law on the Soviet State Enterprise of June 30, 1987, until now the main document of economic reform. To justify its existence, an enterprise is required to make a profit. According to the plan, if losses occur during a transitional period, an enterprise can be financed with state funds within the limit of progressively smaller subsidies established by the state's five-year plan. The enterprise must work out measures to strengthen its financial situation, eliminate losses within an established time, and ensure profitable work. If it continues to show losses, it will be left to bankruptcy.

Perestroika's key feature for economic reform is putting every enterprise under the system of full self-sufficiency and self-financing. An enterprise may use bank credit to reach its manufacturing and social goals but only by strictly observing the credit principles of providing security for loans and meeting payments for principal and interest. The bank will grant short-time credit to an enterprise for those activities that strengthen its operating funds. Long-term credit will be granted for manufacturing and social investments that are gradually paid off by the enterprise through the accumulation of corresponding funds.

An enterprise is responsible for the efficient use of credit and required to meet its obligations in a timely manner. The enterprise systematically delinquent in making payments can be declared in default by the banks, which will so inform its principal vendors and the ministry.

Price determination under reform.   The following principles underlie the proposed radical reform in pricing:

1. The appeal of goods to consumers should be reflected in the price.
2. Competitive market prices can speed up scientific and technical progress, improvement of the quality of products, and creation of new techniques of resource conservation.
3. The transition to market prices is an integral part of the general state plan.
4. The tendency of prices to increase can be overcome by increasing economic competition among enterprises and by increasing consumer pressure on the manufacturer through refusal to buy low-quality goods.
5. The policy of achieving realistic market prices is linked to the task of improving the real income of the population while observing the principles of social justice.

At the present time it remains unclear exactly how the principles will be worked out—in other words, what the concrete mechanism for price fixing will be. Understandably, this is one of the thorniest and toughest questions of the whole Soviet economic reform. The issue is highly controversial among specialists and the greater public.

Reform in foreign economic activity and the enterprise.   Soviet foreign economic policy in effect from the late 1930s to the mid-1980s was characterized by a high degree of centralization of foreign trade carried out by the Ministry of Foreign Trade of the USSR, the State Committee for Foreign Economic Relations of the USSR, and other departments. Enterprises and the ministries of economic sectors did not have the right to conduct import-export operations independently or conclude foreign trade deals directly with foreign suppliers or clients. They were isolated from the foreign market. Now all enterprises and cooperatives have the right to conduct their own import-export operations in the foreign market. In addition, ministries and certain selected enterprises have the right to create joint ventures with foreign enterprises. The government has made possible a significant expansion of trade and joint ventures with firms of capitalist countries on the basis of mutual advantage.

The adoption of the Law on the Soviet State Enterprise is an important step on the road to meeting the goals set forth by foreign economic reform.[6] But there are problems with reform, and the solution to them is linked closely with perestroika's call for more decisive and consistent measures and the shortest possible time frame. One problem is the shortage of qualified executives possessing the professional knowledge and practical experience of foreign economic activity, especially outside of Moscow and Leningrad. The problem for Soviet managers is their lack of information about the current state of foreign markets—the whys and wherefores of dealing with them.

These problems are not surprising. They have been building for 60 years because of a lack of adequate solutions. However, the decisiveness and speed with which the new foreign economic policy is being carried out in the USSR bears witness to the serious intentions of Soviet leaders and to the long-term character of those intentions.

The role of the enterprise legislated by reform.   The principal goals and tasks of the enterprise are reflected in the Law on the Soviet State Enterprise. The main tasks of the enterprise are to satisfy consumers with high-quality products produced at minimal cost, expedite the pace of social and economic improvements in the country, and continue to serve the interests and well-being of the nation's employees.

To accomplish these tasks, the activity of the enterprise will follow certain guidelines and principles:

- Economic and social development
- Full economic accountability and self-financing
- Collectives' self-management
- Economic competition with other enterprises
- State legality

6. Some relevant details of this law appear in Appendix A.

The enterprise is to be managed in accordance with the principle of democratic centralism, with the broad participation of the enterprise's collective in the elaboration and approval of the plans and development targets.

In organizing the sale of its products, an enterprise is expected to meet completely the obligations arising from its contracts with customers in regard to quantity, variety, deadlines, quality, and other conditions. The enterprise is expected to study demand and to advertise. A purchasing enterprise is expected to pay on time for products delivered to it in accordance with the contract. Payment is to be made with the enterprise's own funds, or, in some instances, with bank credit. The enterprise will sell its products according to prices established centrally for state orders, but at prices it negotiates independently for all other orders. Ultimately, the enterprise will devote its financial activity to creating the financial resources for manufacturing operations and for social improvements.

An enterprise's financial resources derive from its own economic activity, and the enterprise will choose between two forms of business accounting to record that activity. The basic difference between the two forms is in the way the wage and salary fund is calculated. (For details, see Chapter 6.)

Within the guidelines established by higher authorities, the structure and process of management for each enterprise are determined by its production system. The typical structure of a large enterprise is as follows: The enterprise is managed by a director general (who represents the centralized aspect of democratic centralism). Deputy directors general (for production, engineering, finance, economic planning, marketing, human resources, and so forth) answer to the director. The deputy director general for production manages production and the workshops. Workshops have relative independence in production, and are granted wide latitude in the area of incentives for workers, although they do not enter into commercial relationships with other organizations. The basic production subdivision of the workshop itself is the section or production unit headed by the foreman. Production units are assembled from production brigades.

The work of the selection, assignment, and education of managers in the enterprise is performed by higher management, with active participation of the council of the employee collective, the party organization, and the union. The selection of managers takes place in the enterprise primarily through competitive free elections. For the senior posts, the employee council conducts the election. For the lesser posts, the election is conducted by the council with the workers voting directly. This election process is applied to the directors of enterprise, production units, workshops, sections, as well as to forepersons and brigade leaders. (It represents an important part of the democratic aspect of democratic centralism.) Elected directors have the right to appoint and to dismiss their assistants and deputies and the directors of functional subdivisions of the enterprise, according to established procedure.

LAWS AND REGULATIONS CONCERNING ENTERPRISES

The principles of civil legislation in the USSR and the union republics govern all legal entities, including state enterprises. Economic reform and the adoption of the Law on the Soviet State Enterprise on June 30, 1987 has supplemented the civil codes in important ways. Under current law, state enterprises are self-supporting legal entities. They control their fixed and working capital; they can acquire property and assume debts; they can be plaintiffs or defendants in court and arbitration procedures. In addition, the civil code that governs enterprises was recently expanded to include laws concerning joint ventures with foreign legal entities. However, this does not mean that the law or jurisprudence concerning joint enterprises can replace the principles of civil jurisprudence and civil statutes.

State enterprises are created on the basis of decisions made by ministries, state committees, and departments of the USSR. If, for example, an enterprise is under the authority of one of the constituent republics of the USSR, then it is created by the council of ministers of that republic. The decision to create an enterprise of one constituent republic in the territory of another republic can be taken only by agreement with the council of ministers of the other republic.

Because laws and regulations concerning enterprises are voluminous and complex, it is practical only to outline here the nature of the laws as they apply to the four decision areas of our research.

The legal system of the USSR closely defines the rules for capital equipment—its acquisition, use, taxation, and disposition. One enterprise has the right to transfer assets to another enterprise, sell them to organizations, exchange them, rent them, lend them temporarily free or for a fee, as well as write them off if they are antiquated or worn out.

The constitution of the USSR has established the right of its citizens to good health and, in this regard, there are numerous regulations to ensure that industrial equipment is safe and sanitary. The constitution also ensures that necessary measures have been undertaken for the protection and scientifically rational use of land, underground resources, water resources, vegetation, and wildlife; the preservation of clean air and water; the guarantee of renewable natural riches; and the improvement of the environment. An enterprise must take measures to compensate fully for any adverse effects its manufacturing activity has on the environment.

Planning in the USSR is subject to many rules and regulations. Once the state orders are given to an enterprise, it bears the responsibility for the fulfillment of the state order. If an enterprise has suffered monetary losses because of a ministry, then the latter is required to compensate the former. If conflict about financial damages arises, the matter will be arbitrated. Soviet law also requires the enterprise to maintain an accounting system and statistics. The leaders of an enterprise bear personal responsibility for false claims of success and other misrepresentation. An enterprise can also be allowed to cease functioning and its assets liquidated as a result of reorganization (merger, acquisition, splitting the enterprise, selling off a section). Moreover, an enterprise can simply be closed down if there is no demand for its product or if there are repeated financial losses and an inability to pay debts.

Hiring and firing is also governed by multiple laws. The constitution guarantees Soviet citizens the right to work. Workers and laborers exercise their right to work by means of a labor contract. A labor contract, in accordance with the fundamentals of labor law, is the agreement between labor and the enterprise under which the workers must perform work according to their specialty, qualifications, or position, observing the rules of the workplace. According to its part of the contract, the enterprise must pay the workers a salary and guarantee working conditions as stipulated by labor laws and collective bargaining agreements. The decision to hire is made by the director of the enterprise, and the director can share this right only with those officials whose leadership affects the whole enterprise. Soviet law also regulates work hours, overtime, and vacation time. Provision is made for workers' compensation for injuries. Workers cannot be discharged from an enterprise without the prior agreement of the enterprise's trade union committee except in those circumstances provided for by Soviet law. Contributions to social insurance are paid in full by the enterprise without deductions from the workers' paychecks. According to the constitution, citizens have the right to form labor unions. Union committees negotiate collective agreements for the workers with management.

Early in 1988, changes were introduced in connection with the switch to self-financing and the reduction of positions in enterprises. During the period of enterprise reorganization and liquidation, the overseeing agency guarantees workers the rights established by the constitution and Soviet law. Workers must be forewarned of their impending job termination not later than two months before the reorganization or liquidation of the enterprise. At the present time, centers or bureaus for job placement, worker retraining, and professional orientation are being set up. Workers placed in new jobs are guaranteed their average salaries for a period not longer than three months.

According to Soviet law, the right to decide to market a new product means the right to decide to develop a new standard. This right is granted to ministries, departments of the USSR, union republics, and enterprises. A *standard* is defined as a technical document outlining all the norms, rules, and standardization requirements approved by the competent agency, usually Gosstandart. The enterprise must monitor its technology closely to guarantee quality standards, reliability, and the safety of its products; it is expected to guarantee repairs and service after the product is sold. As a further assurance of quality, the state has introduced an evaluation system through which the quality of products is indicated by a state seal of approval. On a new product, a seal of approval must be issued within one year; for especially complex products, approval may occur within two years after the release of the first prototype. Gosstandart has the right in certain cases to extend the time limit. The highest quality rating is reserved for those products that according to all technical and qualitative indicators match or exceed the best Soviet and foreign achievements. If an enterprise takes delivery of a product that lacks the quality stipulated by state standards and agreed-upon contracts, it has the right to unilaterally break the contract with the supplier and demand compensation for losses.

An Historical Comparison

Economic histories of the United States and the USSR reveal significant differences. American enterprise has experienced a gradual shift from the seventeenth-century workshop/craft system to the current network/career system. Earlier forms of enterprise remain to a considerable extent as newer forms emerge. Throughout this long period, US economic institutions have been shaped and reshaped by the steady influence of markets and competition along with the checks and balances of governmental regulation and assistance. Despite periodic depressions and four major wars, the nation experienced no real invasions or abrupt shifts in its form of government. Evolution, not revolution, has characterized the nature of change.

In contrast, Soviet economic institutions in this century alone have traumatically changed from an agrarian feudal form, to an early form of capitalism, to war communism, to the New Economic Policy, to the centralized state control of the Stalin and post–Stalin period, and finally to perestroika. The country has now embarked on a new radical restructuring that has scheduled every element of the economic system for major reform. For the USSR, perestroika represents a relatively untested road. The field research findings in Part II offer an early look at its reforms in action at the factory level.

To round out the broad context for our study, Chapter 4 will present the theory of managerial decision making as it is currently understood in each country. It is this theory that informs the managerial practice we will turn to in Part II.

Chapter 4

US and Soviet Contemporary Decision-Making Theory

US Theory of Managerial Decision Making

[*Editors' note:* The following material on US theory was prepared primarily as an introduction for Soviet readers. Much of it will seem familiar to American readers.]

Major contributors to US decision theory are in general agreement about the steps individuals and organizations should follow to make rational decisions (Simon; Cyert and March). The following is a summary of those steps:

1. Searching the environment for information relevant to the interests of the individual or organization—intelligence activity.
2. Defining issues that require decisions (problems or opportunities)—issue-formulation activity.
3. Inventing, developing, and analyzing possible courses of action—design activity.
4. Selecting and weighing choice criteria based on desired end results—criteria activity.
5. Selecting a particular course of action from the options available—choice activity.
6. Implementing the chosen course of action—implementation activity.
7. Assessing past choices—review activity.

US theory recognizes that people commonly fall significantly short of carrying out all of the seven logical steps cited here. Human minds are, after all, limited in how rapidly they can assimilate information, how much they can store in memory, and how much they can focus on analysis at any point in time. The ideal decision process can be time-consuming and expensive, so people tend to use decision rules of thumb that save time but are prone to error and bias.

In both theory and practice, organizations can outperform individuals in decision making for the obvious reason that organizations can provide more expertise and more analysis than any one individual can command. This holds even though organizational decision making is much slower than individual decision making and also falls far short of theoretically optimal decision making. Scholars of organization have identified and described different patterns of organizational decision making that capture the less-than-optimal character of the actual process.

Satisficing is the term that March and Simon introduced to suggest that organizations tend to act on the first decision alternative that is found to meet some threshold level of performance. *Incrementalism* is the term that both Lindblom and Quinn use to suggest the step-by-step, somewhat trial-and-error way of making decisions that many organizations employ. "Garbage-can decision making" is described by March and Olsen as the method where various choice opportunities, problems, and preferred solutions are mixed together in a stew and only sometimes matched up with one another. In spite of these organizational shortfalls, there is evidence of a fair degree of rationality in the process by which organizations make decisions.

Current US theory on how organizations can best make decisions addresses two questions: (1) How can organizations most rationally process a single decision issue? and (2) How can organizations most rationally be structured for processing an expected stream of decision issues?

In regard to the first question, the theory can be summarized in three propositions:

1. Issue formulation, design, criteria, and choice activity should be centered around the organizational level and role where the relevant information is most concentrated (Thompson).
2. Information should be gathered from all organizational members from any level or role possessing relevant environmental facts, criteria, or design proposals (Galbraith).
3. The final choice should reflect relatively more influence (power) from the levels and roles that are most critical to the successful completion of the chosen action (Pfeffer and Salancik).

Both logic and, to some extent, empirical testing (Lawrence and Lorsch) support these three propositions. It should be obvious that adherence to them requires that an organization handle different decision issues in different ways. For example, the selection of an inexpensive piece of manufacturing equipment would be made by production people close to the factory floor, while a decision about introducing a major new product would be taken by marketing and R&D people at a higher level where market and technical information are concentrated. It should be noted that these three propositions address not only the information-processing aspects of decision making, but also the political or power aspects. In reality, organizations fall short of these normative ideas on both dimensions. Every organization needs to be structured in terms of levels, roles, and relationships in anticipation of adequately handling a stream of particular decision issues.

This leads to the second question. Here the relevant US theory begins with the idea that organizations can best be understood as mechanisms that are structured for making a stream of decisions (Barnard; Simon). Because organizations are committed to different purposes and strategies requiring them to make different kinds of decisions, it follows that they need to be structured in ways that reflect these decision streams. For example, one would expect a can company to be organized quite differently from a semiconductor firm.

Organization structures can be specified by the number and type of differentiated or specialized roles they employ and by the kinds òf integration or coordination mechanisms they employ. The differentiated roles should reflect or map the complexity and diversity of the particular environment with which their purposes or strategy commit them to cope. For example, a firm that needs to weld steel to produce its products would be expected to employ one or more experts who can relate to the state of the art of welding. Differentiation must encompass employees' thinking patterns and values as well as their motor skills. To achieve their purposes, organizations must also integrate the activities of their differentiated roles and departments. The greater the differentiation of roles, the more resources are needed to achieve integration (Lawrence and Lorsch). Organizations employ up to six general types of integrating mechanisms to supply the needed decision-making capacities on a regular basis (Galbraith). Listing the six mechanisms from the simplest and most traditional to the most complex and contemporary, they are (1) common boss, (2) rules, (3) plans, (4) individual lateral roles, (5) group lateral roles, and (6) matrix. Organizations are expected to employ the simpler mechanisms and add the more complex mechanisms in order only as the number and complexity of decision issues to be handled exceeds the existing decision-making capacity of the firm (Thompson). The first three are concerned primarily with achieving integration up and down the hierarchy (vertically), and the last three with achieving integration directly among departments by means of a lateral decision-making network.

1. *Common boss.* When two or more organizational members regularly contribute to the same decision issue, integration is achieved by having them report up to a shared or common boss who will resolve any decision choices concerning this issue. As required by the number of organizational members, the common bosses are in turn assigned to other common bosses to create a decision-making hierarchy of line-boss roles. In the United States, managers are generally expected to refer conflict upward to their common boss without skipping an intervening echelon. Likewise, higher authorities are expected to direct their subordinates by acting through hierarchical channels, one level at a time. In this way, no manager's authority will be undermined by subordinates acting on directions from above without that manager's prior knowledge. This practice can, however, seriously delay decision making and cause communication distortions. Line bosses are expected to take personal responsibility for achieving certain defined results on behalf of the organization, and they expect to receive the corresponding authority to direct the needed resources, both human and material, to achieve these results. Thus the common dictum: *authority should equal responsibility.* In addition to the line or chain-of-command roles, US organizations include staff roles. These positions report to line positions and are expected to support the line as expert advisers without undertaking the authority or responsibilities of the line. It is commonly expected as part of an employment agreement in the United States that the boss's prerogative is to issue directives and the subordinate's obligation is to comply. Managers are taught, however, that as a matter of personal courtesy supervisors should request the compliance of subordinates. They are also taught that it is wise to listen to subordinate's relevant ideas and problems before issuing instructions. Managers encourage such employee participation in decisions to improve the quality of the decision and to increase the probability of commitment and implementation. Nevertheless, employee participation has been institutionalized in only a limited way in the United States, by means of collective bargaining where unions represent employees, and by firms that organize semiautonomous work groups (see Chapter 3).

2. *Rules.* Organizations formulate and disseminate decision rules or standards that serve to integrate by specifying what action is to be taken under what specific conditions. As such, rules are a basic way of achieving integration in all organizations. The rules that organizations employ vary from the specific to the very general and are classified across this range as operational, strategic, and institutional. Typically, the middle levels of management formulate operational rules. For example, an operational rule would be one applying to the use of safety clothing. These rules are often compiled into guidebooks that may have obvious practical utility but can become so voluminous and rigid that they inhibit sensible responses to changing circumstances. More general strategic rules, known as business policies or strategies, cover such topics as the types of products and services to be made and sold, the type of customer to be served, the kind of distribution channel to be employed, the manner of setting prices, the conditions and guarantees on sales, and so forth. Strategic rules are usually formulated at upper-management levels with some input from middle management. Strategic rules, like other rules, are not time limited; they stay in force until changed. For example, the early Ford Motor Company issued a strategic rule that lasted for well over a decade: customers could buy Fords in any color they wished so long as it was black.

Finally, there are the most general institutional rules, many of which are specified in state and federal statutes. These rules deal with the purpose of the enterprise and its relationship to other societal institutions, primarily to the state. They cover the legal form of the enterprise (e.g., corporation, partnership, voluntary association, cooperative) and the legal charter that expresses this form. These rules specify who owns the enterprise and what are the rights and obligations of its owners. In this sense the institutional rules specify who benefits from the work of the enterprise. It is customary in US corporations for these rules—particularly those that relate to stockholder dividends, executive salaries and bonuses, general pay scales, and levels of capital investment—to be made at the highest level by boards of directors, as the elected representatives of stockholders, on the basis of recommendations developed by the chief executive officer. Employee interests, consumer interests, and broader public interests commonly influence these decisions indirectly; only on an exception basis is there direct representation.

3. *Plans.* Organizations integrate their affairs by using plans that specify resources to be available and goals to be reached for a given time period. Such plans can be assigned to organizational units designated as profit or cost centers where more detailed decision making can proceed within the scope of the plan. Plans have the advantage over rules of being more flexible and adaptable to changing circumstances. In the United States, plans have evolved into a central means of integrating large enterprises, in particular of integrating their strategic plans with their operational plans. The most important planning period in the United States is the year, which in turn may be broken down into quarterly or monthly plans or extrapolated into longer-term plans, usually toward a three- or a five-year horizon.

The usual yearly planning cycle starts with top management deciding on the planning guidelines to be used by each strategic business unit (SBU). SBUs are the smallest units that are responsible for a complete economic transaction—that is, the design, production, and sale of specified goods and services. The guidelines for planning forecast the level of relevant economic activity and the general targets the corporation seeks in terms of sales, profits, and capital spending. Each SBU then prepares a detailed annual plan that specifies what it forecasts in terms of sales by product and market and what it proposes in terms of new product introductions, costs, profit margins, employment levels, and capital spending. These proposals are reviewed and revised at corporate headquarters, which can involve additional discussions with the SBU before corporate level authorizes final plans for implementation. Results are periodically reviewed against plans at the corporate level, at least on a quarterly basis and often on a monthly basis. Corporations vary considerably on the extent to which they revise plans on an interim basis to deal with unanticipated circumstances. In any event, division management is expected to inform higher management of any significant deviations from the plan as soon as they are known. The degree to which the annual planning cycle is dominated by top-down directives or by bottom-up proposals also varies across enterprises, with most firms striving for a balance of the two (Bower).

The three decision or integration mechanisms considered so far (common boss, rules, and plans) are vertical or hierarchical in nature. When a firm requires more decision-making capacity than these methods can supply, hierarchical decision mechanisms become overloaded, both the quality and the timeliness of decisions deteriorate, and waiting lines form to get the time and attention of senior people. At that point, lateral mechanisms need to be adopted to supplement the vertical. And in fact, most (not all) larger US enterprises now use lateral mechanisms because the number and complexity of required decisions exceeds the limited capacity of the three vertical mechanisms. At this point, organizations are expected to employ, in sequence, three mechanisms that are lateral or network in nature, as follows.

4. *Individual lateral decision making.* Organizations may authorize individuals to make bilateral decisions between separate functional units without reference to their common boss. Although made within the general context of approved plans and rules, these lateral decisions take a shortcut around the hierarchical system. At times the appointment of a liaison officer further facilitates direct lateral decision making by helping to bridge the gap between separate units. Within the context of single business enterprises, or within profit center divisions of larger corporations, individuals may also be appointed as integrators. An early form of integrator was the project manager who was assigned temporary responsibility for coordinating the multiple units and resources required to complete a time-defined piece of work such as a construction project or a new product startup. Another form of integrator is the product manager who is charged with continuously managing all aspects of a product across the functional lines in a division making multiple products. The product manager often coordinates the development of new products as well. Other integrators may be market, technology, or regional managers.

In contrast to the rules of the hierarchy, these integrators have responsibilities that exceed their normal authority to command compliance. They trade primarily on their authority as experts. They have the power of lateral access and can convene meetings with their peers in other relevant units. They can persuade others to take coordinated action on the basis of logic and the overall interests of the enterprise, but they are not line bosses. When integrators carry out this role with energy and knowledge, it can result in balanced, timely decisions without consuming the time and attention of higher authorities (see Exhibit 3.4).

5. *Group lateral roles.* Organizations may appoint temporary task forces or permanent teams composed of representatives of different functional and specialist units and assign them specified decision-making issues for multilateral resolution without reference to their common boss. These groups of managers are an extension of the integrator role, with the individual integrator acting as chairperson for the integrating team. For example, a business team could be named to develop a new product opportunity. Its members could include a representative of each of the major functional departments. One member who has expertise and skills critical to the product's success would be named chairperson, or integrator. Team members usually undertake this role as an extra, part-time responsibility with the support of their line bosses. Together they develop and decide on business plans and implement the plans within the scope of their original charter. These integrating mechanisms are widely used in the United States.

6. *Matrix.* An organization may assign members to report permanently to two line bosses who represent two different chains of command within the firm. One line boss represents a division of labor by specialized function, the other by product or by geog-

raphy (see Exhibit 3.3). It is estimated that matrix structures are used to some extent in at least one-half of the larger US corporations. Many firms have difficulty making the structure work as intended, however, because some managers have trouble handling the ambiguity of more than one boss.

An organization usually adopts the matrix when it faces competitive pressure to excel in both technology and market responsiveness (Davis and Lawrence). Using a functional organizational structure would foster technological excellence, and using a product structure would foster market responsiveness. Since neither structure can focus management concern simultaneously on both performance dimensions, a matrix or dual chain-of-command structure is indicated. Furthermore, unlike the two other lateral mechanisms, the matrix structure gives the integrator, or product manager, line authority comparable to that exercised by the functional department managers. Great care and patience are needed to teach managers how to work effectively in a matrix structure, but when this is done, the matrix can increase the decision-making capacity of the organization. Many interdepartmental issues can be resolved by direct problem-solving effort without the delay of moving the issue up to the common boss.

Exhibit 4.1 clarifies how the six integrating mechanisms are expected to be brought into play. It illustrates that every organization starts by using the base mechanism of a common boss and then adds mechanisms one at a time as they are required by the complexity and quantity of issues to be resolved. In this way additional decision-making capacity is created. Although an organization retains the three vertical mechanisms even as network methods are added, these decision-making methods gradually move the organization from a centralized functional structure (steps 1 and 2), to a decentralized multidivisional structure (step 3), to a network structure (steps 4, 5, and 6). This clearly links to the discussion in Chapter 3 on the historical evolution of organizational forms in the United States. It suggests that US organizations are evolving by adding decision-making capacity to cope with the increasing complexity of decision issues. The reasons for this long-term trend toward increased decision complexity are not obscure. The advance of science and technology adds complexity. Consumers are becoming more demanding and discriminating. Competition has been moving from local to global. Consequently, this trend toward decision complexity and related organizational complexity is likely to continue (Lawrence and Dyer).

USSR Principles and Theory of Managerial Decision Making

[*Editors' note:* This section was prepared primarily to assist American readers by summarizing Soviet theory about managerial decision making. Our

EXHIBIT 4.1   The Six Integrating Mechanisms of US Corporate Decision Making

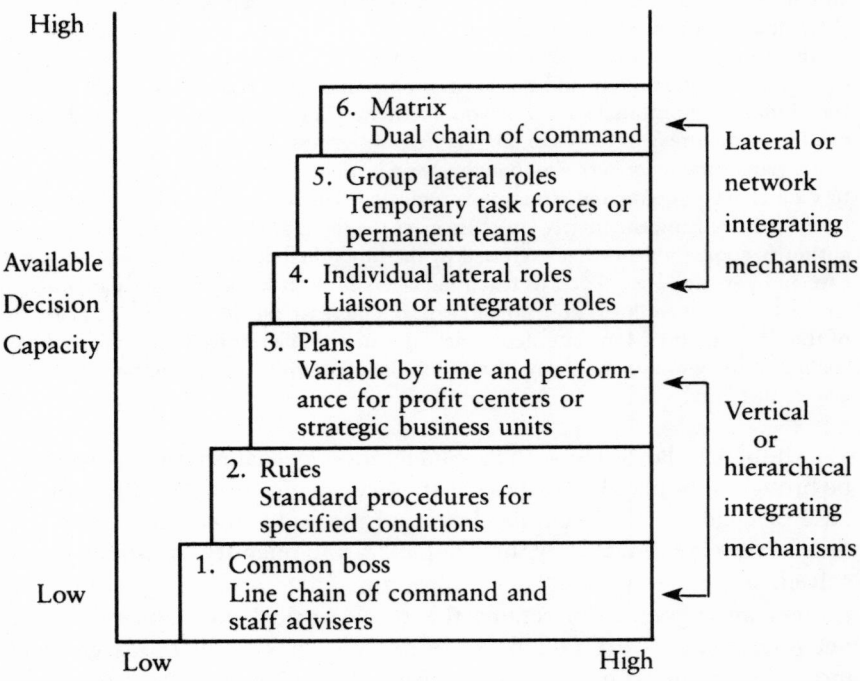

Number and Complexity of Decision Issues

editing has been limited to a clarification of what our Soviet colleagues have chosen and interpreted.]

Managers in the USSR are taught that any decision is the product of management activity. As a process, the decision can be broken down into three stages: (1) the preliminary or preparation stage, (2) the elaboration and adoption stage, and (3) the implementation and review stage. This three-stage process is called the managerial cycle. Each stage of the managerial cycle can be divided into substages.

1. Preliminary
   a. Search and investigate the situation
   b. Identify the problem
   c. Formulate and name the problem
2. Elaboration and adoption

   a. Develop alternative solutions
   b. Assess alternative solutions
   c. Choose the best alternative
   d. Formalize the decision by producing a document
3. Implementation and review
   a. Organize the implementation of the decision
   b. Review and control how the decision is implemented
   c. Assess the final result

The final assessment serves to investigate mistakes and their reasons as well as to identify and build on the positive experience. We will use the term *decision-making process* to refer to the three stages outlined here.

As is known in management practice, it is difficult to isolate a single decision that can be used as a complete and final model; each concrete decision will be unique. The art of management in the USSR means using the principles and patterns of socialist management to seek and find forms and methods that will be most effective in concrete situations. Managers must apply both the general principles and the more specific patterns to the concrete situation.

PRINCIPLES OF SOCIALIST MANAGEMENT

Principles of management articulate stable relationships among different elements of the managerial system. Basic principles have been developed through practice and theory and are reflected in legislation and laws, such as the USSR constitution and the Law on the Soviet State Enterprise. The basic principles are as follows:

- Combination of centralized leadership and grass-roots democracy (CL/GD).
- Pervasive state management wherein the state represents the whole society and manages everything, and everything is managed on behalf of all the people.
- Combination of party leadership with independent economic management.
- Consideration of the numerous different interests (national, collective, individual).
- Planning. Management activity must be organized by a plan; decisions should be made based on real economic facts and consequences reflect both industry and territorial interests.

The foundations for these principles are the collective ownership of the means of production, technological progress, social and political unification of the country, state representation of all people, and Marxism/Leninism. Centralized leadership and grass-roots democracy (CL/GD) is the most important single principle under socialism. It expresses the most significant relationship between management and subordinates and inter-actions among different elements of the management system (including goals, functions, methods, organizational structure, personnel techniques, process, procedures, innovations and so forth). Its essence is that central-ized leadership (managing from one center, subordination of minority to majority, subordination of specific to general interests, tough discipline, one-man power) must be balanced by grass-roots democracy (the power of the workers' collective, shop-floor-level initiative, elections of production unit leaders). Historically this principle, originally formulated as demo-cratic centralism, was used to organize activity of the Communist party. After the revolution it spread beyond the party to state and enterprise man-agement. Under Stalin the democratic aspects of this principle were sup-pressed. In its renewed form, as a key element of perestroika, we will refer to it as CL/GD.

State hegemony. In the USSR the state represents its population and acts as an agent in its behalf. The state is the major owner of the means of production and has full power to force anyone to do anything. The state educates people ideologically to be ready to fulfill societal demands and obligations. State management has many internal hierarchical levels orga-nized by industries and by territory. The Council of Ministers along with numerous industrial ministers and their managing bodies run the national economy. Each industry's management is organized into many different levels, starting with the ministry headquarters and proceeding downward through the enterprise and the plant to the section and the brigade. The im-portant thing is that enterprise management includes managing not only the people, but also the material resources—plant and equipment, supplies, and so forth. All enterprises have jurisdictional status and economic ac-countability (*khozraschet*). They are fully responsible for their own opera-tional decision making.

Territorial management levels range from the all-union level, through the union republic, to the city and the village. The basic territorial management is done by the Council of People's Deputies, which is created at each level of the hierarchy. All management actions fall under state jurisdiction, and the state specifies the approaches to be followed in any decision-making process. The current perestroika trend is to pass more authority in decision making in many fields to the territories.

Communist party participation. The Communist party participates in management, elaborating, and approving basic program documents in areas of general economic policy. It also provides political and ideological support for the development of the economy. This work is done by the party through its own hierarchy, which is built on the territorial chain. In the enterprise, party organizations are used to mobilize workers' efforts to fulfill production targets—to "do [their] best."

Centralized leadership and grass-roots democracy. As the major foundation for the Soviet decision-making process, CL/GD can be reviewed at two levels. On the macro level, the decision maker must balance the needs of centralization and decentralization. On the micro level, CL/GD combines one-man power (*edinonachalie*) with the collegial (*kollegiallnost*) and the collective (*kollectivenost*) aspects of the decision-making process.

The main issue of centralization/decentralization hinges on how much authority is delegated from the top down. The real degree of delegation depends on where in the hierarchy decision making is centered. There could be three types of centralization from this point of view: first, only key decisions are made at the top; second, the majority of decisions are made at the top; and third, all decisions are made at the top level. Because of human limitations, moving many decisions upward means either expanding the top-level staff or delegating its authority downward. For this purpose the USSR has developed the deputy system. But don't be misled. Deputization creates the appearance that the top leader entrusts rights to deputies, whereas in fact this is only a formality, not a real delegation of authority.

On the other hand, higher-quality decisions may be made at a lower level where the most information is available and by the people who will be responsible for implementing the decision. It is clearly perestroika's policy to leave only strategic and policy decisions to the top level and to delegate operational decisions to lower levels. Decentralization not only brings more independence to structural task units (STUs), it has another facet that makes it similar to democratism.

Similar issues arise at the micro level but the forms are different; specifically, one-man power, the collegial, and the collective. One-man power means giving one person all decision-making rights. But an allocation of rights must be consistent with responsibilities. Managers are responsible for overall organizational activity and the results of their enterprises. Both the status of managers in the USSR and their rights are reflected in legislation. The manager is automatically entitled to represent the enterprise and its collective to any other person. He or she controls the assets of the organization (building, furniture, equipment), makes any agreements or gives power of attorney as required, opens bank accounts, and performs other such actions. Within his or her area of responsibility a manager may issue an order, which then becomes obligatory for all in the organization. Naturally, this occurs under the sanction of state management; the manager not only organizes the production process and represents the organization, but also represents state and national authority within the enterprise.

Again, it is important that management's responsibilities and duties be balanced with management's rights. Many rights with few responsibilities create the possibility of lawlessness and ineffective decisions. Many responsibilities with few rights restrict creativity and effectiveness. While in practice a manager's rights often do exceed his responsibilities to some degree (top management tends to have the most rights with the fewest responsibilities), a relative balance remains the ideal.

Just as centralization and decentralization are linked, one-man power cannot be assessed without considering the collegial and collective parts of the decision-making process. The collegial and the collective interact with one-man power in the decision-making cycle. For example, numerous people affect the decision making in the early and final stages, while at the second-stage decision point one-man power usually dominates. To balance one-man power, one needs many forms of the collegial. The most widely used dynamic of collegial-manager integration is when the manager makes a decision after listening to the opinion of a council of experts. The use of the collegial helps the manager build good relations with subordinates. On the other hand, extreme use of the collegial leads to diffusion or avoidance of responsibility, red tape, and bureaucratism.

The third element in the decision process, the collective, is usually accessed through elections. The role of the manager in this situation varies. It could be leading a discussion, mediating conflict, or, more autocratically, determining the amount of collective influence that will affect each decision. In terms of relative collective influence, there are four general categories of decision situations:

1. When decisions for general directions are made by the whole collective, and implementation of the decision is done by individual STU managers.
2. When the collective adopts a decision as well as a general direction and assigns who should do what. Implementation of the decision is done by the managers individually without further interference of the collective into the work process.
3. When the collective gets involved directly in the work process.
4. When the collective makes all decisions regarding who should do what, when, and how.

Decision type 4 is more likely to happen in brigade activity, whereas decision type 1 is more likely to happen with the workers' collective council at the enterprise level.

Key Soviet Management Concepts for the American Reader

[*Editors' note:* The following section was prepared to explicate for the American reader some important Soviet management concepts drawn from both theory and practice as we observed it in the plants. These ideas will be particularly useful for understanding the reports of managerial behavior in Part II.]

It is of crucial importance that American managers who are to be involved in joint venture operations realize that the Soviet system, while presently in flux, has and intends to preserve its own management principles, which have evolved from deeply rooted traditions, values, and priorities.[1] In this manner, the Soviet government is committed to seek indigenous solutions to its problems. These management principles need to be accepted and respected by participating American managers even though they may be difficult to comprehend. Therefore we find it necessary to clarify some points and expand on what our Soviet colleagues have to say about this crucial issue.

The content of authority in Soviet organizations is hard to grasp, as it differs conceptually from that of its counterpart in Western hierarchies. The classic organization chart (see Exhibit 4.2) implicitly reflects the Western attitude toward the type of authority superiors should have over subordinates. Although they must perform assigned tasks, periodically report to, and occasionally seek decisions from their direct superior, subordinates in the US system are recognized to be *separate* links in the chain of command. Whatever authority their positions carry is theirs and is *not included* in the authority of their superiors. Moreover, superiors cannot short-circuit their subordinates. Therefore they often find themselves isolated from the reality of their area of responsibility by the wall that their immediate subordinates form to obstruct their direct contact with lower echelons of the organization, which subordinates consider to be their own "turf."

---

1. "We are looking within socialism, rather than outside of it, for the answer of all questions that arise." Gorbachev, Mikhail, *Perestroika* (New York: Harper & Row, 1987), p. 36.

"Perestroika" represents a renewal "of society on socialist principles . . . under no circumstances must we depart from this path," Gorbachev, Mikhail, Meeting of the CPSU Central Committee with workers, January 6, 1989 (Moscow: Novosk Press, 1989).

EXHIBIT 4.2   Classic Functional Authority Structure in US Enterprise

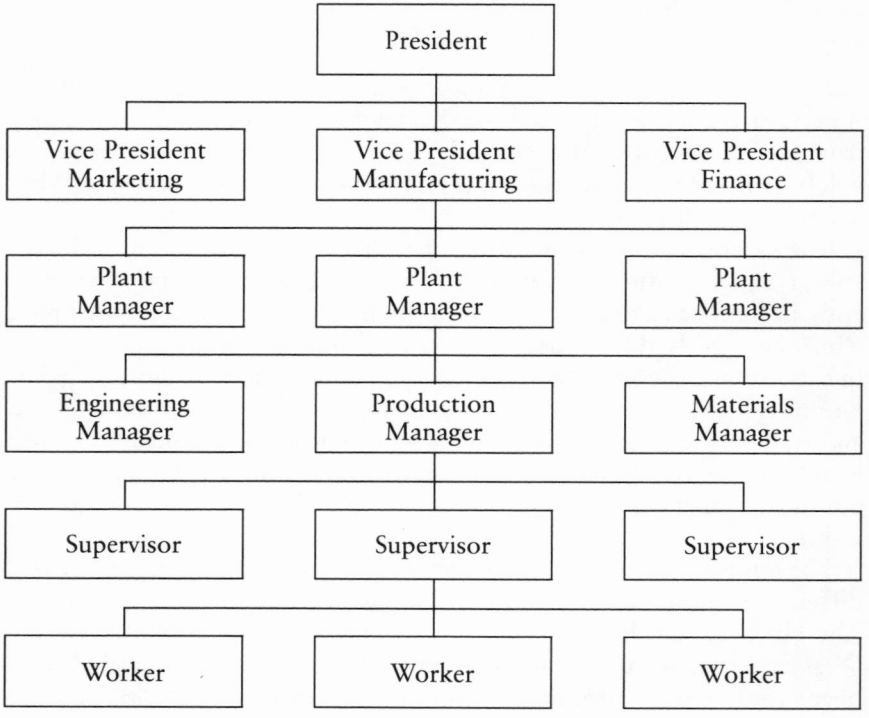

In the Soviet system, authority has a very different connotation (see Exhibit 4.3).

STRUCTURE OF THE SOVIET SYSTEM

The core of the traditional managerial structure of Soviet enterprise is the structural task unit (*podrazdelenye*)[2] or STU. The STU is a group charged with performing a specified task in the enterprise.[3] Soviet enterprises are themselves STUs, and each contains as many STUs as are necessary to perform its assigned tasks. Each STU is a microcosm of all larger ones and a model for all smaller ones. Each STU has as many hierarchical levels as are necessary. As shown in Exhibit 4.3, the smallest STU of an enterprise is the

2. See Para. 6 of Article 5 and Para. 2 of Article 6 of the Law on the Soviet State Enterprise.
3. There are Production STUs (*proizvodstvennye podrazdelenye*) and Administrative STUs (*administrativnye podrazdelenye*). The STU is not to be confused with the US notion of the strategic business unit (SBU), which mainly refers to a profit center rather than to a team of people. Nevertheless, in the Soviet system, especially with the self-financing rule introduced by perestroika, STUs are often also SBUs.

EXHIBIT 4.3   STU System of Authority in a Soviet Enterprise

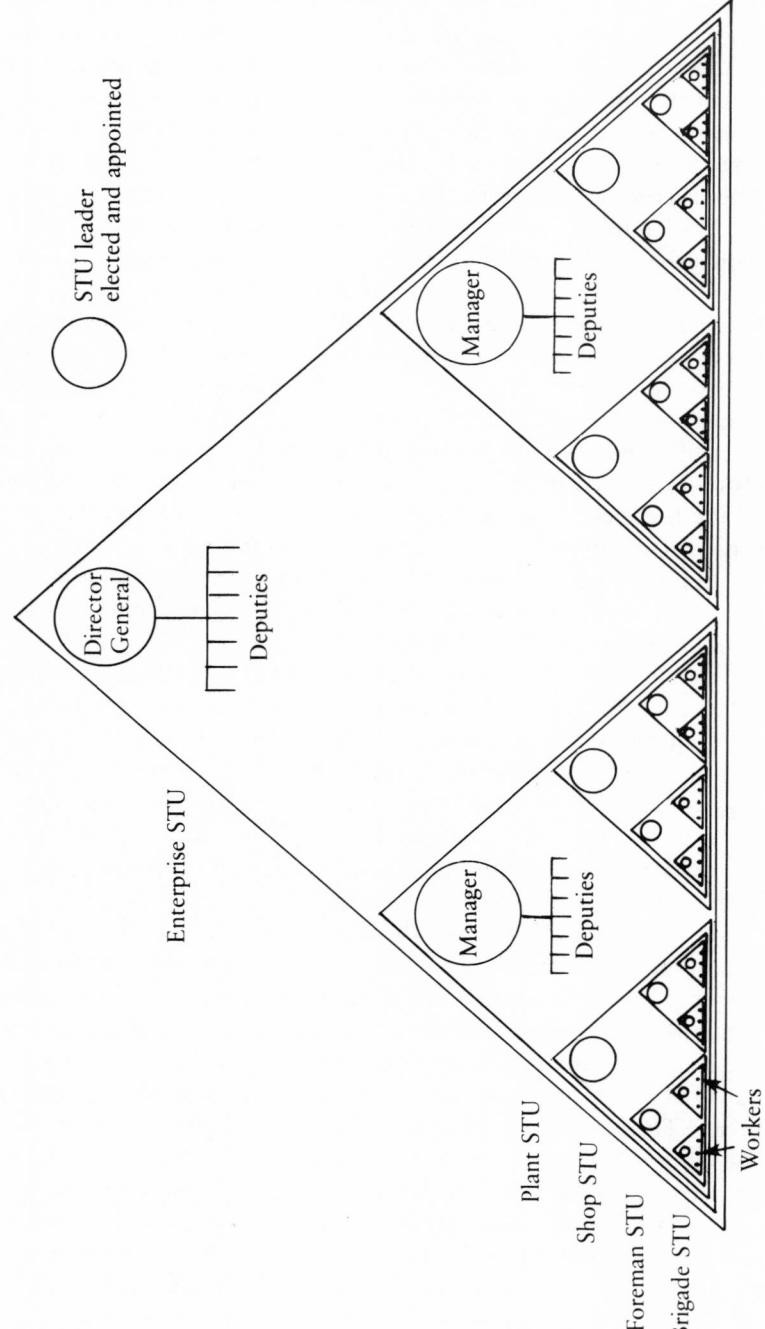

brigade, which has only two levels: the workers and the brigade leader. The largest STU of the enterprise is the enterprise itself. If an enterprise comprises more than one plant, it usually contains five hierarchical levels of line managers: the director general of the enterprise, the plant managers, the workshop managers in each plant, the foremen in each workshop, and the brigade under each foreman. Each Production STU is led by a manager, who, according to perestroika's Law on the Soviet State Enterprise of June 30, 1987, must be legitimated by being elected by his subordinates and subsequently confirmed by superior authority. This two-step legitimation of authority makes the STU manager doubly strong.

We emphasize that the practice of subordinates electing managers cannot as yet be considered established. The election process has been in force only since 1988. With the exception of one plant where two elections have already been conducted, the plants we studied had had only one round of elections, and it's likely that a number of Soviet enterprises have not gotten around to it yet. In our study we did find that candidates and voters were taking these elections very seriously. We stress, however, that Soviet joint venture legislation has not yet clarified whether or not the requirement of electing managers applies to joint ventures. In either case, joint ventures in the USSR would be well advised to develop mechanisms whereby workers have the opportunity to influence decisions.

To help the reader better understand the STU idea, Exhibit 4.3 illustrates each STU as a triangle. Once elected and confirmed, STU leaders are granted a great deal of discretion by superiors and are obeyed by subordinates. At the same time, through voicing opinions openly, making suggestions, and offering criticisms at meetings, group members provide input to the internal decision process of the STU and thus have direct influence on the external input of the STU to the decision process of the entire enterprise.

Members of STUs refer to themselves as "we," and show an astounding cohesion, solidarity, camaraderie, and loyalty to one another and to their leader. These characteristics of the STU often lead to excessive compartmentalization of the affairs of organizations. In cases of weak leadership at the top, they can diminish the unity of the enterprise and enhance the tendency of an STU to give priority to its own interests over those of the enterprise. STU members are bound to one another by total confidentiality as to the inner workings of the group. In fact, divulging information to outsiders, even on trivial matters, needs the leaders' clear approval. STUs function as a collective entity that is practically impossible for outsiders to penetrate. Small, closely knit informal groups have always been a part of getting things done in Russia. Examples include the peasant commune (*obshchina-volost*), the peasants' *artel*, collective labor groups, the village *mir,* and the elected rural councils (*zemstvos*).[4] In the factory, the parallel to these land collectives is the brigade. In essence, all these groups are STUs. STUs can be one of the great strengths of the Soviet enterprise, but these cohesive groups are very hard to integrate horizontally.

Not all Soviet managers are STU leaders. Deputies, for example—including deputy directors and staff people—are not considered STU leaders. STU leaders usually delegate important parts of their authority to deputies, who within the realm of the delegated responsibilities, have the authority to act as STU leaders. A good example of this is the head engineer of each plant. A reliable indicator of which managers are Production STU leaders is whether or not they are required by law to be elected by their subordinates. Elected managers are Production STU leaders and provide the backbone of authority in the enterprise. Managers of Administrative STUs (staff) can be leaders of their individual STUs only by appointment and without being elected. Exhibit 4.3 indicates that the following managers are elected STU leaders in a Soviet industrial enterprise:

- Director general of the enterprise
- Plant manager, if the enterprise has more than one plant
- Workshop manager
- Foreman
- Brigade leader

The power of STU leaders in an enterprise can be compared with a nested set of the familiar Russian *matrioshka* dolls. The largest *matrioshka* doll contains all the smaller dolls, just as the primary STU (the enterprise) contains all the smaller units. And just as each progressively smaller doll contains all the smaller dolls, each progressively lower STU leader has authority over all the smaller units. Even the lowest functionary, the worker (the tiny solid doll inside the stack), can be viewed as an STU leader. Though individual workers are without subordinates, their authority rests in their clearly specified realm of responsibility (*kompetencija*).[5] Thus the director general's authority and responsibility includes *all*[6] the authority and responsibility of all subordinate managers whose authority and responsibility in turn include all that of their subordinates down the line. While this unique combination of tradition and ideology tends to overload verti-

4. Sutton, Antony C., *Western Technologies and Soviet Economic Development 1917–1930* (Stanford, CA: Hoover Institution, 1968).
5. Safronova, I.P., *One-Man Management and Collegiality in the Socialist Industrial Enterprise.* (Kiev, 1978), p. 185.
6. Some subordinates' authority is not totally included in that of their superiors, as they also report to other superiors. For example, the head accountant reports also to the Ministry of Finance. Perestroika is abolishing this double-boss system, and aims to restore authority to the leader of the enterprise.

cal communication channels and reinforce the "doctrinal desire to maintain centralized control,"[7] it does have considerable advantage in the vertical integration of STUs and of the total Soviet enterprise. Exhibit 4.3 clearly indicates the virtual impossibility of lateral integration in the enterprise without the creation of intricate special mechanisms. Here is an example: Because essentially only the leader of each STU makes decisions, members of groups that include representatives of other STUs tend to be reluctant to commit themselves by volunteering opinions unless they have previously consulted with their STU leader. This is the systemic reason for the reluctant behavior of individuals in ad hoc task forces or multi-STU councils. Members of such groups do not consider it their duty to speak up unless explicitly requested to do so by the chairperson of the meeting. Then they will ponder whether or not the issue should be decided by their own STU leader. This analysis suggests that the only effective councils are those in which STU leaders participate directly: meetings of brigade leaders presided over by their foreman, for example, or of foremen presided over by their shop manager. If direct participation of STU leaders is not practical, effectiveness will be in proportion to the degree that each representative has been authorized by his or her immediate STU leader.

HOW THE SYSTEM FUNCTIONS

The "essence of Soviet authority"[8] rests on two deep-rooted traditional management principles: one-man leadership (*edinonachalie*) and collective leadership (*kollegialnost*). The two are closely interwoven and work alternately. Both can be traced far back in the country's history and have evolved from inveterate values and priorities.[9] Throughout Russian history, leaders have sought the optimal balance of centralized and decentralized management methods to serve each phase of the country's socioeconomic development.[10] Only rarely has this balance been achieved.

The central Soviet principle of party and state management has been democratic centralism (DC). The concept of DC was first introduced in

7. Armstrong, John A., "Sources of Administrative Behavior: Some Soviet and Western European Comparisons," *The American Political Science Review* 59 (September 1965), p. 646.
8. From Gorbachev's speech delivered on February 25, 1986 to the Twenty-seventh Congress of the Communist party of the Soviet Union.
9. In Chapter 2, our Soviet colleagues mention the old traditions of self-management and collectivism of Russian peasant communes, while saying at the same time that "centralized governing mechanisms" have very deep historical roots.
10. Gorbachev described the purpose of his economic reform in his Autumn 1987 speech commemorating the 70th anniversary of the revolution as "to assure . . . a system . . . based . . . on an optimal combination of centralism and self-management."

1906 as an organizational party statute of the Russian revolutionary movement. According to its original formula, it comprises four elements:

1. The application of the elective principle to all leading organs of the party, from the highest to the lowest;[11]
2. Periodic accountability of party organs to their respective party organizations;
3. Strict party discipline and the subordination of the minority to the majority;
4. The absolutely binding character of the decisions of the higher organs upon the lower organs and upon party members.[12]

Lenin considered the principle of democratic centralism as the foundation of the economic system of socialism. He showed this principle to be "a combination of centralized direction of the economy by the state toward the solution of the key tasks of development, so as to guarantee the public interest, together with the initiative of the people, allowing for local conditions and the development of democratic principles in management."[13]

Collective leadership has its origins in the collegial decision making of the medieval Russian peasant commune, and is defined by Soviet writers as the system of management whereby leadership is placed in a group of people (*collegium*) that deliberates and *decides* all basic questions of management. Decisions are made by majority. Usually, however, debate continues until consensus is reached. Once a decision is made, all members of the group commit themselves to its implementation. Collective leadership is applied in the Politburo of the Central Committee of the Communist Party of the USSR, the Council of Ministers of the USSR, the USSR Academy of Sciences, and a number of other important Soviet associations and institutions. A traditional problem with collective leadership has been that it encourages the tendency of managers to cover themselves by hiding behind collective decisions.

One-man leadership in the management of organizations is rooted in centuries of centralist traditions. The concept was borrowed from the army and introduced into Russian public administration by Emperor Paul I at the end of the eighteenth century. Lenin first established one-man leadership in 1918[14] as a key management system in Soviet administration. As ar-

11. Before perestroika, the great dichotomy between practice and policy caused this element of DC to hardly ever be applied. Positions were in fact appointed from "above." This is one of the main practices that gave the Soviet system its authoritarian, centralist character.
12. Waller, Michael, *Democratic Centralism: An Historical Commentary* (New York: St. Martin's Press, 1981), p. 62.
13. Aganbegyan, Abel, *The Economic Challenge of Perestroika* (Bloomington: Indiana University Press, 1988) p. 193, and Gvishiani, D., *Organization and Management.* (Moscow, 1972), pp. 31–33.
14. "Edinonachalie and the Soviet Industrial Manager, 1918–1937," *Hiroaki Kuromiya, Soviet Studies,* Vol. XXXVI, no. 2, April 1984; p. 186.

ticulated by Lenin, one-man leadership institutionalizes at one stroke top-man power and autonomy of parts. Legalized by the Twelfth Party Congress in 1923, the concept was established in September 1929 by the Central Committee of the Communist Party of the USSR[15] as the basic management principle of the Soviet enterprise.

Frequent abuses of power in recent years have associated one-man leadership with Stalinist autocracy, and the term seems to have fallen into ill repute. The power of STU leaders has also been diluted by a number of external interventions and controls. These interferences have tended to blur lines of authority and undermine the effectiveness of leaders by subordinating staff managers to outside functional agencies as well as to STU leaders. Advancing technology has also diffused authority from manager to specialist. The basic ingredients of one-man leadership, however, have remained deeply embedded in the Soviet manager's thinking—often at an inarticulate level—and they persist as important elements of Soviet enterprise management.

Under perestroika, the synthesis of one-man leadership and of collective leadership—two apparently conflicting basic forms of management operating within the framework of collectivism[16]—is expressed in the organizational concept that (in order to prevent its being misnamed democratic centralism) we call in this book centralized leadership grass-roots democracy (CL/GD). A significant finding of our study is that, contrary to prevalent Western thinking, the centralization of one-man leadership and the decentralization of collectivism are not conflicting forms of management, impossible to reconcile. This is because the Soviets resolve the apparent paradox by clearly alternating these forms in distinct phases of a coherent system of decision making. We have diagrammed the flow in Exhibit 4.4.

As we have observed inside the enterprise,[17] these alternating centralizing and decentralizing phases of the decision process are separated in time, and the switches from one phase to the next are signaled by social rituals. It needs to be understood that these phases are inseparable parts of an integrated whole: if one of its phases is ignored or exaggerated, the effectiveness of the system is weakened and decision implementation is less likely. Within the STU, this decision system plays itself out between the STU

15. Ibid., p. 185.
16. The Law on the Soviet State Enterprise, while keeping one-man management in the administration of the enterprise, restores a great deal of decision-making power on important issues to the workers' collective, which is made up of the entire personnel of the enterprise.
17. Some might argue that the first phase of the decision process, intended by perestroika for the Soviet system as a whole, is grass-roots participation and not goals from above. They might be right. But we have observed the system at the level of the state enterprise, which, as stipulated by Point 1 of Article 2 of the Law on the Soviet State Enterprise, as a first step, is guided by control figures from its superior authority. The authority of the enterprise's collective is intended by perestroika to democratize the further phases of the process.

EXHIBIT 4.4   Diagram of the CL/GD Decision Process

Centralized leadership

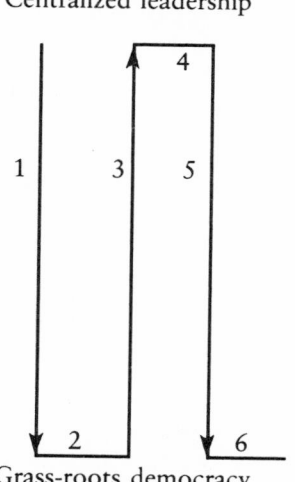

Grass-roots democracy

1. Goals—TOP DOWN—The leader clearly poses the issue and specifies the targets to be attained.
2. Deliberation—Wide and open participation of all levels of the STU, including the workers.
3. Proposal—BOTTOM UP—Submission of proposal to the leader.
4. Deliberation—Careful review of the proposal by the leader.
5. Decision—TOP DOWN—Clear instructions by the leader.
6. Committed and unified implementation.

leader and STU members. Its democratic side offers the clear advantage of achieving a considered and committed decision. What may not be so clear, but probably is equally valuable, is that its centralized side offers the power of clear, strong-disciplined leadership with faithful execution.

A fundamental aim of perestroika is to neutralize the mechanisms producing monolithic uniformity of opinion in organizations, to capture and restore the latent culture of the self-energizing coexistence of grass-roots participation and the STU leaders' authority for decision making.[18] The Law on the Soviet State Enterprise of June 30, 1987 greatly enhances collectivism, i.e., the role of the enterprise's collective in decision making (democratization)[19]—and on the other hand it greatly emphasizes discipline.[20] Neither of these elements are new. However, their democratic features were atrophied under Stalinism and the decision process was rendered ineffective.

18. "The aim of this reform is to ensure . . . the transition from an excessively centralized management system relying on orders to a democratic one, based on the combination of Democratic Centralism and self-management." Gorbachev, Mikhail, *Perestroika* (New York: Harper & Row, 1987), p. 34.
19. "The program of our party has as an aim a more effective utilization of all forms of direct democracy. The direct participation of the people in the preparation, the making, and the fulfillment of state and other decisions." From Gorbachev's speech delivered on February 25, 1986 to the Twenty-seventh Congress of the Communist Party of the Soviet Union.
20. "The movement ahead will be achieved as fast as larger discipline, organization and responsibility of everyone for the work he undertakes will be achieved." Ibid.

The following are some of the elements of CL/GD:

1. All members are strictly accountable for their actions. The authority and area of responsibility assigned to each and every manager are taken very seriously by peers, subordinates, superiors, and outsiders. They constitute an assigned duty, an obligation to society, to the enterprise, and, above all, to the immediate STU. For every employee, even the worker without subordinates (the solid doll in our example), the area of his responsibility is his legitimate turf and is never meddled with by peers and seldom interfered with by superiors. In this manner, everyone in the enterprise is individually responsible for successfully performing the assigned work. As indicated, strict accountability has often been neutralized by diffusion of individual responsibility in collective decisions and in many signature documents.

2. Subordinates are unconditionally and implicitly obedient to superiors. Discipline is an essential ingredient of CL/GD as stipulated in Articles 2 and 14 of the Law on the Soviet State Enterprise. Otherwise, it is feared that confusion and chaos will ensue. This does not mean that there is not plenty of room for camaraderie. The coexistence of camaraderie and discipline is rendered possible in the Soviet enterprise environment by the ritual entailed in switching from one to another. Although managers enjoy joking with one another, when it is time for a working meeting they sit in descending rank along the sides of a rectangular table in the leader's office with their leader at its head, and everyone works seriously. This ritual assures the transition. Serious business is not transacted in a nonchalant manner. Jokes during meetings are only the leader's prerogative, and he or she may use them to make an important point or defuse tension.

3. STU leaders bear the complete responsibility and are bestowed with broad authority and complete administrative power for managing their STUs as a whole. As shown in Exhibit 4.3, the contours of their responsibility encircle *all* areas of authority and responsibility within their domain. An informal, implicit deal is made between STU members and leaders: members must obey the leader's instructions, and the leader must protect them and stand up for them in every way to everyone outside the STU. The top STU leader of the enterprise is the director general, whose influence is felt everywhere, from the executive suite to the production floor. The director general is a walk-around, face-to-face manager. The ideal Soviet manager is an administrative perfectionist who demands discipline and implementation of assigned tasks and creates a sense of purpose and pride in all subordinates. If fulfillment of a task entails crossing STU boundaries, managers go up the hierarchy to their common boss for every decision. To be perceived by subordinates as a good leader, a manager must inspire confidence in his or her effectiveness, as well as show concern for the well-being of all subordinates. The most crucial characteristic of leaders, however, is their strength: their willingness to take responsibility and their readiness to exercise authority by making final decisions and assigning clear tasks to subordinates. As we mentioned earlier, the authority of leaders has been diluted by multiple interventions. Perestroika aims to alleviate this dilution.

4. STU leaders can have direct access to, give instructions to, receive reports from, interfere with, and—for any length of time they see fit—assume part or all of the authority on any issue of any employee on any subordinate level of the hierarchy. If they consider it necessary, they can bypass immediate subordinates and communicate with any member of their STU and of all enclosed STUs (see Exhibit 4.3). However, giving

instructions by jumping echelons or asking for decisions by bypassing superiors is expected to be done only with good reason and intervening managers are expected to be informed after the fact. Subordinates from all levels also have the right of direct access to their leaders. It is common for managers to post office hours when they are available to meet with any employees (or even members of employees' families) who wish to consult them directly on any matter whatsoever. This feature of the Soviet management system not only boosts employee morale and discipline, but also greatly enhances the leaders' realistic perception of what actually goes on in the organization. Direct contact between all echelons of the enterprise hierarchy is one of the most fundamental and distinct characteristics of the Soviet management system and, if not done excessively, enhances considerably the vertical integration of the enterprise.

5. Multiple controls aim to check despotism and mistakes of leaders. The considerable decision-making power that perestroika's new enterprise law restores to the collective is one of these controls. The party organization, the labor union, and other social organizations assist in transmitting messages from top to bottom in the enterprise, help secure commitment to goals, and serve also as monitors on the leader's exercise of power.

6. Formal and informal groups play an important role in integrating the hierarchy vertically. STU leaders use such groups in the decision-making process within their STUs and ask for their deliberations before decisions are made. STU leaders can delegate to such councils the authority to serve as surrogate managers by conducting and coordinating the whole cycle of the decision process except the final decision, which leaders must make or approve themselves. As we have noted, councils comprised of members of different STUs have great difficulty arriving at deliberations unless they are made up of the STU leaders.

7. The enterprise law of June 30, 1987 provides that all STU leaders from director general down to brigade leader are elected by their subordinates and subsequently confirmed by higher authority. This two-step process, which requires STU leaders to be legitimized from both below and above, illustrates one way to resolve the apparent paradox built into the very concept of CL/GD. It combines top-down and bottom-up power into an integrated system of management. Without both powers, a decision cannot be consummated, and if taken will be very difficult to properly implement. It is difficult for Americans to see both forms of power as being real, but they are.

8. All members are expected to maintain complete confidentiality on all matters relating to their immediate STU and the entire enterprise. A tacit agreement binds the members and the leader to one another. STU members expect the leader to represent their interests and the leader expects total confidential and personal loyalty in return.

All STUs are intended to function according to this management system, which consists of an institutionalized signaled alternation between centralization and grass-roots participation. Our study finds that the switching of gears between the centralized and decentralized phases is signaled by rituals: the seating arrangements at meetings, for example, or the articulation of the final decision by the leader and others.

Perestroika aims to substantially increase the disaggregation of decision making at each level of the "down" phases and the aggregation at each level of the "up" phases. It suggests that decisions be made at the closest possible level to implementation. In his speech to the Twenty-seventh Party Congress, General Secretary Gorbachev explained, "Our long experience tells us that exactly in this direction must we seek forms corresponding to today's circumstances of combination of centralism and democracy of one-man leadership and of the elections of management of the national economy."

Understanding the resilient, distinctive features of the Soviet management system requires time and effort. American managers who aspire to successful joint ventures will position themselves to work closely with their Soviet colleagues, applying the optimum amalgam of centralized and grassroots participative management methods.

Summary

Our study reveals that both countries—each from its own history, traditions, and ideology—have developed distinctive managerial systems. While the Soviet managerial system seems more clear, explicit, and uniform than that of the United States, the US system remains firmly established as a result of its gradual shaping by market and competitive forces as well as the checks and balances provided by various government bodies.

In the next part, we will describe in detail the four companies evaluated by our field research teams in the Soviet Union and in the United States. In particular, we will address the decision-making processes applied to four key business activities.

Field Research on
Decision Making

Chapter 5

Field Sites and Managerial Practices

[*Editors' note:* Part II will present the results of the field research conducted in the United States and the USSR. Chapters 6 through 9 will describe, respectively, the decision-making processes for each of the four issues that broadly represent the work of managers: annual planning, hiring and firing, capital investment, and new product introduction. Before we proceed, however, it is important that the reader be able to visualize the research process itself and the background of the enterprises and plants that were studied.]

The Research Process

A unique feature of our research was that a single field research team consisting of two US and two Soviet scholars did all the actual on-site work at the four plants in the United States and the four plants in the Soviet Union. As a team they spent approximately two working weeks taking an intimate look at each of the eight sites. The enterprises that opened their operations to us were remarkably candid with the researchers. In the spirit of glasnost, they let the warts and wrinkles show. The researchers were granted interviews with people at many levels, from the production floor in both countries to corporate headquarters in the United States and the central ministry in the USSR. They attended many different types of management meetings and had access to official documents. They were permitted to audiotape all interviews and a sample of interviews and meetings were videotaped (170 hours). Moreover, the enterprises have remained accessible since the intensive research period to answer questions and confirm the accuracy of our reports.

The entire research team—including the directors—not only visited research sites, but also held intensive analysis and writing sessions in Moscow and Boston. We found that our capacity to be insightful observers kept growing as a result of these interactions, and some highlights of this process need to be spelled out.

SOME INSIGHTS GAINED FROM DOING JOINT RESEARCH

Even though shared interests and motives propelled members of the research team toward collaboration, certain hurdles obstructed our interaction. We brought to this work many different beliefs, experiences, and preconceptions about ourselves and about the other's worlds and systems. A number of myths, and undoubtedly a number of inarticulated fears, stood in the way of our clear perception of one another. And though everyone sincerely desired to be open and reveal these understandings to the others, sometimes we were unable to do so. It was not easy.

The great complexity of the interaction has to be recognized. Pressures that burdened our exchange included unrealistic expectations, conscious and subconscious resistance, suspicions, and memory decay. Differences in work rhythms, decision processes, work loads, and priorities of culture and profession impeded our interaction as well. For example, the practitioner is accustomed to a relatively short cycle of reward/punishment from his or her work, whereas academics expect to wait much longer for positive/ negative feedback, especially when their work involves research or writing a book. A practitioner experiences considerable frustration from the prolonged cycle of feedback.

Working with individuals from different cultures and different professions can create a great deal of strain. We went through stages of anguish and insecurity about what value our knowledge and experience would have, as well as about the authenticity of others' inputs. These doubts created tension. During the two years we worked together, however, a mutual awareness of our varying beliefs and perspectives gradually developed. As we enlightened one another slowly about these perspectives, we created the basis for genuine exchange, which in turn produced mutual understanding.

The most effective form of interaction was not discussing or exchanging abstract views, but working together on a tangible problem or a concrete task. For example, when we shared different interpretations of an event we had all observed, we discovered that each had to help the others if a reasonably balanced interpretation was to be achieved. As time passed we were able to develop the necessary candor and flexibility to integrate our ideas. Only then did insights accumulate and merge to create a new total picture. Then the next stage became possible: jointly mapping out concepts and together organizing the evidence.

This type of interaction became effective only after we had known one another for some time, and only when our working arrangements permitted us to take a more reflective stance. Only then did we shed our rigidity and defuse tension. Again, this dynamic worked best when we were considering specific issues together in groups representing all four dimensions of our team: Soviets and Americans, academics and practitioners. Interaction from a distance—that is, by phone or correspondence—never really achieved insights. The key was to create a setting where all sides could exchange information; then the combined knowledge and experience provided a far richer perspective than any individual had before the interaction occurred. Wider areas of potential gains from cooperation were discovered. We learned of each side's important latent assumptions about the management process. We learned that familiar concepts really meant quite different things. It was during these group exchanges that theory arose from the analysis of actual experiences and from the common emotional involvement, rather than from preconceived postulates.

A major challenge in this multiparty effort was to develop realistic levels of expectation about who could best contribute what. The demands of our project were such that we would often assign tasks to someone who was not ideally suited to complete them. Distributing responsibilities according to each person's special knowledge and experience was critical to our cooperative effort, and in time we learned what each team member could do best.

It is true that initially we avoided some sensitive topics. But as time passed and mutual confidence increased, obstacles arising from the differences in our traditions, systems, and professions receded. We found that we could successfully explore sensitive issues. The process speeded up when we learned that the joint performance of a concrete task, such as compiling a day's field notes, was an effective way to learn about one another's way of thinking and values. A deeply rewarding and satisfying experience ensued. Personal friendships developed that transcended the scope of this project and enriched our lives in a manner that we all hope may pave the way for more work in the future. We have learned that effective cooperation between Soviets and Americans and between practitioners and academics is possible and fruitful. This bodes well for the effective joint management of business joint ventures in the future.

An Introduction to AmElectric

[*Editors' note:* The names of the enterprise, locations, and individuals have all been disguised.]

AmElectric got its start as a manufacturer of electric utility equipment in the late 1800s. Over the next hundred years it grew into a diversified multinational corporation in the *Fortune* 100 group. Our study was conducted in AmElectric's operations division, which specializes in making large equipment for electric utilities. Division headquarters, located some distance from corporate headquarters, is responsible for managing several plants and 5,000 employees. We conducted our detailed study of AmElectric's management practices at two of the plants, as well as at division headquarters.

THE UTILITY EQUIPMENT INDUSTRY

For many years following the 1965 electric power blackout that immobilized the entire northeastern United States for two days, manufacturers of electrical equipment enjoyed prosperous conditions and an annual industry growth rate of 7.5%. Their customers, electric utility companies, added capacity to maintain self-sufficiency and prevent a major power blackout from recurring. Because the utility companies were (and still are) monopolies that have exclusive rights to supply power in specific geographical areas, the utilities experienced relatively weak cost pressures from customers. Utilities were more concerned with getting their orders filled so that they could meet demand for electricity.

In 1973, all this changed. The oil embargo made oil and gas prices shoot up, and construction of new plants virtually ceased. New foreign competitors (e.g., the Japanese) added to the price competition for what little business was left. A third development was that the government began imposing more regulations on the industry. As a result, the industries supplying utilities suffered a steep decline. Workers were laid off, plants were closed, and some firms went out of business. For AmElectric the downturn meant shrinking its work force approximately 25% per year for several years and closing several plants.

Because new plants were not being ordered, the industry began to focus on its service business, the upgrading and replacement of existing parts and facilities. In fact, this business was starting to develop significant profits since many of the power plants in the field were several decades old and in need of repair and rebuilding.

THE PRODUCT MARKET

The AmElectric operations division manufactures and assembles large capital equipment for sale to public utilities throughout the world. Very long lead times are customary for obtaining orders and for manufacturing equipment. For example, AmElectric learns several years in advance whether a utility is thinking of requiring a new plant or of making major repairs. In 1988, it had been a long time since AmElectric had received an order for a new plant. When a large contract for parts or replacements is signed, employees gather to celebrate in the division headquarters lobby, ringing the "good news bell" and rallying 'round for announcements.

Because of reduced demand, customers are in a stronger position to dictate their terms. AmElectric responds to this challenge in several ways. First, it takes a proactive approach to new product development by designing replacement parts that are product upgrades to reduce the utilities' operating and maintenance costs. Second, it has a strong quality-assurance program. Third, it offers reduced delivery times. As a result, the division has shown a consistent annual profit despite declining market conditions.

After an order is placed, manufacture may take as long as a year. (It takes up to eight years to build a new power plant.) Delivery schedules are critical; each day that a power plant is shut down for an outage costs utilities hundreds of thousands of dollars in lost revenues or in expenses to purchase auxiliary power. Thus utility companies write penalty clauses for late delivery into important contracts. AmElectric maintains an inventory of the most common or critical components that can be shipped in one day.

DIVISIONAL HISTORY

AmElectric built its original plant in the northeastern United States. In its heyday, the three-million-square-foot plant employed 18,000 workers. An adversarial union-management environment prevailed with strikes and walkouts common. The union fought for complex work regulations and high wage rates.

When expansion was required in the 1960s, these rigid union practices and high labor rates led AmElectric management to seek new plant sites in the South. The two plants we studied are among them. Built to incorporate the latest manufacturing technology and management techniques, both are equipped with state-of-the-art numerically controlled computerized manufacturing systems. At the time of our study, one plant was the nation's largest air-conditioned manufacturing facility under one roof. The human resource philosophy has encouraged participative management and attractive working conditions to build a committed and motivated work force, loyal to the company. AmElectric brought in some management from the Northeast and trained the local labor force, many of whom had been inde-

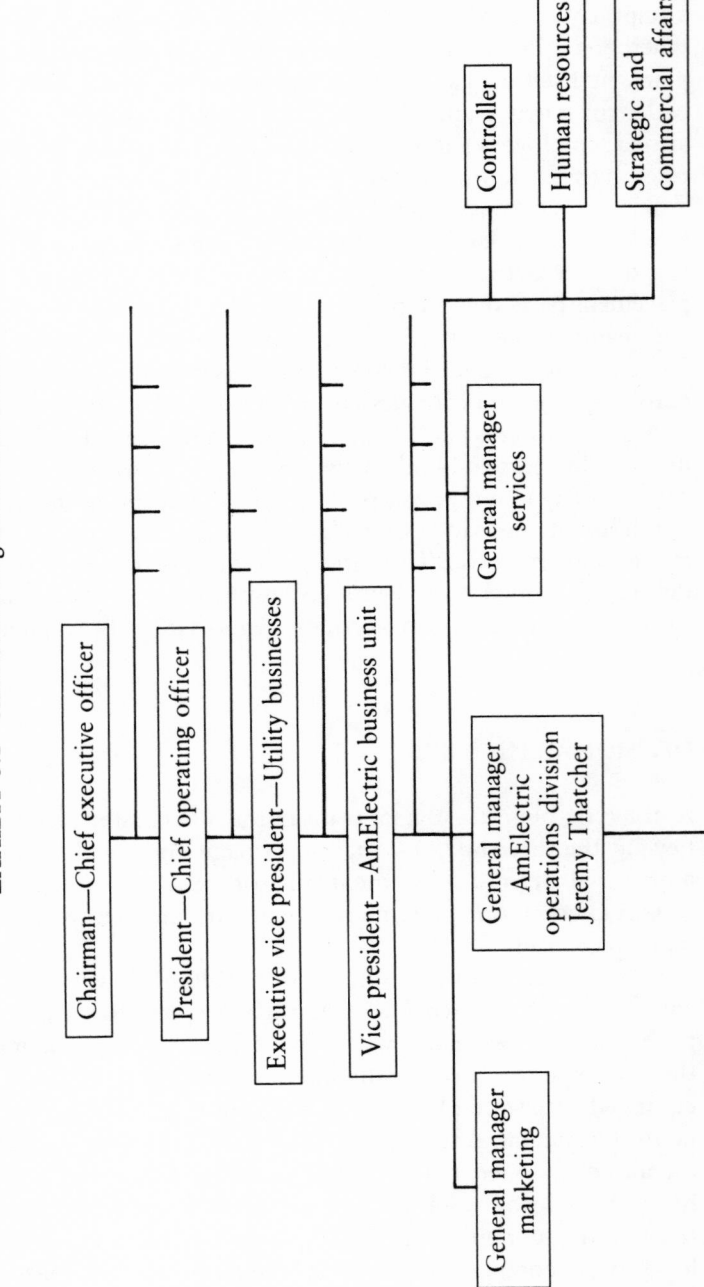

EXHIBIT 5.1   AmElectric Organizational Chart

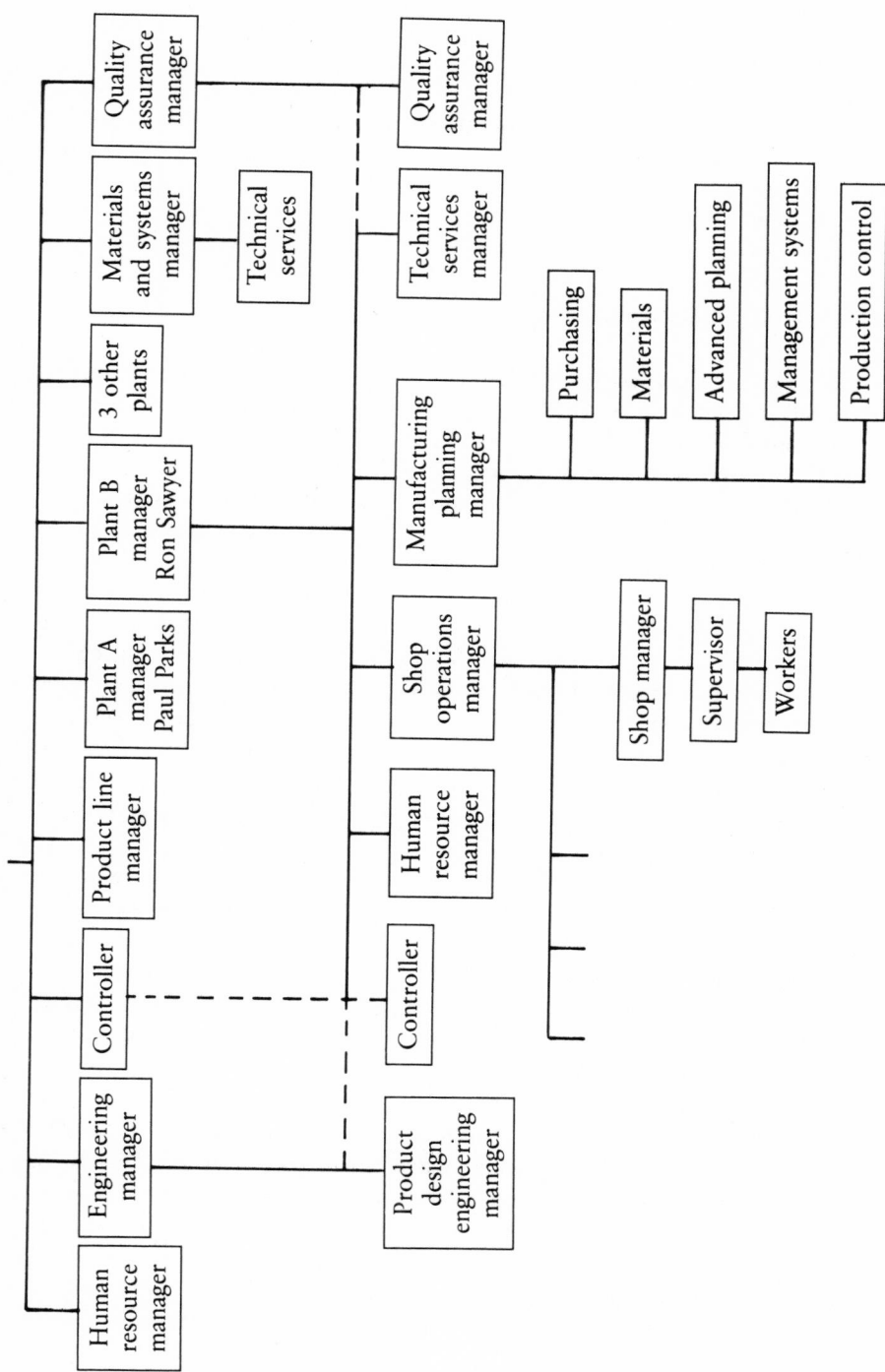

pendent farmers and seemed to adapt well to the participative management approach.

Initially each plant employed up to 1,000 people. But when orders dropped off in the 1970s, both plants were forced to lay off workers and change their production facilities to accommodate downsizing to 60% of capacity.

DIVISIONAL ORGANIZATIONAL STRUCTURE

As a result of downsizing, AmElectric's operations division had undergone several reorganizations by the late 1980s. Staff attitudes had become jaded and confused. The running joke, "If my boss calls, get his name," was a common refrain among employees. Inefficiencies were inevitable. With each reorganization, people would be reassigned and details of projects they had been working on would fall through the cracks. At one point, division headquarters staff had reported to 11 different departments at the business unit. Now the organization has been rationalized into large functional groups to resolve lateral coordination problems among marketing, engineering, and manufacturing and to make preparations for a joint venture recently undertaken with a foreign partner. Under reorganization, the operations division gained the engineering unit and the product line department to serve as its liaison to field sales and marketing (see organizational chart, Exhibit 5.1). According to the division's general manager Jeremy Thatcher, under the previous structure the organization was "an octopus."

Jeremy Thatcher makes a practice of keeping in close contact with the plants through frequent phone calls and regular visits every few weeks. He admits that some may say he overmanages, but his rationale is that he wants to be up to date on financial and schedule details in order to maintain customer and corporate commitments. He also points out that he has to optimize for the interests of the division as a whole because the plants tend to act in their own self-interest.

Exhibit 5.1 shows other strong links between the plants and division headquarters (e.g., the quality-assurance managers report directly to division headquarters). As one plant manager facetiously put it, "This is the separation of church and state that prevents me from giving the order to 'ship that junk.' " Managers of product design in the plants also report directly to division headquarters engineering. The plant controllers report directly to the plant managers but have strong "dotted-line" relationships with the division headquarters controller. These structural features are characteristic of AmElectric's traditional multidivisional form with hierarchical line and staff roles.

The two AmElectric plants that we studied were built in industrial parks on the outskirts of medium-sized southern cities and opened within a year of each other. Exhibit 5.2 presents summary facts about the two plants.

EXHIBIT 5.2   AmElectric Summary Data

	Plant A (components)	*Plant B (assembly)*
Products	Components for utility equipment	Assembly and repair of large utility equipment
Plant size	400,000 square feet	500,000 square feet
Total Employees	850	750
Management and professional	250	264
Production workers	600	486
Year plant opened	1971	1971

Exhibit 5.3 highlights the activities that make up a typical day for the manager of Plant A.

EXHIBIT 5.3   AmElectric Plant A Manager's Day

6:30 A.M.	Sometimes attends plant workshops.
7:00	Arrives at work.
7:30–9:00	Reads mail, does paperwork, makes phone calls.
9:00–12:30 P.M.	Weekly staff meeting of plant management team in conference room. Plant manager chairs the meeting but purposely avoids sitting at the head of the table to allow other managers more autonomy.
12:30–1:00	Lunch.
1:00–3:00	Quality-improvement team meeting with members drawn from various plant departments and levels. (Chairmanship rotates among members regardless of level: plant manager currently the chair.)
3:00 on	Informal meetings with two to four people; meetings with customers; paperwork; tours of shop floor about twice a week to chat with workers, all of whom are known by name.
6:00–7:00	Leaves for home.
Evening	About two hours' paperwork at home; uses computer linked to plant's system and electronic mail to send memos electronically to staff.
Away days	When away from the office for more than a day, plant manager appoints a deputy, rotating the position among management team members.

An Introduction to AmTruck

AmTruck was formed in 1919, when it began manufacturing and selling diesel engines in a small midwestern town. By the late 1980s, the company had grown into a major *Fortune* 500 firm, with $2.8 billion in annual revenues; its 24,900 employees were building and selling approximately 160,000 engines a year.

AmTruck's primary market is the North American truck industry. Two-thirds of its sales dollars and over half the engines it makes are sold in North America. AmTruck has a 57% share of this market, with one major domestic and several foreign competitors. AmTruck also sells to the light industrial market, providing engines for such equipment as tractors and small cranes.

Two types of customers have an impact on AmTruck's product sales. One is the truck manufacturer, whose special concerns include how an engine fits into a particular truck model. The other is the end user (a truck driver or trucking company), who seeks reliability, reduced maintenance, and durability. Both customers want lower costs. An average AmTruck engine lasts several years and requires an overhaul every 600,000 miles.

THE PRODUCT MARKET

In 1983, AmTruck's top management adopted a pricing policy aimed at limiting Japanese competition. AmTruck lowered engine prices 30% and established a five-year goal for bringing costs into line with prices. During that period it eliminated 2,600 manufacturing jobs and cut manufacturing floor space by 30%. At the same time AmTruck improved delivery schedules and made significant cuts in engine inventories. As a further competitive measure, AmTruck began providing special services such as order-sequenced shipping, which often requires computer links with customers. Although these price cuts and technological improvements enabled AmTruck to retain market share, they led to unforeseen expenses when the truck market unexpectedly boomed. To increase production, AmTruck had to rehire laid-off workers, add temporary workers, and institute overtime. This prevented the firm from realizing some of the cost savings it had aimed to achieve.

External suppliers provide many of AmTruck's components, particularly those with costly and difficult technologies such as high-quality engine block castings. Purchased components usually come from a preferred supplier that has been approved along a number of dimensions including cost, quality, delivery, and innovation. Because AmTruck works closely with these suppliers, it accepts their products directly into production without on-site quality inspection. As part of the cost-reduction effort, AmTruck has pared down the number of suppliers and focused on getting a select few up to its quality and delivery standards. It even buys tooling for suppliers, so long as they agree to use the tooling for AmTruck components.

Despite its well-conceived competitive pricing, cost reduction, and quality-improvement programs, AmTruck has experienced some very wide earnings swings. If its stock trades at a low price, management fears investors may purchase the stock and attempt to take over the company.

Government regulations have a powerful impact on AmTruck's bottom line. Emissions standards in particular place heavy demands on AmTruck's budget. One of the key legislated changes affecting AmTruck is the exhaust emissions standards for 1994. Said one engineer, "The EPA has the idea of technology forcing. We have no idea how we can meet their standards, but they figure if they make it law, we'll figure out some way to do it."

AmTruck participates in a number of licensing or joint venture relationships. While several of them are overseas (India, Mexico, the People's Republic of China), some are with US partners and operate in the United States. AmTruck has substantial experience in joint ventures and holds solid opinions on how they should be set up and managed. Above and beyond its profit-oriented programs, AmTruck has made a substantial effort to be a positive influence in the community. It has commissioned the building of numerous important architectural works and attempts to support community efforts such as education and ethnic relations. AmTruck has an internal ethics program that guides its decision making. For example, although it does sell engines for military use, it will not sell them to the government of South Africa or other organizations it feels will misuse them.

AMTRUCK PLANT C

Plant C, with 950 employees, assembles midsize diesel engines and machine components for use in two engine product lines. It is housed in one large modern structure built in 1974 and is located in a rural part of an eastern state.

AmTruck opened the plant with the explicit mission from headquarters to use and test concepts of participative management. Some of its mandates (and its methods for fulfilling them) are the following:

- To use teams as the basic building block of the organization. (The team-member job description applies to all shop-floor employees.)
- To have as few hierarchical levels as possible (The plant has only five: plant

manager, functional staff director, business team manager, team manager, team member [worker].)

- To encourage lateral decision making at all levels among managerial peers.
- To minimize status differences and design a "neutral"—or not demotivating —pay system. (All employees are salaried and expected to work 40 hours a week. Salary increases are based on skills learned, not on seniority.)
- To encourage production workers to learn new skills and undertake a wide variety of tasks. (Possibilities include machine maintenance, quality control, supplies and inventory control, cost control, daily scheduling, and employee discipline.)
- To have workers control the pace of machining and assembly tasks, rather than have machines control the speed.
- To institute organizations and mechanisms through which shop-floor employees have a voice in management decisions. (Representatives from all employee groups convene as a board to discuss plant matters.)

Plant C was designed to accomplish two main human resource management objectives: (1) to create a climate in which the work itself would be rewarding, and (2) to maximize the potential for individual personal growth by providing each employee with challenges and opportunities. During the 1980s, the plant faced, and found ways of dealing with, many difficulties. When corporate headquarters called for personnel cutbacks, Plant C avoided layoffs by freezing all hiring, reducing work hours for all employees, giving voluntary leaves without pay, creating a "swing" team of excess people who could be assigned to miscellaneous tasks throughout the plant, and taking other creative cost-reduction measures. The plant also had to adapt its organization to accommodate just-in-time production and total quality control systems, both of which reduced the individual and team autonomy by requiring more coordination and tighter links among teams. Some workers complained of increased stress. Another major challenge was that Plant C had to compete internally for certain products. For example, because Plant C made the same crankshaft as another AmTruck plant, it had to be sure its performance was equal or superior to that of the other plant.

In 1988, the plant was operating at 70% capacity, producing 100 engines a day, in two shifts that employed 950 people.

AMTRUCK PLANT D

Plant D differs from other AmTruck plants because it is a joint venture between AmTruck and another company in the truck business. This means that some financial deadlines and reporting requirements differ for this plant. Annual plans and expenditures have to be approved not only by AmTruck management, but also by the management of the joint venture partner. The joint venture partner retains the right to hire and fire for specific positions, such as controller.

Built in 1980, Plant D is a large, air-conditioned showcase facility with very modern equipment. Its participative management methods are the same as those at Plant C. Although the factory runs mostly on automated lines, plant management has tried to create an attractive environment by providing open space, cheerful colors, and an attractive cafeteria. Like Plant C, it was designed to be a "flat" organization with only five job descriptions. Workers are salaried, and hiring criteria stress team skills such as performance on group problem-solving tasks. Ultimately, the team with which a new employee will work makes the hiring decision in a "consensus meeting."

At the time of the study, Plant D was operating at only 50% of its planned capacity, building 300 engines a day, and just adding its second shift. The startup plus a recent volume increase had posed some difficulties, partly because the plant employed some temporary workers that imposed additional wage and salary expenses. Also, because of its early emphasis on interpersonal skills, some felt that the plant may have neglected technical skills and now had a work force skilled at communicating and organizing but lacking some of the necessary technical abilities.

For additional information about AmTruck see Exhibits 5.4, 5.5, and 5.6.

A Comparison of AmElectric and AmTruck

This overview of the two US firms highlights some changes that they shared with much of US industry at the time of our study. Both firms were facing stronger competitive pressure, much of it from foreign sources. Both were operating at significantly less than full capacity and searching for ways to cut costs. Both had experienced cutbacks in employment. (This was particularly true at AmElectric.) Both were moving toward a flatter organization with fewer staff positions. Both were using methods to involve the work force in the affairs of the enterprise. Both were moving into joint venture arrangements with foreign as well as domestic partners. In most of these restructuring trends, AmTruck had progressed farther than AmElectric.

EXHIBIT 5.4   AmTruck Organizational Chart

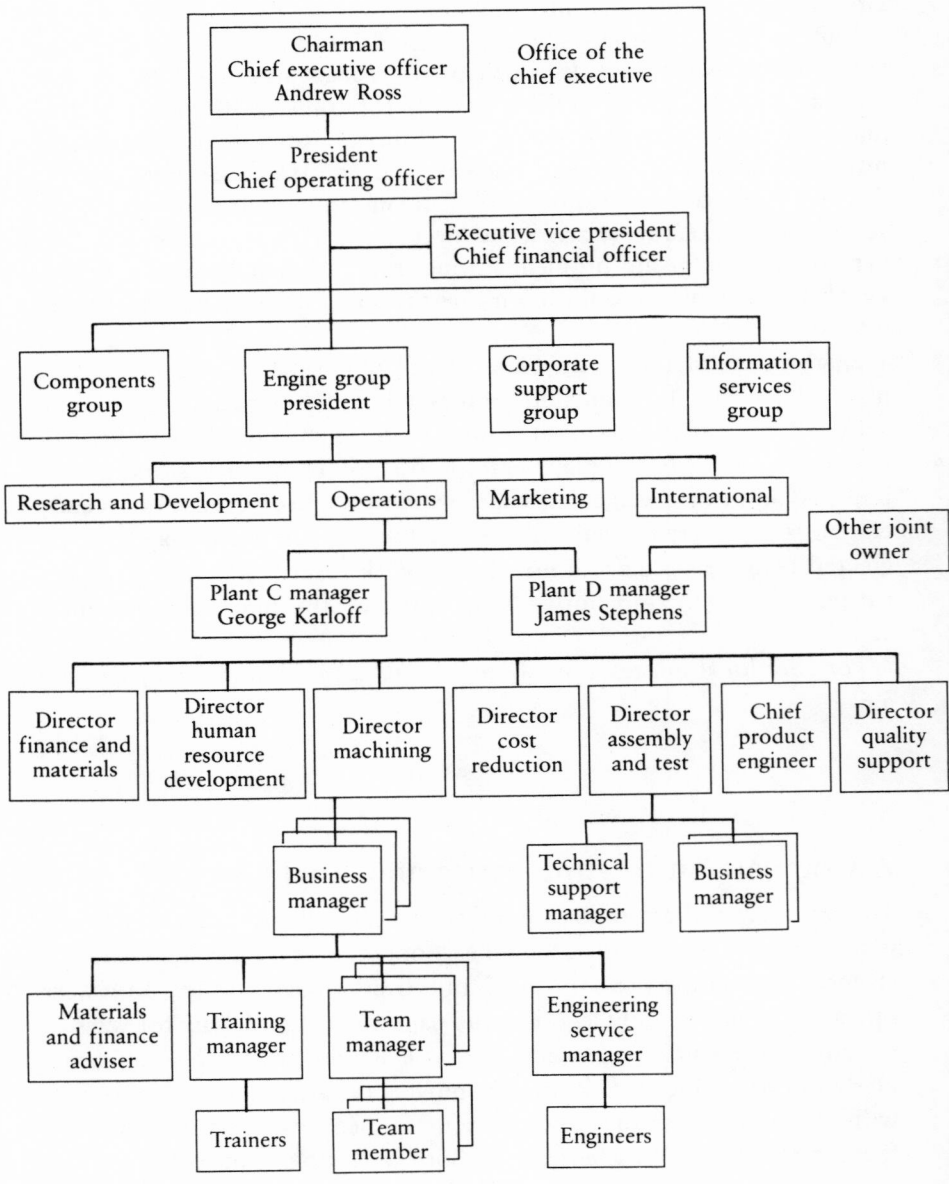

EXHIBIT 5.5 AmTruck Summary Data

	Plant C	*Plant D*
Products	240–300 HP diesel engines and machined components (e.g., camshafts, crankshafts, flywheels)	75–250 HP diesel engines
Plant size	950,000 square feet	1.1 million square feet
Total employees	950	860
Management and support	450	380
Production workers	500	480
Shifts	2	1+
Year plant opened	1974	1980

EXHIBIT 5.6 AmTruck Plant D Manager's Day

7:00–7:30 A.M.	Arrives at plant and prepares for the day; checks the day's calendar; reviews any written or electronic mail that has arrived; reviews last night's production reports.
7:30–8:00	Attends daily production meeting with 20–25 functional and line managers from various levels; reviews issues and today's plans (four out of five days).
8:00–10:00	Attends one of several weekly meetings (e.g., machining and delivery improvement); about half of this time is free for ad hoc get togethers, shop-floor visits, and customer presentations (usually spends about an hour and a half a week with a visiting customer).
10:00–12:00	Attends different staff meetings three times a week: on Monday, a standard staff meeting to review the week's plans, production logistics, presentations, and so on; on Wednesday, a smaller staff meeting (functional reports only) on long-range planning issues; on Friday, an operations meeting that includes next-level-down managers to review the operating side of things (e.g., the quarterly forecast, how to handle labor relations on the floor, and so forth).
12:00–12:30 P.M.	Grabs a sandwich if there's time.
12:30–6:00	Conducts or attends less structured, ad hoc sessions, improvement or production planning meetings; addresses maintenance problems. Every Tuesday, company headquarters people visit by plane and may need to meet; every Friday at 4 is a "fireside chat" with 10–15 randomly selected employees (usually shop-level workers) to hear their concerns and discuss plant issues without breaking the chain of command.
6:00–6:30	Spends time alone reviewing mail and day's events.
Away days	Usually travels 10–15% of the time; visits headquarters once a month for product team meeting and other headquarters business; visits a customer once a month; visits a supplier about once a month—tends to see only the extremes (good and bad).

An Introduction to SovElectric

A HISTORY OF THE ENTERPRISE

The SovElectric enterprise was formed in 1975 and consists of three plants that manufacture four models of electric motors, ranging from .75 to 5 kilowatts. Its product is used in a wide variety of industrial equipment. The enterprise has access to the services of SKB, a nearby research and development institute that develops motor designs not only for SovElectric, but also for other motor plants in the same *Minelectrotechprom* ministry. In 1988, SovElectric produced 25% of the USSR's total output of motors of this type and employed 8,000 people.

SovElectric's three plants are located within 220 kilometers of one another. Although they are autonomous profit centers, each receives strategic direction and technical assistance from SovElectric headquarters and regular visits from the director general. The director general of the overall enterprise is also the manager of the original plant, Plant V. For most regularized reporting, the director general reports through a scientific production organization (NPO); however, he may bypass NPO and go directly to the ministry for special reasons.

There is a growing emphasis on export production at SovElectric. At the time of the study, the enterprise was producing for export to more than 50 countries. In 1987, the whole enterprise earned 1,048 million rubles in sales, realized a 43-million-ruble profit, and produced 2.5 million motors.

THE ORGANIZATIONAL STRUCTURE OF SOVELECTRIC

SovElectric is a self-financing enterprise, and its structure is quite similar to that of other Soviet enterprises. The director of each plant is responsible for the fulfillment of state orders and basic indicators in the state plan such as productivity of labor, profit, and costs. In addition, the director is responsible for cost reduction, new product introduction, quality, social programs, supply and distribution, and personnel.

The next level of line manager in the plant is the shop manager, who is responsible for fulfillment of the plan within the shop. This manager is responsible for meeting targets for his or her shop only, but these targets may include a wide range of criteria such as introducing new technology, increasing labor productivity, educating workers, and reviewing shop equipment and labor conditions. Each shop manager has a deputy for technology, to whom his or her subordinates, the section heads, go for help with supplies, technology, maintenance, and so on.

The managerial level below section head is foreman. In response to a recent government policy, SovElectric eliminated the level of senior or master foreman. However, the wage fund for foremen remains constant, so each may earn more. The trend toward eliminating hierarchical levels began in 1987.

The brigadier is the lowest line supervisor or manager and is responsible for the brigade's fulfillment of production quotas as well as for meeting quality targets and training workers. The brigadier is both a manager and a worker.

The role of the foreman tends to be somewhat ambivalent. Since the brigadier is both a manager and a worker, the foreman may take on the job of hunting down scarce supplies. As is customary, the rights of management are delegated to lower levels when things are going smoothly; but if operations are troubled, senior managers are more likely to be involved in day-to-day detail.

SOVELECTRIC PLANT V

SovElectric traces its origin to a small factory that began operations in 1931, in the midst of a major industrialized city, to manufacture a variety of items from hunting rifles to small calculating machines. The factory added a small electric motor shop the following year. During World War II Germany occupied the city, and damage to the plant was extensive. Some of its equipment was evacuated to the eastern part of the USSR, however, and by 1949, the plant was fully reconstructed. By the end of the next five-year plan, its capacity doubled and the production of motors tripled. In 1950, development of a new electrical insulation material promised significant cost savings. As a result, the ministry assigned the plant to the task of developing a new series of electric motors in three sizes with aluminum alloy bodies.

By the early 1960s, the plant had become the largest supplier of electrical equipment for many industries and exported to 26 countries including GDR, Cuba, Mongolia, Poland, India, France, and Norway. During this period the plant became more specialized as a manufacturer of electric motors and gradually abandoned production of other electrical equipment.

In 1975, the plant acquired equipment to produce the new 4AX series of electric motors. By 1980, they were producing 300,000 motors annually in the 4AX90 series (90 millimeters in height) and 650,000 in the 4AX80 series

(80 millimeters). This product line became their specialty, and Plant V became the main plant of the enterprise.

At the time of the study Plant V had 4,000 employees, 600 of whom were engineering and technical staff. These employees were grouped into 13 shops. Although the plant had an 11% employee turnover rate, reasons for over half the turnover were unrelated to the plant—for example, army leave, retirement, and child-care problems.

Plant V's main products were 80- and 90-millimeter motors with a power range of .75 to 3.2 kilowatts. In 1987, this plant had annual sales of 86 million rubles and a 26-million-ruble gross profit. Sixteen percent of its products were for export, and 36 million rubles of its sales came from consumer goods.

SOVELECTRIC PLANT W

Although it is a self-financing unit, Plant W belongs to the overall SovElectric enterprise. Operating at full capacity, the plant employs 3,000 workers and still cannot meet current production demands. Plant W is the sole USSR producer of motors with a 71-millimeter rotation axis and ranging from .25 to 2.2 kilowatts. It also produces parts for other SovElectric plants and is the only producer of certain plastic components for motors. Seven percent of its products are exported. Production volume was 154 million rubles in 1987 and gross profit was 54 million rubles, 15.5 million of which was allocated to the profit funds (52% to the social development fund, 27% to the fund for reinvestment, and 21% to the material incentive fund).

Plant W's reporting and planning systems connect to enterprise headquarters, although the plant may go straight to the ministry on special occasions. Despite current production problems, the plant enjoys a good reputation locally and has little difficulty attracting employees; people consider it a good place to work.

A SUMMARY OF SOVELECTRIC

SovElectric plants have a reputation for being progressive in introducing new products and new work methods. Starting in 1984, the AIR series replaced the 4AX series of motors. The plants have been the sites of various successful experiments, including a new type of brigade (team) system whereby work teams are paid according to their final output. SovElectric has received awards for product quality and innovative practices.

At the time of the study, however, SovElectric's three plants were insufficient to produce all the needed motors, and SovElectric was forming a consortium with other motor manufacturers to provide a wider variety of motor sizes. It has not yet begun to export directly.

Additional facts about SovElectric are presented in Exhibits 5.7, 5.8, and 5.9.

EXHIBIT 5.7   SovElectric Summary Data

	Plant V	*Plant W*
Products	Industrial motors 80 and 90 mm rotation axis	Industrial motors 71 mm rotation axis
Plant size	61,000 sq meters	54,000 sq meters
Annual production volume	1,250,000 units	1,370,000 units
Total employees	4,000	3,000
Management and support	600	570
Production workers	3,400	2,430
Shifts	2	2
Year plant opened	1932	1958

An Introduction to SovTruck

SovTruck was formed as a large production enterprise in 1971 as part of a general merger movement in the USSR. In 1988, it had 120,000 employees in 15 plants across 12 cities. Its main assembly plant was one of the first auto plants in the Soviet Union, founded in 1916 by the Russian Auto Society and nationalized in 1918.

The truck plant began as a truck repair shop in 1918. In 1924, it produced its first truck and then began producing one truck a day. That model could carry 1.5 tons at 50 kilometers per hour and had a 36-horsepower engine. During the late 1920s and early 1930s, the plant received substantial capital investment (over 400 million rubles), increasing its production capacity to over 70,000 trucks annually by 1937. These models had 73-horsepower engines, a load capacity of three tons, and traveled at over 60 kilometers per hour. By 1948, the large trucks were on a mass-production schedule.

A new model truck was introduced in 1964, essentially the same model that was being produced in 1988. After 1964, however, continuous design

EXHIBIT 5.8   SovElectric Plant W Organizational Chart

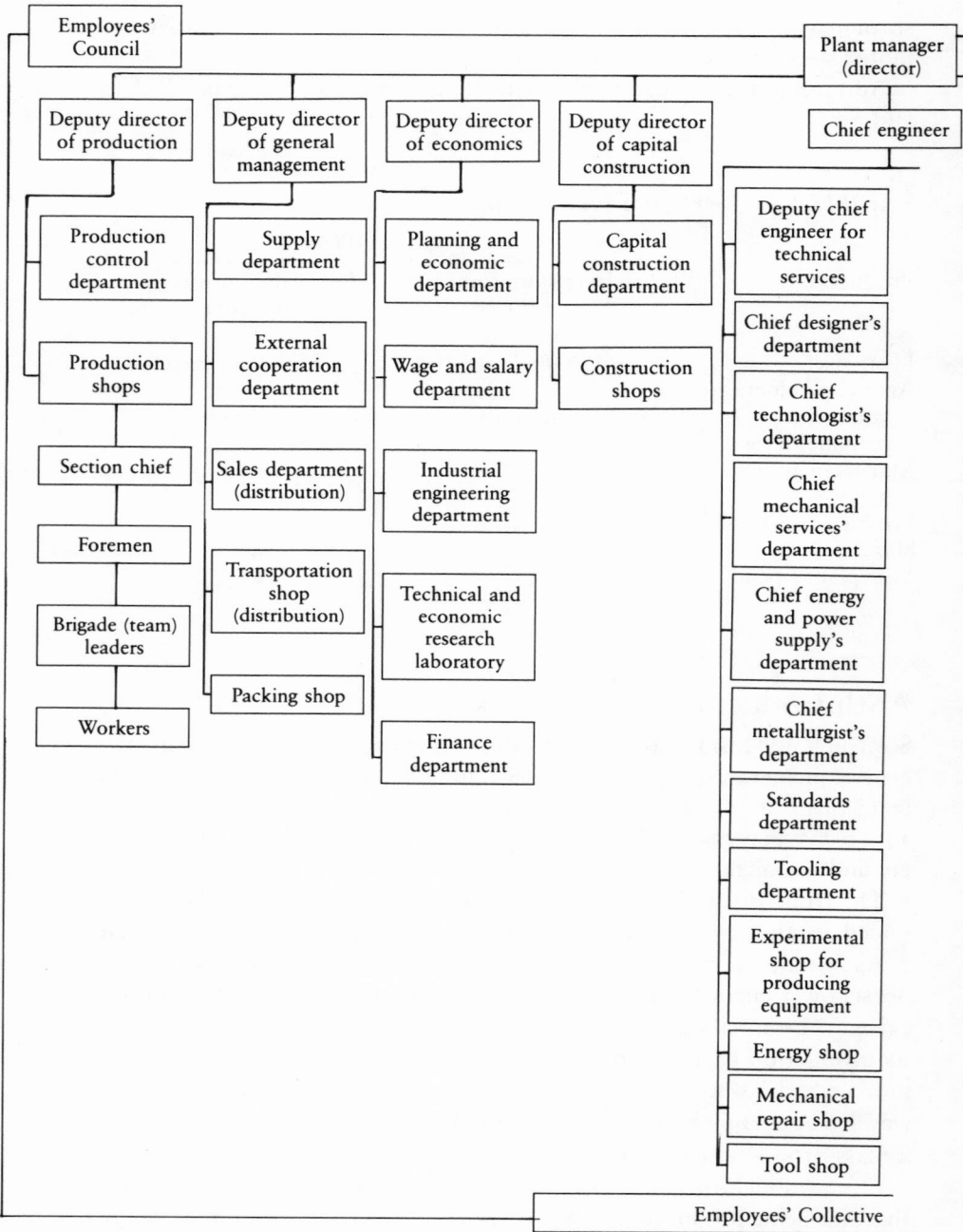

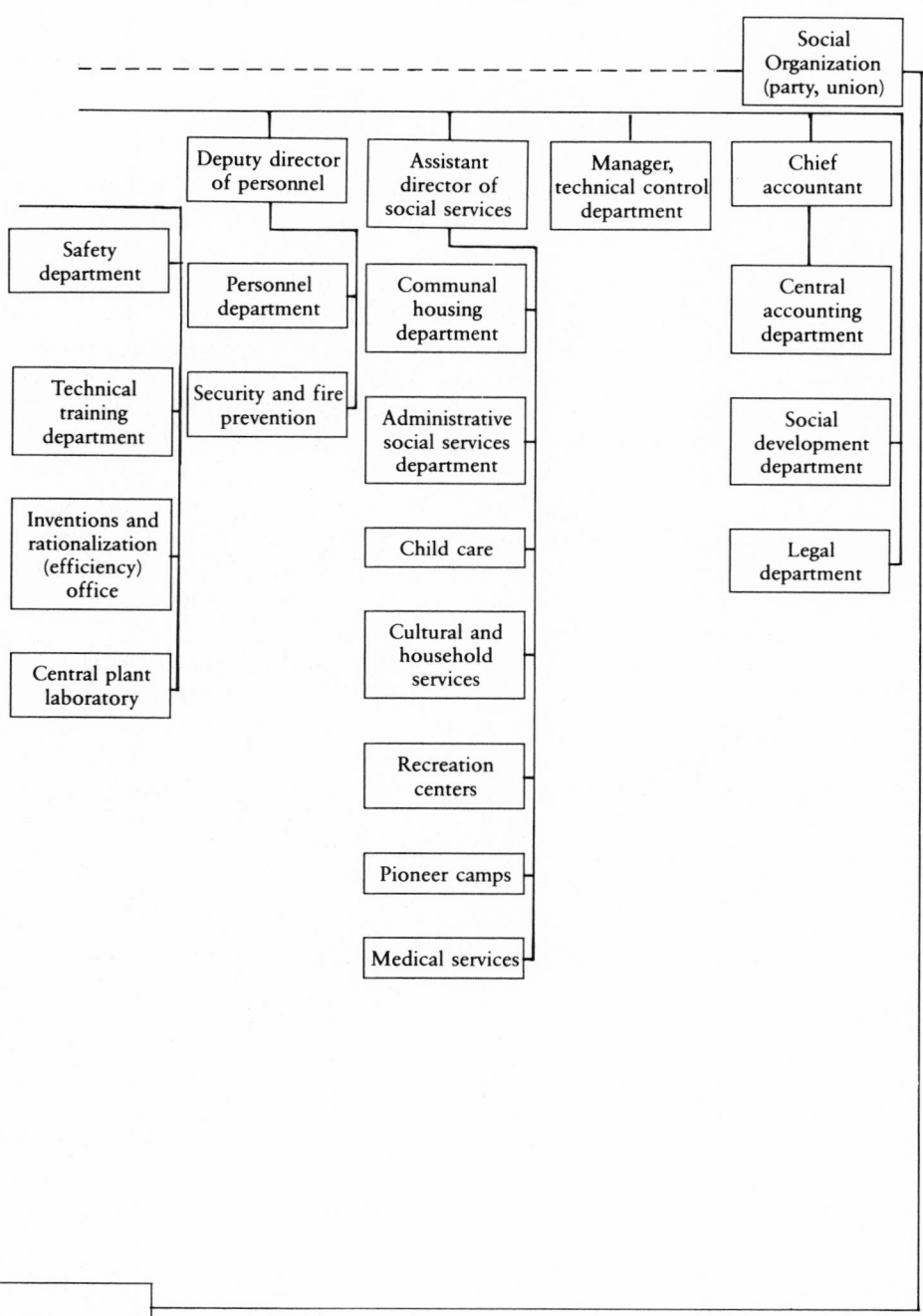

improvements increased the life of the truck from 150,000 to 350,000 kilometers. At the time of our study, annual production numbered 204,000 trucks with 6- to 10-ton capacity, a 150- to 180-horsepower engine, and driving speeds of over 100 kilometers per hour.

SovTruck's 1980 dieselization program was producing 8,500 diesel trucks annually by 1988 and had plans to reach 14,500 by 1989. This substantial investment project was expected to cost close to 3 billion rubles and add 743,000 square meters of new production facilities plus 6,500 units of equipment.

SovTruck produces a quarter of the trucks made in the Soviet Union. In 1988, SovTruck employed 65,000 at its main truck plant complex in Moscow, had 2 million square meters of production space, and 45,000 pieces of equipment. It had 400 automatic machining lines, 800 mechanized lines, and over 100 kilometers of assembly conveyors. The main complex included 10 separate factories, 32 independent shops, 5 independent organizations, and enterprise headquarters. Central headquarters, in addition to managing all the separate factories and shops, has 8 departments for technical development, 21 departments for support areas, and 14 departments for general and managerial purposes. Headquarters also has over 100 scientific units and engineering labs, and connections with 150 scientific organizations.

SovTruck is a fully integrated truck manufacturer, producing everything from raw castings, to final machined components, to truck assembly and finishing. At any given plant site there may be a number of different activities (e.g., casting, machining, and assembly all under one roof). In accordance with central orders, SovTruck must produce consumer goods as well: refrigerators, microwave ovens, decorative hardware, kitchen cabinets and appliances, kayaks, and many other products. Consumer goods account for 5.5% of SovTruck's sales.

The few other major truck producers are located in Kama River, the Ural Mountains, and other regions. Generally, the different truck producers segment the market by truck carrying capacity.

Like other Soviet enterprises, SovTruck has many social obligations. The main plant owns and manages over 100 apartment buildings for employees. It sponsors an evening college and a technical institute, one of which many employees attend, and it runs more than 10 children's schools and summer camps. It supports cultural institutes, numerous sports stadiums, its own football team, a supermarket, its own hospitals and clinics, and a daily newspaper. Moreover, because of its pre-eminence in the city, prominent SovTruck managers are likely to have high profiles in local government activities. For example, the director general of the enterprise is a member of the city council.

EXHIBIT 5.9 SovElectric Plant W Manager's Day

7:30–8:00 A.M.	Tours plant to identify problems and provide solutions on the spot.
8:00–8:30	Prepares in office for selector broadcast (intercom transmission of messages from plant manager, chief engineer, and production manager to all levels of management through shop manager).
8:30–9:00	Selector broadcast.
9:00–9:30	Holds informal meetings with supply and construction department personnel.
9:30–11:00	Tours plant (see 7:30–8:00 above).
11:00–1:00 P.M.	Informal meetings with individual shop managers and specialists.
1:00–2:00	Lunch.
2:00–5:00	Holds regularly scheduled formal meetings.
5:00–5:30	Selector transmission.
5:30–7:00	Tours plant to identify night shift problems and provide solutions.
7:00–8:00	Reads mail.
8:00	Goes home.
Weekly	Chairs production meeting and holds office hours to receive workers, their family members, and others from outside the plant.

THE ORGANIZATIONAL STRUCTURE OF SOVTRUCK

Because of its early reform efforts as well as its size, this enterprise has been managed as a two-level system. In a two-level system, the enterprise reports directly to the top ministerial level rather than to a subindustry department (*glavne upravlenje*) of its ministry. This means that the enterprise may go directly to the minister with requests and proposals. The enterprise may also manage with less interference from above. In fact, one of SovTruck's managers commented that he has not been asked to go to the ministry all year, and the ministry has not issued any orders that directly interfere with his work.

The SovTruck plants in Moscow are organized around the main truck assembly plant. The main plant is a large production complex using about one million tons of metals and many other components and raw materials annually. Every day the plant's main conveyor loads and ships about 700 trucks. This central plant helps coordinate resource and supply relations for the entire enterprise. All other plants and structural units in the main complex are directly subordinate to the main plant and report to the director general.

Other than the specific structures described here, relationships within each plant are nearly identical to those of SovElectric.

SOVTRUCK PLANT X

Plant X is situated in the main truck complex. At the time of our study, it was operating at 100% capacity and producing 900 gasoline engines a day. It runs two shifts with a total of 2,291 workers, but because of a labor shortage, 450 of its workers are temporary, many of them foreigners. This causes some quality problems because temporary workers have less ability or motivation to perform top-quality work. Turnover runs at about 8%, which management feels is too high. Though few are absent without an excuse (effectively, grounds for dismissal), an average 10% of the labor force might be absent on any given day for one of the following reasons: unused holiday, illness, child-care problem, work in a pioneer camp or other social activity, holiday without pay. During the fall, the labor shortage is particularly critical because some workers are required to leave to help bring in the harvest. The worker's average wage at the time of the study was 205 rubles a month, or 218 rubles a month with bonus, which is a bit higher than the average national figure.

Plant X is a critical feeder for the main assembly plant. Out of its daily 900-engine production run, 600 engines go to the main assembly line. Therefore the plant is under substantial pressure to make its targets. Moreover, the situation is exacerbated by a long-term plan to shrink the gasoline engine business. Thus the plant receives few funds for reinvestment or capital improvement. These difficulties may explain in part the high rate of plant manager turnover: in a single year, there had been three different plant managers.

Plant X operates much like a cost center, with an annual operating budget of 230 million rubles. As at all Soviet plants, the Communist party, the trade union, and Komsomol are represented at the plant and at plant manager's meetings.

SOVTRUCK PLANT Y

Plant Y produces truck components such as carburetors, fuel pumps, and shock absorbers, as well as consumer goods such as metal fasteners. Its 2,400 employees—including 80–150 temporary workers—work two shifts in 30,000 square meters of space. At the time of our study, the average wage at Plant Y was 188 rubles per month without bonus, 210 rubles with bonus.

Plant Y is located some distance from the main SovTruck complex and is operated as an independent profit center with its own profit targets. Because of its status as a profit center, Plant Y has far more engineers than Plant X and designs many of its own product changes at the site. (In fact, Plant Y turns to headquarters only for special technology needs such as welding expertise or machine-tool building.)

Plant Y supplies 700 customers, but 40% of the plant's production goes to the main plant. Its annual sales volume is 50 million rubles. Of this, 23 million rubles go for raw materials and parts from outside the plant, 5.2 million rubles for the wage fund, and 900,000 rubles for bonuses. The value-added was 11 million rubles, or 22% of sales. Out of 50 million rubles in sales, 9 million is profit, 2.5 million of which is left for the plant and 6.5 million returns to the enterprise. In the previous 13 years, the plant has increased its sales of consumer goods from 120,000 rubles to 3.5 million rubles.

Additional facts about SovTruck are presented in Exhibits 5.10, 5.11, and 5.12.

EXHIBIT 5.10   SovTruck Summary Data

	Plant X *Engine plant*	*Plant Y* *Auto parts plant*
Products	150–180 HP gasoline engines	Truck components (shock absorbers, carburetors, fuel pumps); consumer goods (fasteners, ovens)
Plant size	17,000 sq meters	30,000 sq meters
Annual production volume	240 million rubles	50 million rubles
Total employees	2,470	2,430
Management	186	150
Support and specialist workers	825	1,080
Production workers	1,459	1,200
Shifts	2 (3 as required)	2
Year plant opened	1963	1935

EXHIBIT 5.11 SovTruck Plant X Organizational Chart

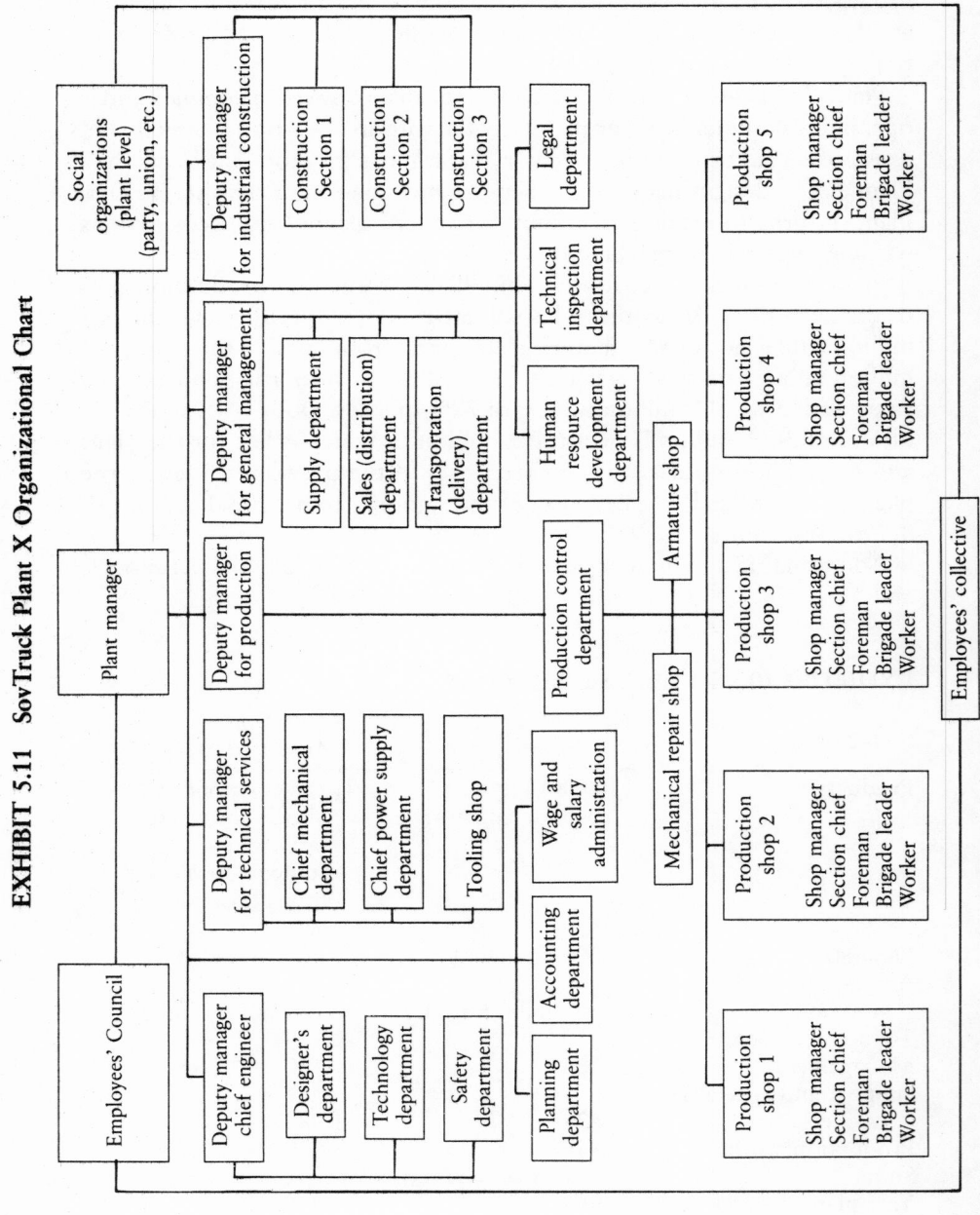

EXHIBIT 5.12 SovTruck Plant X Manager's Day

7:15–7:20 A.M.	Arrives at plant.
7:20–7:40	Receives oral production report for previous day (materials supplied to main assembly line, production against required output); receives written report for previous 24-hour period, to be reviewed carefully with first deputy for production.
7:40–8:30	Notes main points of shift supervisor's report and tours the shops to observe and evaluate the situation.
8:30–9:00	Returns to office to read mail and prepare for daily plant management meeting.
9:00–10:00	Conducts daily production management meeting. (By order of the director general of the enterprise, meetings other than production meetings are prohibited in the first half of the day in order to sustain a focus on production.) Hears details of shift supervisor's report and report of managers and social organizations; clarifies current situation and issues instructions. Announces agenda for meetings in advance to give people time to prepare.
10:00–11:00	Solves problems arising from morning meeting; plans activities for next day.
11:00–12:00	Arranges various meetings for later in the day (finance, personnel, production planning).
12:00–1:00 P.M.	Tours the shop to monitor the situation and correct problems he observes.
1:00–2:00	Lunch time for managers and specialists (workers go to lunch from 11:00 to 12:00).
2:00–5:00	Attends meetings at headquarters and meetings of social organizations; solves plant problems requiring external involvement; may hold plant meetings for quality, engineering, safety, and so forth.
5:00–5:30	Chairs regular evening production meeting.
5:30–6:00	Tours shop floor for second shift.
6:00–7:00	Chairs in-plant technical meetings on most pressing issues.
7:00–8:00	Receives information about second shift; makes corrections; reads mail and does paperwork.
8:00	Leaves for home.

A Concluding Comparison

Although some basic comparisons can be made between the two Soviet enterprises in our study, their comparison with the US firms and plants is more interesting. All four Soviet plants are older and larger than the US plants and, not surprisingly, their capital equipment is older too. The competitive pressures behind various forms of restructuring in the US firms are only now being felt in the Soviet enterprises. Signs of flattening hierarchy and the search for export markets in Soviet plants suggest the changes that will be more apparent in subsequent chapters. The principle of self-financing has just begun to emerge. Soviet undercapacity is in sharp contrast to the overcapacity in the United States. The overriding contrast between the two management systems is, of course, the high degree of centralized decision making in the USSR as compared with the participative management of the US firms. This will become still more apparent as we turn now to the first of our four management issues, annual planning.

Chapter 6 is the first of four chapters that present the comparative evidence on decision practices of US and Soviet managers in the four selected decision areas. The reader will find that we have decided to present a full description of these practices, available for the first time, by drawing out a number of decision histories. At the end of each chapter and in Part III we will present conclusions from these data that have special relevance to operating joint ventures in the USSR. The detailed descriptions, however, offer much more material than we will comment on; it is offered for the reader's reflection and analysis as a vehicle for gaining an in-depth feeling for both management systems. In this regard we have tried to keep intact some of the style of expression and thinking of the managers of both systems. In effect, we have chosen to share our field notes, as an anthropologist might, to assist managers on both sides to develop an insider's understanding of the other—to move behind the factory walls.

Chapter 6

Planning

Planning in the United States

[*Editors' note:* The following description of the planning process in the US firms has been prepared primarily for the Soviet reader. Even though it may be familiar to American readers, they will find it is useful to put the Soviet practice into focus on a comparative basis. This section will briefly present the general approach to planning used in the United States and then examine its actual practice in the two US enterprises.]

According to contemporary US theory, planning coordinates the work of organizations. US companies usually conduct two types of planning activity: long-range or strategic planning, and annual planning. Typically, a small group at corporate headquarters focuses on strategic planning on the basis of market potentials and competition. This planning process is complex, sometimes utilizing planning tools such as econometric forecasts and models from universities. The primary unit of analysis for strategic planning is the strategic business unit (SBU), defined by its ability to operate as a stand-alone business. Strategic planning assesses the future viability and profitability of different SBUs and makes decisions about getting out of certain businesses, acquiring or building new businesses, and so forth.

Annual planning, which has been the primary focus of our research, builds on strategic plans but is more detailed and exact in its specifications. The annual plan becomes the operating document on which the SBU may base its planned production volumes, human resource plans, capital investment plans, and new product introduction efforts and schedules. The annual plan breaks market and production plans into quarterly and monthly plans, and provides targets to the very lowest levels of the organization.

The annual planning process starts with a forecast of the sales of goods and services, moves on to the estimating of costs for the production of

111

these goods and services, and finally arrives at the projection of profits. Within each SBU, managers usually plan for each of the SBU's component units (major departments or plants) by treating them as cost centers to be managed against variable cost budgets. The typical cost budget starts with the establishment of a standard for the number of direct labor dollars expected to be spent for each unit of output. Then, planners estimate from experience other variable costs such as raw materials and supplies per unit of output. Costs that are relatively fixed regardless of output, such as plant and equipment, may either be added to the budget as an overhead charge atop standard labor or left out of the cost budget. The resulting total standard cost per output unit represents a target to be periodically compared on a variance analysis basis (usually each week or month) with the actual direct labor hours and (if they are available) actual raw material costs, supply costs, and so on. US firms use many detailed variations on this basic cost control process, which is a control tool in all firms and provides a major building block (cost of goods sold) in the larger annual business plan.

In addition, it is customary in most US firms for operating units to select a set of key business variables to measure on a regular basis and to compare these variables to historic results and/or projected targets. For example, such variables as yield (percentage of good units completed against units started into production), inventory turnover, age of accounts receivable, and days lost by accidents are carefully monitored in industries where these variables are critical to success.

Planning at AmElectric

The planning process at AmElectric begins anew every two years with a strategic plan. Senior managers at business unit headquarters (one level above the operating division) are responsible for developing the plans. It takes about four months to complete and set base strategies for the SBU according to market scenarios and niches. A typical base plan might include a strategy to get into some area of business or to exit a particular product line. Strategies are planned for a three-year period with an extrapolation to five years, and planners analyze each scenario according to several alternatives such as growth, status quo, shrink, or harvest for cash flow.

The manager of commercial policy and planning for the business unit coordinates the business unit inputs from each plant for the corporate review, but otherwise the plants have no involvement in strategic planning. "We are 'the tail on the dog,'" explained a plant controller. "We get a couple of weeks to crunch the numbers to estimate plant operating budgets. They run 25 to 30 sets of numbers based on different alternatives prepared by the business unit." This information is then fed back to corporate via business unit headquarters. Corporate headquarters reviews and selects alternatives and then informs the businesses and plants of the strategy, which they must then follow. (See Exhibit 6.1 for AmElectric's annual planning process flow.)

EXHIBIT 6.1   Annual Planning Process at AmElectric

March	Evaluating the market, business unit develops strategy and financial plans. Marketing attempts to forecast next year's orders.
April	Plant informed of early strategic and financial plan drafts.
June–August	Plants receive actual plan targets and begin working out the details for each shop; plant receives figures on expected inflation rates, wage and salary increases, inventory guidelines, and so forth. In August, final targets for productive hours are given (broken down into salable—i.e., direct—and nonsalable).
September	Plant manager and key staff present annual plan and budgets to division and business headquarters.
November	Corporate informs plants whether or not the proposed plan will be accepted as is.
January	Business unit transmits official annual plan figures to the plant; figures may still be changed. Plants begin spending funds.
February	Annual plan figures receive final approval and may not be changed.
	Performance is tracked monthly by business headquarters; deviations are to be avoided and must be explained.

The annual plan is built on the strategic plan. Strict comparisons against plant performance are made and plants have to provide a rationale for deviations from the strategic plan. The annual planning process begins with the marketing department's market forecasts. Even though order forecasting is a difficult and uncertain process, 70–85% of production plans have to be based on forecasts, with only the remaining based on backlog or known orders. Forecasting takes two probabilities into account: whether a customer will place an order in a given time period, and whether AmElectric will get that order. For example, AmElectric may be the sole source for a customer, but the customer may not know whether they'll get the funding to purchase or whether their management will postpone repairs. In fact, in 1988, the division had been below target sales by $15 to $17 million because of "a couple of late cancellations" of orders.

As business shifts from new equipment to service work, forecasting is becoming even more difficult. Demand is less predictable than it was in the

1960s when power companies had long-range construction plans. It is difficult to predict when equipment will break down or when forced outages (unscheduled shutdowns of power plants) will occur. Also, many orders come from "upsell" business, which occurs when power companies maintain their equipment and find additional parts need replacement. In 1987, upsell orders constituted 15% of one plant's repair business. Clearly this demand is not easy to predict.

Plant personnel often discredit market forecasts because of past inaccuracies. According to one plant manager, up until five years ago, marketing made conservative forecasts so that they could easily meet their sales goals. The plants would add 15% to marketing's estimates to make them more realistic. By 1984, though, marketing's projections were reasonably accurate because demand had declined and because the business unit would not allow such conservatism. As demand fell further, the marketing forecasts became overly optimistic. The plants claim that in recent years up to one-third of forecast orders never materialized. While plants cannot unilaterally adjust the marketing forecasts, they can challenge them and ask for more information. Sometimes the plants even succeed in getting modifications.

Conflicts between marketing and manufacturing arise partly because each is evaluated on different criteria. Management judges marketing by the bookings or sales it generates and, as one plant engineer said, "They don't care if the company makes a profit." The plants, however, are evaluated according to such criteria as productivity and cost reduction. If the firm sells a product at a low price, the plant will have to struggle to cut costs accordingly. Because of their conflicting goals, internal battles frequently erupt between marketing and manufacturing on issues of price and delivery.

One plant dealt with this problem through informal networking. Carl Bullock, manager of parts and materials, cultivates personal relationships with key marketing personnel. He makes regular trips to division headquarters to "lobby with the marketers" and brings information back to the plant. He believes that using official channels such as coordinating through division headquarters and waiting for paper documentation does not leave enough time to react to problems. The advantage of his informal friendships is that they create an "advanced warning system." For example, while chatting recently with the division parts manager, Bullock learned that his plant was about to lose parts orders from another AmElectric division. The purchasing manager at the other division was planning to buy them elsewhere. So Bullock and his parts manager visited the other division and convinced purchasing to give the business to Bullock's plant.

After the marketing forecast is developed, the manager of manufacturing planning at the plant works closely with division headquarters to translate the marketing plan into load and then into productive hours. First, the manager of manufacturing planning estimates both the production volume and product mix, based on sales volume. Then the plant manager, controller, and divisional manager of manufacturing planning meet to decide whether the load figure is acceptable. Finally, they translate load into productive hours, the standard direct labor hours that will be needed to produce the required product mix and volume. However, forecasts of productive hours may estimate actual labor hours inaccurately due to a variety of factors: incomplete information, insufficient supplies or materials ordered, engineering and drawing delays, and workers' downtime from production for training, housekeeping, and personal time—that is, anything other than the labor time required to make a product.

Planners allocate productive hours by plant department, determining direct and indirect labor, manpower count, and department overhead, and ultimately producing the department or shop budget. The budgets are usually too fat, and a second cycle within the plant is required to make them leaner. This is "a somewhat painful process," according to the plant manager, who said he uses "penknife, axe, and chain saw" to cut the fat. He tries not to make it a game where people *expect* a second cycle, although he admits that there is some element of gaming.

For example, Mike Myers, Plant B's controller, cut $5 million from 1988 expenses proposed by the plant staff. His practice is to ask the department managers to explain their reasons for each projected cost; if there is not a "good business justification," he drops the item. Thus he trimmed $1 million with no argument from the managers when he found that three of them had each budgeted for bringing in the same 15–20 trainers from outside the plant. Proposed budgets are often controversial when department managers want to add people. For example, Myers knew from experience that in one proposed budget manpower expenses "wouldn't fly" in division headquarters, so he proposed hiring temporary workers until the load stabilized. Myers then presented this proposal at a staff meeting and consensus was reached.

Annual planning is an iterative process at AmElectric. Jeremy Thatcher, the operations division general manager, is involved in three steps: he helps in establishing market objectives by examining whether the assumptions are rational; he participates in drawing up the first draft of the plant budgets; and he makes the formal presentation of the plan to corporate. His primary goal is "to ensure everyone is working to the same plan." The strategic plan sets guidelines about which projects to fund and keeps everyone honest. Despite the plan, however, allocating resources is a major task. Thatcher meets with the plant managers to negotiate them downward while he still endeavors to "foster ownership of the plan at the plant level."

The plant controller assembles the plans prepared by each plant department and rolls them into one budget. In early September, the plant manager, controller, and a staff manager present the plan at division headquarters and explain how they arrived at the numbers. One plant controller claimed, "There is lots of give and take in the negotiation process, and that's a good thing," but added that "winning a negotiation is based on solid business justification." He admitted, however, that Jeremy Thatcher usually wins and cuts their budget. At the meeting, the plants also get feedback, which can be both general (e.g., "your plan doesn't fit the overall picture") and specific (e.g., "productivity can be improved").

Back at the plants, senior managers review divisional comments and hold meetings with staff to make adjustments and pare down or redo the plan. Within two weeks they submit a revised plan to division headquarters. These plans move from the divisional level to the business unit level and then on up to corporate. By November, corporate provides initial feedback on whether the plants' plans are acceptable.

In January, division headquarters officially transmits the numbers for the year to the plants. "It's the plant's last chance to amend the plan. Then you're frozen and they become sacred objectives," a plant manager intoned. Final approval may not come until February or March, but the plants can begin spending funds in January.

POST-PLANNING IMPLEMENTATION

Thatcher starts his monthly staff meetings with a comparison of actual results and those given in the plan. In 1988, the anticipated sales load had not materialized and plans were being readjusted accordingly. Sometimes the actual sales indicate that there are too few productive hours to keep the plant's work force fully occupied. When the discrepancy is fairly small, plant managers sometimes adopt a stretch plan to avoid layoffs. Then they negotiate the plan with marketing and financial groups at division headquarters. However, deviations from the plan are taken very seriously, and everybody is expected to conform, barring uncontrollable external events. There are several ways of adjusting the plant to conform to the plan. To speed up the process, the plant may start jobs into production early, using partial engineering information. To slow things down, they may get a customer to agree to a later delivery than projected.

There is usually a big push at the end of nearly every quarter and year to make the production plan. As one plant controller explained, "Headquarters likes to report increased earnings each quarter and asks the plants if they can ship orders by then to contribute to the final result." As a result, independent truckers circle the plants at the end of each quarter and year waiting for last-minute shipments that can be counted in the plan for the period. For example, on New Year's Eve 1987, people at one plant worked at a feverish pitch. Even the plant nurse could be seen helping out in the shipping department as a volunteer packer. The reason for the frenzy was that the plant had not made its target for sales billed in 1987 because some anticipated orders did not materialize. To offset this shortfall, they increased production volume in December by pulling in several million dollars of orders scheduled for 1988. "December has 38 days," the plant manager had said, smiling. In the last days of December, Jeremy Thatcher had called daily to monitor production, and at 5 P.M. December 31 he declared they had met their objectives. The plant controller was in the plant at midnight to cut off shipments for the year officially to keep the records right.

The key business variables that managers watch regularly are load, productive hours, productivity improvement, inventory levels, and capital expenditures relative to budget. However, there was disagreement at AmElectric about how to measure these variables. At one of Jeremy Thatcher's staff meetings, for example, quality assurance manager Paul Hay told the division controller he "would be a hero" if he could devise a system to "stop all the fighting" about the way the business variables were measured.

Nevertheless, there was general agreement about what the critical variable was. So long as the plants fill the orders on schedule, they are not evaluated on production volume. Rather, they are assessed on how well they keep their costs down and on the main criterion: "How many hours did we produce last month?" Hours are the critical factor for spreading out overhead costs, primarily because the plants are operating at 60% of capacity.

A SUMMARY OF PLANNING AT AMELECTRIC

Annual planning at AmElectric is clearly a complex and time-consuming process. It starts with market forecasts, which move to the plant level for detailing in terms of operating schedules and costs. The negotiations around these cost budgets eventually move up the hierarchy in a reiterative manner. As the top is pressing for stiffer targets, the plant is arguing for more achievable figures. Some gaming takes place, and the process often moves through a second or third cycle of negotiations up and down the hierarchy. Once the plan is approved, however, plants make all efforts to achieve it. This results, among other things, in quarterly and year-end "storming" drives to "make the numbers." As we will see, the planning process is quite different at AmTruck because planning is less conflicted.

Planning at AmTruck

Like other US companies, AmTruck has an elaborate planning system. Every level of the organization participates in developing the annual plan, which includes targets for volume, expenses and costs, capital investment, quality, delivery, inventory, and safety. Exhibit 6.2 outlines the general flow of the planning cycle at AmTruck.

EXHIBIT 6.2   AmTruck Planning Cycle

March–June	Members of corporate headquarters planning staff study the market and competition, make estimates of the likely business environment, update strategies for markets, products, financing, and so forth. In June, plan objectives, targets, and priorities are set and approved by top management.
July	One-week planning conference for up to 300 of Am-Truck's senior staff; senior management presents Am-Truck's plans and strategy; participants discuss direction and resolve issues for the next level in the organization.
August	Planning conference participants (plant managers and their planning staff) return to plant and interpret goals for their plant; for example, a corporate target of 3% cost reduction might be translated into a specific breakdown of which accounts or shops savings it will come from; a calendar of planning deadlines is developed.
September	Plant manager and staff share plans with plant organization, shops, and so forth; each business must submit plans for headcount (number of employees needed), capital investment, inventory, and so forth; numbers are given to the finance department, which compiles all the numbers to ensure they meet targets and develops product cost estimates.
October	Plant manager reviews plan with headquarters, makes necessary changes with shops, and approves plan.
November	Headquarters approves and finalizes plan.
December	An organizational audit checks whether the organization is set up to implement the plan (i.e., is there sufficient skill level and are there any training needs?). Each employee develops an individual work plan in accordance with the corporate plan and following the corporate priorities.

AmTruck's approach to planning attempts to force responsibility and accountability downward, and management stresses that the annual plan is "not just numbers." When Andrew Ross, AmTruck's CEO, kicks off the planning cycle in July at a planning conference with all senior managers, he focuses on the broad strategic goals of the corporation. At this point he offers no specific plan but rather a review of strategic points of emphasis and some broad economic targets and guidelines. The managers at the conference bring back the strategic message to their plants, and translate the broad strategic direction into concrete goals and actions for their operations. Plants accept corporate's targets and goals as given. As one planning manager commented, "Corporate knows the environmental demands, what our financing costs are, how much working capital is available, overall market trends, and so forth. We accept their numbers, but we tell them what we need to accomplish the goals they have set forth."

Market forecasts play a critical role in the annual plan. The detailed planning effort begins with a sales forecast initiated by corporate marketing with input from customer service personnel and plant representatives. Normally, the sales forecasts are highly uncertain. The number of known orders for the planning year is about one-quarter of anticipated volume because AmTruck knows orders only two to three months in advance. Furthermore, the order or product mix may change, which also affects the plants' plan. One business manager talked about his experience developing a plan for his machining area, recalling that the volume forecast changed six times during the few months he was working out his anticipated costs and volumes.

Each business team at the plant works as a group to develop a budget, or an estimate of overall expenses, based on anticipated product sales volume and product mix, as well as on experience from previous years. Total costs are broken down into fixed costs, materials, direct labor, and variable costs. Variable costs include overhead costs that may fluctuate with volume, such as support staff, management staff, and indirect labor. Using the business team budget, the plant develops a standard cost per product, a transfer price with which the corporation credits them.

Another goal integrated into the planning process is to find cost reductions of 3% a year. This, too, is a difficult and uncertain task. One manager recalled, "We spent months trying to figure out how to get 50 cents out of the cam-shaft cost. And this year, our scrap costs went up by five dollars. We had no way to anticipate that. It has had a major impact on our cost profile and makes the 50 cents seem trivial."

Once the plants have developed their plans, headquarters generally approves their figures. Occasionally expense estimates may be cut, or capital investment projects refused or postponed, but usually plant plans are sufficiently aggressive that corporate feels no need to tighten up the numbers. AmTruck's general philosophy encourages managers to set high goals, and plants are not severely punished if they fail to meet them. The perceived motivational impact of reaching for a "stretch" goal and for flexibility is seen as outweighing the need for tight control and precise estimates.

Throughout the year, each plant reforecasts sales volume and costs monthly (using a 12-month rolling forecast) and adjusts its operating plans accordingly. Managers also report on monthly performance to headquarters. If performance was not up to plan, they often spend more time explaining. However, one manager said, "Headquarters isn't so much interested in the precise figures as in understanding the process. If they know you're doing your best and following the right procedures, they'll accept negative deviations."

Corporate managers fly to the various plants monthly for a report on performance versus plan. If corporate stays only a day, the plant manager and his operating team make a brief presentation. During longer visits, the business managers themselves present their monthly data. This facilitates communication between different levels of the hierarchy and enhances the commitment of the business managers to the plan.

The planning process facilitates the introduction of change in the plant. For example, one plant knew that its forthcoming volume forecasts indicated it would have to put on a second shift, so the plant operating team and the business managers began planning for this early in the year. By the time the second shift had to begin, the team had completed the necessary training and recruiting.

When the new shift began, everyone had to take a turn on each shift on an "equality-of-sacrifice principle." The shifts were made up of half experienced workers and half new workers. Nevertheless, because of the excellent planning system, management started up the second shift without missing a beat on quality or productivity. In fact, productivity increased by 10%. One manager said, "Productivity probably increased because of some competition between the shifts. We fed this a little bit by providing data on output."

Sometimes the plant and headquarters disagreed. For example, originally, the plant wanted to run a first and third shift, since the time of the second shift is better family time. However, because AmTruck did its data processing during the third shift, the plant needed a second shift in order to roll its daily performance numbers into the data system in time. Said one manager, "This is an example of the tail wagging the dog. We'd like to be a little more independent of headquarters." Eventually, the plant intended to switch the second shift to third-shift hours.

A SUMMARY OF PLANNING AT AMTRUCK

Annual planning at AmTruck involves the same hierarchical levels as it does at AmElectric once the planning cycle is initiated at the company conference in July. As at AmElectric, the detailed planning begins with market forecasts. The forecasts move laterally to the plants, where first-level business and production teams develop cost budgets. As the plans move up the line for review and approval, further discussions and changes occur. At AmTruck there is less mistrust in the soundness of plant plans than there is at AmElectric. We observed fewer top-level orders for further cuts, which led AmElectric to second and third rounds of planning. Moreover, AmTruck plants and headquarters agree that ambitious "stretch" goals are desirable but must be adjusted as the year proceeds if sales and other forecasts are not realized. They recognize that sales estimates are inevitably subject to error. This realization means that AmTruck responds to shortfalls and overages quickly and realistically, rather than calling for "storming" to fulfill budget numbers.

AMELECTRIC AND AMTRUCK: A COMPARISON

The US firms offer some interesting contrasts in the way they handle annual planning. They illustrate the fact that there is a great deal of variability in US managerial practice. While the AmElectric pattern is more traditional in the United States, AmTruck represents the more recent push toward radical decentralization. Despite these differences, though, both firms start their planning cycle with sales forecasts developed by the marketing personnel, and it is this practice that offers the sharpest contrast with the Soviet practice we will turn to now.

Planning in the USSR

[*Editors' note:* This section describes the Soviet general approach to planning as selected and reported by our Soviet colleagues primarily for American readers. It is followed by descriptions of practices we observed at SovElectric and SovTruck.]

Planning has played a central role in the management of the Soviet economy. Most of the basic goods have been produced at the direction of the central planning authorities. The USSR Council of Ministers, Gosplan (the state planning commission), ministries, and similar authorities of the union republics develop the national plan.

EXHIBIT 6.3 · Overall Planning Procedure in the USSR

I. Five-year Planning Process

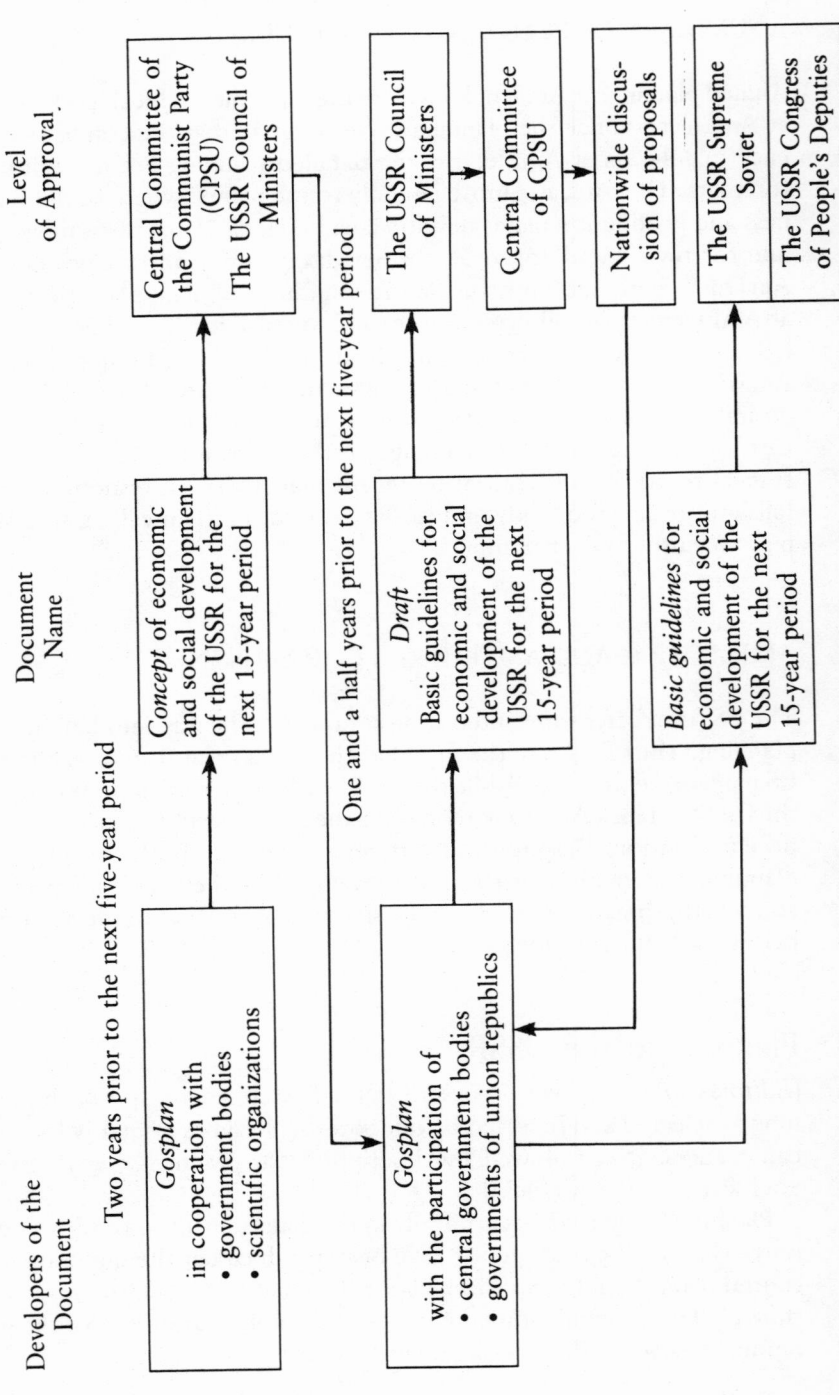

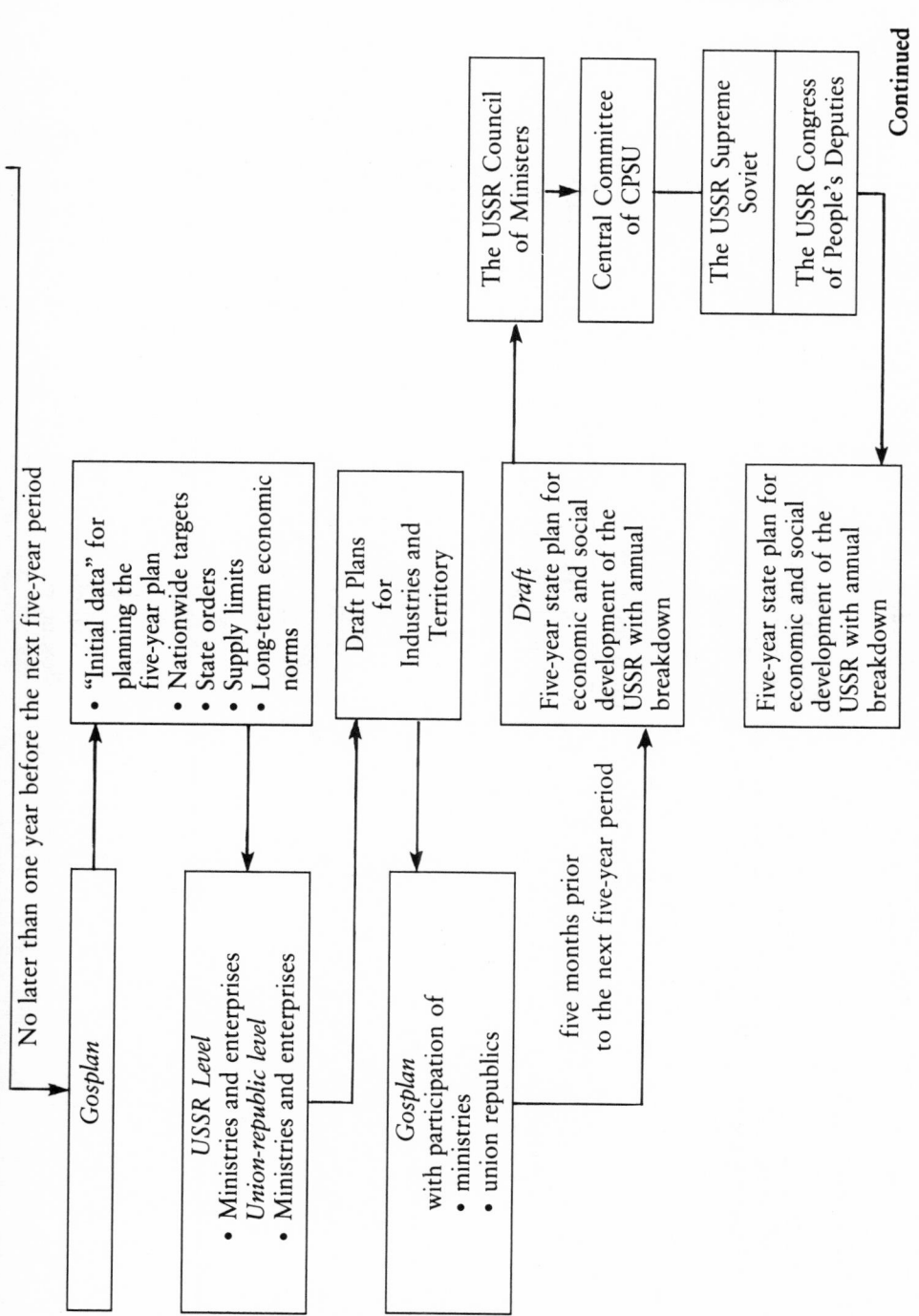

EXHIBIT 6.3   Overall Planning Procedure in the USSR (continued)

II. Annual Planning process

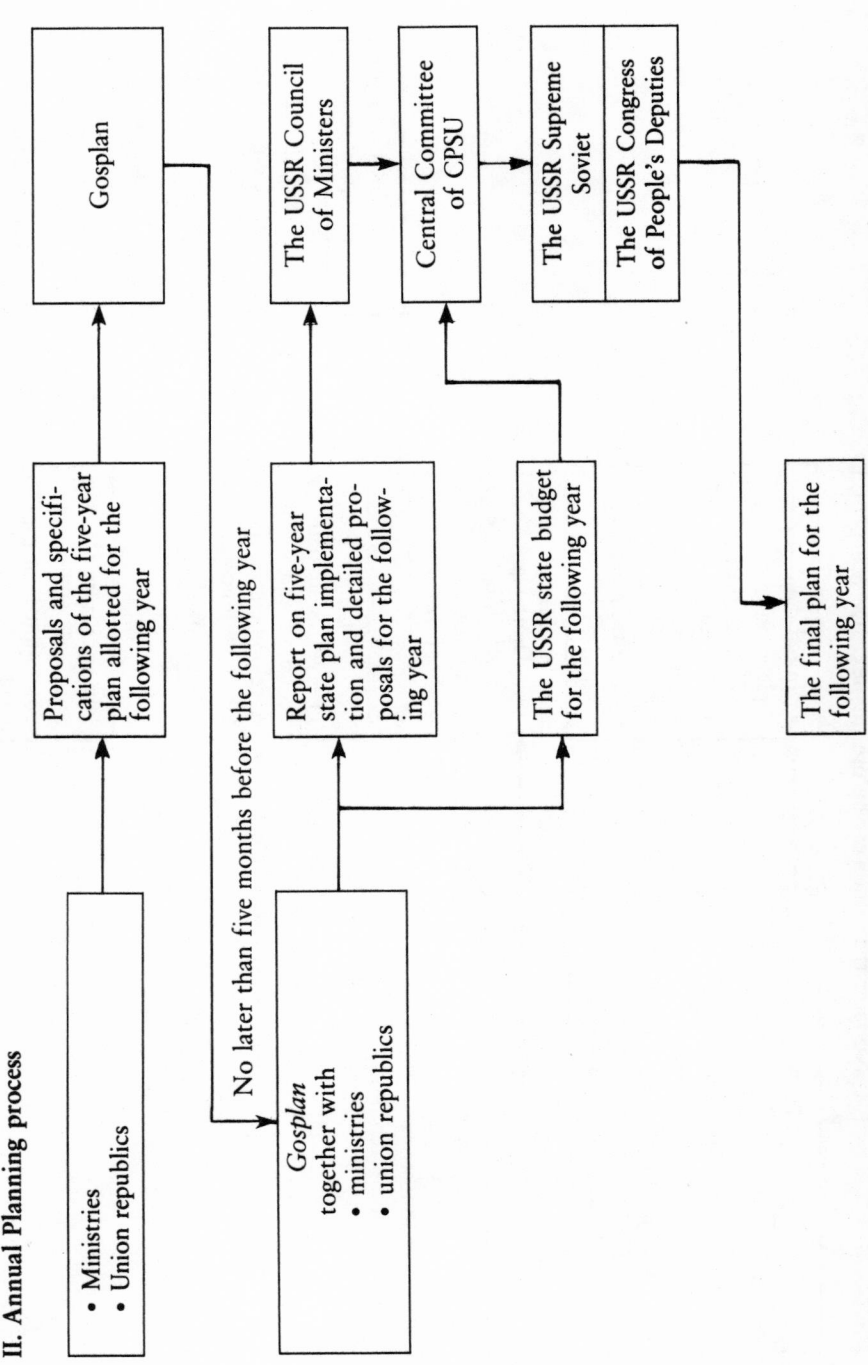

The following procedure is used for nationwide planning in the USSR (see Exhibit 6.3). The process has three major components: (1) a *concept* of the economic and social development for the USSR for a 15-year period; (2) The *basic guidelines* for that development for the same period; (3) and a *five-year state plan* with annual assignments.

The concept is primarily a forecasting document developed two years before the following five-year plan by various governmental bodies and Gosplan. It serves as a base to determine directions for the long-term development of the USSR.

The basic guidelines cover such areas as rates of growth, the economy's structure, intensification methods, industrial and territorial development plans, and priorities for technology and social programs. The guidelines are broken down into five-year estimates; the first five-year period is broken down into annual targets for sectors, industries, and territories. Draft guidelines are prepared by Gosplan with input from central economic bodies, ministries, and the governments of union republics. The draft is presented to the USSR Council of Ministers for approval one and a half years before the next five-year plan. After being approved by the highest party organs, the draft is presented for nationwide discussion. It later serves as the basis of the next plan.

The five-year plan determines the major targets of the national economy of the USSR and is the guide to implementing the aims and assignments of the basic guidelines. It is also the basis for organizing the economic activity of ministries, local administrations, enterprises, and plants.

To prepare the five-year plan, Gosplan submits initial data for planning to ministries no later than one year before the next five-year period. Within a month, each ministry submits more detailed initial data to the enterprises and plants. The initial data includes: macrolevel targets, state orders, supply limits, and long-term economic norms.

Macrolevel targets reflect the forecasted demand for products, expressed in monetary terms and include targets for the volume of products and services required, profit or income to be attained, amount of foreign currency to be accumulated, and productivity level to be reached.

State orders represent the government's assignments for the production of the goods and services needed to meet the targets. Only Gosplan can give a state order to the enterprises. The volume of state orders differs from industry to industry and is geared according to the capacity of each enterprise. On average, the order absorbs 30–60% of the capacity of enterprises and reflects the common responsibility of enterprise and government.

Supply limits are established for enterprises by Gossnab, the state committee for supply.

Long-term economic norms determine the relationship of the enterprise to the state;

local budgets; and the appropriate mix of enterprise funds. The superior ministry approves an enterprise's norms before the enterprise begins developing its own five-year plan.

The list of targets, state orders, supply limits, and long-term economic norms are endorsed by the USSR Council of Ministers. The ministers, however, have no right to add items to the list.

On the basis of the initial data agreed upon with its superior ministry, the enterprise draws up its general five-year plan as well as a detailed first-year plan. If necessary, the enterprise communicates directly with other ministries and government economic bodies, suppliers, and customers to clarify and conclude agreements. In order to calculate wages, salaries, and bonuses the enterprise may choose between two models of self-financing (*khozraschet*). (See Exhibit 6.4.)

Within the enterprise the annual plan proceeds as follows.

Usually, in September of the prior year the enterprise has received the state order from Gosplan, the supply limits from Gossnab, and the long-term norms from its ministry. With those in hand, along with agreements with its customers, the enterprise's chief engineer and chief economist draw up a draft plan for the following year. After being approved by the director general, the plan is sent down to the structural units of the enterprise—plants, shops, sections, and brigades—in the form of written orders. These orders are signed by the plant director and contain a description of the plan in terms of "what to do," and "who should do what," and deadlines for the work to be accomplished.

Then shop managers, in consultation with their subordinate sections and the brigades within those sections, study the possibility of reaching production capacity, determine the bottlenecks, and propose ways to eliminate them in a plan broken down in quarterly periods. The chief engineer analyzes all the proposals and sends them to the enterprise's technical services people—designers, technologists, chief mechanic, chief power specialist, instrumentalist, repairperson, and so forth—to determine the cost and time needed for the work to be done. The draft plan next moves on to the economic departments of the enterprise to be converted into financial estimates and monetary terms. Finally, the plan goes to the planning department where it is transformed into a final plan and a detailed production program for the following year.

Prior to final action, the plan is approved by the employees' council and the enterprise's social organizations (party, union, Komsomol, and so forth). After the plan is cleared by all line and functional managers, it is sent to the director general for approval. He submits it to the ministry for its approval. In the event of a serious disagreement between the enterprise and the ministry about final planning targets, additional negotiations are carried out. If they are unsuccessful, the matter(s) is submitted to an arbitration court for settlement.

Planning at SovElectric

SovElectric embraces a complex system of plans, including five-year, annual, quarterly, and monthly plans. Numerous indicators are given in each plan: sales and profit, productivity growth, wage and salary growth, and others. Recent economic changes have increased the importance of net income. The main planning indicator, however, is delivery schedules and volume, and this indicator specifies the material incentives related to plan achievement.

Although perestroika's changes in the law allow the enterprise to identify its customers independently and plan accordingly, independent planning is still nearly impossible in the absence of distribution channels and independent supply sources for materials, equipment, and components. Furthermore, state orders (*goszakazu*), fulfillment of which is obligatory, account for over 100% of SovElectric's capacity, and supply is still managed by state systems in a centralized manner.

Thus even after the reforms, the ministry gives plans to individual SovElectric plants (because each plant is an autonomous enterprise). Within each plant, they divide the plan into shop plans and work out an internal cost control system and a plan for the cost of sales. Most of this work is done by the Planning and Economic Services Department, which also computes prices to be suggested to the ministry through the industry's scientific production association. This organization also reviews the cost and plan proposals from SovElectric and recommends changes or approval to the ministry. So despite the new law, the ministry requires a lot of information on the internal operational activities of the enterprise; this bothers the planning department, which considers it of dubious legality.

The planning department employs 19 people in a special planning and contract bureau that works with each main customer. The state order specifies a quota that these customers may order from SovElectric, but the contract bureau works directly with the customer to get specifics about technical parameters of the product, needed delivery date, and so on. These customer orders become the input for production planning and are assumed to reflect SovElectric's production capacity. The planning and contract bureau also gets information from SovElectric's research institute about the manufacturing introduction of new product modifications. They combine this information with customer needs to plan product mix. Product mix can have a significant impact on revenue, costs, and profit

EXHIBIT 6.4   Khozraschet, Models 1 and 2

Model 1: Administrative or "profit" model

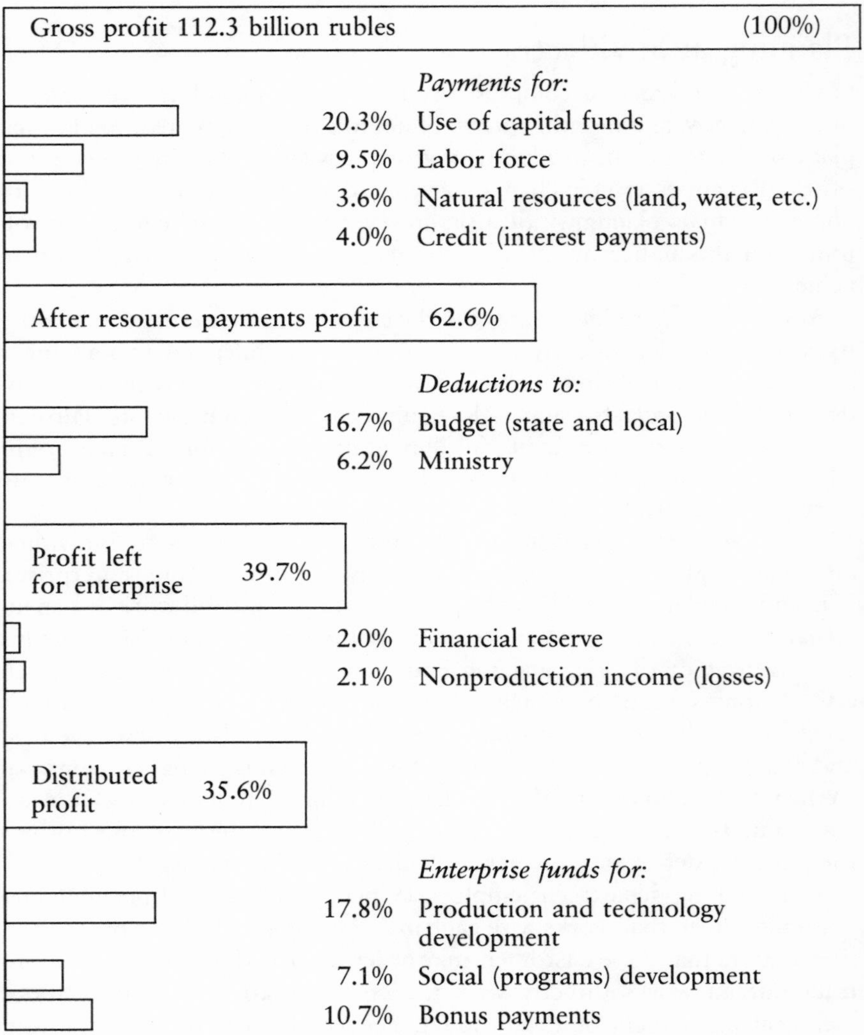

Gross profit 112.3 billion rubles	(100%)

Payments for:

20.3%   Use of capital funds

9.5%   Labor force

3.6%   Natural resources (land, water, etc.)

4.0%   Credit (interest payments)

After resource payments profit   62.6%

Deductions to:

16.7%   Budget (state and local)

6.2%   Ministry

Profit left for enterprise   39.7%

2.0%   Financial reserve

2.1%   Nonproduction income (losses)

Distributed profit   35.6%

Enterprise funds for:

17.8%   Production and technology development

7.1%   Social (programs) development

10.7%   Bonus payments

Note: Data reflect factual distribution of profit in the year of 1987 for all USSR enterprises.

Model 2: Revenue model

Distributed income 200.3 billion rubles (100%)

Payments for:

11.4% Use of capital funds

5.3% Labor forces

2.0% Natural resources (land, water, etc.)

2.3% Credit (interest payments)

After resource payments income   79%

Deductions to:

9.3% Budget

3.5% Ministry

Khozraschetnyi income   66.2%

1.1% Financial reserve

1.1% Nonproduction income (losses)

Khozraschetnyi income for distribution   64%

Enterprise funds for:

10.0% Production and technology development

4.0% Social (programs) development

50.0% Consolidated fund for wage, salaries, and bonuses.

Note: 1) Data reflect hypothetical distribution of income in the year of 1987 for all Soviet enterprises.

2) In 1989, about 2% of all Soviet industrial enterprises used this model.

margins. The planning department also submits volume information to the wage-budgeting office and the wage and salary department so that the number of necessary workers can be calculated, and to the chief technologist so the necessary equipment purchases can be planned.

KHOZRASCHET AT PLANT V: CHOOSING MODEL 2

Plant V is SovElectric's primary plant. Its two other plants report to this plant (though in some instances the subordinate plants can communicate directly with ministry officials). Plant V has had a good track record, particularly since Igor Belig, formerly manager of Plant W, became its manager. Plant V had been an early adopter of motor improvements and in 1984 was selected by the ministry to be part of an early perestroika experiment. The central party and branch ministries had initiated an experiment in broadening the responsibilities and rights of enterprises. The participating enterprises were placed on partial self-financing, given fewer centrally set targets, and allowed greater local control over R&D, capital investment, and wage and bonus allocations. Because Plant V began working under the new rules in January 1984, it is more advanced than many other Soviet firms. Its tasks in undertaking that experiment were two: first, it was to meet strict delivery schedules; second, it was to create more incentives for each production collective to increase production volume. The plant met its plan targets consistently and was generally within its cost budget, although it occasionally failed to meet delivery schedules.

In mid-1987, Plant V was instructed by the ministry to decide which *khozraschet* model it would formally choose. Model 1 was closest to the traditional way of accounting and planning. It offered less risk but little upside potential. Model 2 was the "face of the future," offering a new, more complex method of accounting. Model 2 involved the risk that the plant might not meet its wage and salary obligations and would have to borrow from the bank to cover its costs: the ministry would not fund shortfalls. However, the firm got to apply any savings directly to its material incentive fund or its social development fund (similar to a fringe benefit fund). Thus there was a meaningful upside possibility for the workers and managers to increase their income.

Initially, the plant manager had proposed to follow the more traditional model. However, the branch ministry had been given a target by the government that 52 of the 482 plants in its jurisdiction move to the second model, and the ministry considered this top-performing plant a prime candidate for the newer, riskier model. When the ministry learned of Plant V's initial choice, it urged the plant to reconsider model 2. Because Plant V had been performing well, the ministry considered it likely that the plant could handle the transition to the new model. Participation in the recent experiment had given Plant V some experience in meeting delivery targets, a responsibility strongly emphasized in model 2.

The main criterion for the plant manager was whether the plant could meet its wage obligations. If the plant failed to meet wage payments, it would lose good workers quickly, and this could create a crisis. The amount of money allocated for wages was connected to several indicators, some of which might be more or less under the manager's control. Under model 1, the wage fund was based primarily on the wage fund of the previous year. Under model 2, wages were a residual and could vary. The plant manager wanted to be sure that the chosen indicators would enable the plant to meet its salary obligations to the workers.

Under model 1, the amount of wages given to the enterprise depended on the standard net value of the product. In Soviet terms, standard net value means shipped product and final goods inventory, not what was actually sold. The enterprise might, therefore, affect its wage fund by increasing its finished goods inventories.

The plant could also increase its profit by reducing expenditures. Under the model 1, however, increasing profit would not have much effect on the income of the plant's employees. While 15% of profits were allocated to the material incentive fund, this fund was generally small relative to the total allocation for wages and workers' bonuses. Moreover, the fund was distributed mainly to management and to white-collar workers so that only managers' salaries were affected by profit performance. Workers' wages and bonuses were tied instead directly to production volume.

The primary consideration of plant personnel and management was how wages, salaries, and material incentives would fare under model 1 versus model 2. In June 1987, SovElectric's chief accountant's office began making calculations to compare performance under each model. The early analysis suggested model 2 might be favorable, and even while the department was involved in its calculations, the chief economist strongly suggested looking at the second model. In the meantime, a discussion at a combined party/managerial meeting suggested that there was strong support for moving to model 2.

The chief accountant said, "Based on our calculations, we would be able to meet our salary obligations and possibly achieve quite a big improvement. However, we saw that this would be quite a bit more work for the accounting department, and we did not know how to handle this." The need for more calculations came from two sources. First, since cost performance had a significant impact on profits (and thereby bonus funds) the plant would need to calculate costs more frequently—probably monthly. In the traditional model, if the actual labor cost for a product changed, or if a supplier's price increased, this was not factored into costs immediately, but only over the long term.

Second, an important thrust of the newer model was that it pushed the efficiency incentives lower in the organization. Cost accounting was to be broken out by shops so that each shop could become, in effect, its own "responsibility center." The amount of cost tracking the accounting department would need to do would increase dramatically. Rather than rely on the global, plantwide cost figures used in the old model, the accounting group would need to develop and track figures for "local" costs. Thus every shop would have its own internal "customers" and "suppliers."

Further, there were about 20 ways to calculate costs under model 2, and the ministry wanted more reports, more frequently and quickly under this model. This meant that not only would the content of costing reports become more complex, but the scheduling would be tighter. There was no way to do this with current resources.

For the next few weeks, the chief economist met with specialists to determine the possible workings of the second model; finally, the plant manager (Director General Belig) held an open meeting with all his deputies, all the shop managers, all the staff department chiefs, and the chief accountant. At this meeting, the staff questioned the chief accountant. Because the second model was more flexible and offered the possibility of greater income, there were no serious general objections. However, there was a 45-minute discussion on how the new costing system might work and the need for a computer system to support it. Early estimates suggested that the hardware costs would run to about 2 million rubles and the programming costs might be 300,000–400,000 rubles. There was some money in a general R&D budget that would help the initial funding of this effort, so Belig authorized work on a proposed computer system.

In the meantime, negotiations with the ministry had proceeded. When it first asked Plant V to choose the second model, the plant had declined because payments to the ministry were too high. The ministry wanted the plant to pay 24% of its net income (*virotchki*) to the ministry. The plant suggested it pay the ministry 12%. At the end of the negotiation, the payment to the ministry was set at 18.7%.

As a further incentive, the ministry agreed to soften its target for cost reduction. Plant V's cost per ruble of sales was 69 kopeks at the time, and the ministry charged the plant with lowering the figure to 62 kopeks. When SovElectric's deputy director general in charge of economics declared that target unrealistic and unattainable, the ministry settled on a reduction to 67 kopeks per ruble. Furthermore, because higher costs mean less profits, payments to the ministry out of enterprise profit would be reduced annually by 2 million rubles, for a three-year period.

With the ministry's concession in hand and calculations favoring model 2, management brought the proposal to the workers' collective in January 1988. In preparation, a series of information meetings had been held by the training department, the trade union, the Komsomol, and the party: most workers were familiar with the options. After a short introduction, Director General Belig, along with the chief economist, answered specific questions put by the workers. Most questions revolved around how the second model would affect individual wages. Calculations suggested that if current performance continued, workers would receive the same wage and bonus; if performance improved, they could receive an increase. The decision to try model 2 was approved by the workers' collective at that meeting.

By Fall 1988, the option appeared to be working well. Because work performance had improved, the plant was 1.5 million above its income targets for the first seven months of the year. Product was being shipped on time and up to plan specifications. A 2% growth of average total wage and bonus income was spread more or less equally among the different shops.

Most seemed happy with the plan. Said the party secretary, "We supported it because it was the better choice, not because it was what the director general wanted." The chief accountant pointed out that *khozraschet* improved the status of accountants in the plant, a trend that was reinforced by a state order increasing accountants' salaries by 40–50%.

PLANNING AT PLANT W: CHOOSING MODEL 1

SovElectric's Plant W had experienced far more operating problems than had Plant V. A 1986 ministry decision gave Plant W orders to manufacture a new motor in quantities which put the plant at 130% capacity. Moreover, the plant's substandard tooling and equipment had great difficulty producing the new motor. By the first half of 1987, it became clear that the plan would not be fulfilled. At the end of 1987, Plant W had fulfilled only 85% of its planned volume; the unfilled orders of the new product had to be pushed into 1988 plans. The state quality inspection unit, Gospriomka, had shut down production several times during the year for quality problems and Plant W paid 1.2 million rubles in penalties for late shipments. By August of 1988, production volume was still running 17% below plan and the plant had already paid 1 million rubles in penalties.

In early 1987, initial meetings of the plant manager, chief accountant, and chief economist began the calculations for model 1 versus model 2. They knew the ministry had provided the plant 330,000 rubles toward wage payments in 1986 and calculations suggested a shortfall in the 1987 wage fund as well. Concerned that if workers saw their wages threatened they might resign, management recommended choosing model 1, with a plan to move to model 2 in 1990 or 1991.

During the second quarter of 1987, plant management held information sessions for the employees; assisted by the party, the trade union, and the Komsomol, it explained its calculations and recommendations to the workers. Also in March 1987, the ministry informed the plant of its volume production goal for 1988: 1.5 million motors, some of which were to be replacements for goods not produced the previous year. Plant W management considered this figure unrealistic and held that the 1.45 million target established in the five-year plan was more reasonable. The workers' collective council met twice in April and May 1987 to address the problem. After lengthy discussion and capacity calculations, the plant submitted a 1.45-million production plan to SovElectric headquarters.

Initially, headquarters rejected the 1.45 figure, but Plant W accountants convinced the director general that the plant could not meet the higher production figure. Later in 1987, the director general, the Plant W manager, and the chief of planning met with ministry officials to agree on a plan. The ministry held fast to the 1.5-million target, claiming that their calculations (done differently) showed that the higher volume was achievable.

The manager of planning at Plant W commented, "It was difficult all around. We understood their need for more motors, but felt unable to fulfill this target. No one knew who had the right to decide because perestroika had changed all the rules. We argued that the law allowed us to decide."

In November 1987, the workers' collective conference[1] voted for the lower figure, agreeing to make up some of the volume by increasing production of consumer goods. But the ministry persisted, and the 1988 production goal was set at 1.5 million.

Amid this turmoil the workers' collective conference had to decide which *khozraschet* model to use. During a 40-minute meeting, the plant manager and the trade union chairman spoke briefly, recommending model 1. The director of production spoke in favor of model 2, arguing that the ministry might be willing to offer concessions if the plant took that option. Few considered these expectations well grounded, however, or felt that concessions would be enough to offset the wage deficit. In an open vote, the council unanimously supported model 1.

Plant W continues to experience difficulty with quality and volume. It

1. A workers' collective conference is a formal meeting that everyone working in the enterprise may attend and vote, and every shop is represented by at least one member. The conference is larger than the council and meets less frequently.

has had numerous spot inspections by the ministry for quality and is be-hind on new product implementation. Although the plant receives suffi-cient supplies, they are rarely delivered on time, so the production flow is often disrupted and delayed.

In an effort to begin moving toward the second model, the plant let the shops manage their own social development funds. At the time of our study they were handling the responsibility well. Later in 1988, the workers' council would be given the right to decide the plant's plan by itself.

A SUMMARY OF PLANNING AT SOVELECTRIC

The two SovElectric plants were experiencing markedly different results with their annual plans. Plant V was meeting its targets, whereas Plant W continued to slip. It was in this context that each plant was asked to choose between the two *khozraschet* self-financing models. We were for-tunate to secure details on this decision process and witness enterprise economic reform being implemented in two different ways. Plant V re-sponded to the opportunity to gain more control over its affairs by choos-ing model 2. Its subsequent careful attention to costs, quality, and delivery was being rewarded accordingly. Plant W was beset with adverse circumstances. As we will see in more detail in Chapter 9, Plant W's strug-gle to introduce the new motor demanded by the ministry led to a series of shortfalls that were spilling over from one year to the next. It was out of the question for Plant W to move to the riskier model 2 form of self-financing. In mid-1988, the plant was still experiencing a cascade of prob-lems with no clear end in sight.

One new and important element is clear in both plant situations, how-ever: the increasing role of the workers' collective and its representative council under perestroika. In both plants, the council was taking a key role in the decision process and supporting management in negotiations with the ministry. This seems to be diminishing the relative power of the ministry. The democratization of enterprise management is becoming ac-tive and real.

Planning at SovTruck

Since January 1987, the SovTruck enterprise and 12 of its 15 constituent plants have worked under *khozraschet*. All 1987 shipments were 100% on schedule and the enterprise paid no late penalties to customers. Conse-quently, SovTruck earned 64 million rubles (10%) above preplanned profit for 1987. This profit enabled it to add 24 million rubles to its fund for social development and housing and allocate an additional 20 million rubles for bonuses.

The transfer to *khozraschet* meant the enterprise had to combine its plans for production material supplies, work-in-process, and shipments with the plans of its suppliers. All SovTruck plants worked according to "guiding coefficients" or normatives, which were relatively constant over the five-year planning period. "The principle of our job is now very simple and at the same time very complicated," said Director General E.A. Kratov.

> The enterprise lives and develops on its own money, so that every group, from working teams to the whole plant, can spend their money after they've gotten it from the purchasers. And every member of the collective under these conditions has to know their strategy for reducing costs, not just for today but also to see trends and prospects for the future.

From April through September, both the ministry and the enterprise participate in the development of the forthcoming year's plan. After receiving the plan figures, the enterprise reviews its capacity to meet targets. During this time, it can discuss the targets and figures with the ministry, which may press for its acceptance of tougher targets. Eventually there is agreement on control figures, including items such as the number of trucks to be produced. The consensus figures are submitted to Gosplan for review and approval. Gosplan finalizes plan figures at the end of November. In December, the enterprise receives state contracts and conforms its plan to state orders and special assignments.

In the planning process, the enterprise receives indicators and targets, including normatives for output volume, product mix, profits, capital effectiveness, and wages. Wholesale prices for trucks and components are given by Goskomtsen (state committee for prices). Gosplan and the Ministry of Finance set the normal payment from the enterprise accounts to the state budget. However, payment from the enterprise to the centralized fund of the ministry must be approved by the workers' council before it can be set. Since January 1988, the SovTruck workers' council has the right to participate in planning issues and decisions. In its first joint effort, the council supported management in requesting that the ministry reduce its 1988 export plan. The enterprise argued that it would not have the capacity to produce the export model diesel truck and that gasoline trucks had little demand on the world market. The export department of the ministry checked the facts and supported SovTruck's analysis.

INTRODUCING THE DIESEL ENGINE

Because of technological changes and in accordance with the current Soviet plan, gasoline-powered trucks are becoming obsolete. Still, SovTruck has put a lot of effort into improving its gasoline engine. Its engines are more reliable, lighter, and more fuel efficient than those built 20 years ago; their comparative life has increased from 170,000 to about 350,000 kilometers.

SovTruck's management has thought for a long time that it should start production of a diesel truck, which consumes 39% less fuel. However, in the last five-year plan, it was unable to get the 1.5-billion-ruble allocation necessary to reconstruct the main production complex for startup of diesel truck production. It was unable to make this decision independently, although under *khozraschet* it should have been able to do so with investment funds allocated by the ministry and Gosplan.

Finally, Gosplan allocated SovTruck some funds to build a diesel engine plant, which was estimated to cost between 3 and 5 billion rubles. The plant and the necessary scientific and technical changes involved was a major investment for SovTruck: 40 million rubles annually. But it would also significantly reduce the payments (like taxes) the plant paid to the ministry. Early production runs of the diesel engine have started, though SovTruck continues to produce its gasoline engine. In 1987, more than 1,000 diesel engines were built. It planned to build 2,500 in 1988, 4,500 in 1989, and 6,000 in 1990. SovTruck has started assembling some diesel trucks with engines produced both internally and by another manufacturer. However, the workers' council of the other engine manufacturer voted to reduce their 1990 production target, so it was unclear what SovTruck's 1990 production task would be.

Plans for SovTruck remained unsettled in another important area. Many years of overemphasis on heavy weight truck capacity (3–5 ton) had led to a shortage of smaller (.5–2.5 ton) trucks. Traditional pricing mechanisms did not stimulate the development of small trucks. Also, because truck manufacturers did little in the way of marketing or distribution, there were few meaningful ways of sensing the customers' needs. The oversupply of large trucks became evident in the early 1980s, and SovTruck had to determine (with the ministry's input) whether it would produce smaller trucks.

Although economic reform should allow SovTruck to decide to produce smaller trucks, the ministry believed that SovTruck would not like to invest in this type of new product. The ministry expected the production level of existing trucks to stabilize and believed SovTruck could use its resources more effectively to improve quality. This is because SovTruck, as one of the two major producers in the USSR, can monopolistically dictate what trucks it will produce. Under perestroika it is anticipated that eventually the market will dictate what this enterprise should produce; but in 1988, the Soviet market was not yet ready. The ministry claimed that under perestroika it was no longer able to dictate what SovTruck should produce and had no way of preventing it from producing new trucks. Other observers argued that the power for such production changes still rested with central authorities. The ministry still has most of the administrative and economic force to decide on such scientific and technological questions.

PLANNING AT PLANT X

The planning process at Plant X, the engine plant, begins with the targets, indicators, and schedules set by the enterprise; these include ruble and normative standards as well as volume and product mix targets. Assisted by the production planning department, the economic planning department develops the enterprise's annual plan at headquarters. In September the plan goes to the affiliated plants and their planning departments, where it is analyzed in detail and discussed at the shop level and by the workers' collectives. If a plant's collective does not agree with the plan, it sends alternative suggestions to enterprise management. (See Exhibit 6.5 for the 1988 plan targets for the engine plant.) The profit for the engine plant has not been planned because the plant is on a cost budget. For the same reason, the funds for capital investment and social programs are centralized at the level of the enterprise. Allocations for wages and bonuses are established for the plant by the enterprise.

Following up on the implementation of plans in Plant X is a careful and elaborate process. In measuring compliance to plant and shop plans, performance is reported to enterprise headquarters every 10 days and every month. The plant managers monitor results daily, and often hourly. As we saw in Chapter 5, the manager of Plant X holds a morning and an afternoon production meeting. In both meetings he reviews the results against plan. Usually, shift managers report how much production was achieved and any special problems others need to know about. The meeting is attended by the plant manager and his deputies, shop and functional area managers, and representatives of social organizations. The meeting is held in the plant manager's office at a special rectangular table, with the plant manager seated at the head. In general, the more important employees sit closer to the plant manager. On his right are his deputies and on his left are the shop heads. Representatives from the social organizations and workers' collective are seated on the left, along the wall. Typically, the tone of the meetings is "strictly business," with the plant manager calling on participants to report on the current production situation. When something goes wrong, the plant manager is likely to be quite severe (by US standards) in reprimanding the responsible parties in front of the whole group. The results of both meetings are recorded in a special protocol, with assignments and schedules included. Either the plant manager or his secretary monitors the protocol.

EXHIBIT 6.5 Planning Targets for SovTruck Plant X

The plan of the SovTruck engine plant for the year 1988 includes the following targets:
1. Output target for 1988: R247 million.
2. Productivity growth rate for direct labor.
3. Increase in wage growth as a percentage of production volume growth (coefficient 0.49).
4. Direct labor cost for new production.
5. Normatives/standards for indirect (management, engineering and technical) labor costs (about 7.5% of total labor costs).
6. Average wage growth as a percentage of productivity growth (55%).
7. Marginal cost per unit: 95 kopeks of cost per ruble of sales.
8. The value of consumer product output as a percentage of total output.
9. The total wage payments for indirect labor.
10. The normative/standard payment for capital and supplies.
11. Total value-added of 15 million rubles.
12. Increase of value-added growth over the previous period.
13. The number of workers—2,291.
14. Total labor cost (w/o bonuses)—5,815,000 rubles, of which 5,381,000 is for workers (direct labor).
15. Average monthly wage per employee—204 rubles a month; average wage for production workers—205.
16. Fund for material incentives (bonuses)—505,000 rubles including 349,000 rubles for production workers.
17. Average monthly income per worker under material incentives (with bonus)—225 rubles for all employees, 218 rubles for manufacturing workers.
18. Total expenditures for
    Production funds—37 million rubles
    Fixed capital—31 million rubles
    Variable investment funds—6 million rubles
19. Payments for use of capital, materials, supplies.
20. Total production cost—232 million rubles.

Plan targets may be monitored and pushed in other ways. Phone systems and a computerized production control system link the major plants in the Moscow complex with headquarters. Within the plant, the plant manager has phone connections to all units, including social organizations. There are few phones on the plant floor, however, and daily production flow is monitored via meetings and "walking around." Plant managers regularly visit the shop floor at least once a shift to acquaint themselves with the production situation (see Exhibit 5.12). Managers are also expected to have formal "open door" hours, during which anyone (this includes external customers, employees' spouses, and others) may see them on any issue (this includes social and living conditions, kindergarten, housing, working conditions, and so forth). Though anyone can go to the most senior levels of management with an issue, typically they try to solve it at the lower levels first. Informally, the plant manager always has an open door policy, especially if the caller has a question related to production. In extreme and unusual cases, a subordinate may call a manager at home to help with a pressing production problem—for example, when the assembly line stops.

EXHIBIT 6.6   Monthly Budget—SovTruck Plant X

	Rubles	Percentage
Materials (gas, oil, paint)	1,100	00.47
Scrap (metallic)	1,000	00.43
Natural gas (for testing)	500	00.22
Energy (for testing, technological)	400	00.17
Wages for direct labor	3,100	01.34
Benefits/vacation pay	235	00.10
Social security payments	465	00.20
Depreciation (for specialized equipment)	120	00.05
Operation, utilization, and maintenance of equipment	10,225	04.40
Shop overhead	3,000	01.29
Losses from defective products	700	00.30
Plant overhead	3,800	01.64
Payments to SovTruck computer center	130	00.06
External components	33,900	14.60
Subtotal	56,675	24.84
Transferred semifinished	174,500	75.16
Total	232,175	100.00

In special cases, the plant manager may go directly to the shop floor to make a general appeal to the collective in order to convince workers to fulfill complicated or large-scale work that requires above-normal effort. For example, the director general of SovTruck, in order to prevent a delay in fulfilling a state order, asked Plant X's manager to go to the shop floor and request that workers promise delivery of the required number of engines to the main assembly line. In general, such things are done by the manager only in exceptional cases; otherwise the method will lose its effectiveness.

Social organizations may also help fulfill production plans. For example, in Plant X, the Komsomol helped the administration recruit workers for Saturdays and for the agricultural harvest.

In July 1988, actual spending at Plant X was slightly less than plan because of the savings it had realized primarily on materials and scrap. (See Exhibit 6.6 for a typical monthly budget.) One clever manager had managed to sell excess scrap to outsiders, and this income was added to the budget. On the minus side, new technology and a substantial number of unskilled assembly-line workers led to increased product defects, and costs for rework were well in excess of plan.

THE PROBLEM OF THE WAGE AND SALARY FUND

The planning department at Plant X is headed by V. I. Polova. Nine people report to her, including two economists for overall plant planning and four economists for shop-level planning. One economist is a bookkeeper and another keeps records of the indicators and daily accounts. Polova is responsible for communications within the plant and between headquarters and the plant. She reports management team decisions to the shops and plant performance to the plant manager and the chief economist. The economic planning department is responsible for

- Technical economical planning of all orders for the plant, for the shops (400–900 people), the sections (150–500 people), and the teams (5–60 employees).
- Statistical account reports and final information about work of all departments of the plant.
- Organization of wages.
- Results of competition within the plant (i.e., which shop has performed best).
- Economic effectiveness (growth/improvement) analysis of every technological undertaking of the enterprise.
- Pricing issues.
- Analysis of all plant and STU economic activities.

By November 1987, the plan for 1988 was already developed. Polova recalls,

We had set up the standards or normatives for the wage fund increase to equal .35 for each percentage increase in production. However, during 1988, it became clear that the wage fund's obligations could not be covered if the fund was calculated according to a standard set up in 1987 because production volume in 1988 was lower than planned. Actually, though the plant manager and his staff had known that the method of calculating wages was inaccurate, in the current situation they did not press for a new normative because they had presumed that part of the engine-block production would be transferred to another factory in the enterprise. They had hoped that with the transfer of production, the actual wage expenses would be reduced and that this would allow the engine plant to get out of its underfunded situation.

In January 1988, the engine plant planning department discovered that the actual wage fund spending exceeded the planned budget. However, since the engine plant had performed poorly on its plan indicators, including the indicators dealing with labor productivity and costs, engine plant management decided not to ask enterprise management to revise the volume of the wage fund. Instead, they waited to see their performance in February, and to try to correct the production problems. As the production performance improved during February and March, the planning department drafted a letter for enterprise management asking them to consider the possibility of increasing the wage fund, taking into account the final results of the first quarter of the year.

Because the plant manager was ill during March, the letter was delayed. When he did see it, he sent the letter to the enterprise where it was reviewed for a long time. Because the plant manager [only acting plant manager] did not fully understand the issue, he then asked me [Polova] to go directly to SovTruck's chief economic planning director, Ushinksi.

Polova suggested that the overage was due not only to having to handle production tasks that she hoped would be done at another factory, but also to structural changes in product mix for the 1988 plan. Certain products have more favorable labor content, but in 1988 the plant was producing products whose standard labor was low relative to the actual labor required. The most recent calculation of labor standards had been made in 1963. Ushinski asked Polova to analyze this question carefully at the plant again. For three weeks in April the department worked almost solely on the task. It collected data and analyzed the situation from the time when the new normative for the wage fund had been introduced to prove that the real reason for additional spending was excess work and the structural shifts in the product mix.

Armed with her calculations, Polova and the newly elected plant manager, A. S. Gorian, went to Ushinski. The outcome of their meeting with Ushinski was that they "proved" their point of view and received authorization to revise the wage fund normatives. The new standards increased the plant's wage fund by 1 million rubles.

In 1988, Gorian promised to reach the production level planned for Plant X. But in Polova's opinion it would be impossible to avoid additional wage expense. In fact, they might once again need to ask the economic planning department at enterprise headquarters to increase the wage fund. They were considering alternative solutions. One legitimate option was to make up the difference from the fund of material incentives.

PLANT X RESULTS COMPARED TO PLAN

Production problems at Plant X were far from over. At 250,000 engines a year, the plant was at full capacity. Production volumes were not stable, and programs were behind schedule: Plant X met its production plan in only two out of seven months in 1988. Partly because of the tight goals, equipment was running at or over capacity. With little or no downtime, maintenance and repair workers had difficulty accessing machines. Said one, "I was scheduled to repair equipment this weekend, but they canceled my work so they could use the machines for production." He complained that he was too often called in to do emergency repairs. Once a machine broke down, it was harder to fix; preventive maintenance would have been more efficient.

Quality remained low. A lot of money went into engine and component repair, which did not affect normatives or labor standards. The wage fund was spending 10,000–13,000 rubles a month for repair, against a planned or allocated 5,000. Furthermore, half the incoming supplies needed technological rework.

Plant X also faced a labor shortage. Turnover was high, and the plant imported contract labor from Asian and other socialist countries to work on the assembly line. The temporaries had few technical skills and often performed poorly, particularly with regard to quality defects. The problem was exacerbated by the typically short contract term of these workers.

These difficulties, which had been going on for several years, created a tight financial and production situation for the plant. Further, because of the problems encountered during preproduction and production, the plant had been unable to meet its goals for the six new items in its product mix. It was punished with a bonus fund reduction, from 40% to 18%.

In August 1988, Gorian had gone to SovTruck's *khorzraschet* commission with his chief planner, chief accountant, and chief engineer to discuss the problem. His reasoning: "The manager should not only see the problem but also he should identify the reasons and causes for this problem. If it's required, he should immediately ask for help and try to convince his superiors to improve or to correct the situation." He had honestly explained the plant's problems and clarified some of the mistakes made by the previous plant manager. His truthfulness and sincerity won the commission's trust. He convinced its members—representatives from the planning and economic department at headquarters, financial administration, and other services of the enterprise, chaired by Chief Economist Ushinski—that many of the repair problems had been due to supply problems beyond the plant's control (poor quality of components/supply) and that many of the production problems reflected not only labor problems, but also overburdened and undermaintained equipment. The commission discussed Gorian's explanation for about 25 minutes. Ushinski criticized Polova for not being more proactive in bringing the problems forward sooner. The commission analyzed the data and at Ushinski's suggestion, decided to help.

Reflecting on the events, Ushinski said, "Ms. Polova, the chief accountant, was right. She is very smart and knows her numbers well. This is the way to succeed in your requests. Sometimes I think she may be a little too clever." Ushinski also wondered how such a situation could arise:

> Previously, the plant was generally meeting its plan and budget. It was within the limits of wage and salary, and the costs and productivity were more or less up to the standard. In late 1987 and early 1988, scrap and rework costs had increased noticeably, but this change might have been resolved by a variety of measures. All together, these indicators should have provided a signal. Such situations usually develop step by step as a result of certain trends and also some subjective factors. And economic services should pick up that signal and they should analyze and take some action. It may have been that the economic analysis was not deep enough and they missed these signals. It may also have been that they knew of emergent dangers but were reluctant to tell upper management. Numerous areas were aware of the problem [accounting, technical services, chief engineer's staff] yet kept the information to themselves. If the problems had become public earlier, they would have gotten help earlier. I think there was a block on the information flow in this case.

Although Gorian put together a plan for solving the problems, disagreement persisted as to the needed reinvestment. Because SovTruck is moving to diesel engines, Plant X is expected to be obsolete by 1998. While all agree that capital investments should be cut back, thereby "shrinking" the plant, opinions differ on how much money will ensure quality and the timely achievement of production goals. Given the targets for engine production for 1989 to 1992, plant personnel felt 3 million rubles annually would be necessary to maintain effective production. Corporate management expected to give the plant about 1 million rubles.

Conclusions

The annual plan is a significant and powerful document for large enterprises in both the United States and the USSR. It is the most formalized activity of all the decision processes we studied, and its timing is the least flexible. Planning in the USSR is linked to a national five-year plan, whereas US firms adopt annual plans in conjunction with shorter-term (two–three-year) corporate strategic plans.

THE PLANNING CONTEXT: SIMILARITIES AND DIFFERENCES

Plans in both countries were "blueprints" that the enterprises tried to follow with varying degrees of success. Just as the Soviet Union has never perfectly realized a five-year plan, neither do corporate strategies of US companies always work out to the letter. Thus there is a degree of uncertainty or error in both planning systems. The sources of errors and the methods for dealing with them vary considerably between the two countries, however.

The primary source of uncertainty in the United States is the difficulty of predicting customer demand and market competition. US companies experience far more uncertainty in plan numbers because of market fluctuations. Plans may change quickly when customer orders increase or decrease, and a company's responsiveness to changing demand is critical to its survival. The companies we studied, as well as many others in America, deal with this uncertainty or likely error by increasing their flexibility in two ways. First, they shorten planning horizons (a two-year strategic plan instead of a five-year strategic plan, a rolling forecast and plan target adjusted every month instead of a fixed annual target). Second, they reduce lead times, or the time it takes to make and deliver a product once an order has been received. US companies also try to reduce uncertainty by getting "closer to the customer": inviting customers to product planning meetings, offering plant tours, using computer tie-ins such as order sequenced shipping, and offering special services such as quality inspected shipments. In general, US companies look for ways in which to tie themselves to their customers and secure advance information about sales orders.

Because of competition and declining demand, most of the US plants we studied were operating beneath their potential production capacity. This meant that their major task was to keep expenses down and cover overhead. Because they were operating under capacity, the plants were often looking for more volume. Plant managers pushed marketing for more orders and asked headquarters for more product allocations (e.g., if there were several plants within the enterprise producing crankshafts, the plants might fight among themselves for a given order). They tried to make anything they could sell. Plant managers spent little time tracking production and far more time managing costs and dealing with customer problems. Supplier relations posed little problem. The US plants had few problems finding necessary supplies or influencing suppliers to meet quality and delivery targets.

In the USSR, because planning encompasses the whole economy or system, error tends to accumulate at the national level and show up as dislocations or disproportions in the national economy. Even when many individual plants are able to meet short- and long-range targets, planning errors may appear in the form of national shortages or overproduction. Given the country's history of shortages, market fluctuations are not a problem for Soviet plants. Plants traditionally have been certain of the production levels they must meet and have had no further concern once the product was placed in final goods inventory; however, this is changing.

For the Soviet manager, the great uncertainties arise on the supply side and are caused by pervasive shortages of supplies and components. Short-term shortages can cause failure to meet plan targets. However, because many firms are in a monopoly position, going "offtrack" in this way does not threaten their market, as it would that of a US firm.

USSR plants do have less flexibility when faced with planning error. If production problems or supply delays prevent a plant from reaching its targets, it is unlikely that the system will provide an alternative way to make up the difference. For example, when SovTruck sought a new rubber part and the rubber suppliers had all their output spoken for, the plant found it could not "step outside" the bureaucracy and find a supplier with excess capacity. Soviet plant managers are also more constrained to internal solutions, such as building a backup assembly line or doing work by hand when machines aren't functioning. In contrast, when one AmTruck plant fell behind in production and was unlikely to meet its delivery date, it shipped its engines airfreight to the customer. When AmElectric's primary business, building plants for the utility industry, declined, it closed two production plants and shifted into service and repair work. Such adaptations, or variance from plan, historically have been difficult in the USSR.

Partly because of the problems with supply, Soviet firms have brought more and more activities in-house with the hope of controlling or managing their critical dependencies. Thus the Soviet firms and plants we studied had a broader range of in-house activities (casting, plastic injection processes, finish work, and so forth) than did the typical US plant we studied. This complicates the planning process even further, since more diverse and differentiated activities must be integrated and combined in one enterprise's plan.

Other contextual differences also limit the Soviet enterprise's flexibility. With an average equipment age of 28 years, an ever-increasing volume target, difficulty obtaining new and improved equipment, and unreliable supplies and labor, the Soviet plant is stretched—indeed, very often *over*stretched—and has little slack for improving the situation. In many plants, scheduled repair and maintenance work is postponed because the plant must run nights and weekends to meet plan targets. Volume tends to be an all-important target, and even the most senior managers track it closely.

Finally, the reader may have noticed the reference to structural task units (STUs) as key planning units. It can be seen that the STUs work to foster communication within themselves, but, as the Polova case illustrated, intra-STU loyalty inhibits communication and integration among the numerous units within the enterprise.

THE PLANNING PROCESS: SIMILARITIES AND DIFFERENCES

One clear difference between the planning processes in the two countries is their starting points. In the United States, the starting point clearly was the market. Forecasts of sales, as developed from the ranks of sales and marketing personnel, initiated the process at both AmElectric and AmTruck. The forecasts moved up to corporate or division headquarters and back down to the plants in the form of planning guidelines. The plants then prepared budgets, which in turn moved up the line for negotiation and approval, down for implementation, and up again for reporting results.

The planning cycle in the USSR started with the national goals (although research institutes might inform the central authorities about customer needs). Drawing on the resulting five-year plan and the overall annual plan, the ministries in turn developed a master plan for each industrial sector. It was this step that started the planning cycle from the top down. The plan was studied at the enterprise level, detailed at the plant level, and, with the agreement of the collective, sent back to the enterprise and, as needed, to the ministry for adjustments and approvals. The fundamental decision-making phases of the Soviet planning system were clearly revealed. The six-step pattern outlined in Chapter 4 was supplemented with the new practice of negotiating the final agreement with the ministry. The contrasting patterns and practices highlight important differences in the way Soviet and US managers think about planning and their responsibility for the process.

US and USSR plants are managed with different portfolios of goals. In the USSR, volume receives an inordinate weighting in the goal portfolio (because wages and other key items are driven by this target). Also important is that failure to meet the plan in the USSR was long considered ground for demotion, firing, or even imprisonment. Thus meeting annual plan numbers has a significant personal implication for plant managers. Lower-level managers also feel great pressure to meet the plan numbers. They are likely to accept plan targets even if they personally feel the targets are unreasonable. They may even try to achieve plan targets ahead of schedule, because they can use the extra days to produce above-plan volume that may garner them and their staff extra bonuses. Of course, exceeding the plan by too great a margin can be dangerous; overachievement may lead to substantially increased targets for the following month or year.

When it appears that targets will be hard to reach, Soviet managers may ensure meeting targets by altering product mix. When failure to meet targets appears imminent, managers may try to get targets altered by proving that some required inputs (supply, equipment) were unavailable; then they will not be held responsible for the lower output. Although it is a frowned-on practice, managers will also attempt to get goals adjusted downward if it appears mid-month that the shop or plant cannot meet its original targets. What makes this so important is that if targets are not met, workers will not receive their bonuses; then good workers will leave, creating an even more difficult production management situation. It should be noted that Soviet workers are permitted to quit their jobs. Currently, new jobs in their home areas are usually readily available. As enterprises become more cost conscious under perestroika's self-financing principle, the availability of jobs may diminish.

In some cases, Soviet plant-level managers may let a bad situation get out of hand in order to force upper-level authorities to take action. For example, if certain equipment is failing, rather than constantly take the problem to an upper manager who is likely to deny requests for new equipment or equipment rebuilding, a plant manager may wait for the equipment to break down completely so that it has to be replaced.

In the United States, plant-level goals (cost, quality, delivery) tend to be more equally weighted, though cost often has a primary influence. The plan's purpose is not only to set goals, but also to provide an educational tool that tells lower-level management about the strategic direction and important values of the whole enterprise. Often different goals are assigned to different departments. For example, the manager of quality figures out how to meet quality goals, the controller may champion cost goals, engineers work on new product goals, and so forth.

US plans are adjusted more frequently as customer information changes. Several of the plants we studied found their planned production volume had to be lowered as predicted orders failed to materialize, and the one plant that received more orders than were forecast was having difficulty keeping up with the increased volume.

US managers receive fewer and less severe sanctions for failing to meet plan goals than Soviet managers do. Bonuses are usually given at year's end—perhaps even when plans were missed, if there is evidence of good performance under adverse circumstances. US plant-level managers also seem more willing to alert upper management to likely future problems and unrealistic expectations.

Top-down, numbers-based goals have unintended effects in both countries. The pressure to "make the numbers" (output in the USSR and budgets in the United States) drives the behavior of plant managers. For example, in both countries we found instances of "storming," a big end-of-month or end-of-year push to ship or make the required amount of product. In SovElectric, forcing Plant W to meet higher targets than it was prepared for was hurting its quality, deliveries, and the ability to implement new products. At AmElectric, limitations on investment funds created a rule calling for no additional "bricks and mortar"—i.e., no square-foot expansion of existing plant space. Instead, one plant leased as an expense item a trailer home in which to warehouse huge machine tools. Nicknamed "the dog house," it was pulled into the plant on an as-needed basis.

In both countries, managers and headquarters play "the budget game": headquarters tries to toughen goals, and lower-level managers try to ensure goals that are more easily achievable. This may take the form of hoarding supplies (the USSR), biasing market forecasts (United States), overspending or underspending a given account in order to have more leeway in achieving budgets. Only AmTruck had found a way around this. It encourages plants to undertake ambitious plans and then to adjust them quickly as circumstances dictate. It has created a high level of trust from top to bottom.

While plans play an important role for enterprises in both systems, their aims, significance, and functions differ. In the United States, plans serve as a basic management tool to help harmonize production with market demand. In the USSR, they serve much more as compromises between the enterprise and the insatiable appetite of superior authorities for production, and as monitoring instruments for the authorities. This tends to keep Soviet plans detailed and rigid.

CONVERGING PRACTICE: MOVING RESPONSIBILITY DOWNWARD

Both systems display trends toward increasing the planning responsibility of lower levels. AmTruck had moved away from a planning-by-the-numbers approach to one of mutual information and negotiation between upper and lower levels. AmElectric still has a very top-down, manage-by-the-numbers approach emanating from corporate headquarters, but is considering changing it; all AmElectric employees are informed of the strategic direction.

Recent changes in the USSR have given the workers' collective council authority to approve or reject the plan proposed by the ministry or plant management. One of the plants studied actually did modify the 1988 plan handed down by the ministry. It is likely that the Soviet Union will see more lower-level decision making as perestroika advances. This lower-level input, however, is still more sequential than integrative. While AmTruck's planning process creates a dialogue among all levels of the plants and headquarters, the Soviet system is still more a sequence of decisions and approvals at the various levels than the working out of some mutually designed plan.

Other recent changes in the Soviet Union have increased enterprises' and plants' flexibility. In some cases, buyers can refuse to buy products allocated to them. In another example, SovTruck is "taking over" an unprofitable agricultural combine factory and will retool the plant for refrigerator production. In the electric motor industry, one factory will switch from valve drive to DC motors. Recent reports also suggest that some plants have been allowed to fail, or to go bankrupt.

Chapter 7

Hiring and Firing Managers

Hiring and Firing Managers in the United States

[*Editors' note:* This section presents a review of US ideas about the hiring and firing of managers and human resource management issues in general. The material has been prepared primarily for Soviet readers and much of it will be familiar to the American reader. It is followed by several examples of hiring/firing practices at AmElectric and AmTruck.]

In most US firms, the hiring process begins with a written job proposal that explains the departmental need and describes the rights and responsibilities of the position. If the proposed job is not related to the existing annual plan, it must be justified as an exception. Then the position must be classified by the personnel (or human resource) department to fit into the existing wage and salary system. If the proposal is approved by the designated higher authority, the hiring search commences. The personnel department usually assists the responsible manager by preparing a short list of candidates who seem to be qualified for the position. A number of firms require that at least some candidates be from other parts of the organization or even from outside the company. Personnel locates outside applicants through advertising, personal referrals, or separate professional recruiting firms. Candidates who make the short list are usually screened through a series of interviews conducted by prospective superiors (two or even three levels up), peers, and occasionally subordinates. Interviewers may meet to share impressions and offer recommendations, but usually the final selection is made by the prospective line boss.

The firing of managers (or of rank-and-file workers) in US firms is almost always preceded by a lengthy series of performance reviews and remedial attempts, except in extreme cases that involve theft, fraud, violence, or flagrant violation of orders. Problems associated with inadequate job performance customarily are addressed first in the periodic performance review that every employee receives on an annual or semiannual basis. The performance review, which is discussed by employee and supervisor and signed by both parties, creates a written record of work deficiencies and planned remedial steps. If necessary, warnings become progressively severe to the point where the review states explicitly that continued employment is conditional on improvement. Such documentation protects the firm from legal charges of discrimination that can arise subsequent to a firing. Superiors from two or three levels must make the final decision to discharge an employee. Many companies offer discharged employees, as well as employees laid off due to lack of work, an "outplacement" service designed to help them find suitable employment elsewhere. Exit interviews are often conducted to hear the employee's version of the situation. If the employee is a union member, the discharge situation will be reviewed with union officials according to the company's labor contract. In most firms, union or not, employees have the right to appeal their discharge to higher authorities if they wish, and beyond that to the courts.

Behind the hiring and firing process in most US firms lies a set of complex procedures developed to ensure a longer-term supply of competent managers and skilled hourly employees. Growing firms create annual plans for recruiting college graduates. They also develop long-range plans for management succession, scheduling managers to move through a succession of jobs to provide them with the full range of experiences they will need to qualify for higher responsibilities. Frequently these plans provide for managers to take specialized training in company programs or in management programs offered by universities. Each manager's personnel record describes his or her qualifications for promotion, and the annual review process updates the record.

Hiring and Firing Managers at AmElectric

Founded a century ago, AmElectric has evolved a series of human resource policies and practices that are traditional in the United States. In its earlier years, AmElectric established a functional structure and a market human resource system in keeping with the times. In more recent years, it changed to a multidivisional/technocratic form with labor union representation, except in its newer plants (including those reported here) where it adopted a career form of human resource system with a participative management method.

The plants we studied at AmElectric have consistently remained nonunion, although each has been the site of union-organizing attempts over the years. When Plant B first opened, the hopeful union actually set up an office down the road, but by 1987 it packed up and moved on. AmElectric's new plants endeavor to keep their operations union free by providing benefits and job conditions at least equal to those of a union environment; for example, job classifications are tightly defined, and promotions and layoffs are based on seniority if more than one party qualifies. At the time of our research, a union-organizing campaign at Plant A was under way. The causes appeared to stem from communication problems between management and workers regarding a pay-for-skills program (encouraging workers to learn additional skills by paying them for mastery), a proposed joint venture with another firm and the associated fear of losing AmElectric benefits, and a general perception that management's attitudes toward the work force had become somewhat negative.

Each plant at AmElectric has an appeal board that hears employee grievances. In addition to two representatives from management, the board includes two hourly employees whom the grievant may select from a list of volunteers. In one case, the appeal board had to decide whether to terminate an hourly employee who did not report to work. Management had merely suspended him; but when he appealed the suspension, the board fired him. Clearly, the appeal board not only had teeth, but could at times be tougher than management in interpreting rules.

HIRING A HUMAN RESOURCE MANAGER AT PLANT A

According to the plant manager, hiring a human resource manager at AmElectric Plant A was "a frustrating and painful experience" that took four months to complete. The manager initiated a formal search process and went through the proper channels at corporate in hope of getting the best-qualified candidate that AmElectric could offer. The corporate human resource department at headquarters provided files on four candidates. Three declined interviews and the fourth did not seem suitable: his estimate-of-promotability form indicated poor performance. Somehow the corporate human resource group had selected him as a candidate anyway.

Although the plant manager was frustrated, he solicited corporate's help again and received information on two more candidates. One declined to be interviewed, and the other was less suitable than two potential candidates within Plant A itself. When the plant manager asked for help yet a third time, corporate sent him personal history forms for three more candidates. Because all were unsuitable on paper, none was even called for an interview.

The manager of Plant A decided to explore the possibility of promoting from within. Both Plant A candidates reported to the director of human resources; one was manager of salaried staff and the other was manager of hourly employees. The manager of salaried staff was new to the plant and not ready for promotion. The manager of hourly employees was quite young—29—but he had established excellent rapport with managers and workers alike. Although he lacked the breadth of managerial experience and intuition to make solid judgments on sensitive personnel issues, he appeared to have great potential. The plant manager consulted his immediate subordinates to solicit their input. They recognized the risk of promoting the young manager, but they committed themselves to helping him grow into the job.

Satisfied with this commitment, the plant manager reached his decision. Before making the announcement, he met with the manager of salaried personnel, who was very supportive of the decision to promote his colleague. There would be no hard feelings.

Placing an inexperienced person in such a sensitive job was "a little scary," but the decision worked out well. Plant A's management staff provided coaching and support, and the new human resource manager learned quickly. Predictably, he made some mistakes that the plant manager was quick to correct. On one occasion the new manager announced four upcoming layoffs when, in fact, the plant manager had told him that five would be necessary. To maintain the new manager's credibility, the plant manager laid off only four workers but immediately spoke in private with him about the error.

DEMOTING A MANAGER AT PLANT A

Plant A's quality assurance (QA) manager reports directly to the director of quality assurance at divisional headquarters and has only a dotted-line (advisory) relationship with the plant manager. The particular QA manager in question had been appointed by a former QA director and a former plant manager. The new QA divisional director and the new plant manager soon realized that Plant A's QA manager was not performing adequately. An excellent engineer in his previous job as a specialist, he had no prior supervisory experience; his managerial skills were undeveloped, and he was unable to delegate effectively or build rapport with his staff. He never felt he had enough data to make a decision and "analyzed things to death." Most people considered him a very weak manager who "was in over his head."

Together the new plant manager and the new QA divisional director developed a performance improvement program featuring specific goals and guidelines for the QA manager to meet. Three months after the new plant manager took charge, he met with the QA manager for an hour and a half to discuss the latter's performance problems and to present the plan. The QA divisional director visited the plant every few weeks to coach him, and the plant manager supplemented these visits with counseling sessions. The QA divisional director presented the manager with a formal written appraisal once a month for three months. Little improvement was evident. At that point, neither boss felt they could do any more for him. "He knew he was failing but he couldn't help himself," said the plant manager.

The plant manager and the QA divisional director sought the advice of human resource managers both at the plant and at divisional headquarters; they explored various alternatives for dealing with the poor performance. Everyone agreed that the employee had valuable engineering skills and should be retained in the company. The challenge was to find a way to demote the employee from the managerial position to a professional position in engineering without destroying his self-esteem. The divisional QA director devised a plan to capitalize on the employee's technical competence by creating a new job tailor-made for his skills: specialist in statistical process control. The plant manager agreed that this was the best course of action to take.

The divisional director of quality assurance timed the announcement to coincide with a meeting at divisional headquarters of QA managers from all the plants. He said he did it this way to avoid rumors and to handle the matter in a dignified way. Immediately prior to the meeting, he met privately with the QA manager in question. He spent the first five minutes explaining to the QA manager that he no longer had that job. He then spent an hour and a half "building him up for the statistical process control job." He assured him that his technical expertise was highly valued and that he would keep the same pay level. He then escorted him to the meeting of QA managers, where he announced the transfer to the statistical process control position. He also announced who had been appointed to take over QA management at Plant A. The whole process, from the plant manager's initial meeting with the QA manager to the eventual transfer, took eight months.

At first, the reassigned employee protested the change. After a few months, however, he visited the QA divisional director and thanked him. He said he had never been happier and that it had been a wise move to transfer him to a job he was good at. In fact, he did so well in the new slot that two favorable consequences ensued: He won a corporate recognition award for exceptional performance in engineering, and the position of statistical process control was created in other plants.

This episode illustrates the thought and care that AmElectric usually takes in demoting or firing a manager. The firm has a general policy of treating such poor performance situations with care because, as the plant manager explained, "it maintains our credibility with the work force." The methods include repeated counseling sessions, a performance correction plan, and formal documentation. In this instance, the plant manager also addressed the problem by means of direct lateral contacts with the divisional QA director and the divisional human resource office, using the human resource office as an adviser but not as a place to dump the problem.

Hiring and Firing Managers at AmTruck

The plants of AmTruck operate under the following explicit human resource philosophy: The firm highly values employment security for all employees; the organization has strong expectations for high performance of employees, including individual growth, growth in job responsibilities, and self-motivation; decision making at the firm is characterized by participation and consensus; the company presents few barriers to development and growth and it focuses on helping people be successful.

The organization is characterized by a flat structure with few hierarchical levels. This enables the firm to provide employee growth opportunities by means of lateral transfers, reducing the emphasis on vertical power relationships. AmTruck also has a policy of promotion within position, whereby people learn new skills within an existing job and receive pay tied to skill, knowledge, and performance over time. This practice gives people meaningful careers without making them feel they have to get to the top of the pyramid.

In order to provide flexibility in reassigning people, the company has no written job descriptions. Jobs fall under generic classifications and only the following titles are used: plant manager, director (for staff functions such as finance), business manager, team manager, adviser/consultant (for accountants, engineers), and team member (i.e., production workers and administrative support personnel).

The firm also downplays pay as a motivator in favor of growth and satisfaction by paying all employees, including production workers, a salary rather than an hourly wage. This encourages everyone to feel they are "on the same team." AmTruck does pay production workers overtime in accordance with federal law, but no other employees receive overtime pay. Few people other than the human resource manager know other people's salaries. Managers are not even aware how much their subordinates are paid. The human resource manager noted that sometimes employees ask her how they are doing relative to their peers, but they do not ask for specifics. She will give them the ranges and tell them whether they are in the middle or near the top or bottom. She claimed that, in general, people are not particularly concerned about their pay relative to that of others.

AmTruck is very devoted to its work force. When extreme competitive pressures during the 1970s forced the company to cut staff for the very first time, it attempted to effect its cuts as fairly as possible by implementing programs such as early retirement, under which a 48-year-old employee with 30 years of service could retire with full benefits. AmTruck cut everyone's hours before it cut staff.

Job movement within the company is the joint responsibility of the individual and the company. One support staff member who changed areas recalled, "I thought it was time for a change, and I looked around to see what I was interested in. I basically created a job for myself in this area, and it has worked out great."

AmTruck has created a standard hiring process. First, the manager seeking a hire obtains the authorization to interview (either for a vacated position, or a new position) from both the human resource department and the plant manager. The position is posted and all interested employees are free to apply.

Next, a team of individuals who would work with the new hire interviews candidates. The team could include the prospective manager, the peer staff, and key subordinate staff such as engineers and maintenance workers. The team will develop a list of desired characteristics and rate each of the candidates accordingly. After the interviewing is finished, the team holds a "consensus" meeting at which all must agree on the first-choice candidate.

Other techniques may complement the interview process: sometimes, for example, a candidate is asked to work on a group task. Of course, resumes are studied and reference checks are made. In an emergency situation, some of the steps may be skipped to fill the job quickly. However, the human resource office is responsible for ensuring that all hirings follow a fair process.

Firings occur infrequently and often take the form of a mutual agreement. The displaced person may be given an excellent severance package or moved to another position. Causes for sudden firing are limited to theft, fraud, risking the safety of self or others, and drug or alcohol abuse at work.

HIRING A BUSINESS MANAGER AT PLANT C

In early 1987, a business manager's position opened at Plant C. Because such job openings are considered corporate resources, plant manager

George Karloff's first step was to notify the corporation that this position would be available. After an informal conversation, his boss verbally approved the open position, and Karloff prepared the authorization-to-interview form.

The human resource department posted the position within the corporation; after three weeks, five candidates had applied. During that time the plant put together an interviewing team made up of the plant manager, a business manager (i.e., a peer of the person to be hired), the human resource director, and four subordinates of the position (material adviser, financial adviser, a work team manager, and an engineering services manager). This represents the standard composition of interviewing teams at AmTruck.

Initially, Karloff identified five key criteria by which candidates would be judged: leadership ability, interpersonal skills, manufacturing technical skills, managerial administrative skills, and being a "concept reinforcer" (i.e., enforcer of AmTruck's values). The team suggested two more criteria: future potential and motivation or interest. The latter was added by the four business subordinates, who did not want someone to take the job primarily as a stepping stone. After much recent turnover, they wanted a manager who would provide continuity by staying in the position for several years.

Each member of the interviewing team received background information on the five candidates and was assigned a special area of responsibility to explore during the joint interview. For example, the human resource manager was to investigate a candidate's "people skills," while the business subordinates were to investigate technical skills. Four of the five candidates were internal to the plant, and one was from headquarters. After the interviews were complete, the interviewers ranked each candidate individually according to each of the criteria and gave each candidate an overall ranking.

After two weeks of interviewing, Karloff called a meeting of the entire interviewing group. Members shared their individual rankings and then created an overall evaluation chart to compare their rankings and work toward a consensus.

The team agreed quickly on three candidates to "deselect," but it soon became evident that the four business subordinates had a different first choice than did the rest of the interviewing team. The situation became sticky, and the plant manager suggested that the group take two–three days to reevaluate the candidates.

The two front runners differed dramatically. The one favored by the plant manager, business manager, and the HR director had a college education and was being groomed for growth in the hierarchy. Further, management already had made some commitments to the man, and the plant manager himself had indicated to him that he was the most likely candidate for the job.

The candidate favored by the business subordinates had only a high school education but substantial manufacturing experience. While he was not viewed as particularly high on people skills, or on upper-management potential, the four subordinates felt he had the technical skills they lacked. Given their experience with frequent turnover and managers who were relatively unskilled technically, a technically qualified candidate had substantial appeal.

During the three-day break, Karloff had several conversations with the HR manager. Mainly they discussed what role Karloff should play in the hiring decision. While the plant manager could "force" the hiring of his preferred candidate, both he and the HR manager wondered what costs this action might have. Would the subordinates from the interviewing team—and other workers—lose faith in the consensus process?

When the interviewing team reconvened, the subordinates felt even stronger about their initial choice, but indicated they were willing to go along with the three managers who favored the other candidate. They reiterated their concern for stability and emphasized the importance of technical skills. So sound was the subordinates' reasoning that the three managers on the team agreed with them, and the value of the consensus process was upheld.

An advocate of the consensus process, Karloff recalled his very first consensus hiring decision with these comments:

> At the time I was in favor of one candidate while the group was in favor of another. We had a long discussion about it, and toward the end I suppose I became quite forceful in advocating my candidate. Suddenly, a member of the interviewing team started crying. I was confused and asked her what was wrong. Hadn't she understood the consensus decision-making process? She replied, "I understand the process, but I didn't think you could be so stupid as to force your decision on us and destroy the process." That's when I realized how important the process was, and how fragile it is.

Two days after the interviewing team had reached its decision, Karloff called corporate for approval. He had to explain their choice, especially because corporate had expected the team to select the other candidate. After receiving corporate approval, the team held "deselection" interviews with the other candidates to explain to them why they had not gotten the job. The first runner-up left the plant for headquarters very disenchanted. Six months later, he left the corporation. By that time, however, the selected candidate was doing well in the job.

REPLACING A BUSINESS MANAGER AT PLANT C

Plant C had a business manager in assembly, Ted Albright, who had been there since the plant startup four years earlier. Ted was very popular among subordinates and support staff and had been identified closely with the plant startup philosophy. Ted formerly worked in human resources but had asked for a line assignment when the plant started up. After Ted assumed the line position, however, his assembly results were consistently poor. His unit was chronically behind on orders, and management came to feel that Ted's lack of technical competence might have a role in the problems. The job itself had become increasingly technical; product changes required more technical skill than Ted apparently had. In response to the situation, the plant manager observed Ted's performance carefully for two months.

Finally, the plant manager deemed Ted's performance as a line manager unacceptable and approached corporate human resources to determine what kinds of arrangements could be made to "remove" him. Corporate proposed two options: assign Ted a job in human resources within AmTruck or fire him and offer him a severance package. When the plant manager presented these options, Ted accepted the severance package, presumably because he would have lost face by accepting a transfer back to human resources. He left the plant within a week.

Commented one manager: "It was really a difficult situation, because he was so highly regarded and so closely associated with the plant startup. In some ways, his departure was viewed as symbolic, that the plant was losing its original 'people' commitment and now was emphasizing cost and traditional management approaches. We just kept focusing on the numbers and the objective facts and tried to minimize the negative attitudes."

The plant manager already had some ideas about a replacement a few weeks before Ted left. Nonetheless, the job was posted, and several people interviewed for the position. In the end, the plant manager's original choice was given the job. Said one human resource manager, "We probably shouldn't have posted the job in this case, because most people ended up feeling that we were only going through the motions. The process lost credibility."

The new hire succeeded in improving results during the first six months of his tenure. He let the team engineer run his first team meeting because he felt it was important to demonstrate respect for the team's existing skills as well as commitment to the team concept. One of his strategies was to educate the workers about performance, and to this end he hung huge posters in the team meeting room reviewing monthly performance on key indicators. He believed that by highlighting objective performance indicators, he helped the team identify goals and focus on the necessary tasks to be accomplished.

FIRING A BUSINESS MANAGER AT PLANT C

Before being promoted to business manager for the machining line, Joe White had no supervisory experience. He had worked for several years at AmTruck's Plant C as a specialist in purchasing parts for the machining line. He had a strong technical background and had apparently achieved good results in his previous job. Moreover, Joe also had good relationships with managers at headquarters and was considered very astute politically.

During Joe's first few months as business manager of the machining line, his performance on cost, quality, and delivery was good, and his technical understanding of the machining line was excellent. However, after a brief honeymoon period, it became evident that there were problems in his supervisory style. Some characterized Joe's attitude as "If you want to get along here, you have to go along with me." Some even questioned his results, feeling that he had manipulated calculations almost to the point of fraudulence—though no one could prove these suspicions. Beyond his questionable reports, his authoritarian management style conflicted directly with the team concept the plant had adopted at the time of its founding.

Soon after these concerns surfaced, one of Joe White's workers went to the human resource department claiming that she did not get a fair pay increase because she had refused his requests for a date. However, the human resource manager discovered that she had a poor performance record and that she did not deserve an increase. Moreover, there was no proof of any sexual harassment.

As time went on, many other women spoke up about harassment incidents they had heard of, but none of the targets (those women with first-hand experience) were willing to speak up, so the human resource department could not build a case. It was also difficult to differentiate the managerial style issues from the sexual harassment issues. Several times the human resource manager talked with Joe White about his style problems. They sent him to management skills training programs. The human resource manager explained, "We spent a year and a half focusing on the wrong problem."

Eventually, more stories circulated about his asking women for dates. Finally, it became clear that he was having a blatant affair with one of his workers. "It wasn't just simply a matter of a sexual relationship between two consenting adults," recalled the human resource manager, "but they would team up against the people they didn't like. Finally, the whole plant became politicized." Eventually the gossip spread beyond the firm to the community. One manager recalled, "I was stopped in the supermarket by a friend who asked: 'What's this I hear about the engine plant becoming a Peyton Place'?"

Thus, after a year and a half, Joe White's behavior had become entirely unacceptable to the plant manager, who considered it damaging to the firm and became concerned about potential lawsuits. He told corporate that he was going to fire Joe White. Corporate, however, offered to transfer him, an action that the plant's human resource manager attributed to several underlying dynamics. First, corporate values careful termination decisions and ethical due process. Second, corporate considers itself a good judge of character and would be reluctant to admit it had made a mistake. (As one manager commented, "It was hard to believe someone could have gotten so high in the hierarchy and be so bad.") Third, members of corporate may have been influenced by White's social connections with them—he had been a good friend and golf partner.

Joe White was transferred to an older, more traditional plant. His new plant manager had been told over the phone by a colleague at corporate that the employee possessed skills desperately needed at her plant. She was given no other information about the circumstances surrounding his job transfer. Within six months, similar complaints surfaced at the second plant. This time the plant manager took the allegations to the headquarters' human resource department, seeking advice about what to do. The description of the harassment was identical—word for word—to claims that had been made in the previous plant, and it seemed undeniable evidence of sexual misconduct. The plant manager fired Joe White immediately. "He was a sick man, pathological," she recalled. "He should have received counseling."

Reflecting on the incident, the human resource manager suggested that the problem could have been handled more effectively and rapidly if the firm's official procedures had been followed carefully. Because of the issue's sensitivity, management and human resources had approached the problem more tentatively than they approached other kinds of performance problems. Recalled the first plant manager, "He was getting a mixed message. We were saying, 'change your style, and don't ask women out on dates, but keep up the great production performance'—so he was also hearing, 'you're great, we need you.' It's not surprising he didn't take our warnings to heart, and got cocky. In the end, he hung himself."

A SUMMARY OF HIRING AND FIRING AT AMTRUCK AND AMELECTRIC

The AmTruck examples of hiring and firing managers have much in common with those at AmElectric. This is true even though AmTruck has some distinctive ways of managing human resources, priding itself, for example, on maintaining a flat, egalitarian structure. In terms of hiring and firing, though, both firms paid a great deal of attention to due process. Both were very deliberate in searching for remedies other than discharge. The one unique aspect of AmTruck's decision process came up in their hiring practices. AmTruck not only used a firmwide posting system but also gave a heterogeneous selection group considerable power in making the final hiring choice. The selection group contained potential peers and subordinates of the candidates as well as superiors. Furthermore, we saw higher management deferring to the preferences of these peers and subordinates. However, this semielection process was not a formal or mandated procedure. In the USSR, as we will see, management elections are now mandated as part of the selection process.

Hiring and Firing Managers in the USSR

[*Editors' note:* This section presents Soviet theory about the hiring and firing of managers and human resource issues in general as selected by our Soviet colleagues primarily for American readers. It is followed by several examples of actual hiring and firing practices at SovElectric and SovTruck.]

PERSONNEL POLICY IN THE USSR

Article 40 of the Soviet Constitution of the USSR ensures the right of citizens to employment. This means that they are guaranteed a job with pay in accordance with the quantity and quality of their performance. The pay level is guaranteed not to be below the minimum, which is established by the state. Citizens also have the right to choose a vocation, type of occupation, or job in accordance with their abilities, vocational training, and education, while taking into consideration the needs of society.

The constitution of the USSR also gives to Soviet citizens several other rights connected with their work. Such rights include: preservation of health, social security, shelter, and education. Many state bodies and social organizations are involved in implementing these rights. Regulations and procedures for hiring and firing and conflict resolution are written in labor legislation and in the extensive regulations of central state bodies—for example, the State Committee for Labor and Social Affairs. Finally, all these rights are respected by every enterprise and organization in the USSR.

There are three categories of employees in the industrial enterprise: managers, professionals, and workers. In enterprises utilizing the first model of *khozraschet* (see Exhibit 6.4) there are standards for the number of employees and administrative personnel and for salaries. Production workers are usually paid a piece rate plus bonuses according to the number of units they produce. Hourly wages and bonuses are usually paid to indirect labor supplying technical services, repairs, and toolings.

There is a job grade system—six grades within production workers' jobs (*tarifnaia sistema*); for example there are six grades of welders—and a salary range for engineers and support personnel, with the maximum and minimum stipulated (*vilka*).

There is additional pay for extra qualifications and mastery, which can reach up to 50% over the base rate. There are also regional coefficients that provide additional pay for all kinds of personnel. These extra payments are made from the salary and wage fund of the enterprise and are included in the cost of production.

Professionals and managers are paid in accordance with a salary system that breaks down specific posts into four categories. The higher the position, the higher the wage. The salary of a shop manager and a department manager will usually be 60–90% higher than the wage of a grade-six worker. The basic salary of the director general of an enterprise is somewhat higher than the maximum salary of a professional and can be even higher if the proportion of high-quality products produced by his plant is more than 25% above the average quality in his industrial sector.

Both blue- and white-collar employees get bonuses, which are oriented to short-term targets. In the past, workers tended to consider bonuses part of their regular pay; however, under self-financing (*khozraschet*) this practice has changed. For example, in the machine-building industry the piece-rate workers' bonuses cannot exceed 25% of their base rate (10% for plan fulfillment and 15% for quality). For hourly workers and foremen the limit is 40%. For line managers and professionals bonuses cannot exceed 30% of their base salary.

Enterprises provide many fringe benefits to their personnel at very low cost or without charge—health care, housing, education, recreation, and so forth. These are tools that can be used by managers to motivate workers.

In the Soviet machine-building industry approximately half of the production workers are women. There are very few women in managerial positions. Formally, pay for men and women is the same. Some jobs, however, are considered women's jobs and are relatively low paying. At the same time, women—especially those with children—receive additional benefits.

According to the law, children can be employed to a limited extent from the age of 16 on, with some restrictions. At age 18, the person becomes a regular worker. Managers usually do not employ children.

There is a personnel department at the ministry level, as well as at the enterprise level and the plant level. A system of management training exists within industries. Some progressive enterprises even support career management systems. Every enterprise has an appraisal and assessment system, and this process has been taken very seriously since perestroika. Today's trend is to demote people for poor performance.

In personnel more than in any other area, the opinion—and in some cases the approval—of the party, Komsomol, and the union are crucial. For example, party approval is mandatory for top-level management appointments even with the employees' council in place. Party approval, however, is not as important now for selecting middle managers.

Involvement in social organizations (party, Komsomol, union) provides experience in managing people since this is one of the prime functions of these organizations. Consequently, an important career path to top management is to work closely with (or even within) social organizations and gain experience as a member of the party or union committee. Some people alternate stints in production with stints in social organizations.

A critical role of the union is to formally authorize the firing of personnel at any level. The union's function is to protect the rights of employees; only in case of serious crimes do state directives automatically authorize firing.

Every Soviet working person has a work booklet (*trudovaia knizhka*), an official file listing all the full-time and part-time positions he or she has held, and the duration, place, and duties the positions entailed. Introduced in the 1930s, the official file is used to calculate pension benefits according to number of years worked. Honors and praise can be listed, but it is illegal to include mention of punishments or salary. Employees have the right to see it at any time and can petition to have errors corrected. Personnel departments of enterprises have files that can be utilized for employee selection, placement, promotion, appraisal and assessment, and development and training. In addition to political loyalty, commitment to work, education, and experience, there is an increasing emphasis on entrepreneurship and the ability to make independent decisions in the selection of employees. The average time between promotions is 5–7 years, but for young people with higher education, it can be 2–3 years. Most enterprises promote from within.

People tend to stay a long time in one enterprise. Until about 20 years ago, in fact, legislation granted people regular pay increases if they stayed in the same enterprise. This rule has been eliminated, and there is now less of a tendency to stay a long time in one enterprise, but it is still fairly common. People may remain tied to an enterprise because it is difficult to find alternative housing, or because they have transportation problems, or because they have their name on the plant's list to get a car. In addition, people may be promoted faster if they stay in the same enterprise. Nevertheless, people are changing jobs more and more as conditions slowly improve and restrictions are eliminated.

Middle- and top-management jobs require higher education. At leading enterprises such as SovTruck, people who aspire to management positions must also take two years of night classes in management at the enterprise's training institute. Most managers have technical backgrounds in fields such as engineering. Most supervisors and foremen are trained by the enterprise in special programs. In big enterprises there are programs for middle managers who also may take courses at sectoral and regional training centers. Furthermore, strong moral character is a requirement for any managerial position.

When it comes to hiring and firing managers, special attention needs to be given to the managerial evaluation system. Constant evaluation of managerial qualities and the selection of people who best meet the requirements of specific jobs make up the most important element of an effective personnel policy. The senior managers of enterprises and the party and union representatives are key figures in the selection of executive personnel, their training, and the administration of their work incentives. Especially significant is the study of how well foremen and brigade leaders perform the following operations: gearing up for production (planning the work, giving technological instructions, and so on); operational control of subordinates; reviewing and evaluating subordinates' records; planning and conducting shift meetings. In particular, the director of the enterprise must discuss with the party and union committees the effectiveness of shop managers and give a systematic and detailed analysis.

As a rule, upper management is also the subject of such an evaluation, but its evaluation is based on economic indicators of the enterprise as well as on executive discipline and personal initiative. Competition based on creating and reviewing personal improvement plans is a special way to evaluate and stimulate the creative activity of managers and specialists in many enterprises. The results of these personal plans are evaluated every quarter and on the basis of the whole year's results. Managerial evaluations come in the form of informal approval or criticism in meetings, bonuses, fines, and sometimes severe disciplinary sanctions.

Personnel files play an important role in work with executives. One of the most complex problems in using the personnel file as a document, though, is overcoming the tradition of avoiding any negative comment and regarding any flaws that are noted in the personnel booklet as blocking career advancement.

The personnel file is also an important source of information during regular certifications of executive personnel. In accordance with directives from the Council of Ministers of the USSR, all engineering and technical workers undergo certification every three to five years. Likewise, foremen and heads of shops and enterprises undergo certification not less than once every two years. A committee in each enterprise does the certification according to a special schedule. The manager's immediate superior reviews each employee's file with the employee and then forwards the pertinent documents to the chairman of the certification committee. The committee, in close cooperation with the plant's social organization, interviews the managers under review, who are given the right to express disagreement with entries in their personnel file, explain the motives for their conduct, and make comments about higher-level managers. The committee then makes a decision not only on the candidate's certification, but also on raising or lowering the salary.

The training of managers is carried on at the shop level and in the plant as a whole. Top-level managers personally train people for the jobs of shop steward and section manager. Shop stewards in turn train personnel as foremen and shift heads. The majority of those in the applicant pool for managerial jobs are current workers who are considered as candidates for certain jobs on the basis of their records.

A number of factors beyond their individual control influence the effectiveness of shop managers: type of work and working conditions, contributions of higher-ups and the party organization, opinions of the collective, and the moral and psychological climate of the workplace. Two basic reasons account for shop managers being replaced: difficulties in performing the work and difficulties in relations with senior managers and the collective.

The performance of managers depends to a significant degree on the management style of those higher up in the chain of command. Negative influences—such as petty interference, voluminous directives and unrealistic deadlines, insufficient justification for and agreement on assigned tasks, difficulties in providing enough information about the work, and excessive emotional tension in communications—can suppress managers' abilities. The negative influences compound whatever difficulties managers face because of their own lack of experience or incompetence. Usually the resignation of a manager takes place on the basis of a gentleman's agreement with his superiors. Dismissal is rare and resorted to only when the violation is serious.

Perestroika has introduced an important phenomenon: the election of STU leaders. This election process brings more democracy to the workplace but does not weaken one-man leadership (*edinonachalie*); once STU leaders are elected and confirmed, they have full authority to exercise strong leadership.

Hiring and Firing Managers at SovElectric

The hiring and firing of managers at SovElectric must be considered in the context of the entire personnel situation. SovElectric operates in an area where there is a general shortage of qualified employees of all ranks and specialties; as a result, employees are encouraged to work past their normal retirement date. Turnover at SovElectric had been running about 10% and recently dropped closer to 7%. However, 70% of turnover by resignation is due to conditions beyond the control of the individual or the enterprise—military service, for example.

The personnel office at SovElectric performs two functions: supplying the enterprise with required personnel, and developing and training personnel. After preliminary discussion with a job candidate to identify interests and skills and match them with the needs of the enterprise, the personnel office refers the candidate to a manager who is seeking such an employee. The candidate then has an interview with his or her potential boss, who explains the duties, the workplace, and the working conditions. Then the manager informs the personnel office of the hiring decision.

A group consisting of the immediate supervisor, the personnel manager, and the union and party secretaries makes decisions regarding punishment. There are four types of punishment for violation of discipline and rules of internal order: a warning, a serious warning, demotion, and firing. The director general can publicly announce a violation at a plant meeting and name the person who is involved.

With regard to firing, the role of the employees' council as stipulated in the Law on the Soviet State Enterprise of 1987 is very important because it has a right to challenge the administration's decision to dismiss an employee. A special group within the employees' council takes responsibility for hiring and firing issues.

HIRING A DEPUTY DIRECTOR GENERAL FOR PERSONNEL AT PLANT V

Prior to his appointment to the position of deputy director general for personnel, Aleksandr Savelev had been director of personnel for a larger enterprise in the city. As Savelev explained later, he was told in May 1987 that Director General Belig of SovElectric would like to see him. Savelev had known the director general from their days at the local polytechnic institute because of the latter's well-known work with the Komsomol. They had not been classmates, however; Belig was three years older and had studied in a different department.

Savelev had a one-hour meeting with the director general and the party secretary. The director general asked him about his ideas concerning the personnel function and if he had reasons for being interested in the job. Savelev said he wanted greater autonomy; he had little latitude to make independent decisions in his current position. Savelev asked about the situation in the plant and about its personnel policies. The director general assured him of the opportunity for autonomy and offered him the job on the spot, with the proviso he meet with the local city party committee and officials at the ministry in Moscow. They briefly discussed salary, and the director general noted that SovElectric's initial offer would not be much of an increase (290 rubles per month versus Savelev's current 250 rubles, with a comparable bonus) but that he could expect more after the pay system was revised. Savelev asked for time to think over the offer and learn more about the enterprise. He made two more visits and was briefed by the personnel manager.

On June 12, Savelev met with the director general again and accepted the job. The enterprise party secretary then took him to a half-hour meeting with the local city party secretary.* The city party secretary asked Savelev about his professional background and his activities as a party member. Savelev had become a party member in 1973 when he took his first job after graduation and had been very active in party activities. He had been a group-level Komsomol leader and chairman of the council of mentors at the institute and had served as full-time assistant secretary of the plant Komsomol committee where he currently worked. The meeting concluded favorably.

---

*Since these events occurred, the requirement for approval by the local party committee for senior management appointments has come under review. At the time of this appointment, the party district organization still worked closely with personnel directors in deciding human resource issues.

Two days later, Savelev went to see officials in the ministry in Moscow. Without disclosing his secondary purpose, he coordinated the visit to coincide with a trip to Moscow authorized by his current employer. He presented ministry officials with the letter of offer from the director general of SovElectric, which also bore the signature of the local party secretary. The ministry's director general of personnel and the personnel manager specifically responsible for SovElectric questioned him about his professional and party background and were interested in how his current employer would react to his leaving. Savelev predicted that the reaction would be one of displeasure. The ministry officials interpreted this as a good sign.

Returning to his current enterprise, Savelev learned that its director general was seriously ill. He decided to postpone his resignation until the director general returned to work, and the director general at SovElectric agreed to wait. In August, when Savelev did break the news, his current director general reacted negatively and offered a pay increase to persuade Savelev to stay. But Savelev was not interested. He felt he had no opportunity for advancement there; the two people above him were his age and unlikely to move.

In mid-August, Savelev finally got permission to accept the new position. Later he learned that the director general of SovElectric had gone to higher authorities, who in turn put pressure on his director general to grant official permission. (Savelev was not told who these authorities were, or how the director general at his former enterprise was persuaded to change his mind. Such matters are not disclosed.) Nevertheless, he did not start his new job until November 2, agreeing to stay while both his immediate superior and he himself (at the request of his new employer) took vacations.

Savelev explained that nothing officially prevented him from leaving without the permission of his former director general. He could simply have resigned and been hired into the new position, rather than being transferred. However, Savelev wanted to take everyone's needs into consideration and make as smooth a transition as possible. (Although he did not mention it, perhaps Savelev was also concerned that simply leaving of his own accord might be recorded unfavorably in his work booklet and therefore held against him in the future.)

Savelev was pleased that his new job met his expectations. In fact, he was given more autonomy than he had expected. Within a month of his appointment he got approval from the director general for two new sets of personnel policies and procedures—one on turnover and the other on vacation. Unlike his previous employer, who had resisted many of his ideas, Savelev found that Belig was very receptive.

THE FIRING OF THE PLANT W MANAGER

Ivan Bandura had been plant manager at Plant W for ten years, and until the last few years the plant had enjoyed a good reputation. As a manufacturer of small industrial motors, the plant had been touted in the press for quality work and had successfully completed experiments in quality control. However, with the onset of several changes, conditions deteriorated. One change was the transition to the AIR series of motors; another was the delay of technical upgrades; a third was the increase in quality requirements instituted by the state quality control commission, Gospriomka; and a fourth was the economic reform of self-financing and cost accounting.

The problem became serious in 1986 when production was short by 100,000 motors, for which the plant paid customers 1,200,000 rubles in nondelivery fines. The situation continued into 1987 when they paid fines of one million rubles in the first six months. The ministry and the director general decided to dismiss Bandura, and the party committee agreed.

Meanwhile, the newly promulgated Law on the Soviet State Enterprise required that dismissal of a plant manager must be done with the approval of the employees' council. In April 1988, representatives from the ministry came to the plant to get the employees' council to approve the dismissal and consider other candidates for the position. The ministry representatives, the employees' council, the party committee, and the plant manager met. The chief of personnel administration from the ministry said they were very unhappy with Bandura's performance and proposed to dismiss him on the ground of not meeting the standards to be a plant manager. This severe judgment would ruin Bandura's career because his work booklet would contain the number of the article in the personnel statutes on which they had based his dismissal. The party secretary told ministry officials that the party would agree to dismiss Bandura but on a less severe charge, and the ministry officials agreed to the compromise. Members of the employees' council had known Bandura for ten years and did not want to be unduly harsh. Nevertheless, they too were prepared to dismiss him. Like their constituency, they were disgruntled over bonuses lost in the wake of low production. Numerous administrative and production workers had left Plant W for better opportunities elsewhere.

The party committee and the employees' council decided on the procedure to follow in announcing Bandura's dismissal. Although their plan was to have the party secretary explain the situation to everyone at an employees' conference, he gave the floor to Bandura to make the first statement. Perhaps the party secretary felt uncomfortable performing this unpleasant task and wanted to give Bandura some dignity. The party secretary may also have been following the new policy of diminished party interference under perestroika. Although Bandura was aware of the agreement that he would be dismissed on less severe grounds, he announced that the ministry had come to punish him and to dismiss him according to the more severe article. The director general believed that Bandura used this tactic to elicit the employees' sympathy. Bandura talked about his long service at the plant and claimed that the ministry had not given him help when he had asked for it. He explained that he had repeatedly asked the ministry for help with such issues as housing and supply of critical raw materials but that his calls and letters were unanswered. Finally, he had gone to the ministry in Moscow on his own to try to get action. He said that it was not fair for the ministry to blame everything on him and to dismiss him. He then made an appeal to the employees for their support in helping him get the plant to move forward.

Upon hearing Bandura's version of the story and unaware of the compromise that had been reached, the employees' council felt that the ministry was using Bandura as a scapegoat to cover its irresponsibility. Consequently, the employees' council decided to fight the unfairness of the ministry by holding an election for the plant manager's position. Council members said they had known Bandura for ten years and that they would be the judge of his abilities. The council posted notices and set up a nomination box for one month, seeking internal candidates. Bandura was the lone applicant.

The chairman of the workers' collective felt that Bandura was not strong enough to turn the plant around. He was disappointed with Bandura's plan for the coming year and for the future. For example, although Bandura knew the bottlenecks and had some ideas about how to solve them, he did not provide enough clarification in his plan. Nevertheless, the collective decided to proceed with the election; and though the director general had an outside candidate in mind, he did not say so. The director general wanted to let the workers' collective try its wings without his interference.

On May 12, the election was held with the 400 delegates representing the workers' collective, the director general of the enterprise, party and union officials, and Bandura in attendance. Bandura spoke for half an hour about his "self-critical" plan for the plant for the next five years, outlining both positive and negative aspects. A dozen others made statements and asked questions. They criticized him on a number of counts and warned him that he had to improve and get the plant running smoothly. Then they called for an open vote. Bandura was reappointed with 396 in favor, 2 opposed and 2 abstentions. The meeting concluded with a 15-minute speech by Bandura, and the workers' collective submitted written notification of its decision to the ministry for confirmation.

The chairman of the workers' collective admitted that the reelection of

Bandura was the collective's way of exercising its authority and rebuking the ministry for its perceived unfair treatment of Bandura. Without that additional provocation, the chairman was convinced that the collective would have dismissed Bandura without an election.

Five months passed, and the situation at Plant W did not improve. The director general now had the legal right to raise a question about Bandura's performance with the employees' council. Accordingly, the director general proposed dismissing Bandura and holding an election one month later, and the employees' council agreed in a vote of 26 to 2. A selection board was organized and seven candidates applied—four internal and three external. The external candidate proposed by the director general won by a majority, and one month after the new plant manager started work the plant fulfilled its plan. Bandura took a position in city government.

FAILURE TO REELECT A FOREMAN AT PLANT W

The senior foreman in the Plant W machine shop was unpopular with the workers because of his authoritarian management style. He did not listen sympathetically to their problems or address their needs effectively. For example, he refused a worker permission to get off early to meet her son after his first day of school. The shop party secretary accumulated such information and became concerned about the social climate of the shop.

In late 1987, as a part of a mandated program, the plant manager was arranging to abolish the position of senior foreman in all the shops. Before perestroika, a staff reduction like this would simply have been announced by management. But with the new economic reforms, the shop party secretary and the machine shop manager informed the deputy director of personnel that in connection with eliminating the senior foreman's position, they would like to hold an election for the two foreman positions in the machine shop. The shop party secretary felt it would be best for everyone concerned if the problem of the unpopular foreman were solved through the democratic process rather than by administrative means—that is, by the plant manager punishing or dismissing him. Therefore the manager of the machine shop, the plant manager, and the party secretary gave their approval for an election to be held in December 1987. There were four candidates for the two positions: the senior machine-shop foreman, the two incumbent foremen, and a white-collar worker from the shop's technology section, who nominated himself.

Since this election predated the formation of the workers' collective, the shop's party secretary presided over the process. Ninety-five percent of the shop workers attended, and one worker suggested that the shop manager speak. He described the vacancies and read the personnel department's statements about the candidates. Each candidate followed in turn with a five-minute speech outlining his plans for the shop. Candidates then answered questions.

After a short discussion of what voting procedure to use, the group decided on a secret ballot and appointed a five-person commission to supervise the balloting. The commission counted the ballots in front of the group, and the chairman of the commission announced the results. Of the 74 people present, only 11 voted for the unpopular senior foreman. The white-collar technologist received only 14 negative votes, and of the two incumbent foremen, the workers chose the one who was most principled and consistent. The chairman of the voting committee and the party secretary signed a special protocol, and the elected foremen were officially appointed by the plant manager two weeks later.

All four candidates have found a place in the organization. The deposed senior foreman took a job in the production control office and is no longer in a management position. The technologist who became foreman is doing well, as is the incumbent foreman who was reelected. The foreman who was not reelected took a job as a worker, but the shop party secretary reported that he was satisfied because he was making more money.

A SUMMARY OF HIRING AND FIRING AT SOVELECTRIC

The hiring and firing episodes at SovElectric display in some detail the changing nature of personnel-oriented decision making since perestroika. The episodes clarify some of the different procedures for electing and confirming STU leaders and appointing non-STU managers: The personnel assignment was a non-STU post, and no election was held; Director General Belig, who was an STU leader, simply decided with the agreement of the party secretary to offer the job to Alexandr Savelev at the end of their first interview. However, his decision required clearance by the local party and the ministry.

The other two cases did involve STU positions; hence elections were held. In the Bandura firing, the newly established employees' council directly opposed what it considered to be the recommendations of the ministry and the opinion of the director general of the enterprise. And it prevailed—even though Bandura eventually withdrew and an outside candidate proposed by management was voted in at the second election. Again we saw the plant party committee consulted at every step until it ultimately agreed that Bandura should be replaced.

In the case of the unpopular senior foreman, the shop party secretary took the initiative to recommend an election and chaired the election meeting. Because his official role was to alleviate the poor morale in the shop, he was instrumental in the process. The voters then made their decision, which was officially confirmed by higher authorities.

At SovElectric, the employees' council was moving into a central role in personnel matters. This seems to reflect a genuine attempt to use the council as the democratic mechanism it was intended to be. The director general of SovElectric was patiently contributing to the education of the employees' council in making wise choices by a trial-and-error process. The success of the employees' council might in fact have depended on the support of the administration as well as on the competence and experience of the council members.

Hiring and Firing Managers at SovTruck

ELECTING A MANAGER AT PLANT X

Plant X had experienced serious difficulties over the past several years, and repeated turnover had plagued the plant manager's position. From 1981 to 1986, I. F. Ptichkin held the position. For a few years he was a strong manager and did a good job, but then he seemed to run out of new ideas, and the plant began to decline. Headquarters reassigned him as production manager at the carburetor plant, which was consistent with the enterprise's personnel policy of rotating managers every four or five years. The move was considered a lateral transfer: a lower-status position in a larger plant.

G. F. Priakhin succeeded Ptichkin as plant manager in 1986. A. I. Ushinski, the enterprise controller, reported that SovTruck headquarters helped Priakhin a lot, trying to ensure his success. Headquarters increased the wage fund and replaced some equipment. However, Priakhin did not fare well in the job. The assistant Plant X union leader said, for example, that Priakhin had tried to solve the plant's problems by having people work overtime, but this upset the workers. In April 1988 after a year and a half, Priakhin resigned voluntarily and was transferred to the carburetor plant as chief technologist. As in the case of Ptichkin, the move was considered a lateral transfer and a fairly comfortable transition. The manager of the carburetor plant had worked in Plant X in several capacities and was probably instrumental in Priakhin's reassignment.

The vacancy left by Priakhin provided the first opportunity for the employees' council to elect a new plant manager. It proposed an internal candidate, A. S. Tumanov, who had been Priakhin's first deputy. Tumanov had joined the enterprise in 1970 as a mechanic but had spent most of his career as a union representative and a personnel administrator. Enterprise management considered Tumanov unsuitable for the position and initially expressed its reservation to the employees' council, suggesting an alternative candidate from headquarters, A. S. Gorian. The enterprise personnel director of engineering and technical staff believed from the outset that Tumanov would not be an effective plant manager. That individual had worked with Tumanov in personnel and considered him competent there because of his good people skills, his ability to help others and communicate well, and his mild disposition; but the engineering personnel manager believed Tumanov lacked the strong technical skills essential in an effective plant manager.

However, headquarters soon backed off and left the decision to the employees' council when it realized that the shop managers, party, and union wanted Tumanov. The personnel manager said that headquarters did not press its opinion on the employees' council because "we didn't want to put pressure on them." It also did not push its own candidate because "it wasn't the right time, and they probably wouldn't have elected him anyway because they preferred a nice guy who was an internal candidate." At the April balloting, three workers gave Tumanov a negative evaluation, but the others favored him and he was elected.

It was obvious from the beginning that Tumanov was in over his head, and in July—three months after taking the job—he resigned. The enterprise personnel director of engineering and technical staff said that Tumanov had probably known he was unqualified but took the job because he did not want to go against the workers' wishes. Also, his pride probably played a role in that he did not want to admit his lack of technical expertise. He even persisted in the job despite serious health problems. In his three months as plant manager he had been ill three times and needed a back operation.

Tumanov returned from sick leave in late July and tendered his resignation. The Plant X personnel manager and party secretary discussed it and agreed that there was no suitable internal successor. They informed the enterprise personnel director of engineering and technical staff, who in turn informed the deputy director general of personnel. E. A. Kratov, director general of SovTruck, learned of it from his deputy. Kratov met with Tumanov before he left, and Tumanov admitted that he had overestimated his own abilities and that he could not handle the situation. He also mentioned his health problems. Kratov said he "didn't blame him personally," but "put the blame on the workers who didn't do a proper analysis."

There were conflicting opinions about the causes of Tumanov's failure. The enterprise personnel director of engineering and technical staff said that Tumanov was not qualified and did not have enough experience managing a large-scale operation. He felt that Tumanov should have understood that such a large production operation could be improved only with a strong initiative from below—from the shop-floor level. But Tumanov did not organize such an initiative. Several units in the enterprise helped him, but he could not set the most important priorities for developing the plant.

One member of the employees' council, a 41-year-old brigade leader with 19 years' experience in the enterprise, disagreed. He said he thought that Tumanov was a good person, well qualified, with a lot of drive. Although he personally felt that Tumanov lacked technical expertise, he believed that Tumanov had the employees' support and that if Tumanov had received help to repair the old equipment, he might not have resigned.

Ushinski, the enterprise controller, felt that Tumanov did not get help because "he didn't signal to the enterprise finance group that he was having difficulties." Director General Kratov said much the same thing: "To get support you must analyze the situation and make concrete proposals. The key is for a manager to make sound proposals and then he will get support. Tumanov was only on the job three months and didn't make any proposals."

Kratov explained why he did not interfere with the employees' council's choice of Tumanov:

> We knew that in the end we would win the game. Election of managers is completely new, and often the collective doesn't understand that electing a candidate gives him full power to make decisions. If the manager wants to solve these problems, he must be demanding and persistent. And not everyone likes that. Often people in such situations overestimate a manager's potential and may elect a candidate who is softer and less demanding, not understanding that in the end the collective itself will suffer. In August we went to the collective and told them they had made a poor choice and got themselves in a bad way. After that incident, headquarters will have definite advantages in future elections throughout the enterprise, and people will put more faith in the candidates we propose. It taught them a lesson.

The member of the employees' council who had doubted Tumanov's ability before the election expressed doubts about the election process. He personally felt that plant managers should be appointed rather than elected because workers are unable to evaluate plant manager candidates. He felt elections were appropriate for the lower levels of management that workers are more competent to evaluate. He noted that the employees' council had discussed the issue but did not agree. The issue was also included in a survey conducted by the enterprise sociology department in late 1987.

On August 1, Tumanov submitted his resignation to the director general and withdrew his name for reelection. The next day, representatives of the administration, the party, the union, and the employees' council met to discuss the matter. At that meeting the enterprise personnel director of engineering and technical staff said that the group had made a mistake and that a plant manager with a strong technical background was needed. If they couldn't find a good candidate themselves, headquarters would. He then nominated A. S. Gorian, deputy chief engineer at headquarters, pointing out that Gorian had done a good job for Plant X in that capacity and emphasizing that he would be able to open doors for the plant at headquarters. Furthermore, Plant X employees had worked with Gorian and knew his reputation—for example, the fact that he had turned the truck assembly plant around.

At the same meeting one member of the plant party bureau spoke in favor of Tumanov, while the rest kept silent; only 2 of the 33 council members voted against letting Tumanov go. The group then decided to invite delegates representing all the groups in the plant to the employees' council on August 3 and to hold the election on the following day.

Gorian's nomination for manager of Plant X had been personally initiated by Kratov, the director general of the enterprise. Kratov reported that he tries to keep in mind all the high-potential managers and "had set [his] sights on Gorian," as well as on two others. Gorian had gone through the enterprise's training and development program and had been assigned to various positions. Of Kratov's other two candidates, one was needed at another plant and the other, unlike Gorian, lacked the potential to advance into top management after the assignment.

Kratov had known Gorian a long time and had observed his performance as deputy chief engineer. Although he had planned Gorian's advancement at headquarters, Kratov felt that the troubled Plant X needed Gorian more than headquarters did. (He had told Gorian that he wanted him to be plant manager when Tumanov was being considered for the job.) The party organizations at headquarters and Plant X also discussed Gorian's candidacy, and the enterprise personnel director of engineering and technical staff nominated him at the plant's council meeting on August 3. The election for Plant X manager was held on August 4, 1988; 300 people attended, including members of the employees' council. The employees' council was authorized to elect the manager, and its choice was to be confirmed by the enterprise director general. If he disagreed with the election results, the director general could cancel the election but must give reasons and call for another election.

The following account of the election proceedings appeared in the enterprise newspaper:

> The meeting was chaired by the party secretary of the plant who invited the delegates to give their opinion about the proposed candidate, Gorian. A metal repair worker named Andreenkov stood up and asked: "And this new man, will he be in the job long? Will he stay for three months and then leave? Once you start something, you need to stay and finish it. And is he coming to the plant willingly?"
>
> The room started to buzz in support of the worker's question. Then it was the candidate's turn to answer and present his action plan:
>
> "I'd like to begin with a few words about the problems in the plant. First, with respect to materials, the forging shop sends us oversize pig iron, the casting shop sends us defective castings, and other plants send us poor quality parts. Deliveries of most of our supplies are irregular. Second, the equipment is old and worn out. Most of the machines are more than 25 years old and no longer meet precision specifications. And third, there is a labor shortage. One-quarter of the work force is temporary, and there is an acute shortage of adjusters and mechanics."
>
> He then answered the questions posed by the worker:
>
> "Whether I take the job voluntarily or not, what's the difference? They offered it to me, and I accepted. That's what's most important. Will I stay at the plant for a long time? Yes, for as long as I'm needed. I give you my word.
>
> "And now a bit about myself. I'm 35 years old. Born and educated in Moscow. I started my career as a shop foreman in plant number 1. Then I became senior foreman, section manager, shop manager, deputy plant manager, and plant manager. In May 1987 I was appointed deputy chief engineer for production at headquarters.
>
> "If elected plant manager one of the challenges I see for myself is fitting into the organization. It was easier in plant number 1 where I started, grew, and got to know people well. Here I'll have to get to know people and start from scratch.
>
> "I know the plant's problems. The plant isn't so bad to have worked so hard. That's the way things are. A lot of things were neglected while you were getting ready to introduce state quality inspection standards. Perhaps it was due to the frequent changes of plant managers. Technical measures weren't taken on time. And you had to prepare very seriously for the state quality control, and a large investment needed to be made to satisfy state requirements.
>
> "I don't promise to fulfill my plan tomorrow. That's impossible. But as for the bottlenecks I see right now, I have ideas how to overcome them. In the plant there are practically no supply services that meet today's requirements. We'll create them. And they'll be strong and work properly.
>
> "I believe it is the responsibility of every worker, regardless of his position, to come to work and contribute to the output of the assembly line. Be they accountants, financial officers, managers, or repair persons—all work to get the product out. This is a principle that I will strictly uphold.

"Every manager has two types of responsibilities to workers: material—to provide them work without stoppages, and moral—to pay them well to feed their families. And I mean well paid for their regular work hours. That is, bonuses should be used as an incentive for conscientious work and not as payment for overtime.

"I have the following requirement: Whatever is given to you—do it. If you don't like the suggested way of doing it, do it your own way, but not any worse. Just do it and report the result. And not finishing it or keeping quiet about it won't do."

The candidate's speech was followed by a question from the audience: "Will headquarters help the plant? Why didn't they help us when Tumanov was plant manager?" This was a concern of many of the workers who were tired of rush jobs and poorly run shifts. The headquarters deputy director general of personnel, Kalinin, replied,

"I disagree. I spoke with the manager of the diesel plant in another city and he promised to send 150 to 200 workers to the plant for two years. They would help the plant, train them and give them experience in producing diesel engines."

The newspaper report concluded with a commentary:

> The answer was concrete, but it didn't reduce the mistrust and resentment of the people gathered there. This was because the workers didn't come when Tumanov was plant manager, and because only now was headquarters promising help.
>
> So the ice of mistrust and resentment didn't melt away. And outsiders would raise other questions. For example, where were the workers? If there was no help from headquarters, why didn't the workers themselves help their plant manager? Where was the workers' council of the plant? Realizing something was wrong, why didn't they go to the headquarters workers' council? Why didn't the party intervene? Why did the union keep silent?
>
> The workers' collective had not yet become owners of the plant or a real power under democratization and glasnost. It is fair to blame headquarters and the social organizations. But it is also fair to blame the passivity of the workers themselves.

The delegates decided to take an open vote on Gorian's candidacy. Gorian remained in the room. Everyone was in favor except for one abstention.

Gorian commented after the election that he expected to get new equipment. He said that the plant produces 1 million rubles worth of engines a day and is very valuable to the enterprise, so the enterprise must help the plant replace its 827 pieces of faulty equipment: "Everything needs replacement from top to bottom. Headquarters has no choice: if they don't help, there will be a disaster."

Ushinski, however, noted that the plant would be shut down in 10 years when they switch over to diesel: "It would be a waste of money to put in all new equipment since we are winding down the gasoline engine."

Commented Kratov, "Of course, Gorian still doesn't know the limits of the help that he can expect to get from the enterprise, but his desires are greater than the possibilities. He is asking to replace all the equipment, but we can't do it."

E. S. Kalinin, the enterprise deputy director general for personnel predicts Gorian will stay in his new job for three to five years and then be moved laterally or vertically. "If we left a manager longer, he would stagnate, so we have a management development plan to rotate managers."

Six months later the director general reported that Plant X was operating smoothly and successfully under Gorian's leadership in spite of not having received new equipment.

DEMOTION OF A SECTION MANAGER AT PLANT Y

A new production manager was appointed for Plant Y in December 1987. One of the first assignments was to look with a fresh eye at the performance problems of a section manager.

The new production manager was an engineer by training but had spent several years as a Komsomol leader. From 1972 to 1975, he had worked in the personnel department at headquarters, and his people skills were well developed. He believed that using the full capacity of a person was more important than solving production bottlenecks. Happy people tend to do their best. With this philosophy he tackled the case of the section manager, who proved to have an inappropriate, autocratic style. In an attempt to understand the section manager as a person, the new production manager went directly to his work site to talk with him. Then he looked into the production situation and visited each shop to talk one-on-one with some of the section manager's subordinates.

The production manager eventually came to doubt whether it was possible to change the section manager's style. One shortcoming was that the section manager did not say anything when he encountered problems. In addition, he was passive and did not try to solve his own problems. He knew that he was performing poorly but could not help himself. Moreover, when the deputy for production tried to help him, the section manager refused his help.

The production manager arranged for the section manager to be transferred to another shop as a mechanic, a job he had performed very well in the past. He explained the situation openly to that shop's manager, who accepted the employee voluntarily because he had a shortage of skilled mechanics.

The former section manager was happy with the transfer and probably had the opportunity to earn more money as a mechanic than he had earned in his managerial position. The production manager said that the situation worked out well for everyone concerned but added that not all situations had such a happy ending.

Conclusions on Hiring and Firing Managers

The account of the selection of Tumanov and Gorian at Plant X is a rich example of the decision process for management selection. Of particular interest is its illustration of how centralized management and self-management are combined. The alternating sequence of action back and forth from a democratic mechanism to a centralized mechanism is the key to understanding how the election process for STU leaders is conducted. As it did at SovElectric, SovTruck headquarters backed off and let the employees' council dominate the first election. Kratov explained this as a learning process. The second election, in which Kratov nominated Gorian, was dominated by the STU leadership. However, the chosen leader assumed his position with the support of both rank and file and higher authority. Again, the secondary role of the party is apparent. It is also interesting that in reporting the election results, the enterprise newspaper did not hesitate to question the enterprise leadership.

The case involving the demotion of the section manager bears a remarkable similarity to the two US demotion episodes. Both systems respond to poor performance with the same sequence of action: first, search for ways to help the person improve his performance; and second, if this does not work, search for a transfer offer that will move the employee to an area of competence with minimum loss of status.

The most dramatic difference between the two countries' corporate decision-making processes is reflected in the mandated and institutionalized procedures under perestroika for conducting elections for STU managers. AmTruck had an informal consensus process that was similar, though not nearly as official as that required by the current implementation of centralized leadership and grass-roots participation (CL/GP) in the USSR. The Soviet procedure was clearly a serious process and the results in these instances were positive. The process was neither totally democratic nor totally centralist but an amalgam of both.

Chapter 8

Capital Investment Decisions

Capital Investment Decisions in The United States

[*Editors' note:* This section presents a review of the general US approaches to capital investment decisions. The material has been prepared primarily for Soviet managers and will be familiar to some American readers. It is followed by examples of capital investment practices in the two US firms.]

US theory is quite clear that the best way to decide whether to proceed with any significant capital expenditure is by calculating its net present value (NPV).[1] The formula for calculating net present value is comprehensive. It takes account of all anticipated cash income and all associated costs over the entire expected life of the investment. It then translates these cash flows, revenues less expenses, into today's dollar value by discounting future returns by the interest income those dollars could earn over the intervening time in other equally risky investments. If the resulting net present value is more than zero, the investment is worth making—it will add to the value of the firm. However, the analyst should examine the net present value of other options—including delaying the investment—and choose the alternative with the highest net present value.

In practice it is not so easy to use this formula. In many instances it is difficult, if not impossible, to calculate with reasonable accuracy what the future cash flows will be. This in turn can lead to setting such high discount rates that few, if any, projects will generate a positive net return. This problem is particularly likely to occur in regard to research and development (R&D) investments. Such investments are made if deemed necessary either to satisfy the market's demand or to secure a competitive position in the market. However, R&D investments may be rational even with a negative

---

1. "Net present value" is a somewhat more precise term for what is also frequently referred to as "discounted cash flow."

present value if they dissuade a competitor from making a similar investment (Baldwin). Partly because of these difficulties, other ways of judging capital investments are also used in practice. These include calculations of how long it will take to recover the capital investment, how the investment will impact the current year's earnings per share, and how the rate of return compares to the firm's overall rate of return on assets. These methods are used even though it can be demonstrated logically that they lead to less-rational decisions than does the net present value method.

No matter what decision method a firm uses, the method must be fitted into its overall system for planning and approving capital investments. Most US firms develop an annual capital budget that lists the projects approved or anticipated for funding in the coming year. The overall budget is prepared by top management, mainly on the basis of proposals developed at the operating levels. Proposals are expected to reflect in-depth research and analysis in the areas of issue formation, intelligence, design, and criteria evaluation. Analysis will be technical as well as financial. Operating-level proposals are summarized and considered and authorized by the board of directors as a total package. Top management and the board must judge at this time the merits of the entire capital budget, given the existing financial resources of the firm and its capacity to raise additional capital.

Capital Investment at AmElectric

THE ANNUAL CAPITAL INVESTMENT PROCESS

The capital investment process at AmElectric can be considered in three phases: budgeting, appropriating, and monitoring. Planning for capital investment begins in July, as production forecasts and budgets get under way.

Budgeting for capital investment. In August, a technical manager from each plant area submits proposals of his or her projects to the manager of advanced manufacturing technology; documentation includes return on investment (ROI), timing, and so on. The technology manager and the manager of accounting services meet with the plant staff and select the projects to promote. Then they present their proposals to the plant manager and prepare a description of the projects, set priorities, and determine how the funds will be spent annually for the next three years.

Projects are first evaluated according to their support of strategic objectives and then by the net present value, rate of return, and risk category. In terms of strategic objective, there is a fairly even division among equipment replacement, cost reduction, and product improvement; few projects are based on volume increase.

There are four risk categories. Category A, the lowest risk, is for investments in existing product or technology, existing facility, and existing market. Risk increases when any or all of these factors are new. Therefore category D, the fourth and highest level of risk, is assigned to projects that involve a new product or technology, a new facility, and a new market.

Whether a project is considered *annual* or *major* depends on a combination of its cost and its risk category. A project is classified as major when the investment exceeds $5 million in risk category A, $2 million in category B, $1 million in category C, and all projects in category D—all other investments are classified as annual projects. Authorized approval levels are based on these classifications.

The upward routing of approvals in the capital-investment plan approval process is as follows: plant manager, divisional general manager, capital review committee of the business unit, business unit, group, and corporate. The investment approval process continues when the plant manager submits the plant's plan in September to Jeremy Thatcher, divisional general manager; Thatcher sets priorities among plants. In November, the revised plans move on to the capital review committee of the business unit, which consists of a technical representative from each division. The committee meets for two or three days to review all divisions, and each one is allotted 30–40 minutes to present its major projects. Each plant sends a technical expert as its spokesperson to explain the technical justification for the investment. Plant managers do not attend but are aware of the issues and the money involved and trust their subordinates to represent their interests.

The capital review committee reviews all projects over $100,000, rates them, and recommends funding levels based on the following criteria:

1. *Strategy.* Does the project support division and business unit objectives, and is it included in the financial plan?
2. *Quality.* Will the project help meet quality requirements?
3. *Technology.* Are we using the appropriate technology (for example, mature, key, base, or leading)?
4. *Risk/innovation.* Is the amount of risk appropriate? Does the project have a good probability of success?
5. *Rate of return.* What rate of return will be realized? Is it enough for the risk involved? Is the payoff time acceptable?
6. *Implementation.* Is there clear division commitment to the project? Does the division have command of all resources needed? Is the project only the tip of the iceberg (first step of a much larger commitment)? Is the timing right? Can the project be deferred without causing an impact?

The capital review committee devotes approximately five minutes to a discussion of each project. Members complete a rating form to evaluate projects according to the six criteria, vote on which projects to fund, and send their recommendations to the business unit. Major projects must also be approved at the group and corporate levels.

One plant engineer explained that there is no personal favoritism in the capital-investment allocation process because the capital review committee is composed of peers of the technical specialist representing the plant. He noted that it would be simpler, though not as fair, if the plant manager "fought all the battles," adding that it is the plant's capital plan, and it is up to the plant to prepare it and justify it. The plan is not dictated from above. Sometimes hourly workers and lower-level salaried staff become frustrated that the plant does not promote their projects, but the plant technical manager explains the criteria to them and emphasizes that they submit to the capital review committee only those projects that they are confident will be accepted. He does not recall any projects being rejected and says that the committee trusts the plant's judgment. Even after a project is approved for the annual capital budget, it must still be reviewed again as a separate appropriation request.

Approving capital appropriations.   Preparation of capital appropriation requests often takes months, and people strive to get it right the first time because there is seldom a second chance to plead their case. Plant engineers research and write the specifications with the help of purchasing and other staff. Detailed descriptions are provided on the following items: benefits, personnel effects, market and economic risks, level of utilization at which the project breaks even, technology and implementation risks, alternatives, key milestone schedule, and breakdown of specific items and costs. Plant personnel spend weeks and even months fine-tuning the proposal to "ensure it will sell." They also inform Jeremy Thatcher early with the hope that he will approve it without revisions. Within the plant, the signature route for appropriation requests moves from department head to controller, marketing, human resources, engineering, and the plant manager.

It usually takes about three weeks for an appropriation to be reviewed at divisional headquarters. Then it is submitted to the capital review committee at the business unit level, which meets monthly. The plant usually sends the appropriation a week before the meeting. If the request involves a lot of money or is urgent, the plant manager calls the secretary of the committee to make sure everything is in order and to answer questions before the meeting.

Jeb Boxer, head of technical services at divisional headquarters, coordinates the plants' capital appropriation plans and discusses them with

Jeremy Thatcher. (Officially Boxer reports to the materials manager, but for capital appropriation matters he reports directly to Thatcher.) The plants' technical specialists write the appropriations and Boxer communicates directly with them. Sometimes plant managers feel it is unnecessary to go through Boxer because they have already told Jeremy Thatcher about an appropriation during one of his plant visits. However, Thatcher has instructed Boxer to not let himself be bypassed even though he is hierarchically lower than the plant managers. Thatcher relies on Boxer to see that the appropriations are prepared properly and formally and to ensure that all appropriate organizational members are involved. This had been a problem because people in different parts of the organization did not always talk to one another. Boxer is able to informally give Thatcher "the inside scoop" on which of the plants' capital appropriation justifications are "shaky." Boxer is also responsible for coordinating refinements of proposals by going back to the plants and sometimes revising the appropriations line by line with them.

Jeb Boxer explained his relationship with the plant management:

> I'm straight with the plants. I tell them, "Don't lie to me because I'm going to be the biggest help you've got." We have a relationship where they trust me, and I give them a hard time, but I go to bat for what I think is right. So I think I have a reputation that I make them happy if I feel comfortable about the approach they've taken. It usually does work out.

Boxer's self-assessment of his role was confirmed by Jeremy Thatcher: "Jeb's a super-straight guy. He's the keeper of the books, and he ensures the quality of the documentation to support our capital projects."

Some of the plant management staff are frustrated with the present situation in which the plant manager does not have authority to make capital appropriation decisions. They believe that the staff assistants to Jeremy Thatcher at divisional headquarters have the real authority and that Thatcher is too busy to do more than "rubber-stamp" the appropriations. Some plant management personnel believe that the plant manager is more experienced and competent to make such decisions than Thatcher's assistants are, but they cultivate good relations with the assistants in recognition of their authority. They also "prime" Jeremy Thatcher approximately six weeks in advance of submitting an appropriation request to smooth the way during the limited time they ultimately get with him to obtain his approval.

To alleviate the problem of accountability for appropriation requests, Jeremy Thatcher authorized Jeb Boxer to monitor a signature sheet on which individuals acknowledge exactly what they are responsible for. Seven functions are represented: the divisional headquarters managers of marketing, engineering, technical services, information systems, the plant human resource manager, plant controller, and plant manager. For example, the plant controller signs the following statement: "All financial data is correct including cost justification and NPV (net present value) and ROR (rate of return). All required financial forms have been attached and are correct. Source of funds is correctly identified." On a separate summary sheet of the appropriation request, additional approval signatures are recorded: plant department head, plant manager, divisional controller, divisional general manager, business-unit general manager, group executive vice president, and corporate president (as required by the size and risk of the investment).

In the past, plant managers were authorized to approve capital appropriations within the limits set by the approved capital budget plan. When business conditions worsened, approval levels were "bumped up the organization." A plant engineer noted that while this process keeps good control of expenditures, the negative side is that it takes months to get an appropriation approved. Staff at divisional headquarters are currently trying to streamline the complex approval process.

Monitoring capital investments. Throughout the year, actual capital spending is tracked against the plan by routine accounting procedures; managers devote their time only to variances. The budget may be modified if business conditions change. It may be cut if a downturn develops, or projects may be substituted in midyear. For example, a project may be stopped despite the availability of capital funds if the expense budget contains no money to install the equipment; there is a policy against letting equipment sit idle. Hedge buying (buying tooling in anticipation of a project being funded) has also been curbed.

In the midyear review, plants may be asked to prepare contingency plans—that is, to prioritize their projects in case available funds increase or diminish. Overall, about 80% of the projects in the plan get implemented. The remaining are not pursued by the plants either because they are not viable or because conditions have changed and the plant has submitted substitute projects.

If a project was originally proposed as a cost improvement but did not meet the criteria, it could be reclassified as a replacement project and funding sought on that basis. Cost reduction is a priority, however, and the current cost-cutting campaign seems to be paying off: Plant A generated more cost reduction proposals in 1988 than it had in the previous 10 years.

Throughout the year, the division asks for "make good reports" giving updates on how well the projects are doing. Only about 50% of the projects meet all expectations because it is difficult to implement projects that successfully achieve the forecast cost savings. It is hard to squeeze out cost savings in direct labor because hourly workers have been cut to a minimum. Costs now must be reduced from overhead and professional staff.

Another kind of problem arises when money is unspent at the end of the year. If a piece of equipment was not available from the manufacturer as scheduled, the plants must find ways to reallocate the money to other projects because the money is not rolled over to the next year. Division has recognized the phenomenon and has recently instituted a rule whereby a certain percentage of the budget must be spent or allocated at the end of each quarter. Jeb Boxer, coordinator of capital appropriations at divisional headquarters, says the plants are overly optimistic about their ability to spend capital funds, and they seldom spend all of them. Plants lose credibility, however, if they ask for new funds after failing to spend the previous year's allocation.

The plants can also ask for extra funds for a "hot" or high-need project that was unforeseen. If the project fits with corporate's strategic thrust, a plant can bypass the formal procedure and get quick approval from the corporate executive vice president by preparing a simple justification. For example, Plant A acquired robots this way when productivity improvement was a key corporate strategy.

Monthly reports and midyear reviews of capital expenditures are conducted regularly to monitor activities. These reviews are an integral part of the management information and control system that helps everyone keep an overview of the situation and address problems in a timely manner.

A summary of the process. The official investment process at AmElectric can be characterized as elaborate and extended. For the most part it conforms to traditional US capital investment theory. Action starts at the bottom of the organization, then moves to the top (or close to the top), and back down in three waves: budget, appropriations, and monitoring. This builds into the system many checks and balances that reduce the possibility of serious error but consume a great deal of management time. There is, however, sufficient flexibility in the system to accommodate special late projects and adjust approved projects to fit changing circumstances. In practice, as we are about to illustrate, managers have devised ways to streamline the process and get the "right" things done by circumventing the rules without technically breaking them.

AMELECTRIC'S TRANSFER SAFETY PLAN

The original budget decision. In May 1987, the AmElectric management committee announced its decision to shut down a Northeast plant and transfer a main-product manufacturing line to southern assembly Plant B. The decision was based on recommendations of a five-member team that for a year had studied ways to rationalize the plants and reduce surplus capacity. Jeremy Thatcher, the divisional general manager to whom the team reported, had instructed its members to take a no-frills approach and budget only for transportation and installation of existing equipment. Equipment upgrading was to be funded by the receiving plant and would have to be justified on an item-by-item basis. Because of the issue's sensitivity, the study team was kept small and secret. According to the Plant B staff, the team lacked sufficient knowledge of detail and did not budget enough capital for the transfer. However, Thatcher noted that he himself had pruned the team's capital budget by one-third before presenting it for corporate approval.

To facilitate that approval, Thatcher spent three days at corporate headquarters explaining the plan to management committee members and key corporate staff. At its decisive meeting, the committee approved the transfer plan but cut the capital portion of the budget by another one-third; then it added several million dollars for expenses such as equipment transfer, employee benefits, and capital writedown. Jeremy Thatcher recalled his thoughts at that meeting:

> I was not sure we could do it all for the budgeted amount, and I probably should have said so. But I thought there might be a way to make it as a pure transfer plan excluding process and technological improvements. This project was the most important strategic program we had. Our whole business survival depended on it. We were going to lose money and just bleed to death if we didn't do it. So at that point I accepted the budget cut. I just wanted to get out of the room and get on with the job.

In the fall of 1987, midway through the transfer, Plant B staff proposed a change in the plan: upgrade certain equipment, buy some new machines, and transfer other equipment not designated initially. These changes would cost several million extra. A few of the items were justifiable and were approved as productivity improvements, but some equipment upgrades could not be justified this way.

The decision to request an additional $3 million.   In March 1988, Thatcher, Jeb Boxer, and Vic Hoffman, the division controller, visited the plant to see if the proposed equipment was really necessary. They agreed that it was and sought a way to obtain the money. Thatcher knew his career was on the line if he were to exceed the budget by $3 million with a string of disparate appropriation requests:

I could have been in real hot water. When I accepted the budget cut, I owned the problem and was responsible for it. That's where the ownership thing comes in. It wasn't the plant's fault. They could have said to me, "Look what you did, boss." It was up to me to fix it. I thought, "We're about to go off the cliff. What are we going to do?"

While his staff worked on a solution, Thatcher asked the plant to keep a separate set of records on the project. This showed that the overall project had a reasonable chance of beating its budget. Ultimately, Thatcher and his staff made a collective decision to adopt the plant controller's suggestion to repackage the items under the umbrella of a safety plan. Analyses had shown that the Northeast plant's facilities did not meet current safety standards, and each new expenditure could be justified on the ground that it would improve plant safety. For example, for the test facility the plant wanted an explosion-proof concrete bunker, which would double the amount originally allocated for the facility. A major test failure could result in extensive damage and personal injury. One manager at Plant B admitted that the chances of that happening were one in a million, but pointed out that plant staff insisted on safety precautions before accepting responsibility for any equipment. Another request had to do with replacing a machine that was considered too hazardous to transport from the Northeast plant. The machine contained PCBs, a known carcinogen and violated the Occupational Safety and Health Administration (OSHA) regulations.

Thus safety and environmental issues were the common thread linking the capital equipment requests that "just so happened" to result in the technological upgrades that the Plant B staff wanted. "Everything is true. It was just so cleverly packaged," confided a manager in the plant. "And we thought, who would have the audacity not to approve these things? And we went all the way up and got approval."

Before taking the proposal to corporate, however, Thatcher made the plant staff rewrite their justifications with great care. He jokingly explained that they had become so convinced of the legitimacy of the safety plan that initially they had taken the approach of "'Please send me a million dollars' written on the back of an envelope."

In May 1988, Thatcher presented the plan to the strategic capital review committee. Committee members were sympathetic to the issues but approved the plan reluctantly; in their opinion the safety features should have been included in the original plan.

While admitting that the safety plan was "one of the more unnerving things that happened to me in the past couple of years," Jeremy Thatcher staunchly defended it: "We haven't wasted a nickel. We'll end up with the world's best assembly shop. The problem was it didn't fit the original plan."

He added that in the end he "didn't get [his] wrists slapped" because the expense side of the transfer came in considerably under budget. Hence the total cost of the transfer would be done for the allocated $47 million; although the capital cost was higher than originally budgeted and accounting rules would not permit mixing capital and expense budgets.

The transfer process.   Cooperation from the Northeast plant was critical to the success of the transfer. The Northeast plant's priority was to meet its own production goals during the transfer period, but this priority could conflict with getting the transferred equipment operational in the southern location. Ron Sawyer, manager of Plant B, strongly recommended to Thatcher that the successful transfer of operations be included in the Northeast plant's goals. That approach had been very successful in the transfer and shutdown of the "mother" plant a few years earlier, so Jeremy Thatcher met with the Northeast plant management staff in the fall of 1987 and set this goal. The plant also reported to Thatcher throughout the transfer and closedown. Sawyer said that as a result there was a noticeable improvement in cooperation: "It worked. It made machine tools and people available that wouldn't otherwise have been."

Another way of enlisting the Northeast plant's cooperation was to include it in the planning and design of layout for the new assembly facility. According to Sawyer, "We sent plant layouts to them and got their blessing. We wanted their input. We looked at them as being experts, and we also wanted them to be on the same team. We didn't want them second guessing what those jerks (we in the southern plant) did."

Sawyer oversaw the transfer from a general perspective. In his words,

> I'm a process person. I didn't even study the detail, but I wanted to make sure that all the appropriate people were involved—the Northeast plant, the area manager. I didn't offer detailed suggestions, as I didn't want to be part of the technical decision-making process. I did some devil's-advocate questioning during the review process. For example, what are the load assumptions, can we handle peak periods? But I didn't offer solutions. The team knew I'd approve it after they had all approved it. Mine was the last signature.

As ambitious as the transfer and installation of equipment was the retraining of the Plant B work force to manufacture and assemble the unfamiliar product. Workers who might otherwise have been laid off were retrained by technical specialists brought in from the Northeast plant.

Summary of the product transfer project.   The study of the AmElectric transfer demonstrates that an official capital investment plan is followed carefully and monitored closely. Managers up and down the hierarchy have learned to prepare in great detail the many kinds of studies and justifications that go into a capital investment proposal.

The tightened review and approval process contributed to the "creative packaging" of some parts of the transfer capital budget as a safety proposal. Safety was a valid selling point but not the primary motive of plant managers, whose foremost concern was in equipping Plant B to be a low-cost, high-quality, high-volume producer. To achieve this, the divisional head opted to take a professional risk in supporting the additional safety package. In this case, it was a successful move.

FLEXIBLE MACHINING SYSTEM (FMS)

Phase 1.   Plant A's flexible machining system was a multimillion-dollar project to be implemented in several stages. FMS was the largest capital investment program undertaken at Plant A since the plant was built. Its strategic thrust was threefold: (1) to improve competitive advantage by reducing costs, (2) to add flexibility in meeting customer needs with engineering changes to upgrade products, and (3) to reduce lead time. FMS would be not only a metal removal system, but also a software system. The system was expected to enable new styles to be introduced quickly and phased out promptly when demand was met and other styles were required.

The project was the brainchild of the plant's manager of manufacturing planning, Juan Carerra. It was "his baby," and he pushed it all the way to the top of the corporation, striking up a friendship with AmElectric's chairman, with whom he could converse in Spanish. Carerra even gained the chairman's informal support for the project during one of the chairman's plant visits.

In January 1985, Juan Carerra began holding weekly brainstorming sessions with 25 plant engineers and, in his words, "planting seeds at divisional headquarters for FMS projects." The weekly meetings were "participative to the extreme" and became unwieldy. At that point the group was trimmed to include just 10 engineers who met on a monthly basis. Finally, a five-member FMS review team was formed: Juan Carerra; Tom Aster, Carerra's subordinate manager of advanced manufacturing technology (later to be named FMS project head); the manager of shop operations; his subordinate, the area manager for machining (where the equipment was to be installed); and the manager of quality assurance. The review team was responsible for providing justification for FMS, allocating staff resources to the project, and planning for implementation. The shop operations staff contributed data on what the costs and lead times had to be to make FMS worthwhile.

In late 1985, Jeb Boxer, the divisional technical services manager, reviewed the situation with Jeremy Thatcher and suggested that Carerra and the plant facilities manager submit an appropriation even though they did not know exactly what equipment they wanted. FMS technology was changing rapidly, and Plant A had been hesitant because its personnel lacked sufficient expertise to evaluate the options properly. However, the plant had not spent all of its appropriation for the year, and Boxer saw FMS as an opportunity to allocate some of the remaining funds. He warned the plant that it might not get its requested funds the following year if it had funds remaining in the current budget. Carerra's team decided to write an appropriation for phase 1 of the FMS project, consisting of some large machine tools. This was consistent with the corporate policy of phasing large projects and calculating benefits at each stage. In phase 1 of FMS, the plant could already claim cost savings from the machine tools.

Phase 2.   By the second quarter of 1986, Plant A engineers had homed in on what products would work and what additional machine tools would be needed for FMS. Late in 1986, Plant A began preparations for phase 2. The FMS team met with the divisional managers of marketing, engineering, and manufacturing and got them to commit to the changes in production volumes that could be expected based on proposed cost reductions. In September 1986, Plant A prepared a $4.9-million appropriation request for phase 2. However, as Jeb Boxer said, the figure looked "too fishy"; it barely fell under the $5-million threshold for major projects that require approval by the board of directors. Boxer believed that political problems with corporate would ensue when it became apparent that the entire project (phases 1 and 2) would actually cost more than $5 million.

Boxer presented Jeremy Thatcher with two options: "Should we throw in a few more bucks to make it $5.1 million so it doesn't appear as though we're trying to skirt the fact that it's a major? Or should we cancel the first appropriation [for phase 1] and wrap the whole thing up into one?" The first option was unattractive because "there's so much more pain involved that you don't want to do a major unless you really have to." The second option's drawback was that it violated the chairman's preference for phasing large projects.

Thatcher conferred with his superiors in the business unit and Boxer contacted the secretary of the corporate capital review committee (SCRC) for advice. The SCRC suggested that the appropriation be written as phase 2 for $4.9 million as originally proposed. Remarked Boxer: "It was a revelation to me that the board of directors didn't want to spend time on it. They don't want to be messing around with things unless they are well over $5 million or risky."

So Thatcher agreed to keep the appropriation under $5 million but was "up front with the review board" about the scope of the project and its total cost. With the groundwork carefully laid, the project was approved by both the capital review committee and the executive vice president without requiring approval by the board of directors. Not only did the project as a whole show a very good rate of return, but phase 1 would realize savings on its own.

At the time of our study, the FMS project was in its implementation stage. During the summer and fall of 1987, a team of engineers from Plant A toured machine-tool manufacturers in Europe and Japan to study the technology. Tom Aster, the FMS project head, had 13 professionals in his group work on the project's design phase and write bid specifications for equipment. By the end of June 1988, all equipment purchases were to be finalized, but some ordering delays occurred because Juan Carerra was out of the country. Nobody wanted to order the equipment in his absence.

Another major problem was the selection of software to run FMS. The AmElectric in-house software developers, a separate business unit, had a history of not always delivering on their promises, and Jeremy Thatcher expressed initial concern about the capacity and commitment of that group. He resolved the matter with the head of the unit and Plant A signed an agreement with the in-house group. The 200 pages of specifications were revised six times, and negotiations went back and forth between Tom Aster's staff and the software group. Aster would have preferred to contract with an outside firm, but admitted that those arrangements also can cause problems.

The goal to have FMS fully operational by the end of 1989 was viewed as unrealistic by some plant management staff. Nevertheless, pilot operation was scheduled for early 1989. According to the manager of shop operations, "The rest of the world is moving in the direction of FMS. The sooner we get it up and running the more competitive we'll be in the world market. It will impact new products and should lower our costs."

Summary of the FMS project.   In the FMS instance, again we see a relatively junior AmElectric manager taking on significant personal responsibility to sponsor a major capital project. Juan Carerra's informal relationship with the corporate chairman helped support the project, but FMS still had to move through the specified approval steps. Informal advice from the divisional and business unit levels helped smooth the approval process, and the cumbersome procedures were made to work.

Capital Investment at AmTruck

THE ANNUAL CAPITAL INVESTMENT PROCESS

The capital investment process at AmTruck is closely related to the planning and new product introduction process. After marketing and manufacturing have developed in sequence their product and production strategies, financial planning runs a financial simulation to determine the level of capital expenditure the corporation will be able to fund during the implementation period; determination is based on profit and cash flow generated.

After the financial planning group simulates the overall budget, it establishes capital spending targets for each engine business. These are based on strategic needs of the target engine business—for example, to maintain capacity or to increase it. The manufacturing groups then develop a capital spending plan that will meet capacity planning volumes, and they attempt to stay within the spending targets. Using a computer, they prepare a base plan and identify exposures, namely overexpenditures or failures to meet capacity requirements.

The manufacturing groups submit their plans to manufacturing planning, which rolls them up into one engine business plan. Risk factors are identified to senior management, and adjustments are made as necessary. This plan may go through two or three iterations involving lateral and vertical interaction. Finally, the totals for appropriations and cash flow are submitted to the board of directors for authorization at its December meeting.

If the plan is approved, it is put into place as an operating plan at the first of the new year. Then the plan is sorted into a number of categories by means of budget codes. The main category is the purpose of the expenditure: capacity expansion, cost reduction, new product change, quality assurance, research, environmental compliance, or business support.

When the plant manager receives the overall budget, he or she asks for proposals from engineering and production employees. For example, someone may generate a cost-reduction idea. First, the general idea—how it works, the anticipated savings, and what will be required to implement it—is presented to management and financial planning. If preliminary business management approval is obtained, the proposer then prepares a formal request for appropriation (RFA), which is submitted for approval. The RFAs should correspond to the projects described in the plan. RFAs up to $100,000 may be approved by the plant manager, up to $250,000 by corporate officers, up to $500,000 by the president's staff, and over $500,000 by the president. If the RFA is approved, a purchase requisition is approved to release an order to the supplier. When the equipment is delivered, an invoice is prepared and vouchered for payment. Actual payments and cash flows are tracked throughout the year and reported monthly.

During the approval process, key questions are asked: Where will the funding come from—approved budget or out-of-budget? What is the cash flow timing? The payback? The return on investment? Projects must clear a 15% hurdle rate, or cost of capital charge. A sensitivity analysis is performed to determine, for example, how cost and ROI estimates fluctuate with production volume.

Said one AmTruck manager, "For most projects we do what we call 'greasing the skids.' Senior management should be familiar with your proposal long before it arrives on their desk as an RFA. If they just get an RFA cold, they're a lot less likely to approve it. And once an RFA has been rejected, it's hard to get it approved later."

The AmTruck philosophy of participative management is inculcated in the capital investment process. The finance manual specifies the role of approval levels, the rationale for delegation, and the role of staff functions in the process:

Since delegation is at the heart of approval, we have asked ourselves why do we delegate. Clearly we delegate because we consider it to be both productive and profitable to do so. Not only does it eliminate unnecessary review of decisions where little value is added, but it builds commitment throughout a responsive organization.

However, there are powerful inhibitors to delegation—lack of trust, lack of shared values, lack of confidence in an adequate flow of information. If a manager can trust his subordinate to have the same information and apply the same values in making a decision, he becomes eager to delegate. Lacking that trust, the manager will revert to control, reserving authority to himself. The implied lack of productivity is accepted rather than attacked.

Because approval levels are highly visible throughout the organization and shape our work on a day-to-day basis, they convey a powerful message as to how we want to manage.

What is the role of corporate staff? In the various approval processes, corporate staff has played a diversity of roles: initiate, coordinate, and control. While these roles are important, the tendency to either drive or control these processes centrally has too often led to duplicate staff functions at the corporate and group levels with the potential for adversarial conflict.

While we must ensure that adequate decision and transaction control processes are in place and working (as well as expand the role of "checking" where it supports improvement), corporate staff does not need to review decisions that are best made within the line organizations.

CAM LOBE MILL PROJECT AT PLANT C

The cam lobe mill investment followed the standard approval procedures. The engineer for the machining shop in the large engine plant discovered that there was substantial room for improvement in the camshaft machining line. The work was very demanding physically, and there were significant quality problems.

The engineer met with machining team members and asked them to begin thinking about possible solutions to this phase of camshaft machining. Some workers proposed that they visit other factories to see how it was done there, and some members of the group later visited the supplier factory to determine how the cam lobe mill would work.

Once the team began to develop a clear idea of the kind of machine it wanted, the engineer worked with it to develop the cost and rate of return estimates. She recalled, "This was a very easy project. Management wanted improvements like this. The team was committed to technological change. And the return on investment was 135%." The RFA forms were submitted to plant management and quickly approved. The new machine was ordered, delivered, and put into service on schedule.

REDUCING THE CAPITAL INVESTMENT BUDGET AT PLANT D

Because AmTruck's capital investment process is flexible, a plan can be adjusted to meet changing conditions during the year after it is approved. For example, Plant D found in the middle of 1988 that it was likely to spend 10% over its $11.3-million capital allocation if it invested in all its approved projects. This was a new phenomenon; historically, the plant spent only about 50% of its budget. But in the 12 months since budget preparation, production volume had increased and new personnel had been hired. Furthermore, human error had occurred: some needed items had been omitted from the budget.

Finding an additional 10% to cut from the capital budget was complicated by the categories and sizes of the various projects. Some projects are "must dos," related either to legal requirements or new product needs. For example, a change in how the serial numbers are displayed on the engine had been mandated by marketing. While the plant could not refuse to make the change, a senior accounting or production executive at corporate might successfully challenge it.

A second category of projects that were considered vulnerable to cost reduction caused some disagreement because of data-gathering problems. Because the capital budgeting system was not integrated with the overall expense tracking system, a request for appropriation might claim substantial cost savings in terms of headcount reduction, but there was no systematic procedure for deducting the cost of that personnel. The controller noted, "One technique we used was when someone said that a project will eliminate two engineering jobs. We said, 'Fine, what expense account should be debited for next year?'" This bound the managers to their cost savings projections.

An additional difficulty in cutting capital spending was that fully one-third of the overage was in one "must-do" project. Thus cutting many smaller projects did not do much to reduce the total amount of the overage. No latitude was provided by projects that were already under way and for which funds had been spent.

The plant manager called on his staff to pare the budget rather than ask corporate for additional funding. "Corporate isn't in a position to give us more money. We'd rather beg forgiveness on a slight override as opposed to asking for permission for a large override on the front end." The first criterion was to throw out projects unless they either affected the customer in the current year or facilitated a large cost reduction. That left new projects—some of which had already been approved, others that were pending approval from corporate, and others that were in the planning stages. The plant manager felt they ought to do them all, but it was a matter of postponing some until the following year to keep expenditures within the original plan as much as possible.

The manager and the controller of Plant C carefully planned how to get the staff to sacrifice capital projects. They developed a procedure and a set of guidelines for deciding which capital projects should be funded first. Two days before the plant management team meeting, they distributed a memo outlining the process.

At the meeting, the controller spent a fair amount of time laying the groundwork. He told the management team, "If you can't wear a plant manager's hat in this meeting, then you should leave right now." Then he went through the projects line by line. To get the ball rolling, the controller had obtained advance agreement from one manager to cut his own project voluntarily. The general degree of commitment to the reductions turned out to be so high that several managers gave up pet projects in which they had already invested time, energy, and resources.

In the end, the plant manager and the controller were pleased with the capital reduction process. Despite the potential for acrimonious debate and outright resistance, the managers cooperated with one another and cut $700,000 of the unfunded projects. This was probably due in large part to the successful implementation of participative management and delegation of authority at AmTruck. Noted the plant manager:

People have a fair appreciation of the situation. We've involved people down to the team manager level in trade-off meetings. There is a real willingness of people to give up projects when they see it in a larger context. We're in a sharing mode and our message is getting through. Although a particular group of engineers may wonder if we really know what we're doing and why their project wasn't funded, nobody said it. It's just human nature. But there wasn't this feeling at the plant business manager or team manager level. They have a real understanding of the trade-offs. They won't necessarily be happy. At the monthly business review meetings, I hear small pleas. For example, the QA people say: "If only I had my electron microscope." So people will make their points. And that's healthy. You don't want that to go away.

THE TEKCONTROL LEVER MACHINE AT PLANT C

In response to increased capacity demands for current products and the introduction of a new large engine in 1991, Plant C needed new equipment to assemble the 18 cam box levers in each engine. Plant engineers recommended a numerically controlled, fully automatic machine tool with a unique design that had not been manufactured before. When the specifications were put out to bid, one of the three bidders was Tekcontrol, a newly formed AmTruck subsidiary that specialized in designing and manufacturing computer-automated technology.

Tekcontrol's bid of $600,000 was considerably lower than those of its competitors. Despite reservations about Tekcontrol's inexperience, Plant C management agreed to award it the contract.

The project ran into serious difficulties, and everything came to a head in May 1988. Tekcontrol was more than a year late on delivery of the machine, and the price had skyrocketed to $1.2 million, double the original quote. However, when outside machine tool experts were called in to evaluate the equipment, they assigned it a value of $1.1 million: they were impressed with its capabilities and elegance. Because Plant C did not have the funds in its capital budget, corporate agreed to absorb the unanticipated additional cost, viewing the expense as its commitment to the Tekcontrol startup.

The technical problems associated with the Tekcontrol machine could not be solved as easily as the financial ones. Plant C engineers discovered in a one-hour test run that while the machine produced high-quality output, it could not meet the six-second cycle time required for current products (it ran at 91% efficiency because it was based on an "unrealistic" assumption of 100% uptime). Furthermore, in its present condition it would be unable to assemble the levers for the 1991 model.

In May 1988, Tekcontrol notified Plant C that it was stopping work on the machine. "Without major additional funding we can't make it do more than what it is doing. We've done our best." Plant C engineers claimed that Tekcontrol knew from the quotation stage what the cycle time requirements were, but they doubted whether Tekcontrol took the requirements seriously. For their part, Tekcontrol engineers claimed that Plant C engineers kept adding bells and whistles and calling for modifications to the design.

The plant manager met with his engineers to discuss the options. The meeting began with one engineer summarizing the situation: "Basically the gun is to our head. Either we accept the machine as is, or Tekcontrol has said they will scrap the machine." By this time the Tekcontrol machine had become as much an emotional issue as a technical one for Plant C engineers. They no longer wanted to deal with it and were more interested in seeing Tekcontrol punished. Said one engineer to the plant manager, "We feel that Tekcontrol has not done its job and that ought to be recognized somehow. If it had been an outside manufacturer, we probably would not accept the machine, nor would they be putting this kind of pressure on us. And right now we'd be talking about what our lawyers would be doing." (However, a corporate vice president argued that many advanced machine-tool manufacturers "low-balled" and were often late on delivery.)

The plant manager listened calmly to his staff and then set about finding workable solutions. He said,

> It's a Mexican standoff. We don't want Tekcontrol to do the major overhaul required to equip the machine for the 1991 model. They won't do the upfitting in terms of the right cycle time for the current model. We don't want to scrap a $1.2-million machine. We've got a sticky situation here. It's not going to go unnoticed in the corporation. It's going to reflect on Tekcontrol. They'll be looking for references and we can't give them a positive one on this one. Plus we need more money.

The plant manager asked his staff for advice on the best strategy. It would cost $70,000 to redo the hydraulics to improve cycle time and an additional one-third the cost of the machine to retool it for the 1991 model. Should they have Tekcontrol get the machine up and running or bring it in-house and try to get it working themselves with some support from Tekcontrol? One engineer responded, "I doubt we can get much support from Tekcontrol once it's off their site. They won't come here and help. Plus, I don't think we have any confidence in Tekcontrol's ability to do the job." The plant manager felt that because the machine was the first of its kind, Tekcontrol should expect problems. "I would think Tekcontrol could fix the sucker," he ventured.

One plant engineer agreed, noting that Tekcontrol had other successes, but argued that "it would take an attitude change by Tekcontrol" as well as additional money, which Tekcontrol was unwilling to forfeit from its profits. "The only viable solution is to bring it in here and get agreed-on funding from corporate to make it work for existing and 1991 levers," he concluded.

The plant manager agreed with the proposal to bring the machine to the plant and ask corporate for $70,000 to rework the hydraulics to improve cycle time. If scarce skilled trades personnel were assigned to the project, the new machine could be operational within six months. Plant C would keep the existing machine operating as a backup. With corporate's approval, the job of retooling for the 1991 engine could be contracted to an outside machine-tool manufacturer.

Immediately after the staff meeting, the plant manager telephoned the president of Tekcontrol at corporate and advised him of the decision.

SUMMARY OF CAPITAL INVESTMENT AT AMTRUCK

While both US enterprises begin their capital investment planning with an evaluation of market demand and competition, the process at AmTruck is significantly simpler and shorter than at AmElectric. Because AmTruck applies its decentralized approach to the capital budgeting process, straightforward projects like the cam lobe mill can go forward promptly. Consistent with that practice was the Plant D staff's full responsibility for trimming its capital budget to a figure within the approved level. AmTruck's system, however, is not error free, as we saw in the Tekcontrol situation when cost overruns, delays, and technical shortfalls were experienced. However, the magnitude of the lever machine project assured its review at both budget and appropriation stages by the corporate president, who favored giving the contract to AmTruck's new subsidiary. That corporate felt responsible for the sourcing decision is indicated by its willingness to fund the overrun. Moreover, because this was prototype equipment, a more-than-usual amount of technical uncertainty was to be expected.

The Capital Investment Process in the USSR

[*Editors' note:* This section describes the standard Soviet approach to capital investment decisions as selected and prepared by our Soviet colleagues primarily for American readers. It is followed by examples of investment practices that we observed at SovElectric and SovTruck.]

In accordance with the policy of radical economic reform promulgated by the Twenty-seventh Party Congress in 1986 and developed by the Nineteenth Party Conference in 1988, capital investments are funded in one of three ways: by the enterprise itself (mainly through the development fund), by bank loan, or—if necessary—by government monies. (See Exhibit 8.1.)

An enterprise is limited as to the amount of government capital funds it can acquire. The limit is determined to be the smallest sum needed to achieve the desired industrial capacity. Capital investment decisions involve many state organizations: the Planning Committee, the Supply Committee, the Standards Committee, the Pricing Committee, the Labor Committee, the Ministry of Finance, and the State Committee for Science and Technology. Although funds from the ministry require extensive justification, other state organizations may help enterprises and industrial ministries get more funds, get them faster, get equipment faster, introduce new equipment, and so on.

Self-financing enterprises use their profits to renew and modernize plant and equipment, drawing on their own funds either for industrial development or for science and technology. The central ministry for each industry determines what portion of an enterprise's profits will be added to the two funds and, in general, how the money in the funds will be allocated. In 1988, enterprises funded 85% of their capital investments from their own internal funds. Science and technology funds finance scientific and research work, testing and design work, the introduction of new products and technological processes, and the quality improvement of existing products. Industrial development funds are used for plant expansions or replacements.

New technology and improvements in manufacturing must pay for themselves; that is, measures taken for the sake of technological progress must turn a profit (or savings) over and above the money spent on them. If preliminary estimates show that a profit or savings will not be forthcoming as a result of measures taken during the course of the accepted payback period, then the project must, as a rule, be rejected. The accepted payback period ranges from five to seven years depending on which sector of the economy is involved.

As in the United States, a distinction is made in the USSR between capital and expense. There are two kinds of currency used in regard to capital investments: rubles and hard currency—that is, currency exchangeable in the international market. Hard currency is available through the ministries, and

EXHIBIT 8.1 Capital-investment Process in the USSR

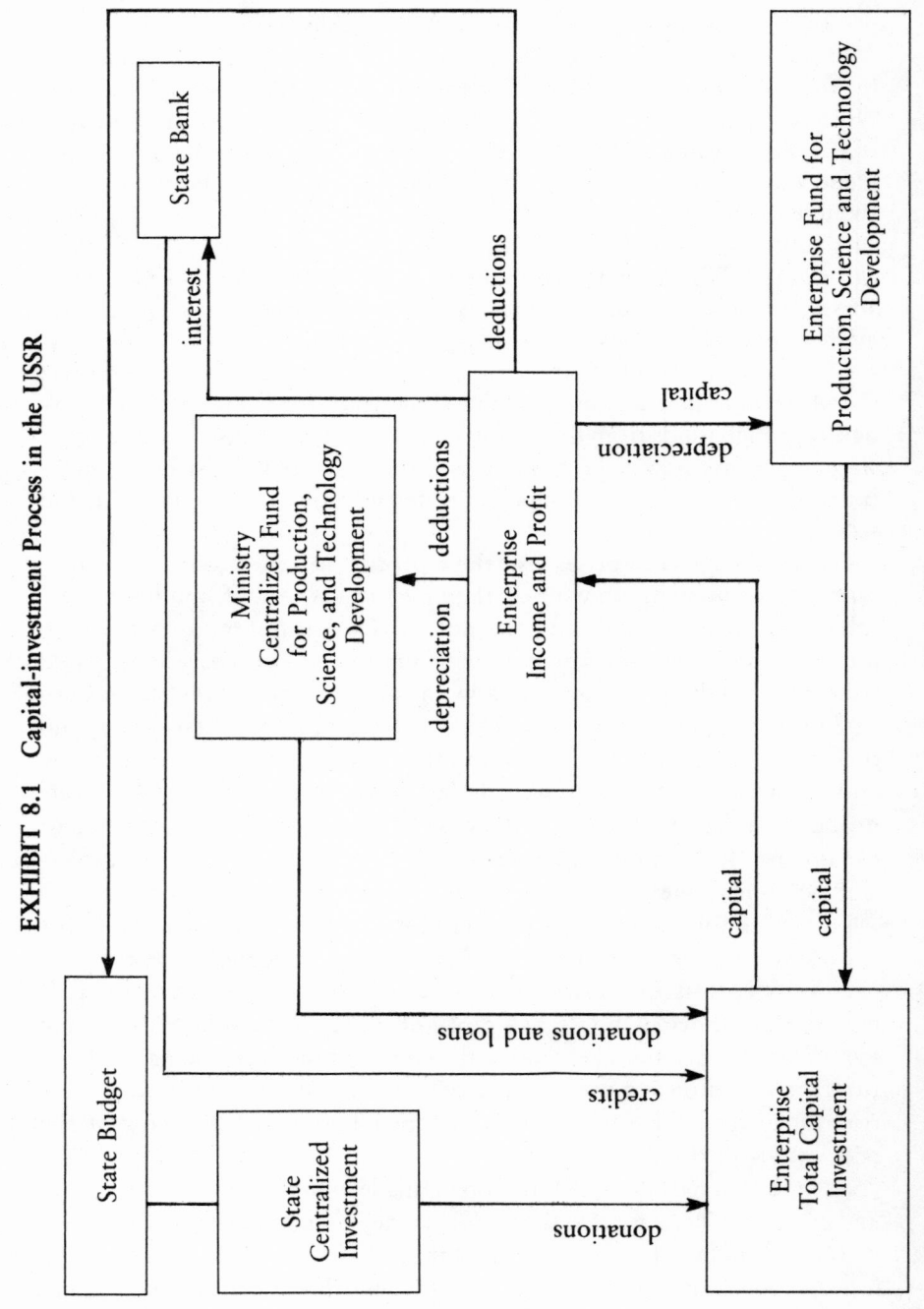

firms themselves may also earn hard currency through exports of their products.

Equipment depreciation periods are much longer in the USSR than in the United States. Capital investment funds are used for repair far more frequently than for replacement of equipment. There is a policy of replacing worn-out equipment, but it is very difficult to get authorization to upgrade equipment that is still functioning. No accelerated depreciation is used. Furthermore, overloading of production capacity forced by tight production plans leaves little opportunity to carry out preventive maintenance programs, so there is little time for quality repairs to be done. Enterprises often suffer too from a shortage of floor space for new equipment.

In general, plant personnel prefer foreign equipment because it is often of better quality than Soviet equipment. A common practice when purchasing equipment, though, is to produce the tooling in-house rather than obtain it from the outside manufacturer. This cuts costs, reduces dependence on the supplier, and enables the enterprise to use its own tooling specialists. Many large enterprises produce their own equipment.

Even after funding is secured for capital investments, an enterprise faces many problems in procuring the authorized equipment. Procurement is arranged in one of the following ways.

The principal way (accounting for 85% of all capital purchases in 1988) is through the centralized allocation of resources by the ministries. Ministries allocate capital goods in accordance with the national priorities developed by Gosplan and Gossnab. Enterprises can facilitate these supply arrangements by making their own contacts with supplier enterprises and wholesale agencies. Purchasers and suppliers that have had long-standing relationships have recently been allowed to deviate from established prices by agreeing to discounts or extra payments for meeting special customer requirements.

The second way of acquiring capital equipment (accounting for 15% of such purchases in 1988) is through direct wholesale trade between suppliers and purchasers. These trades are made without reference to central ministries.

Finally, the enterprise can move to a new organizational form and thereby change its way of handling capital investments. An enterprise may now join one of the intersectoral associations—created in 1988—that do not report to a ministry. It can also leave an association and proclaim its independence or link up with another ministry or join another association in its own ministry. Such moves usually mean the enterprise assumes more self-financing responsibilities.

The national priorities for capital investment are to increase production volume and improve quality. However, production volume is of such critical importance that quality has suffered.

The capital investment plan is treated as a part of the consolidated annual plan, initiated and eventually approved by the enterprise's superior authority. Therefore unexpected purchases are not viewed favorably. Each shop in the plant provides input into the capital investment plan by submitting requests for equipment. The technologist in each shop coordinates the capital investment plan. The plant's chief engineer is involved also, but not in as much detail as the technologists during this initial stage. The plans are then forwarded up the hierarchy, where they are reviewed and consolidated. At headquarters the chief engineer of the enterprise has considerable decision involvement. And when the plan reaches this point in the process, the chief technologist of the enterprise coordinates the enterprise capital investment plan. The employees' council then approves the size of the capital investment budget, and it is signed by the director general of the enterprise.

In Soviet industry, centralized industrial ministries establish standard procedures that they expect enterprises to follow. These detailed procedures have the effect of law for state enterprises and are familiar to Soviet managers, who expect to move through them a step at a time in sequential order. It takes time and generates significant paperwork, but as we discovered at the two Soviet firms, managers have found ways to streamline the process.

Capital Investment at SovElectric

Several stages mark the process of capital investment and new equipment introduction at SovElectric. First, the policies and procedures are set from above. Second, requirements for equipment are identified and the request is introduced. Third, allocations are approved, a contract agreement is made with the manufacturer, and the equipment is paid for and received. Finally, the equipment is installed and introduced to the user.

Usually the chief engineer's office at each plant is involved in the preparation of production equipment proposals, as is the chief technologist's office. Both offices identify the specifications of the required equipment. Financing decisions are commonly made by top management—that is, the director general, chief engineer, and deputy director general of economics (controller).

Capital investment proposals are also considered by the technical council, a group of about 60 people representing different departments and echelons within the enterprise: plant manager's deputies, chief engineer, managers and deputies of all technical subunits, chief designer, chief engineer of the design office plus design managers and senior specialists, tooling shop manager, chief metallurgist's and chief technologist's personnel, as well as the party secretary and union chairman, who attend for informational purposes but do not have input on technical issues. The technical council typically meets quarterly but may be convened more frequently if needed. It discusses each issue and brings it to an open vote. The plant manager and the director general of the enterprise have veto power.

In January, a list is prepared of the equipment approved for purchase along with the contracts and the time when equipment is due to arrive. The variety of capital equipment is limited, and users normally try to buy equipment that already exists. However, the industrial ministry supports a special institute that researches and develops specialized types of equipment, which is produced by a separate enterprise. SovElectric runs a specialized section for the production of certain kinds of equipment that is not produced elsewhere. This workshop employs 110 people.

GENERAL PROCEDURE

Two typical problems occur in capital equipment acquisitions at SovElectric. First, the type of equipment that will meet specifications is not always available. Second, once the appropriate equipment is chosen, it is not always easy to secure delivery. Under the system in place prior to recent economic reforms, the plants did not buy their own equipment. Because there was a rationing system (*kartochnaya sistema*), plants did not always get the equipment they wanted. At that time SovElectric was not using its own money to purchase equipment, so not much thought was given to the issue.

The deputy chief technologist in Plant V explained that equipment is allocated among the shops according to the following priorities: increasing production capacity, freeing up bottlenecks, and replacing obsolete equipment. Before economic reform, the shops would order as much equipment as possible because they did not have to pay for it themselves. Now they are more reasonable about equipment orders because they are on a self-financing system.

Information on capital equipment starts being collected by late February or early March. The shop technologists and shop managers work with the chief technologist to determine capital investment needs. By midyear the chief technologist's office receives specific orders from the shops and begins consulting with suppliers. Many managers are involved in following through on the detailed equipment-purchasing procedures mandated by the ministry. When the supplier contracts are complete, the chief technologist's office gives the detailed documentation to the construction department, which is responsible for receiving and paying for the equipment.

The party does not appear to play a significant role in capital investment decisions, nor is it involved with technical issues in general. Its function is to monitor the impact of technical decisions on workers' morale and job satisfaction. The party might become involved if a proposed piece of equipment threatened to simplify the work and reduce wages. The party secretary chairs a weekly meeting of the shop-floor party representatives and tours the shops daily to confer with them.

The union's role is to ensure that the equipment improves working conditions. When the equipment is installed, the union also helps train workers to operate it and tries to convince them to train themselves.

EASTERN EUROPEAN AUTOMATIC LINES FOR ROTORS

In 1983, the industrial ministry authorized its technical institute in Petrovsk to investigate technology that would enable Plant W to produce a new model of motor. The plant's design office provided the institute with specifications of the new motor. The institute studied the situation and recommended automatic lines from a firm in Eastern Europe that had supplied the plant with similar equipment a decade earlier. The order was placed by the Ministry of Foreign Trade office responsible for ordering equipment from abroad. The technical institute then selected the equipment as standard issue for the entire industry.

The purchase quickly ran into financial, technical, and personnel problems. Plant W actually needed a machine that was smaller and more flexible to change from one product modification to another. Moreover, while price had not been a key consideration before the purchase because capital investment funds came from the ministry, the plant had switched in the interim to self-financing and now sought a less expensive machine.

Since becoming subject to self-financing on January 1, 1988, SovElectric is extremely cost conscious. Indeed, the chief technologist at Plant W said cost has become the number one concern. As he explained, facts speak for themselves. Plant W needs nine million rubles per year for technical development, but the ministry has allocated only three million per year out of profits. At that rate it will take 25 years to replace all the equipment. Financial difficulties sprang not only from the change in financial responsibility, but also from a price increase. The equipment purchased a decade earlier had cost 600,000 rubles, but the new model cost over three times more.

In early 1987, at a meeting of the plant technical council, the plant manager proposed substituting newly developed Soviet numerical control equipment for the Eastern European automatic lines. The Soviet equipment cost only one-third as much and was more precise—precision was a particularly important consideration because the rotor is the most sensitive part of the motor. However, there was a national shortage of the numerical control equipment, and its manufacturer could not meet the demand for orders. Another drawback was that the Soviet equipment had no automatic lines, hence it required more workers and resulted in lower productivity than the Eastern European lines. Because of these factors, the order was left with the Eastern Europeans.

Still the plant was very upset about having to pay for equipment that came in over budget and was not what they wanted. "Those who are paying the piper didn't get to call the tune," said the chief technologist. To make matters worse, the plant and the import office were at odds with one another because they were evaluated according to conflicting targets. According to the chief engineer, the plant wanted to buy equipment as cheaply as possible to keep costs down, but the import office wanted to buy expensive equipment because its targets were based on the value of imported equipment. Ultimately, the plant refused to pay for the equipment; in fact, it did not have the money to pay. The bank was insisting on payment, so Plant W was in a difficult situation.

Technical problems started as soon as the equipment arrived in the spring of 1988. The Eastern European manufacturer claimed it had no space to set up the line and test it before shipment, so it sent specialists to test it on site. Because they had not been informed of the plant's specifications, they could not get the electronics working. As a result, the new automatic line sat idle for several months, and the rotor shop manager had to make do with the existing Eastern European automatic line, which was ten years old and constantly breaking down. Furthermore, the contract for receiving spare parts from the manufacturer had expired, and the adjusters had to develop unconventional ways to repair the old equipment. The director general decided to send a task force of specialists from the main plant to repair the old equipment, since the personnel on site had simply been "firefighting" the problem. He selected the most skilled of the eight adjusters from each of the seven production lines and sent them full time to Plant W. The job was successful but was only a temporary solution. The manager of the rotor section explained that his staff had been unsuccessful in repairing the equipment because there was a shortage of skilled adjusters to maintain it. It takes years of experience to do the job, and adjusters are in great demand throughout the plant as well as the country. It is difficult to attract people to the job, he said, because although the work is hard, adjusters do not earn much more than regular, less-skilled workers.

An additional complication was that the standard model ordered by the technical institute was incompatible with three other machine tools on Plant W's rotor line, and those machines would be difficult to modify. Plant W was faced with the choice of not accepting the equipment (and thereby having nothing) or accepting it and substituting manual production for the three incompatible machines. They adopted the second alternative, which required fifteen people to produce what two people formerly had produced.

In March 1989, the deputy minister of the ministry that manufactured the automatic line in Eastern Europe visited the USSR to discuss the equipment problem with the deputy minister of the industrial ministry responsible for SovElectric. N. P. Belig sent the first deputy of the chief engineer as his representative. The director general later reported that the Eastern European equipment was paid for from the ministry's budget and that SovElectric would not have accepted it if it had to pay for it itself.

THE WESTERN EUROPEAN ALUMINUM CASTING PRESS

The purchase and installation of the Western European casting machine went smoothly. The machine was the third of its kind to be installed in Plant V, so management was familiar with the technology as well as with the purchasing procedure.

The decision to allocate capital funds to the casting shop was based on the fact that casting is a critical operation. As the first step in the production process, it is a frequent bottleneck. The plant had considered a locally produced casting machine but its electronic components were of poor quality. The Western European equipment had proven effective in reducing production costs and increasing quality.

In 1985, the director general earmarked several million rubles for the casting shop and other bottleneck areas. The chief technologist's staff defined the bottlenecks, and the director general of the enterprise (who was also the Plant V manager) decided the funding allocation on the advice of the chief engineer and the deputy director general for economics. Although the chief technologist is responsible for most capital equipment, the complex areas of metallurgy and welding require special attention. In the case of the casting equipment, the chief metallurgist was in charge and reported directly to the chief engineer.

In January 1988, Plant V management prepared a preliminary agreement to purchase the equipment. In February 1988, the matter was brought before the technical council. In March, the chief metallurgist, chief of mechanical services, and the mechanical services manager of the casting shop examined the

Western European casting machine at an exhibition in Moscow and agreed to buy one. In late May, the same team went to Western Europe for a week to study the machine and receive operating instructions. The contract specified that the plant would install the equipment.

The shop-floor layout for the new machine was approved in May, and it took three to four weeks to clear and prepare the space. The casting machine arrived from Western Europe in June. Delivery was fast because the plant had ordered the standard model. The equipment cost 400,000 rubles in hard currency, and SovElectric had taken a hard currency loan from the bank at a 10% interest rate.

A special task force of 15 technicians and managers was responsible for making the new machine operational. E. A. Aleve, the deputy chief engineer responsible for industrial engineering, held a daily meeting of the task force, which included the deputy shop head for technical services, the chief of mechanical services, the chief metallurgist, and the chief of energy services. Timely completion of the project was important to Aleve because his bonus depended on it. To facilitate matters, he wrote a special order stating that everyone on the team would share a bonus of 500 rubles if the project was finished on time. The director general approved the order.

Installation went smoothly except for a problem with an electronic part. The part had worked properly at the demonstration in Western Europe, but one of the Soviet specialists discovered a glitch. He suspected the Western Europeans had intentionally caused the problem so that they would be called in to fix it. Working nights and weekends, the team had the machine producing at full capacity by September and received its bonus. The document releasing the equipment for production bears the signatures of the shop manager, the chief of mechanical services or his deputy, and the shop technologist. It is worth noting that this example of successful Soviet cross-functional cooperation seems to have worked because it was led by a senior manager designated by the enterprise director general and involved lower-level STU managers.

A COMPUTER FOR MOTOR SHOP #2

P. S. Goldman came to Plant V in February 1988, and several months later was elected to the position of manager of Motor Shop #2, responsible for assembly, testing, and shipment of motors. He soon found many problems with record-keeping in the shop, and he succeeded in getting a computer installed to alleviate the situation.

The planning department spends a lot of time calculating the load of components needed for Goldman's shop to assemble motors, and it gives him a list of orders to produce on a quarterly and monthly basis. Motor Shop #2 then calculates the number of components needed per day for assembly and makes recommendations to the plant's planning and dispatching office. The planning and dispatching office serves as a liaison between the various shops because it has an overall picture of the whole plant, including the facilities and capabilities of all the shops.

Goldman wanted a computer to help resolve two types of record-keeping problems. The first was monthly production figures. At the end of the month, his records did not match reality. It was difficult to make an exact count of the materials remaining at midnight on the last day of the month. The second problem was that the assembly line could not account for all the materials and components that came from other shops. The accounting department wanted an accurate count and made the shop take financial responsibility by preparing special documents that reflected the losses in the technical indicators and in production expense.

At the end of July 1988, Goldman discussed his record-keeping problems with an old friend in the design office. The designer advised him to ask for a computer and introduced him to a catalog of various models. The designer recommended that Goldman write a letter to the director general requesting a computer through the design office. (Under the new system of self-financing, the design office makes money this way. It reports to the director general of the enterprise but is semiautonomous. It can also sign agreements to do design work for other enterprises.)

Goldman wrote the letter a few days later. He did not ask for a particular type of equipment because that would depend on where the computer was bought. A Soviet computer would cost between 30,000 and 60,000 rubles, but he preferred a foreign model. He mentioned the computer request to the director general during a discussion of his production management problems. The director general discussed the request with the chief engineer, the manager of the computer center, and the chief technologist, and then gave his approval for the computer.

Two things were in Goldman's favor and helped him get the computer without delay. First, the chief engineer was a good friend who had hired him from another enterprise. Second, and probably more important, Motor Shop #2 produces motors for export to the West and is a generator of hard currency, which can be used to purchase foreign equipment.

A SUMMARY OF CAPITAL INVESTMENT AT SOVELECTRIC

The capital investment system has gone through a rather dramatic change under perestroika. For the first time enterprise managers are concerning themselves about the cost and effectiveness of capital equipment and beginning to take responsibility for many aspects of the decision process. We can also see the important function of groups in the capital decision process. The technical council, for example, serves an especially important purpose in the capital investment process. The council unites various separate functions under a common boss, facilitating coordination. Overall, the move to self-financing seems to have simplified and shortened the decision process.

Capital Investment at SovTruck

PLANNING FOR DEVELOPMENT OF NEW TECHNOLOGY

At SovTruck there is no single research center, but historically there has been a structure of chief specialists: chief designer, chief of energy services, chief of mechanical services, chief metallurgist, chief technologist, and so on, for a total of 15. Each chief specialist has his or her laboratories and design offices that formally report to a member of top management, usually at the level of the deputy chief engineer. This organizational structure is used for both new technology and solving operational problems.

In the 1950s, to link all the chief specialists horizontally with the departments of the enterprise involved in new technology, the position of deputy chief engineer for science and new technology of the enterprise was created. This deputy's principal duty was to organize research and development for new truck prototypes. At that time, the entire office of the deputy chief engineer for science and new technology consisted of an assistant and a secretary. As the need to solve more complex technical problems increased, however, the position of deputy director general for science and technology of the enterprise was created, and V. D. Razin was appointed to the position.

Whereas some enterprises may develop two plans, at SovTruck the consolidated plan is the basic planning document for both research and development and capital investment. It is compiled annually but includes themes and projects that span several years, so it is modified on a rolling basis. Although the planning, funding, and justification are similar for R&D and capital investment, the procedures are different for each. Thus, Razin's consolidated plan consists of four basic parts:

1. "Blue-sky" R&D for untested ventures.
2. R&D for the next product cycle.

3. Development work for prototypes and working models, new materials, equipment, and production units.
4. Introduction of new technology for production, including
   a. introduction of new models and batches,
   b. new technology for existing models.

In 1988, the consolidated plan included 530 R&D and capital investment projects, and the activities of every division of the enterprise were coordinated according to the plan.

The funds for R&D and capital investment are apportioned at a meeting of the employees' council that defines the funds for the following year. The basic criteria for the consolidated plan are that it include projects mandated by national programs, cost reduction projects, and projects that increase profit. To be included in the consolidated plan, a unit of the enterprise must submit to the science and technology department a request and list of measures for introducing progressive technology, mechanization, automation of production processes, and computer technology.

Work on the consolidated plan begins in May for the following year, and by June 1 the engineering and production units have submitted their requests and lists to the science and technology department. The requests are granted according to three sets of criteria:

1. Effectiveness for the national economy as a whole.
2. Cost reduction of the finished product calculated at the level of the enterprise.
3. Effectiveness within plants and shops.

The investment requests must also contain recommendations for sources of financing, and these recommendations must be approved by the production planning unit and various other services of the enterprise involved. However, if the investment costs less than 50,000 rubles, it is not subject to budgetary review other than verification by the financial and legal units of the science and technology department. If it is over 50,000 rubles it is sent to the financial and planning unit of the enterprise (reporting to the deputy director general of finance and chief economist, A. I. Ushinski), where it is carefully checked and revised if necessary.

Every engineering unit of the enterprise prepares for its technical council its portion of the consolidated plan, and in October–November the engineering units defend their proposals at meetings of the special council chaired by Razin. Each unit has one day to present its proposal. Then the special council sees whether the proposed project fits with research and technical programs. The special council is composed of technical specialists as well as financial officers and lawyers. The proposals are also reviewed by the national Scientific and Technological Society, which can both review and improve proposals, though its role is not very significant compared to that of the special council in the enterprise.

In December, a draft of the plan is reviewed by the technical-financial council of the enterprise, which consists of the director general, E. A. Kratov, and his two deputies: E. P. Nekrasov, chief engineer, and Razin, deputy director general for science and technology. The council meets quarterly to review only large, important projects and decides whether to create future scientific and technical programs based on the projects. The final version of the consolidated plan is cleared by Razin, Nekrasov, and Ushinski and submitted to Kratov for approval. Kratov then issues a special order for the enterprise.

As a rule the final consolidated plan is completed before the next planning year, which begins in May. However, the profit for the enterprise is determined in mid-January of the planning year, and then the capital budget must be approved by the employees' council. As a result, the consolidated plan is actually approved in early February. During the period between February and May, spending is financed on credit.

Since the consolidated plan includes projects budgeted over a multiyear period (usually not more than five years), the level of financing may change during the annual review. On average, up to 20% of the projects are cut back, though in 1987 the figure was 7%. For projects having important significance at the national or industry level, the enterprise may turn to higher agencies (the ministry and the State Committee for Science and Technology) for additional financing.

The department of science and technology is responsible for monitoring the projects, the capital investment, and the new technology plan. The plants are responsible for making short quarterly and annual reports on their projects, but there is an informal rule that if everything is going smoothly, the department for science and technology does not bother with the report. If problems arise, however, all efforts are employed to solve them. This is also the case with respect to the entire R&D and capital investment fund. If it is not overspent, then Razin does not monitor anyone, but in the case of overexpenditure, the controller, Ushinski—and if necessary, higher organizations—get involved. Razin exercises personal control over expenditure of R&D and capital investment funds received from higher organizations. He commented,

> This is an example of the informal rule that how you do something is your business and responsibility and up to your discretion as long as you are not caught breaking regulations. You are the leader of your domain of responsi-

bility. We are not supposed to, and do not, interfere when things are going smoothly. However, we will get deeply involved if things go wrong.

According to the chief engineer of Plant X, the party's role in technology is rather insignificant. At meetings on the introduction of new technology, the party secretary can say whether he or she thinks it is good or bad but has no authority to intervene from a financial perspective. The chief engineer does not recall any interference from the party secretary, although the party secretary complains about projects falling behind schedule. In fact, the party secretary may want more modern equipment to be introduced, but he or she is primarily interested in quality, as that is a political issue. The party secretary does ask the chief engineer about volume, quality, and schedules at the morning plant management meetings, at special sessions of the party committee on new technology, and in personal discussions.

LASER EQUIPMENT FOR THE ENGINE BLOCK IN PLANT X

In 1975, while serving as SovTruck's deputy chief engineer, V. D. Razin was one of four people who developed the idea of using a laser beam to strengthen the metal used in truck manufacturing. He collaborated with scientists at the laser center of a leading academy, the industrial ministry, and a prominent university. Because of the national importance of the technology, the State Committee for Science and Technology provided funding, and the university funded and produced equipment to test the capacity of the laser. The process was patented.

In 1976–1977, the enterprise began exploring ways of using the laser in its manufacturing operations and involved engineers from Plant X. They discussed the possibility of using the laser to strengthen the piston, but in 1978 decided to use it to strengthen the surface of the engine block. The engine block was one of two major bottlenecks in Plant X. The laser process would enable the cylinder to withstand a higher degree of pressure, thereby reducing the amount of metal required. The lighter weight of the engine would result in fuel economy for the truck. The process was also expected to increase the life of the engine from 250,000 to 400,000 kilometers.

Enterprise designers worked on the development of the laser for the engine block throughout 1979–1980. The project was included in the 1981 capital investment plan, which provided the necessary financial, material, and human resources. It cost one million rubles but was expected to yield a return of 1.7 million rubles a year—that is, a payback period of less than one year.

The equipment was manufactured by the laser lab of the enterprise with the help of the outside organizations involved in its earlier development. A year and a half was spent designing experimental models. An engineer from the maintenance shop of Plant X was involved in planning the installation of the laser. However, the manager of the shop that received the laser recalled that although engineers and designers visited the shop in 1982 to discuss the laser, the shop did not participate directly in development.

The laser was installed in 1985 and was used frequently at that time. It became fully operational in 1986, but very soon thereafter serious problems arose. Plant X's maintenance foreman and seven mechanics had to constantly service the equipment and make adjustments, with help from SovTruck's laser lab. Late in 1986, the shop manager and the chief engineer of the plant went to Razin for help, and the next day Razin held a meeting with the managers of the plant and the laser lab. Razin also met with outside contractors and ministry officials. Their first decision was to repair the existing laser machine, but it continued to function poorly.

Next, the chief of SovTruck's technical department held a meeting at the plant. This time dirty water was discovered and a decision was made to install filters. But the laser still failed to operate properly, and another meeting was called the next day. Acknowledging the severity of the problem, the parties agreed to study it for a week and meet again. With the chief engineer of Plant X chairing that meeting, the maintenance shop engineers prepared a set of alternatives, and the engine shop prepared data on the breakdown of the laser. The shop manager reported that the laser was idle as often as it was operative and that production volume had declined. The laser had also proven to be incapable of withstanding 24-hour operation and so could not fulfill capacity requirements.

In May 1988, after many meetings and deliberations, the enterprise approved the decision to replace the laser with a newer model that was more powerful and reliable. Razin said it took two years to discover that the problem was with the laser itself, rather than with other parts of the equipment. Although the laser was only a small component, it was the heart of the machine. It had worked well in laboratory conditions but could not withstand the temperature in the shop. The decision was made to sell the original equipment. Because it was in high demand, it was sold for three-quarters of its cost.

A NEW SANDBLASTING MACHINE FOR PLANT X

Since 1970, SovTruck's Plant X machining shop had used a sandblasting machine that cleaned metal filings from the lubrication channels of the crankshaft by spraying a mixture of sand and water under pressure into the channels. The crankshaft had an unusual configuration in which metal particles tended to accumulate, and it was important to remove these particles because they could destroy the bearings and stop the engine from operating.

By the early 1980s, the high pressure in the hydraulic mechanism caused the sandblasting machine to break down. Quality control found that the breakdown created two problems. First, on inspecting the engines visually as well as with magnets, it found a large quantity of metal filings in the crankshaft. Second, the high pressure could itself damage the machined surface and cause defects to the crankshaft.

On quality control's initiative, the shop manager asked the mechanics to repair the machine, but the limited measures they took failed to solve the problem. In 1985, quality control finally refused to accept the defective parts, thereby creating a bottleneck in the machining shop.

The manager of quality control and the chief engineer of Plant X studied the problem. The manager of quality control believed that the design of the sandblasting machine was defective because it could not withstand the pressure. So the team got the plant manager's support to request a more advanced replacement from the deputy director general for science and technology at headquarters. Team members discussed the idea with the designers in SovTruck's department of custom (nonstandard) equipment, who agreed they could design it. They also enlisted the support of SovTruck's chief technologist.

The chief engineer of Plant X recommended presenting the request as a quality improvement, and the plant manager took the matter to the chief engineer of the enterprise, who readily understood the importance of improving the quality of the product. The controller's office estimated that the machine in good working order would result in savings of 100,000 rubles. Managers from the enterprise level met at the plant and agreed to help speed up the process of getting the new machine. In late 1985, in accordance with established procedure, Plant X submitted a request for the equipment, signed by the chief engineer and the chief technologist of the plant. The enterprise approved the request.

The plant immediately began a search for an outside plant that could manufacture the machine. However, no plant could meet its quality standards. Engineers in Plant X spent the next year preparing the technical documentation required for the appropriation request. Six weeks later, SovTruck's scientific and technical council approved the request as part of Plant X's annual plan and allocated 15,000 rubles for the initial stages of development. Total cost of the equipment was in excess of 100,000 rubles.

The chief engineer of the enterprise agreed to have the equipment manufactured in-house and issued an administrative order to that effect.

Three units of the enterprise were involved in the installation of the new sandblasting machine—the machine-tool installation unit, the construction unit, and the engineering and technical support unit. Because units within the enterprise cannot force other units to start work or to speed up, the deputy chief engineer of the enterprise was appointed by the director general as the responsible coordinator of the project. The chief engineer of Plant X said that this individual performed the task very effectively. Not only did he have the necessary formal authority, but he had previously worked at Plant X. The line people whose support he needed knew him, respected his knowledge, and appreciated his eagerness to help them. Among other things he assisted them in preparing a schedule to coordinate the installation. The development plan was to be completed in 1987, the machine was to be manufactured in 1988, installed by August 31 and tested by October 1 of that year, and made fully operational by 1989.

B. F. Kirpichev, the chief of production development (preparation of production) in Plant X, was coordinator of the project within the plant. Preparations on the shop floor for the sandblasting machine involved dismantling and removing the old equipment, digging a pit for the foundation, building the foundation, and providing electricity and water. The manager of the repair shop noted that his crew had begun work on the electrical connections in early 1987, before they received the formal order. They started in advance because it is very difficult to alter the connections once the machine is installed.

Kirpichev drew up a detailed schedule, which he distributed to all participants. They returned their comments, and he called a meeting to discuss the schedule. Once they came to an agreement, the schedule was approved by the deputy chief engineer of the enterprise as overall coordinator.

The sandblasting machine was manufactured in April 1988, but the plant was far from ready to install it because the pit for the foundation had been started only the month before. Kirpichev admitted that it was mostly the plant's fault that it was not ready in time. The facilities were old and production volume had been dropping. There were three plant managers in the past six months, and there was also a shortage of workers to do the job.

From March through August 1988, Kirpichev held four coordinating meetings to clarify the work schedule and solve problems. Representatives from the enterprise, the plant, and the shop that would receive the sandblasting machine attended, usually seven or eight people in all. The meetings usually lasted about half an hour. At a meeting at the end of April, Kirpichev prepared a schedule with May 10 as the completion date. An experienced designer, however, argued that it would take until the end of August. At first Kirpichev was shocked, but after the meeting he started to believe the designer was right. It turned out that he was.

A big problem involved finding workers to prepare the site for the sandblasting machine. The enterprise refused to assign its construction unit, saying it was a relatively small job. This meant that Plant X had to use its own workers. A few people from the plant's housekeeping unit helped dig the pit, but most of the work was done by production workers whose official job was to make crankshafts. Kirpichev noted that the practice of using line workers to do extra jobs such as construction had been common in the plant for decades. However, this is an expensive way to get the work done because the workers are paid overtime at a higher hourly wage than the relatively unskilled work is worth. The inability of Plant X to solve the problem directly with the construction unit is an example of the difficulty in implementing lateral relations.

Several problems developed. First, because the production line was not to be stopped during installation of the equipment, the pit had to be dug on weekends when the line was not operating. But when production fell behind schedule, the line was put into weekend operation. Each time this happened it delayed installation by a week. The digging crew tried to make up for lost time by working late at night or early in the morning when the line was shut down. Despite these efforts, delays continued. Kirpichev believed that it was very difficult to modernize such an old facility without shutting down the production line. To dig the pit, for example, workers had to move ten machines.

A second problem involved obtaining the workers to do the installation. The shop manager was unhappy about having his people do the digging because it was not their job, and he cooperated only reluctantly. It was also hard to predict the number of workers who would actually report for the job. Five might volunteer, but only one or two would actually show up.

On one occasion there were no workers available because they had been reassigned to a rush job to install ventilation boxes. The union had urged that the boxes be installed for workers' safety, but management had put it off until it suddenly realized it was about to have a meeting with the union on the issue. At that point, plant management made the ventilation boxes top priority to ensure it had complied with the union's request. This is an indication of the union's area of responsibility and authority.

In spite of the difficulties, the sandblasting machine was finally installed in August. The Soviet managers had demonstrated their ability, given time, to cope with shortages; but at the same time they had revealed some of the problems created by a lack of effective lateral mechanisms among STUs. Kirpichev, the plant-level coordinator, was a staff manager and did not seem to be able to secure the needed support from other STUs such as construction.

EQUIPMENT FOR THE VORTICAL CHANNEL ENGINE CYLINDER AT PLANT X

In 1984, in accordance with a national quality improvement plan, SovTruck issued an order for the next five-year plan to redesign its gasoline engine to reduce fuel consumption by 6 to 7%. Enterprise designers proposed changes in the configuration of the fuel combustion cell and the fuel line, and the vortical channel engine cylinder was designed. This in turn required a different configuration of the casting and new machining of the cylinder head, so corresponding changes were made in the carburetor and distributor. The first experimental batch of 100 engines was produced in 1984 and generated the expected fuel savings. As a result, the truck's industry rating improved, and the enterprise received additional financing for the project. Plant X was in favor of the project because the improved engine would be more durable and reduce the need for production of spare parts. The chief engineer of the plant worked closely with the designers during the development stage.

This was a major project costing 500,000 rubles; 100,000 of that sum was earmarked for Plant X. Because the benefits of the new engine were calculated at the enterprise level and several units in the enterprise were involved, the project was coordinated at the enterprise level by the chief engineer and the chief technologist, who set deadlines for the major phases of the work.

The order for new equipment and tooling was included in the 1985 consolidated plan for the development of science and technology and capital investment for the enterprise. Plant X was to manufacture the vortical channel and needed new equipment to machine the new engine block and perform other operations. Existing equipment also had to be modernized. In 1985, the enterprise issued an administrative document developed jointly with Plant X and agreed on by the other units involved. Plant X then developed detailed schedules for implementation with the agreement of the other units and prepared a document. It was critical to meet the tight deadline if the truck were to qualify in the national quality improvement campaign. Headquarters and plant personnel would lose their bonuses if they failed to meet the deadline.

Several problems arose in introducing the new equipment for the vortical channel engine cylinder. One problem developed because the plant that supplied castings to Plant X experienced delays in getting the proper tooling. The casting plant, too, had to deal with the problem of shortage. This affected Plant X adversely, and in late 1985 the chief engineer asked Razin, the deputy director general for science and technology of the enterprise, to extend the deadline. Razin called a meeting of half a dozen people—including the plant's chief engineer, representatives from the casting plant, and specialists involved in key phases of the project—and decided not to extend the deadline. Instead, he authorized funds for a new casting machine that would use a different technology from the one that was causing problems.

Another problem involved getting the cooperation of the enterprise's tooling shop. Again, this was a failure in lateral relations. Initially, the tooling for the new equipment needed by Plant X was assigned to the tool shop and included in its plan. However, because the interplant transfer prices and tariffs made the project unprofitable for the tool shop, it was not interested in doing the job and held the work up in every way possible. The manager of the tooling shop explained that it was more profitable to manufacture the equipment itself than to manufacture the tooling it required. The shop agreed to do the tooling provided it was officially designated as equipment and charged as capital rather than expense. The chief engineer of Plant X explained that his plant initially designated the tooling as an expense rather than as a capital investment in order to speed up the project. The manager of Plant X's technical office asked the manager of the technical department of the enterprise to force the tool shop to fulfill the order; he was unsuccessful.

The matter was put before a dispute settlement commission chaired by Razin. Members of the commission were the deputy director for production preparation of Plant X, the deputy manager of the tool shop, and four tooling specialists involved in the development of the new engine block. The chief engineer of Plant X recalled that the tool shop representatives were so insistent that the dispute settlement commission decided not to argue with them. The commission rewrote the order as a capital item, and the tool shop produced the tooling. It was clear in this instance that skilled workers such as toolmakers have significant power when they control production processes that others depend on.

Other difficulties arose when the tool shop began installing the tooling in Plant X. In order to meet their deadline, the tooling specialists did their work quickly and left. But plant management did not accept their job as complete or sufficiently precise. It wanted the tooling specialists to stay until everything worked properly. The two sides were deadlocked and searched for a compromise. Plant X finally agreed to accept the tooling shop's work as long as it was approved by the designers. The engine plant mechanics would then take care of the minor remaining problems. The tooling shop also resisted when the production people in Plant X pressed them to make the equipment compatible with existing technology. This would take more time and the tooling workers wanted to finish the job quickly. The chief engineer and the designers pushed them to make the equipment to their specifications and the work finally had to be monitored by the chief technologist and the chief engineer of the enterprise.

Because of shortage of capacity to meet planning targets, the modernization of existing equipment and installation of new equipment were to be done without interrupting current production. Crews worked primarily on the weekends, but some production stoppages occurred in order to keep within the schedule. In such cases the deputy manager of the mechanical repair shop would determine on the spot what could be done to meet the deadline. In addition, the project manager, the deputy chief of tooling, the deputy chief of maintenance, and sometimes the chief engineer of Plant X would work on the job site on Sundays to solve problems on the spot.

SUMMARY OF CAPITAL INVESTMENT AT SOVTRUCK

These cases illustrate the difficulties in coordinating various lateral functions to implement capital investment projects at SovTruck. The heads of the units had to rely on going up the line to a common boss to achieve coordination between separate STUs. Problems were created by shortages of critical supplies and labor, and the ingenuity of managers and workers was instrumental in overcoming adverse conditions.

Conclusions on the Capital Investment Process in the United States and the USSR

Both the United States and the USSR use an annual capital investment budget as a key to their capital investment decision process. But apart from this significant common denominator, their practices diverge.

The hierarchical starting point for capital investment is different in the two systems. In the USSR the process starts at the top—at the level of national priorities that are defined for each industry by the relevant ministry. The capital priorities are passed by the ministry to the enterprise level through a statement of national priorities and allocation of capital for the year. The message moves down to the plant level, where specific projects are defined and proposed. Then the proposals move back up to the enterprise level where they are approved or rejected if within the allocation, or referred to the ministry for approval if needed.

In contrast, the process in the United States starts at the bottom of the organization where people are in direct contact with the market's needs and the competitor's initiatives. At the level of plant management, and even at the level of the hourly employees at AmTruck, people are given a general sense of what is possible, and with this in mind they develop capital project proposals. These hundreds of proposals move from the bottom upward through a review process. At the top they are studied in terms of feasibility, rank ordered, and approved up to the limit of available capital. The approvals then move down again to start the capital equipment purchasing process. However, funds are not finally committed until each project is separately approved at the appropriation stage. Then the purchasing starts and in due course is reported upward to be compared against the budget. The point of difference is the starting point. In the USSR it tends to be triggered by national priorities and in the United States by market and competitive conditions.

The two systems can also be characterized by the rules that specify the number of check points that proposals must pass before they go forward. The number of such checks is large in the USSR, but tends to vary in the United States. The procedures for approval in the USSR are mandated from the level of the ministry or higher for funds that come from the ministry, from the bank if the funds come from the bank, or within the enterprise itself if it uses its own funds. Rules specify in detail who needs to approve each project and in what order. At AmElectric, the number of such check points for projects almost rivaled the number in the USSR. At AmTruck, the number was much fewer. In the USSR the procedure called for the necessary documents to be passed from office to office in a sequential approval process. It was more customary in the United States for approval to result from a meeting in which various specialists gathered at one time to review and act together on a capital project. The rules for approval in the USSR emphasized one financial test—the number of years before the investment would pay out. In the United States, a number of financial tests were used. In addition to the test of net present value emphasized by US theory, the two US firms we studied used tests of the length of payout, an investment return hurdle rate, a test of return against the corporate average, and a test of levels of risk.

In both countries, various informal practices were used to supplement or circumvent the formal approval process. This was seen at AmElectric in the FMS situation when the sponsor gained the support of the corporate chairman through informal channels. In the USSR this happened at SovTruck in regard to the laser equipment and the purchase of a computer. In both systems there was a certain amount of gaming about the capital budget, but it took different forms. In the United States it was seen in the product transfer project when a number of projects were packaged together to seek approval under the priority of "safety." In the USSR various projects were put forward for approval under the banner of the current national priority. The one organization where such gaming or the use of informal channels was not seen was AmTruck. The simpler rules followed there plus the high level of trust and flexibility the firm had cultivated among different levels of the hierarchy seemed to eliminate the need for these practices.

The capital-investment decision process in both countries was not error proof. The most conspicuous error seen in the United States was the Tekcontrol equipment purchase at AmTruck. The biggest error in the USSR was the purchase of the Eastern European machine tools at SovElectric. It may not be coincidental that both episodes involved the investment decision being made at the top of the organization: at the ministry level in the USSR and at the corporate level at AmTruck. According to the US theory described in Chapter 4, the best place to make such decisions is at the level where the relevant information is concentrated. In each of these cases, this would be at the plant or shop level. This theory was ignored in each case—and at a cost. The high-level decision in the USSR was part of the standard procedure, while at AmTruck it was an exception.

The discussion of investment errors draws attention to the level at which capital investment decisions are typically made in the two systems. The pattern in each system is obvious but it is worth highlighting. Capital investment decisions are usually made at a higher organizational level in the USSR than in the United States. Most of these decisions are made at the ministry level in the USSR and at the corporate level in the United States. However, we saw this beginning to change in the USSR. Now managers at the plant and enterprise level are beginning to take a more active interest in capital equipment decisions. Under self-financing, the managers at lower levels see that they have an important stake in the process. Again, AmTruck practiced the most radical decentralization: the cam lobe mill decision was virtually made by the production workers themselves.

The system of CL/GD in combination with STUs has numerous strengths, but one of its shortcomings is that it requires decisions that affect several units and specialties in an organization be made by the shared common boss. Lateral cooperation is difficult at best. In the case of the tool shop, self-financing seemed to make lateral cooperation even worse. In contrast, in the United States the development of a legitimate way for peers to make decisions together on a direct lateral contact basis makes such escalation to superiors unnecessary. This practice not only saves time and paperwork but, more important, it puts the decision in the hands of the people who have the greatest expertise on the subject. In the United

States, this lateral decision was seen in the product transfer and FMS cases at AmElectric and in the Plant D budget-cutting case at AmTruck.

Generally, US managers had a preference for buying capital equipment from outside vendors, while Soviet managers were often forced by shortages of outside supplies to secure equipment from another unit of their own enterprise. The Soviet phenomenon of self-supply has developed from the lack of a specialized machine-tool industry. It is admittedly an inefficient system that can result in costly equipment. Purchasers of equipment can be much more demanding of outside suppliers than of a sibling division within one's firm. And being demanding can influence all elements of the purchase including delivery, quality, and price. This contrast can be seen in the comparison between the Tekcontrol episode and the Eastern European machine-tool case.

The reason for the different perspectives in the "make or buy" decisions is probably clear but needs emphasis. Many decisions in the USSR are influenced significantly by the constant reality of shortages. With time, the perestroika reforms can change this situation, but it will not happen overnight. The situation in the United States is the opposite: overcapacity is the norm.

Chapter 9

New Product Introduction

New Product Introduction in the United States

[*Editors' note:* This section reviews the general approach to new product introduction in the United States. Because it has been prepared primarily for Soviet readers, much of the material may be familiar to Americans. It is followed by examples of new product introduction observed at AmElectric and AmTruck.]

The ability of US firms to develop and manufacture new products on a constant basis is so critical to their long-term success that most firms have installed systematic procedures for managing the process and making the required decisions. The somewhat haphazard process of the past followed three sequential steps: design, manufacture, and sell. But too often that approach led to the production of goods that customers did not buy. Today most firms have placed marketing at the front end of a four-step process that features three or four review points between the steps.

The first step focuses on the idea or concept. Ideas for new products and new businesses are solicited from all parts of the organization as well as from customers. Viable concepts are channeled into a new product department where specialists help develop them into preliminary business plans. This involves both market and technical feasibility assessments. If a proposal looks promising, it is added to the set of such concept proposals to be reviewed and assigned priority by a top-level new product committee that represents a variety of organizational functions. This committee provides general guidance to the entire new product process.

If the concept gains support in the review, it moves to the second step, product design. The best designs emerge when marketing experts and technical experts learn to collaborate in design work. Their preliminary designs are reviewed by product engineers for manufacturability in terms of cost, quality, durability, and so forth and are redesigned as needed. The improved design is then analyzed to estimate unit costs, sales price, margins, sales volume, and potential net returns for several years out. At this point, a promising design and business plan is sent back to the new product committee for its second—and probably most important—review.

If the design and business plan passes its second review, it moves into the testing stage. Many large firms have prototype development and testing departments staffed with product and process engineers and technicians. Often these innovators must devise new manufacturing methods as well as refine the design to make its production practical. As prototypes are produced in sufficient quantity, they are usually submitted to a market field test to see if they attract customers and perform properly in regular use. The results of both laboratory and field tests are used to revise the product as necessary and develop a full-scale business plan based on more accurate assessment of cost and market potential. If the prospects are still promising, the new product committee gives the product a third review to see if it merits an investment in full-scale manufacturing and marketing.

The fourth step is the move to full-scale production on a regular basis. Now careful attention is paid to the details of coordinating quality control, inventory buildup, product promotion and advertising, distribution channels, and sales launch. Often a product manager is assigned full time to manage the process directly with the many functional specialists who will be involved. Under the product manager's leadership, representatives of all the necessary functions may form a business team. Some new-product business teams are temporary, but others become permanent product teams and are the beginning of a matrix structure.

At any of the four steps a project can be dropped. Many more projects start the process than complete it. The key is to make mistakes on a small scale and successes on a large scale. At each step of the process, the firm is "buying" more information that can increase its certainty about the outcome. Further, the review committee has the option, at any stage, to send the project back to repeat an earlier step or to put it on hold awaiting other developments in technology or market opportunity. Naturally, the new product process is handled differently by industries serving consumer versus industrial markets; it varies too with degrees of technological sophistication and levels of capital requirements.

New Product Introduction at AmElectric

CONTEXT

As we discussed in Chapter 5, few power plants have been built since the boom days of the 1960s. The fuel crises in the 1970s halted plans for new power-plant construction, and power utilities focused on increasing the efficiency of existing plants. Thus the operations division of AmElectric had to find new outlets for its products. Demand came primarily in the form of replacement parts and improved parts for the existing 956 power plants built by AmElectric.

AmElectric customers specify a number of criteria for replacement parts, not because of the actual cost of the parts, which may be small, but because of their effect on power-plant operating costs. Perhaps the most important criterion for the power company is the reliability of the part. An unexpected breakdown or malfunction in a power plant may cause a forced outage. When the power-generating station is shut down because of failure, the company must provide its customers with electricity by buying it from other power stations at extremely high rates. A forced power outage may cost up to $1 million a day. A second criterion is the durability of the product and its required maintenance schedule. All power stations have a schedule of planned outages, times when the plant is shut down for regular generator maintenance and replacement of parts. While planned outages are not as expensive as forced outages, anything that either lengthens the time between power outage or shortens the downtime necessary for replacement and maintenance is likely to meet with substantial customer interest. A third criterion is delivery time. Though the schedule of planned outages allows AmElectric to provide needed parts well in advance, the possibility of a forced outage means the customer may need replacement parts at a moment's notice.

Other factors affect the customer's buying habits. For example, some power companies in the United States are publicly held and receive reinvestment funds through a government budget. This means that the budget for parts may be canceled or reworked depending on the state's financial position. When most of the plants were built, states and municipalities had substantial funds, so each utility commission requested a "custom" generating station. This means that the power plants built by AmElectric are not standardized, and even the simplest replacement parts may have hundreds of design modifications based on the different plant designs.

Lack of standardization caused complaints among many of the product engineers. A simple order for replacement blades could require the engineer to consult more than 20 documents (the original plus numerous technological modifications). A worker on the line complained that often when he got the working kit (a set of tools and parts) from supply for a given order, the parts and tools provided were not those needed for the particular blade or rotor he was machining. This unwieldy system was scheduled for a major streamlining via computerization. One marketing manager took a positive view of the complex maze of design drawings, pointing out that, "If someone steals an engineering design of our chief competitor, they can make the part with no problem. If they steal our engineering draft designs, they probably can't make the part because they don't have all the necessary modifications."

Finally, while it used to be a "given" that power utilities with AmElectric plants would buy AmElectric parts, some AmElectric customers were now buying replacement parts from both domestic and foreign competitors.

These changes in the marketplace forced AmElectric to become more aggressive in its new product development. In its earlier days, AmElectric was considered an imitator that waited for its main competitor to make modifications and then copied them. However, in the scramble for business, AmElectric introduced an elaborate new-product planning system in the early 1980s (see Exhibits 9.1 and 9.2). The process includes four steps:

1. Situation analysis: marketplace environment, competitive issues, product line, customer perceptions, product performance.
2. Investigation of areas of opportunity: potential for product value-added (improved availability, reduced maintenance, efficiency improvement, and so forth), market potential, financial goals, engineering and manufacturing capability.
3. Conceptualization: ideas and seed money, make-or-buy decision, engineering and conceptual designs, manufacturing review, commercial strategy.
4. Commercialization: financial objectives, priority setting, customer benefits, engineering and design review, marketing strategy, initial order.

This outlines the ideal process; in practice, product introduction may jump phases or cycle back to earlier phases.

A typical new product takes one to two years to make its way through the process, but some can take as little as six to eight months or as many as four years.

SITUATION ANALYSIS

New product ideas are evaluated according to many criteria: customer satisfaction, potential market, contribution to margin, earliest ship year, re-

EXHIBIT 9.1 AmElectric New-Product Development Process

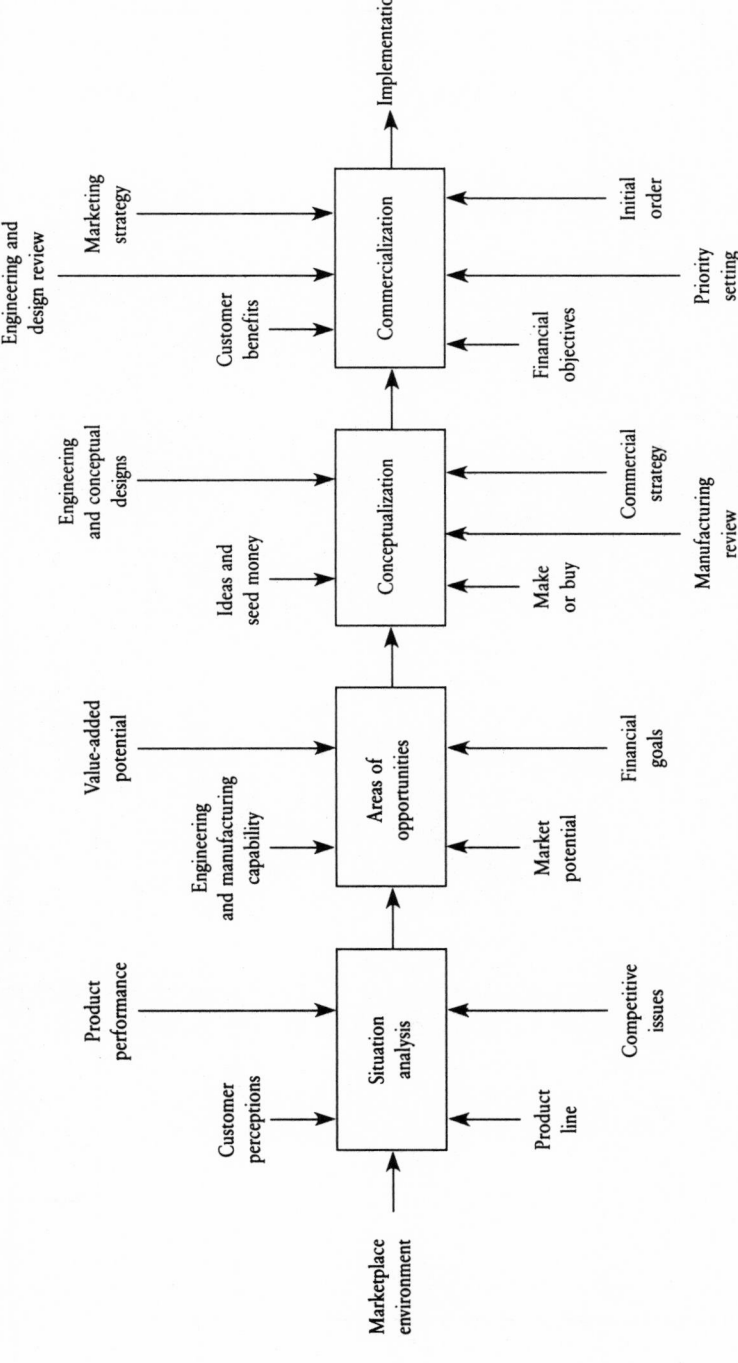

EXHIBIT 9.2 AmElectric's New-Product Investment Model

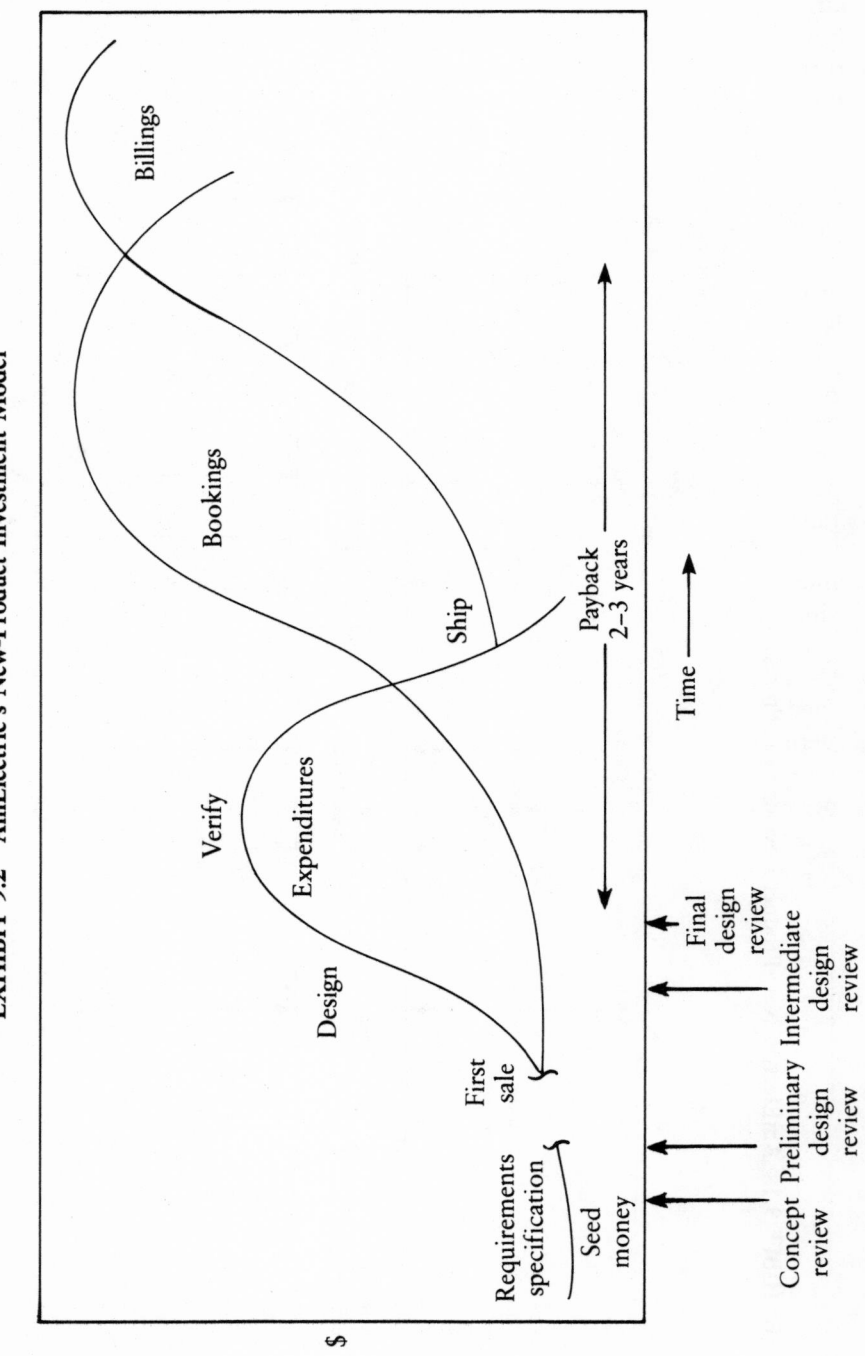

sources requirements (engineering, manufacturing, marketing skills), number of units for break-even, payback years, new technology requirements, return on resources, and so forth. A new product is defined as one that requires significant effort and funding to design and develop. Therefore, an extensively modified existing product could be classified as "new," while a totally new product that is low cost and low risk would not be so classified.

In theory, marketing plays a key role in the development of new products. It aims to get close to the customer and stay abreast of industry trends and competitors' offerings. New product introduction ostensibly begins with marketing's forecasts but in practice marketing has difficulty fulfilling this role because engineering and production staff often doubt the validity of the information marketing provides.

At the time of our study, we were told that marketing's forecasts often had been inaccurate. Some plant personnel felt they knew customers better because they worked with the utilities on operating problems. Tension between marketing and the production organization was exacerbated by an organizational structure that split marketing off from the rest of the power systems production group. This led to a lot of finger pointing and miscommunication. The problem was partially corrected in 1988 when the parts business manager joined the power systems group staff as a marketing liaison. In another effort to close the gap with marketing, the parts manager at Plant A hired a marketing representative for blading from headquarters and trained her in the plant's systems for three weeks. With her substantial engineering and plant experience, she served as the focal point for blading changes. This procedure cut down on "being inundated with inane, trivial, unprepared requests for quotes from the commercial staff," said Plant A's manager of advanced planning and manufacturing information.

AREAS OF OPPORTUNITY

The business development group at AmElectric operations divisional headquarters coordinated marketing, engineering, and plants; it also initiated new product introductions based on information from marketing. For instance, a customer complaint about a blade cracking created an impetus for a new product. The business development group got approval for seed money to evaluate new product feasibility (in this case, $100,000 seed money for a $5-million project). The business development group manager requested that his boss release some engineers to develop paper studies and computer simulations. At any given time, about 10 engineers were working full time in new product development, and other engineers worked on these projects in addition to their regular responsibilities.

Unfortunately, although the business development manager was very dependent on this group, he sometimes had to "plead with them to work on new ideas." The business development group had a hard time spending all its seed money ($1 million in 1988). One problem was getting enough good new ideas. Only 40 products were under consideration at the time of our study. The manager of technology explained that he had to create a climate for productivity: "You can't simply mandate to an engineer: 'You *will* come up with three creative ideas this week.' " Another problem was that engineers did not want to work on a concept that might be shelved, so they avoided risky ideas.

Engineers and production people also complained that there was no priority system among marketing's new product plans. One senior engineer commented, "There are simply too many projects we *have* to do." However, marketers claimed that dealing with the many projects should simply be a management problem of trading off long-term error reduction and product improvement with the need to meet current production goals.

CONCEPTUALIZATION

At AmElectric, the conceptual design provides information on performance characteristics, cost, and delivery. Once the conceptual design is prepared on paper, the decision is made about whether to manufacture the product; so a few thousand dollars of seed money can be the basis on which the firm undertakes a multimillion-dollar product investment. The new-product development group then works with manufacturing to determine the price for the product.

One serious problem in product engineering has been accountability for new product design. In February 1988, the manager of engineering commissioned a task force of five of his top performers to study the design review process. Over a three-month period the task force interviewed nearly everyone in the product engineering group (some 300 engineers, technicians, and managers) to map the existing situation and gain input about the problem. Marketing's views were solicited also. Frustration with the current situation was so great that the interviews lasted far longer than planned, some continuing into the night. The task force produced a lengthy report with 37 categories for performance improvement. The biggest single issue was "ownership": when six people signed a design change order, no one knew who was responsible. In one case of a product field breakdown, no one could identify the engineer whose design failed because the design was done "by committee." This also meant that management was unable to distinguish the skilled engineers from the poor ones.

The engineering manager wanted to instill pride of ownership in his staff: "The engineer owns that drawing. This is essential." His solution was to have the project boss sign the document. This proposal met with opposition from engineers, who felt it threatened their independence, and from the bosses, who feared the responsibility.

The design review report raised other issues around the limits of authority, elimination of errors on the most important tasks, the extent to which procedures were being followed, quality of management skills in engineering, and how to best use resources. The engineering manager concluded that the "very negative report detected cancer" but that it was "not terminal."

COMMERCIALIZATION

AmElectric will not develop a new product unless it can be sure of enough demand to justify the investment. Therefore new product proposals are taken to various customers to see if the customers are willing to "fund" product development. New products are priced to earn a quick return because they are unlikely to have a long life (i.e., new modifications will supplant them). AmElectric provides the customer with information on performance, delivery, and price, and the customer bases its decision to sign a contract on that information. Customer negotiations may take six months, and changes to the conceptual design are usually proposed. After the contract is signed, the project is translated into goals and schedules to determine lead times for manufacturing. The plant's manager of manufacturing planning is aware of the product idea before the seed money document is prepared, and he or she gives input on cost in the conceptual design stage. He or she delegates production responsibility and holds biweekly meetings to get updates and to help staff as necessary. However, Plant A's manufacturing planning manager notes the difficulty of the process: "It is impossible to quantify all the variables on market, cost, and price. There is always a risk involved, and it gets down to gut feeling."

Once a new product is approved for development, there is a need to coordinate the functional roles involved. Members of the product engineering organization perform the coordinating function. They prepare flow charts to track the schedules of various phases of the project and assign responsibility for them to appropriate functional groups. Key personnel from each functional group (marketing, product engineering, and so forth) meet monthly to discuss progress and make decisions. The composition of the group changes according to the phase of the project. For instance, marketing personnel may dominate at the early stages, design engineers at design stage, and plant manufacturing engineers at the production stage. The meeting location depends on the location of the majority of the members. For example, during the production phase, meetings take place in the plant.

The 1988 reorganization of the operations division was expected to help coordinate the headquarters engineering schedule with the manufacturing schedule. Both engineering and the plants will now report to the division manager.

THE RUGGEDIZED BLADE PROGRAM

Ruggedized is a term denoting a more durable component. There are three categories of ruggedized products: rotors, moving blades, and stationary blades. A ruggedized blade is generally shorter, thicker, and heavier than its predecessor and has a bigger "root" (the part that holds the blade in the turbine). The ruggedized program has been ongoing for several years and offers three advantages: (1) it resolves certain technical problems, (2) it constitutes a quantum improvement in technology, and (3) it results in a superior product that can be marketed strategically to fend off European competitors and gain more business.

A major ruggedized project is Building Block 72 (BB72). In the project number, 70 refers to low-pressure turbines, and 2 refers to the last two rows of blades. Blades are the most critical component of turbines, and the last row of blades is the most important row. This row is most susceptible to problems because moisture collects on it in the power generation process. Malfunctioning blades in the last row can have catastrophic consequences for a turbine. If one blade breaks, it can be sucked into the turbine and destroy all the remaining rows of blades, causing millions of dollars worth of damage. Furthermore, the last row of blades poses the greatest engineering challenge. Because it is relatively expensive and has a large potential market, BB72 is a high-priority project with a shorter than usual product development cycle. Production will be on an overtime schedule for the first three years to meet the initial demand for retrofitting turbines. Demand will then moderate and become more manageable.

The BB72 ruggedized program was initiated in response to customer complaints. Five turbine generators using blades of the original 1962 design had recently experienced breakage in the last two rows. A major utility that owned three of the units complained to AmElectric top management. Engineering tried to modify the existing design with little success. A new conceptual design had been done in 1985, but at that time no customers were willing to pay for the new product (they wanted it under the warranty agreement).

In 1987, several customers (utilities) visited Plant A to discuss the problem. Representatives from division, shop operations, and engineering did a "show and tell" of the hardware of similar ruggedized blades and highlighted the manufacturing and verification processes. In September 1987, the manager of commercial programs and policies, Fred Hart, commissioned a study of the funding, manpower, and production resources that would be needed. He assigned Don Jewel, a commercial group representative, to gather information on the costs of similar existing products from cost accounting, as well as production information from the plants. Dr. Ravi Prasad, a turbine engineering adviser, gathered data on the engineering aspects of the proposal. The plan took two months to prepare; Hart then took the proposal to corporate headquarters where it was approved in November. The development costs for the BB72 program were in excess of $7 million.

Prasad and Jewel became the two program managers of BB72. Prasad coordinated engineering development of the new design, and Jewel coordinated commercial policy and customer support. Jewel's responsibilities included ensuring that the product was delivered on time and within budget. He would also develop commercial policies for the blade when it was introduced to the rest of the industry. Jewel had been working full time on the project since September 1987.

At the same time, marketing finished preparation of a list of all potential customers and a requirements specification that utilized significant input from design engineering.

In March 1988, the first major customer signed a contract to purchase BB72 ruggedized blades. At that point, the formal design and development cycle was established.

Finally, in April 1988, the manager of engineering at the division determined that coordination of testing and manufacturing with design engineering should be kept in the engineering department. Prasad was replaced as project manager by two engineers from that department, who coordinated manufacturing schedules, drafting, and budgets and held regular meetings with people involved. At Plant A, the manager of advance planning was notified officially by Jewel in April 1988 to start the full-scale development and production of the new ruggedized blade.

Starting in April Jewel held meetings twice a month with personnel working on BB72; 10 or 12 people usually attended. Because there were hundreds working on the project, coordination was a major challenge. The fundamental problem was scheduling to meet the delivery date: not everyone accepted the schedule set by engineering. Jewel had had running battles with the plant over their different priorities. For instance, the shop operations manager at Plant A, Norman Pickford, was unwilling to put the blades into production before testing was complete, but Jewel insisted that production begin in order to meet the promised delivery date. Jewel called Paul Parks, the plant manager, and after a long conversation promised to pay for any defective blades due to engineering problems out of his marketing budget. Plant A then began producing the blades.

Jewel also managed a conflict over the production of a mixed tuning blade. Pickford, Plant A shop operations manager, was reluctant to spend funds on a special die to make the blade because he had other needs for the money. When Jewel's boss two levels up "reminded" Pickford's plant manager, Parks, that the die machine was essential in meeting the promised delivery schedule, Parks ordered Pickford to get the die.

Jewel included design engineering representatives in his meetings with production people. This gave the designers a preliminary look at the existing technology and the problems that production people were facing. Feedback resulted in design changes that otherwise would not have been made at such an early stage.

At AmElectric, conflicts between design engineering and production occur routinely throughout most projects and are usually resolved at regular meetings. Final product design tends to be the result of compromise between the two groups. In the BB72 project, design engineers tended to have the final say because AmElectric authorities had charged them with solving the blade breakage problem. For example, there was disagreement over a blade root design. Production was unhappy: the root design was costly, time-consuming, and hard to produce because it took a lot of grinding. Production was familiar with the component, which had been featured on previous products, so they complained early in the project (late 1987), calling for a new design. But other designs failed to solve the problem of stress on the root. Design engineering went to the production boss, Dom Short, and insisted that only its proposed design could be used. Short held a meeting with the plant manager within a week and the proposed design was kept. Despite the conflicts, the BB72 project in mid-1988 was on schedule to meet its delivery date; the new product appeared to have a lot of promise.

AN ORDERING SYSTEM FOR COUPLING BOLT

A new way of processing orders for coupling bolts resulted in a reduction of delivery time from over three months to a single week. The impetus was competitive pressure. AmElectric had been losing market share to Asian competitors who could provide quick delivery. Carl Bullock, the Plant A parts manager, wanted to institute a computer-integrated manufacturing

(CIM) system. The CIM cell is a parts-ordering system that stores and produces thousands of drawings.

Bullock visited division headquarters in May 1987 to persuade Steve Kinicki, manager of parts, to give him the money for a CIM cell. Impressed by the potential reduction of lead time, Kinicki agreed to fund the project, although his office was not a typical funding source for plant projects. The appropriation took six weeks to prepare, however, and was not submitted to business headquarters until July 1987. Plant personnel became frustrated by the subsequent slowness of the approval process because the return on investment promised to be excellent, and the cost of the equipment was relatively small. Although Jeremy Thatcher verbally approved the project, standard AmElectric procedures had to be followed. Furthermore, many people involved in computers at headquarters repeatedly asked technical questions of plant personnel. The delay was also due to poor preparation of the appropriation request. Jeb Boxer, manager of technical services in business headquarters, had to have the plant staff rewrite it because it was vague and incomplete. The system finally became operational in January 1988, even though formal approval was not granted until May 1988.

The new ordering system has led to increased sales and many customer compliments. Said the manager of parts and materials, "It used to be that about 16 people had to handle the order before the plant could produce it. Now only two people need to see it." Kinicki, who was subsequently made manager of customer service in an AmElectric reorganization, hopes to identify other parts suitable for CIM order processing with a similar reduction in lead time.

SUMMARY

New product development at AmElectric followed basic US theory quite closely. Marketing expected to initiate the process and remain in close touch with engineering throughout the design stage. Production was brought into the planning at a fairly early stage to influence the design in terms of its ability to be built. A program or project management system was used to achieve coordination across functional lines. Though the theory seemed logical, in practice the process generated significant conflict among the functional groups. Some of the conflict was little more than a healthy clash of priorities and was brought to a timely and rational conclusion—usually by negotiations among peers, occasionally by a higher common boss. At the time of our study, however, the conflict between marketing and engineering was not being quickly or rationally resolved; there was mutual distrust, and different groups were acting on different market assumptions. A recent structural change within the AmElectric organization was expected to help solve this problem.

New Product Introduction at AmTruck

AmTruck introduces new products and product improvements through a formalized process known as New Product Planning and Development Process (NPP&DP). Exhibit 9.3 depicts the process graphically. The philosophy behind NPP&DP promotes continuous product improvement and a diversity of projects from which to choose. It has two new product planning tracks: a short-term planning approach in which immediate customer needs and available technology and engineering ideas are matched with new product ideas over a short term (approximately 3 years); and a long-term product introduction process in which "visionary" customers are identified—customers likely to be first users of products that will later become industry standards. The long-term product planning process is far more difficult because AmTruck has to search out visionary customers and gain access to them.

Engineers from all parts of AmTruck may work up proposals and ideas for product changes. The primary impetus is customer demand, but product changes may also result from management dictum or strategic direction; a proposal may even be the pet project or unique inspiration of a particular engineer.

Labeled M1 through M6 in Exhibit 9.3, six stages mark the process of new product development at AmTruck. At the early review stage (M1), product change suggestions are compared with one another on a variety of dimensions, including market demand and cost impact. The overall budget determines how many of these projects will be pursued.

After a project has passed an M1 decision, the company commits to seed money to elaborate the idea and test for market and technical feasibility, and manufacturability. To survive the second decision point, M2, the design must look feasible on paper. Between the M2 and M3 decision points, engineers and production people build prototypes and identify sources for parts and components. Once the M3 decision is made, the corporation commits to investing in the manufacturing expenses associated with building the new product. Engineers continue testing, conduct performance optimization, and produce the product documentation. Manufacturing works through make-or-buy decisions, cost tracking, tooling and equipment purchases, and volume decisions. These steps constitute the M4 decision areas. Marketing develops important customer options, sales and service literature and support, pricing, and pilot installations. When these activities are complete, the corporation reaches the M5 decision point,

EXHIBIT 9.3 AmTruck New-Product Planning and Development Process

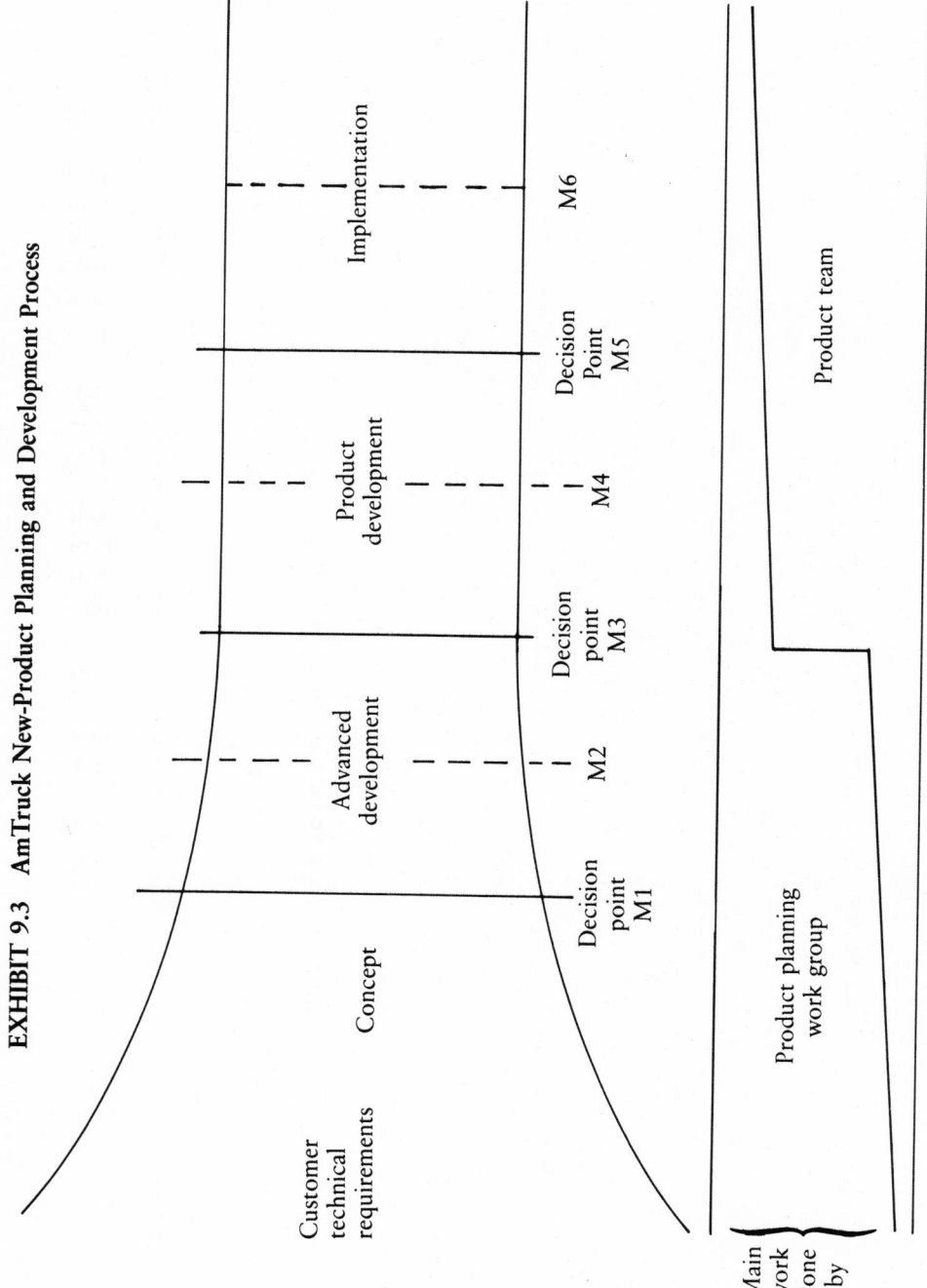

EXHIBIT 9.4   AmTruck Product Management Operating Group

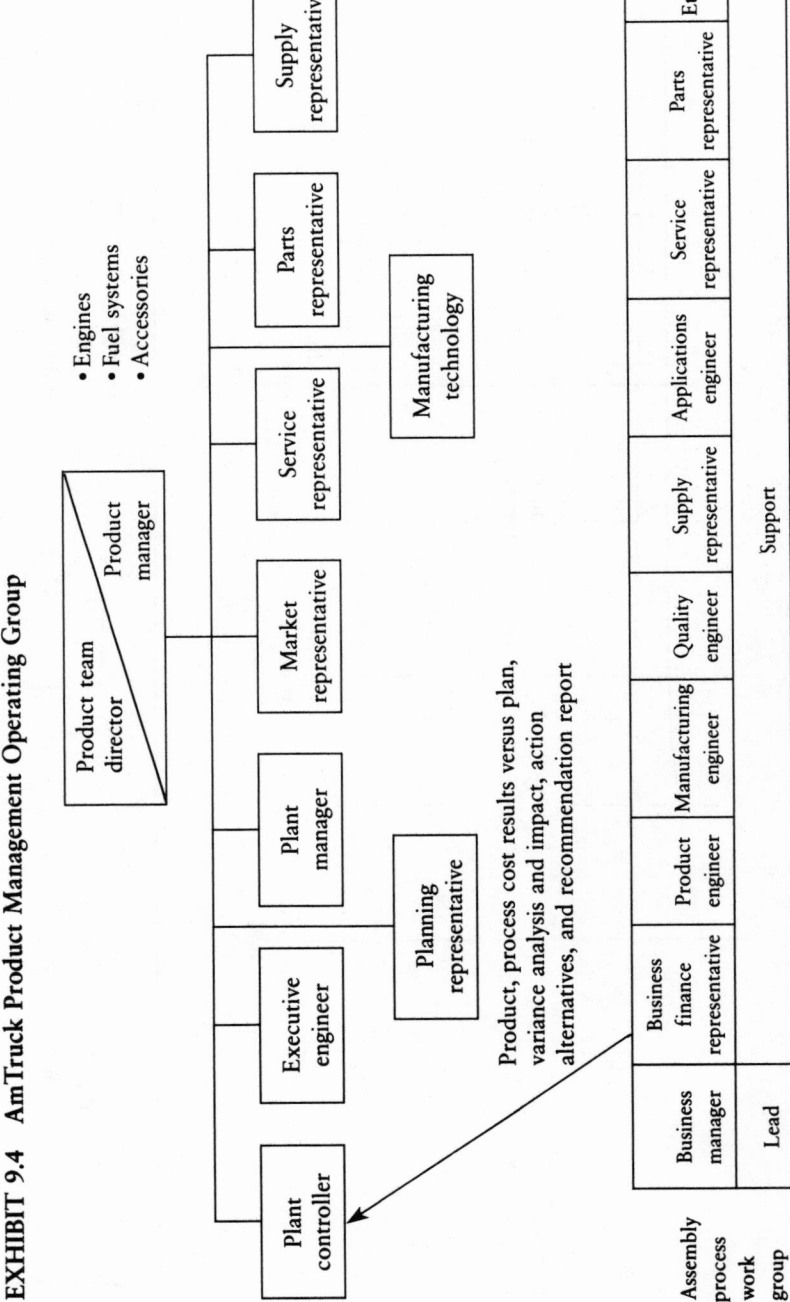

where it may confirm program viability and begin full production. The M6 decision is a follow-up to determine whether or not the product is carrying its weight in terms of performance, quality, and cost goals. The six-step process typically takes between five and seven years.

While customer needs are paramount, other external factors also drive innovation and product change. For example, government regulation on emission standards and fuel consumption directly affects the AmTruck product line. Competitive moves also may shape AmTruck's product strategy. One marketing manager recalled,

> When one of our main competitors came out with a new higher-torque engine, we were really surprised by how much the customers valued this feature. Our customers demanded the same performance, and we had nothing to offer them. We really had to scramble to catch up. We planned our response, our product change, to bring it to market in six months. It actually took about a year.

When new products are developed or special projects undertaken, AmTruck designates program managers and makes extensive use of teams (see Exhibit 9.4). In the following new product introduction, for example, a program manager worked with two teams. The team at headquarters included representatives from marketing, finance, production, engineering, service, and parts. Another team handled design and production development at the manufacturing site.

THE 1.5C ENGINE

When the US Congress enacted the Clean Air Act in 1970, AmTruck management knew it would have to undertake some product redesign. The government's emissions targets for 1992 were significantly below the emissions of AmTruck models.

In the early 1980s, management began funding experimental ideas for a new engine. Research included international trips to understand manufacturing and design in countries such as Japan and the United Kingdom. In addition, because of the lower-priced engines offered by Japan, management set a 30% production cost reduction target for the new engine.

By early 1985, design engineers had formed three strategies—known as designs A, B, and C—to meet the upcoming emissions requirements. Initially, they expected design B to prove superior, but many different considerations went into the assessment and in July 1986, management reviewed the three options and chose design C. Thus began work on the 2C engine.

Soon the engineers realized that some of the benefits of the proposed 2C engine could be achieved earlier than 1992. Certain cost-saving and performance-improvement features could be introduced in the late 1980s. With management approval, a group of engineers began to work on the 1.5C engine, proposed for introduction in 1988 or 1989.

The new engine offered several advantages customers wanted: first, it was more durable than older models and had reduced overhead wear; second, it was much quieter; third, a larger oil pan meant longer oil-drain intervals, which further enhanced durability. Moreover, the 1.5C introduced some of the changes that were planned for the 2C engine and would therefore ease AmTruck's introduction of the latter engine. By September 1986, AmTruck had worked out the engineering analysis for price and performance specifications for the 1.5C.

Engineering studies during this early period suggested that the 30% cost reduction was probably unreasonable. Though some engineers had suspected this earlier, none had taken the problem directly to top management. When a staff reorganization brought one senior new product manager in close contact with the figures, however, he informed corporate decision makers, and the cost reduction target was lowered.

Throughout 1986 and 1987, work continued on the design and production plan for the 1.5C engine. The product team included a broad range of individuals and approaches (marketing, finance, production, and so forth). Not all its proposals were accepted. For example, the team director recalled that the design engineers kept proposing an overhead cam shaft. While this would have given the engine higher RPMs and the truck greater speed, these features were not particularly important to AmTruck's customers; fleet buyers, in fact, do not want their drivers to drive fast. Although the engineers promoted the overhead cam shaft as a cost reduction factor, the idea was eventually scrapped.

As design work on the 1.5C engine progressed, corporate began to foresee funding problems; in late 1987, the design team was told to stop plans for the 1.5C introduction. Although their effort had not been given an official M3 decision (corporate commitment to manufacture and introduce the product), the engineers were surprised. The product team director was skeptical, in fact, and allowed one member to keep working on a particularly critical element of 1.5C. He said, "I know that sometimes these projects are put back on track, and then headquarters acts as if you haven't lost any time at all. The schedules will be even tighter."

"We thought it was a good project," one engineer commented, "and we wanted to keep working on it. We thought it would pay for itself eventually." Engineers from quality, cost, and production all pressed for the benefits their areas could achieve through the 1.5C. Furthermore, competitors were introducing new products at a rate that suggested AmTruck should keep pace. After about six months, the coalition of groups and functions eventually convinced headquarters to continue the project. Engineers resumed working on the product with a focus on the planning of manufacturing, which was scheduled to start in late 1988.

In early 1988, however, it became evident that some of AmTruck's major customers would not be able to accept delivery of the modified engine until 1990. Apparently marketing had anticipated that customers would be so enthralled with the new engine that they would make all possible efforts to incorporate it into their production quickly. However, the new engine's dimensions meant that original equipment manufacturers (OEMs) must redesign part of their truck bodies. Although small OEMs seemed to have little difficulty doing this, large ones took longer to incorporate changes. AmTruck was reluctant to sell 1.5C engines to some but not all of the OEMs, because those that bought them would gain an advantage over those that could not yet offer the improved engines to final buyers.

AmTruck faced a difficult choice: Should it favor its small customers by introducing the engine immediately? Or should it favor its large customers by delaying the engine's introduction until they could accept it? The decision was complicated by the fact that AmTruck had recently discontinued its volume discounts, which had substantially benefited the larger customer. Finally, AmTruck decided to introduce the 1.5C in Europe in early 1989 and to delay the US introduction until late 1989, thus giving the larger manufacturers a chance to prepare for the new product.

Reflecting on this "last-minute surprise," the product director offered these comments:

> First, project management is difficult because everyone is working in parallel—it might be better if actions were more sequenced. Second, marketing was reluctant to approach the customer with the new design earlier because the applications engineers hadn't proved out the benefits of the new design. So the marketing department didn't want to talk to customers about improvements they couldn't be sure of. Finally, I think that the marketing person on our team might not have had enough clout. The people above her in the marketing organization should have been making calls on the customer, but she wasn't able to convince them. Maybe if they had been involved in the project directly, they would have acted earlier.

AMCAR'S RECREATIONAL DIESEL TRUCK

In late 1978, Amcar, an important US automobile firm, developed an interest in installing a diesel engine in its household/recreational truck, a vehicle likely to be sold to individuals who would use it for leisure activity such as off-road driving. The consumer market for small trucks was growing, and buyers were interested in fuel economy.

Given AmTruck's greater experience with the diesel engine, Amcar approached AmTruck with a proposal that it design and manufacture the engine for the Amcar small truck. AmTruck had strong engineering skills and staff, whereas Amcar had cash but lacked the internal expertise to develop the new motor. Said one AmTruck project manager, "It was really a first for us. We were essentially engineering design subcontractors. Management had to think this commitment over."

AmTruck planning and manufacturing engineers began research into the feasibility of the proposal in late 1978. By early 1980, the Small Engine Development Center (SEDC), made up of headquarters marketing and engineering personnel, began to work up specific proposals for the engine design. In January 1980, a rough planning review committed the firm's resources to the project.

The startup was less than smooth. To facilitate necessary coordination among Amcar, the SEDC, and the plant that would produce the engines, two major leadership/project-management roles were established. One position considered the engine from the broad perspective of the "whole truck," and the other from the narrower perspective of marketing and production engineering issues. Between the two teams were liaison people who exchanged ideas and information as the project progressed. The engineering drawings were computerized, and the groups issued engineering change orders on a constant basis.

Coordination was not always easy. For example, the design of the engine's oil pan posed a unique problem for AmTruck because of the special demands for depth, capacity, and fit in a relatively small space. The SEDC evolved different designs and sought advice from suppliers, manufacturing, purchasing, and plant engineering. The ultimate design was a joint effort of all these groups. After numerous iterations, the SEDC finally obtained a full release of the design, even though Amcar still complained that the oil pan should have been insulated because the engine was too noisy.

Manufacturing strategy proved to be another area of disagreement. Amcar was accustomed to a high-volume, low-modification production strategy. This approach was not welcomed by AmTruck, where a low-volume, high-modification environment was the norm. Often, volume estimates differed broadly, as did the willingness to incorporate additional options. "Plain vanilla meant different things to different people," said one engineer, while a team leader commented, "We did a great job holding back the number of options. It doesn't take too many options before you have an overwhelming number of specifications." Differences were eventually worked out by the two teams.

Two other developments affected the new product's introduction. First, initial demand was well below forecast. Because of several factors, but primarily the 1981 recession, consumer interest in diesel trucks was far below what Amcar had predicted. This left the new factory desperate for any orders to fill its anticipated 600-engine-a-day capacity. Second, as the engine approached product launch, Amcar found it lacked space for some of the truck assembly work it had planned to do. Amcar and AmTruck subsequently renegotiated the relationship so that AmTruck did the assembly. This, of course, provided AmTruck with additional revenues but also meant that it must plan for additional manufacturing and warehousing capability.

In February 1988, the initial prototype was approved for production, and the M5 decision was reached on May 16 that year. As the product launch approached, excitement mounted. Said one project leader, "The big guys get involved. There's a lot of mother-henning and hovering. I might as well keep my calendar clear until the launch." The product attracted a lot of attention because it targeted a new market segment for AmTruck: the retail consumer. This meant television advertising and media events. For example, the new Amcar truck was scheduled to climb Pike's Peak in record time, a feat calculated to attract truck buyers. All the retail hoopla was unique for AmTruck.

SUMMARY

New product development at AmTruck followed standard US theory closely, as it did at AmElectric. Emphasis was on a step-by-step process with periodic reviews that signaled go or no-go decisions. Practices varied somewhat from case to case, and predictable conflicts surfaced when multiple divisions had differing goals. Most conflicts were resolved through lateral task forces. This device worked even when the groups spanned two separate organizations in AmTruck's joint ventures with Amcar.

The common denominator of both firms was their sophisticated use of lateral decision-making groups to integrate and expedite the complex decision-making process.

New Product Introduction in the USSR

[*Editors' note:* This section describes the Soviet general approach to new product introduction as selected and reported by our Soviet colleagues primarily for American readers. It is followed by descriptions of practices we observed at SovElectric and SovTruck.]

Historically, new product introduction in the Soviet Union has involved numerous organizations—from central government bodies headed by the USSR State Committee for Science and Technology, including the USSR Academy of Sciences; to industrial ministries and their research institutes; to scientific-production associations; and, finally, to enterprises, the largest of which have special design bureaus. It was customary to go through the various stages of the innovation process in many different organizations. This process generally resulted in a highly centralized system of new product introduction. Every new product required approval from the industrial ministry and some required approval from the USSR Council of Ministers.

Statewide new product budgets primarily covered long-term, basic research, interindustrial scientific and technical programs, and the development of products that would revolutionize world production. The USSR Council of Ministers made state budget financing decisions. Ministry financing for new product development usually covered interindustry activities, the early stages of innovation, the training of scientific personnel, and the costs of advertising and exhibitions. At the enterprise level, the fund for production, science, and technology development can be spent for new product development, including the purchase of licenses, materials, and equipment. In addition, product organizations may count on, within limits, bank credits to pay for new product development (see Chapter 8).

Typically, Gosplan determines the scope and quality of new products demanded. The research institutes of the ministries make calculations of customer demand and give them to Gosplan. The research institutes may also design prototypes and pass them on to the enterprise. These are then issued as production orders to the enterprise, where engineers and designers plan the manufacturing introduction of the new product.

Large enterprises have their internal scientific capacity to develop new products, but they may use outside sources like a university, the Academy of Sciences, or other industrial research institutions. At headquarters there is a large staff with many technical specialists, while the plants have specialists only for the specific products they manufacture.

The USSR has relied on the supply side of innovation for product improvement, allocating resources to the desired scientific-technical institutes that design, engineer, build, and test new product prototypes (or experimental models). Very often, stages of product development are divided among the different organizations.

Authorities attempt to influence demand for new designs primarily by directives, orders, and goals requiring an enterprise to accept new designs. However, the enterprise's bonuses for achieving timely introduction of a new product design are usually outweighed by the risk of production disruptions that will prevent the firm from meeting volume production targets. Moreover, since prices are set by central authorities, the enterprise and its workers may profit little from introducing a new product.

The planning process for new product introduction is similar to that of capital investment (or introducing new production processes). That is, the general approach to R&D has been to "design down" to cope with deficiencies in supply and manufacturing capability, as well as to deal with controls imposed by ministries and standards committees.

Soviet R&D decisions seem to be based on the following criteria:

- Simplicity in design, aimed at facilitating manufacturing operations and user performance. Strong emphasis is placed on avoiding difficulties in severe physical environments or where support services will be minimal.
- Continuous design improvement, introducing small changes in product components. Small changes help shorten the design-engineering-production cycle and allow engineers to use components that have already been developed and tested in design institutes.
- Commonality of parts, using "group technology" and interchangeable parts to minimize the proliferation of parts in related product areas.
- Prototype modeling. The Soviets prefer to build experimental models rather than rely on design analytics. This facilitates the use of incremental design changes, as new designs can be modeled, tested, and proven.
- Use of foreign standards as yardstick for new product design. The Soviets have used foreign models to upgrade their own products and equipment.

Together, these criteria reduce the risk and uncertainty associated with new product introduction.

At the time of our study (and especially under perestroika), the USSR had recently been experimenting with new structures and relationships to improve their science and technology utilization. Some specific steps were the establishment of the following mechanisms:

- *NPOs.* These are science and production organizations, numbering about 500, that coordinate and bridge between research institutes and factories.
- *MNTKs.* These are interbranch scientific technical complexes that combine research and production facilities; 12 of the 21 MNTKs are run by institutes of the Academy of Sciences, considered more enlightened about

technology and management than the production ministries, which control 9 of the MNTKs.

- *Cooperatives.* Groups or individuals may legally run service organizations that provide research or facilitate the introduction of new technology. For example, the cooperative Iskatel makes controls that connect Soviet-made personal computers to automated factory machines.
- *Scientific organizations have turned to self-financing.* Their revenue is dependent on fulfilling R&D contracts with industrial customers. This means shifting from financing the organization to paying for its output.
- *Extension of Gospriomka.* This system of state inspectors who have the power to reject products that do not measure up has long been used for military products but only recently been extended to certain sectors of the civilian and consumer goods economy. In conjunction with a tough program of quality control, these inspectors now enforce the standards. For example, if new products do not meet quality standards, their price is cut by 5% the first year, by 10% the second year, by 15% the third year; after that they must be discontinued.
- *Improved productivity through plant modernization and cost reduction.* Because the Soviet accounting system has not allowed for rapid depreciation or replacement of obsolete equipment before it is worn out, one aim of perestroika is modernization. However, standards for material and supply usage on new products are tougher. Manufacturers are to decrease costs by cutting out scrap and reducing metal content in their products.
- *Aggressive product improvement goals and standards.* An increasing role in new product development is now being played by joint ventures, with foreign counterparts contributing to the integration of new techniques.
- *More customer input.* Customers may now have more influence on new products through their refusal to accept products they do not want to pay for under *khozraschet,* or self-financing. Further, ministries sponsoring new products must reach agreements with ministries that will use the products. Product samples are tested and the results guide the product development process.
- *New wage incentives.* Personal compensation levels have been increased for new product development work. These measures allow increases of up to 40–50% for workers, 30–35% for engineers, and 15% for managers. All increases depend on the quality and effectiveness of the work.

Under perestroika new product development has significantly changed. Centralization has increased with regard to quality and standards at the same time that the application of self-financing to research and development has decentralized these activities. These measures have had some success, if not the degree of success hoped for. Not all the changes have been well received. In some enterprises, for example, workers have been angry that Gospriomka can interrupt production without providing any help.

New Product Introduction at SovElectric

Like all Soviet state enterprises, SovElectric follows new product introduction programs outlined by the state authorities and related research institutes. Major new designs for electric motors are developed by the SKB Research Institute, which is part of SovElectric but also designs for other motor manufacturers.

In general, the new-product introduction cycle in SovElectric proceeds in six stages.

1. A study of the problem
2. A search for scientific ideas and the construction of initial prototypes
3. Research and prototype development
4. Technological development
5. Introduction to production
6. Full production

The first stage focuses primarily on deciding the direction of new products. SKB's department for patents and licenses performs most of this work, and its results are given as suggestions to SKB management, which decides whether a particular new product should be included in the current plan for new product introduction.

In the scientific research stage, the work consists of making an experimental prototype model of the future product and testing the product for performance features. In stage 3, SKB's R&D unit modifies its hand-built, working prototypes in various ways to investigate performance features. This is a critical stage for new product development because it is here that the research institute's top management chooses exactly which design alternative will be produced. When each alternative has been tested for efficiency, manufacturability, cost, and so on, the information is consolidated, and the final design is selected. During this stage, the department of patents and licenses works with the R&D department. Together, they prepare a special patent form for the USSR and provide suggestions about patenting the product in other countries. Either the whole product or new components may be patented.

At the fourth stage, technological development, two types of specifications are involved. One is a designer's documentation (*konstructorskia documentatzia,* or KD) and the other, a preliminary pattern (*opitnje obrazjetz* or OO) of the working model. The KD and the OO are reviewed by an interministerial commission, MVK1, which includes customer, designer, and producer representatives. MVK1 decides whether or not to move forward with production. If the decision is affirmative, MVK1 passes the KD and OO on to the plant's chief technologist.

The technological development stage is likely to take longer than the first three stages because critical manufacturing determinations must be made. Essentially, there are three alternatives: (1) to use existing manufacturing technology; (2) to modernize existing technology and equipment; or (3) to improve existing technology and add manufacturing capability by increasing plant space, installing new equipment, instituting new processes, and so on.

At the fifth stage, introduction to production, the plant's chief technologist and chief engineer's office, with information from the SKB chief constructor, put together the new manufacturing technology. This includes construction and installation of any new tooling or machinery and placement, setup, and startup of new equipment. Test batches of the new product are run. Now the plant technologist produces technological documentation (*tecknichiskja documentatzia,* or TD) that describes the manufacturing technology needed for the first run. The technical documentation goes to MVK2, a second commission, which will decide on design and manufacturing technology. With MVK2 approval, the product moves into production.

At the national level, the five-year plan has orders for every ministry, every industrial subsector, every enterprise, and every plant, regarding the economic criteria for new product introduction. The plan specifies the amount of savings to be achieved through greater manufacturing efficiency as well as the savings to be realized by the product in use (e.g., more efficient motors, more durable motors). The plan describes the annual economic effect of the savings, specifying how much the new product should contribute to the gross national product. The relevant indicator at the plant level is the cost savings or the additional profit that may be realized in the given planning period.

The National Plan of Science and Technology Development, which is a derivative of the State Plan for Social and Economic Development, has a subsection called Introduction of New Products in Industry. This subsection gives the main targets for type of new product to be produced, technical characteristics of proposed new products, and special arrangements to be made with foreign countries.

Typically, the entire process takes four years: six months for the first stage, a year each for the second, third, and fourth stages, and from nine months to a year for the fifth and sixth stages combined.

A product change may be treated as a new product introduction. So may the initial USSR manufacture of an item that is an established product elsewhere in the world (e.g., home laundry machines or microwave ovens). Modernized products that meet new, higher quality standards or incorporate new features may also qualify as new products, and new products may be intermediate goods as well as final goods. For example, a change in the motor that becomes part of an otherwise unchanged machine tool qualifies as a new product introduction. Any change that is classified as a new product introduction legitimates a request for a higher price.

AIR MOTOR IN PLANT V

Electrical motor production is usually done by series (class). In the USSR, the main asynchronic series produced in industry is the 4A, with a capacity range from .06 to 400 kilowatts and a 71-millimeter standard axle of rotation. These motors are used for many purposes in a variety of industries, including machine tools and equipment. Within each series or class are many modifications based on specific customer needs.

In 1980, a new production series of asynchronic engines called AIR began in the USSR. This new product was designed at the SKB Research Institute, and SKB played a main role in the project, partly because of its highly successful design of the D100 and 4A motors. These machines were well received and produced for export.

In the early stages of project planning for AIR, SKB had designed a series of motors in conjunction with the Organization of the Interelectric Program, members of which included the Comecon countries' research institutes. At the national level, the project was monitored by the State Committee for Science and Technology and called for the new AIR series to be manufactured in ten plants, three of which were SovElectric plants.

AIR had several advantages over the previous 4A model. It was expected to last an additional 6,000 hours, to weigh less, and to use less electricity. The new motor in use nationally could save 32 million kilowatts annually over its predecessor. The AIR project was particularly needed at this time because manufacturing allowances for materials, energy, and labor resources had been tightened. In general, since new product introduction and cost reduction were high national priorities, the AIR introduction was a high priority for SovElectric's management.

Annual materials savings for the new motor were 1,260 tons of metal (260 tons of copper and 1,000 of aluminum); annual labor savings were 3,250 weeks of work. This could save SovElectric over 23.7 million rubles annually in the production of 2.6 million motors. For this reason, too, increased production of the AIR motor was a high priority.

Though the plant received central orders to introduce the AIR model, it had its own internal reasons for wanting to do so. In 1973, SovElectric had introduced the 4A, with which it had tremendous success. Because few other organizations were able to put this new product into production in as timely a fashion as SovElectric, and because Goskomtsen (State Committee on Prices) allowed a very favorable price increase, SovElectric was able to improve its financial situation dramatically. Before producing the 4A model in the 1970s, SovElectric was in difficult fiscal straits, but the price for the model 4A was so high that the entire enterprise soon became profitable.

SovElectric presumed that the new AIR product would give it similar advantages. For this reason, the 1980 decision to introduce the new AIR motor met with the ready acceptance of the plant manager, the technical council, the chief engineer, and other relevant parties. In 1983, AIR went into production at SovElectric's main plant, Plant V, two years ahead of schedule. The plant expected to get a six-ruble price increase based on improved quality and a new product. All the written rules and regulations of Goskomtsen, the Ministry of Finance, and the State Committee for Science and Technology provided calculations and standards that led SovElectric to expect that six-ruble increase. Moreover, SovElectric's customer, a metal-cutting equipment institute, also vouched for the improvements in AIR, which further led SovElectric to believe it could convince Goskomtsen to increase the price.

Although new product introductions usually take four years, AIR took only one year and four months. The introduction moved quickly, in part because SovElectric skipped stages. For example, one part of the motor (a plastic shield) was not supposed to be given to manufacturing until the motor was totally redesigned. But in this and other cases, it gave the part to the chief technologist and the tooling shops ahead of time, thus overlapping the second, third, and fourth stages. And according to the director general, "It could have been even faster if we had CAD/CAM technology to help us."

Despite the rapid pace of development, the introduction was not without hitches. For example, the winding equipment was too slow, and SovElectric eventually had to buy new equipment from abroad. In manufacturing, insulation materials for AIR melted and contaminated the internal grooves of the motors. It took a lot of time to raise the product to standard.

After the model had been introduced into production, the director general found that a six-ruble price increase would not be forthcoming. A new person was in control of pricing policies for the electric motor industry, and in his opinion, SovElectric had benefited too much from the previous new product introduction of 4A. Further, the administrators at Goskomtsen said that a six-ruble increase for the nine million motors produced in the USSR would amount to an expensive 54 million rubles. So the new price control administrator determined that SovElectric would receive no price increase for its new model AIR. The director general met with the chairman of Goskomtsen to protest, but he held his subordinates responsible and did not make any favorable decisions. Finally, Goskomtsen proposed a 1.5 ruble price increase. SKB's design engineer said, "It's as if they were being punished for introducing the new model early. It's very sad to see innovation punished. Enterprises that follow a wait-and-see policy actually benefit."

The chief economist's section kept strict records of the costs associated with the new product AIR. Through documentation, she showed that costs for the new product were seven kopeks per unit higher (or 1.45 million rubles for the plant), partly because new manufacturing technology had to be developed for producing the new motor. She also found that nearly all the over-budget costs could be attributed to difficulties associated with equipment for the new AIR. A principal reason for the elevated costs was that manufacturing technology development for AIR was done by an affiliated institute in Petrovsk, while SKB did the product design development. The new AIR model was not compatible with manufacturing technology designed in Petrovsk. Ideally, Petrovsk and SKB should work together and report to the same ministry, but there had been a lack of coordination. Because the Petrovsk institute was planning manufacturing design for the 10 plants that would produce AIR, they chose an automatic line that could be used everywhere. However, the equipment was more appropriate for larger AIR models, and SovElectric was producing small models. The equipment took up too much space and did not perform the required machining well.

After a year and a half of negotiating, the director general, the chief controller, and the chief accountant went to appeal the price decision to the Goskomtsen. After studying their calculations, Goskomtsen agreed to give them a three-ruble price increase. However, the chief accountant believed that this price still would not compensate for increased costs.

AIR IN PLANT W

A 1986 ministry decision gave Plant W state orders for producing for the first time a different model of the AIR motor. From the startup of AIR production in 1987 Plant W experienced difficulty in meeting its quotas. Early on, the ministry had expected to divide production of the AIR model between two plants, Plant W and a plant in Kaster. When it subsequently found that the Kaster plant was unable to produce the AIR motor, all production was scheduled for Plant W, putting Plant W at 130% of its rated capacity. Because technical reconstruction for the new product was behind schedule, Plant W could not meet delivery schedules and was paying fines.

The new model introduction posed an array of manufacturing problems for Plant W. The Petrovsk institute had chosen inflexible automatic lines for mass production of the new motor, failing to consider the requirements that might arise from various customers' modifications. The chief designer commented, "From the beginning of the new product introduction, we had to make one product design concession after another because we couldn't produce the new modifications with existing equipment." For example, no machine at Plant W could perform the copper-winding task on the new motor, so this operation had to be done by hand. The increased precision required for the AIR motor meant that many available machines with wider tolerances could not produce the new product.

Another obstacle to introducing the AIR series at Plant W was the organization of the tooling shop. While large equipment was purchased from external suppliers, much of the tooling (such as press forms and smaller machine tools) was produced by an internal machine-tool shop. In late 1987, the shop was behind in production, and the tooling designers shared their frustration with the plant manager. He took the problem to ministry officials, who suggested that Plant W acquire more machine tools and reorganize its tooling shop. Previously, the tooling shop had been treated as an auxiliary shop, with its budgeting and wage and salary administration done by the plant economics department. Now it was to be treated as an independent shop and given the same powers and responsibilities as other main shops. Many small service shops were combined into this new independent shop to which all Plant W machine toolmakers were to report. Moreover, a plan for transferring equipment to the new area was developed, and the new shop had the right to purchase some resources and machine tools for itself. A new post, chief of tool services officer, was created, and that person was responsible for supply, maintenance, and production. Under him were the chief tool designer, the bureau for tool maintenance, and the tooling shop. The reorganization took place in January 1988. Because the designers and technologists now worked directly with tanners and toolmakers, they could see and monitor the results of their design jobs. Operational speed and quality improved markedly.

Each main shop was given a monthly allocation of work hours and rubles for machine-tool production that it might need. Shops were directed to notify tooling of their requirements by the 20th of every month, and the requirements were to be signed by the chief engineer. When the deadline was not met, or when quality was low, the main shops now complained directly to the machine-tool shop. The machine-tool shop could also buy materials and instruments from outside vendors.

The tool shop, which had now achieved the status of an independent shop, was so pleased with the new setup it decided to increase production volume targets by 131%. The new equipment would increase the rest of Plant W's productivity as well. In addition, the new machine-tool capacity would help it scale up the new AIR product more rapidly.

The plant and tool shop developed plans for capital investment. They decided that 30 new highly productive machine tools would be made and that nine of the plant shops would become highly mechanized or automated. They were also planning to introduce automatic manipulators, robots, and equipment with numerical control devices, as well as machining centers. The improved equipment would help them meet the tighter tolerances of the new AIR motor. As a result, the plant manager planned to scale back Plant W's older products, believing the plant could now meet AIR production volume goals.

Despite its best efforts, the tool shop began to fall behind on its ambitious reequipment plans just as the AIR motor was supposed to be produced in larger quantities. At the same time, Gospriomka, the state quality inspection unit, rejected some of Plant W's current products. It seemed that the reorganization of the tool shop and the implementation of reequipping the factory had been started too late to avoid a major crisis.

SUMMARY

It is clear from our examination of the SovElectric plants that new product introductions do not always go smoothly. The types of difficulties experienced by the two plants, however, were very different. Plant V had a record of success in introducing the earlier 4A motor. Based on this record, it enthusiastically undertook the AIR introduction, remaining ahead of schedule despite some local problems. However, Goskomtsen denied it the expected price increase over the previous model, seemingly punishing it for the earlier success.

When AIR was introduced into Plant W a few years later, troubles arose from two other sources. First, the ministry loaded the volume target planned for another plant on Plant W, putting Plant W at 130% capacity. Then the reorganized tool shop undertook a reequipment and retooling plan that, in hindsight, was overly ambitious. These factors, in concert with the state inspection unit's rejection of some current production, put Plant W into a serious production crisis. The pattern is clear. The fact that new product introduction is easily influenced by government agencies outside the enterprise can be a source of serious problems.

New Product Introduction at SovTruck

At SovTruck, new manufacturing technology is grouped with new product technology; therefore, the proposal and introduction of new products follow the capital investment process that we examined in Chapter 8.

The general rule is that new product concepts are mandated by the ministry. Unlike smaller organizations, which receive new product designs from research institutes, SovTruck has a sizable scientific staff and does much of its product design internally.

Functionally, a plant design department is subordinate to the enterprise design department and Plant X has 70 employees in its design department. In 1987, it developed 170 technical innovations, but only 100 were actually introduced into production. Two types of engineers—designers and technologists—are employed at the plant level in approximately equal numbers. Only seven or eight designers actually make the drawings and elaborate new product design. The others work on improvements and technological adaptations. Technologists evolve the plans for manufacturing introduction.

More engineering time is spent on continuous improvement of existing products than on the design of completely new products. For example, most of the 100 changes introduced in 1987 were product improvements, 20 of them modifications of the carburetor alone. The last overall truck-model design was introduced in 1968. Since then, SovTruck has been doing continuous improvement to the designed truck model, and only in the last three years has it started to design an entirely new truck.

At SovTruck, totally new products are mandated from above by a formal document called a *prikaz* (literally, "order"), which announces a decision. For new product introductions, the *prikaz* specifies the parameters, abilities, and other requirements of the product. The introduction procedure is managed by the plant's chief technologist and carried out by his department. After the designer produces a product change document, a technologist begins working out recommendations for production implementation. If questions or problems arise, the technologist makes recommendations to the designer about anticipated production difficulties. The designer then resolves the problems, prepares a new version of the change order, and sends it back to technology. This process may be repeated many times. After the technologist receives final recommendation from the designer, he or she establishes technological cycles and develops and prepares the equipment and materials. Technologists also place orders for new supplies or equipment as needed.

Continuous improvement changes usually come from the shop floor or from plant-level designers, not from the top. Sometimes, though not typically, the changes are in response to customer requests. Many changes are introduced in response to guidelines and targets set by headquarters—for example, cost reduction, metal content reduction, or scrap or waste reduction. Most involve replacing materials rather than changing product design.

Continuous improvement changes are documented by a formal change order (*izveshenia*), a special technical document issued by the plant to inform the enterprise of its ongoing improvement activity. The *izveshenia* is prepared by the chief designer in accord with the chief technologist. As soon as production is ready to absorb the product change, the order becomes operative as law—the product must conform to the new standards set forth in the document, and the old product must be taken out of production.

In general, these kinds of changes have a preplanned character, because they are very closely associated with the targets or programs established at headquarters. If headquarters mandates a cost-reduction or a defect-reduction program, for example, shop floor-level and plant-level engineers work on these as continuous improvement projects.

A NEW SHOCK ABSORBER

SovTruck's Plant Y was responsible for producing several components for the main truck models. Its new product goals and standards were mandated by overall targets set for SovTruck by the automotive ministry. Plant Y had been directed to make changes in its shock absorber; the shock absorber's length was to be increased and mounting mechanics modified. In addition, the plant was directed to reduce the shock absorber's metal content by 30% and reduce its overall weight. The plant's designers considered these restrictions very tough.

Plant engineers resolved the problem by making the metal pipe of the shock absorber thinner and by changing some metal parts to plastic parts. The development of the new shock absorber 4331 was then included as a project in the Consolidated Plan for the Development of Science and Technology (CPDST) for 1986. The project was to begin in 1986 and be completed by 1990 at a cost of 50,000 rubles to the plant and 180,000 rubles to the enterprise. The estimated savings were 10,000 rubles annually, to result mostly from the reduction in metal.

For a project like this, the chief designer, chief technologist, and chief engineer work first on its justification. There are standard criteria that each project must meet, such as a six-year payback period and the fit of the product with the overall truck design. A special form, the technical economic justification, is prepared by the project designer; it gives estimates of the expenses, including materials, time, and external services. All the calculations are reviewed by the enterprise deputy director general for economic issues, Ushinski, and financed from the CPDST. Since this fund is controlled by the deputy director general for science and technology, his approval is also necessary for the project.

The new shock absorber was developed primarily by Plant Y designers. As is customary, SovTruck headquarters gave the assignment to the plant in the form of a *prikaz* that described the technical characteristics and the parameters of the new product. As soon as the plant manager received the *prikaz,* he submitted it to the plant's design office.

EXHIBIT 9.5   Procedures at SovTruck Plant Y for New Product Introduction

- *Experimental model or early prototype stage.* For the shock absorber, this took one month; more complicated products could require two to three months.
- *Test prototype stage.* Building a prototype for testing usually takes from four to six months.
- *Lab testing stage.* Simulates travel over 100,000 km; takes three to four months.
- *Road testing stage.* Can be done in parallel with the lab testing; takes three months.
- *Field tests.* These take a year to a year and a half. To save time, SovTruck sometimes conducts field tests with a coefficient of one to ten—for example, putting ten times more pressure on the shock absorber than it would be likely to experience in real use. This significantly reduces the nature of the product testing and field test time.
- *Running tests.* Determined by agreement with customers; formal running tests take 300,000 to 400,000 km running and up to 10 years' time.

The typical product development cycle follows prescribed stages (see Exhibit 9.5). In the first stage, designers develop a prototype and determine whether the product will work as the design analytics suggest. If the product's technical characteristics hold up, the next step is to test this early prototype on the truck itself. If it tests well, the designers refine technical details and drawings and move to the next stage. They produce more prototypes and perform lab tests in accordance with a testing program approved by SovTruck headquarters. After lab tests come road tests, which are extensive and real: the new product is installed in a number of trucks and subjected to different climates—temperate, arctic, tropical—with widely ranging road conditions. If the product survives its road test, the designers prepare a report recommending its introduction into the plant's production. Throughout these stages and the subsequent field and running tests, they continue to modify and improve the new product design. After testing and final documentation, the designers pass papers to technological services to prepare documents to introduce the new product into production.

A crucial aspect of this process is the modification of original product design. During the early stages, SovTruck fine tunes the design whenever performance feedback indicates room for improvement. Even during the last stage, when the product has been proposed for production and is in production planning, SovTruck may continue to make improvements in response to production technology or material supply constraints.

The production launch of the shock absorber took less than the standard procedural time. This speed was possible because of a special agreement with the customer (SovTruck's main factory) that waived field testing. Because early tests were positive, the plant's chief engineer decided to put the product directly into production, saving a year and a half of introduction time.

The relationship between headquarters and the plant during new product development is that of a customer and producer. Headquarters is an internal client for the new products of Plant Y. Their relationship is both formal and informal. Headquarters' design and experimental works department includes specific groups for product design and testing, specialized in such areas as corrosion, noise, vibration, special technologies, and so on. Plant Y has a design department that specializes in its specific product designs. The plant designers actually make the new design, develop the project, and provide some lab testing. Headquarters designs the overall truck and performs special services (such as the road testing of the shock absorber), but the plant designers are responsible for the actual new product design.

The close association between enterprise headquarters and the plant's designers continues during the new product introduction stage. Plant Y transfers all design and technical documentation on the new product to headquarters' department of production preparation (or production engineering). That department then issues a document called *predpisanje* (literally, "instruction"), specifying all assignments related to the new product introduction and their distribution to the other STUs involved in the work. The leading roles here belong to the technological and the machining and tooling departments. After the plant's staff has prepared for manufacturing the new product, headquarters' production engineering department issues a new directive (a second *predpisanje*) to produce a trial run of the new product. When all STUs involved in production preparation have submitted a full report on the trial run to headquarters, the department of production engineering issues a final directive (a third *predpisanje*) to release the new product into full production. In the plant technologist's opinion, the use of multiple directives or *predpisanje* illustrates the high degree of centralization in new product introduction. Plant Y is merely the executor of the enterprise's order at the production engineering stage.

After the plant finishes the design work, the chief technologist may request equipment from an affiliated SovTruck plant. The plants work out an agreement on the details of the equipment needed for the new product. Typically, the representatives would be the chief technologist from Plant Y and the chief engineer from the machine building plant, although other special representatives could be designated. During their discussions, the plant representatives consider three questions: Will the new equipment be more productive than existing equipment? Will it fit in the same space as the existing equipment? Will it be more energy efficient than current equipment?

During the production planning for the new shock absorber, the chief technologist realized it needed a new rubber part, a gasket. Plant Y first asked its previous supplier, which Gossnab had directed to supply 150,000 rubber parts to Plant Y, to change their old rubber part to the new gasket. But the rubber supplier rejected Plant Y's request, arguing that under perestroika, it could decide which orders to fill; the supplier claimed that it was at full capacity, could not meet its obligations, and certainly could not meet any new product demands.

After the refusal, Plant Y's deputy director for supply and distribution prepared a letter to the ministry, which was sent out under the director of supply's name. After sending the letter to the appropriate ministry department, he personally went to the ministry to push the issue. Eventually, the deputy director, the ministry, and the rubber supplier agreed that the new product would be produced and delivered to Plant Y on the condition that Plant Y would first send designers to the rubber plant to prepare equipment for the new part. Preparing the equipment and technology would take about six months.

The chief technologist reflected, "We wouldn't have taken them to court if we had believed they couldn't make the part, but we thought they had the capacity. Now it's incumbent upon us to make sure they get help with the equipment and get the press forms in time, or else they will be sure to use this as an excuse for failing to make delivery."

By the fall of 1988, development of the new shock absorber had been completed. It was put into parallel production; that is, the main line continued to produce the old model, while a second line produced the new shock absorber. Its complete transfer to the main line was targeted for 1990.

THE K90 CARBURETOR

Based on the annual assignment to increase fuel efficiency and the 1990 emissions requirements established by Gostandart, designers at Plant Y knew in the early 1980s they would have to develop a more effective carburetor. Such improvements were part of an overall SovTruck effort to increase fuel efficiency of its gasoline trucks.

The new carburetor project was designated K90. Annually, Plant Y ships some 45,000 carburetors, which account for 15% of its ruble volume of production. With its 158 different pieces and parts, the carburetor is the most complicated device produced by the plant. Furthermore, only 7–8% of the carburetor's components are purchased externally; the other parts are manufactured by Plant Y itself.

Development of K90 was the responsibility of the plant's chief designer, E. S. Puzhov. With 20 years' experience in engine design, Puzhov had in fact come up with an idea for improving carburetor fuel efficiency ten years earlier, but found it impossible to implement through available manufacturing and design technology. At that time there was no appropriate electronic technology for the carburetor.

The essence of Puzhov's idea was that the carburetor should cut off the engine while the truck was going down downhill. Electronics in the carburetor could accomplish the task. Project K90 was included in the CPDST for 1980–1987 and financed at 1.5 million rubles. The nationally projected annual fuel efficiency savings for the new carburetor in use was 11 million rubles.

From 1981 until 1984, the product was in its testing stage. While it was assumed that the K90 would meet the emissions standards set for 1990, emissions testing by many SovTruck departments as well as by specialists from other organizations was required. For example, the deputy director general for science and technology, Razin, noted that he had to get information from the ministry because it was the ministry that could perform the emissions tests. It has many stations throughout the country and uses them as emissions testing labs. Its data were used to calculate or compute economic efficiency for the new carburetor, and as a result of the testing, about 50 different technical reports had been prepared. In 1983, however, the technical council of the headquarters' design department shifted further development of the K90 directly to Plant Y, and in 1984, after the initial design had proved itself, the research funds were provided to Plant Y in the CPDST.

Once established in the plant, further product development was regulated through the special order of the plant manager. The changes in the carburetor required some changes within the engine and in other electrical equipment in the truck. The enterprise gave money for the changes in 1985, one month after Plant Y's request arrived at headquarters.

The control for the fulfillment of project K90 was done according to established protocol. The plant manager prepared a special schedule of how to put K90 into production. The schedule was then reviewed by the plant's technical council, which prepared a very detailed protocol paper indicating the measures to be taken, deadlines to be met, and delegation of responsibility for various activities.

Usually the responsibility for a protocol item lies with people at the level of deputy director or chief specialist (people who report directly to the plant manager). In other words, responsibility is designated by the plant manager, and deputies have formal rights to ask others to do work outside of their traditional job function. If the chief technologist is responsible for achieving a task that requires design work, for example, he or she may go directly to the designers to request they do this work according to the responsibility assigned him or her in the protocol. The protocol also includes schedules and a final deadline for the whole project. On a monthly basis, the plant manager checks fulfillment of the protocol and each protocol item. If everything is going smoothly, the plant manager will not check further. After the first new product prototype comes off the production line, the plant manager then formally passes his responsibility to the chief technologist. However, when something goes wrong, the deputy director responsible again takes control of the project.

Although SovTruck wanted to introduce the K90 into production with as little disruption as possible, it ran into problems in 1985. When the time came to assemble the K90, it found that the press for making one of the new gears was not ready. Production had to use an old press form, and assemblers had to rework the gear when they assembled the carburetor. In December 1985, they were still having trouble assembling a carburetor that would work. Finally, the deputy director went to the welding services for the enterprise; with its help, Plant Y got the production process working by late April of 1986.

After the new press form was installed, it became evident that the new carburetor with the new gear did not have the expected fuel efficiency. Solving that problem further complicated the manufacturing task but led to the production of a high-quality gear.

The chief technologist (the deputy director for ensuring that protocol was met) wrote a memo to the plant manager and asked that blame for failing to meet quality and delivery protocol requirements not rest with him alone. He argued that the chief designer should also be held responsible. The plant manager supported the chief technologist, and "blame" was shared by designers and production people.

However, the pursuit of the proper gear had delayed the project by a month and a half; since a shift of the deadline for the new carburetor would hold up the main truck assembly plant, the K90 was introduced into production in a makeshift manner. Management had arranged for additional work space for the K90 assembly, but that required moving the assembly line and much equipment. Tight schedules and manpower shortages prevented plant management from making the move in time for K90 production. Because it would improve working conditions, shop-floor personnel were interested in the move and noticed it was being delayed, but they did not know why. When the issue came up in a shop-floor union meeting, union officials resolved to ask plant management for an explanation. After discussing the matter with management, the union called a plantwide meeting to request help from other shops. With the assistance of workers from those shops, the necessary moves were made.

After moving one part of the carburetor assembly line, management decided to consolidate its two-shift schedule into a single daytime shift; the increased space would allow everyone to work at once. However, most of the 300 people employed on the evening carburetor assembly line were women and students who disagreed with the decision because daytime work would not be convenient for them. By working the second shift, mothers had time to shop and care for their children, who could be watched by day-shift fathers in the evening. Students liked the evening work schedule because it allowed them to attend classes and study during the day.

Management did not change its decision. Instead it asked the party organization for help in explaining the situation to people who were dissatisfied. With the help of the party, management finally convinced the people to go along with the change.

Conclusions

New product introduction is one of the most complicated tasks an organization faces. It requires the coordination of efforts across all groups of employees. It involves basic design, production engineering, manufacturing, and, of course, marketing. Each group has its own outlook on the new product introduction process. Typically, design engineers are interested in developing a technically advanced product, manufacturing personnel want a cost effective product that fits their existing technology, and customers are likely to be concerned with cost reduction as well as with how the product fits their needs (for example, how the engine or shock absorber fits with the rest of the truck). Myriad unknowns—such as whether the new model will work as expected, whether new equipment will perform as required—demand great flexibility and cooperation among the specialists involved in planning for new product introduction.

For these reasons, we see in both countries the development of lateral integrating mechanisms. In the United States, AmTruck had instituted a complex system of teams to help the new-product introduction process. This system worked well, particularly since the company already had good horizontal linking mechanisms (for example, design engineers worked at the plant and a special group of engineers linked marketing with manufacturing, and so forth). AmElectric's equally complex process worked less well because of conflicts between headquarters marketing and plant manufacturing personnel. The most efficient changes occurred with the help of special relationships, as in AmElectric's coupling bolt situation.

In the USSR, SovTruck uses a chief specialist system, in which all R&D and new product introduction was coordinated through the deputy director general for science and technology and the Consolidated Plan for the Development of Science and Technology. The deputy can horizontally connect all chief specialists and all units of the enterprise that are involved in the new product introduction. Moreover, vertical links within the hierarchy, especially in functional areas, remain very important. We saw in the shock absorber case how all enterprise-level departments maintained close contact with their respective plant units throughout the effort. These contacts are especially important during the technological adaptation or development of the product.

In the United States, of course, new product introduction is largely market and customer driven. Customer involvement in the design stage is often crucial to the new product's success (e.g., AmTruck's 1.5C engine). Many of the changes result from customer feedback, either directly or through market performance indicators. In AmElectric's case, the improved delivery time for the coupling bolts prevented the plant from losing more orders than it had already lost to foreign competition. The ruggedized blade program meant increased sales because the new components were more durable and reliable.

In addition, a new product offered exclusively by one US enterprise may enable that enterprise to increase sales by attracting new customers, by getting current customers to replace older products with the new product, and by luring some customers that previously bought from another enterprise. Because they offer a competitive advantage to the enterprise, innovations and new products are carefully guarded secrets. Furthermore, the new-product introduction process itself may be a competitive secret. At the time of our study, AmTruck had recently developed a complex new-product introduction program using specified steps, computers, and other aids to innovation. This process was considered highly proprietary.

In contrast, the Soviet Union pushes innovation by emphasizing the supply of new product ideas. Thus research institutes like SKB must meet new product targets set forth in national plans and according to national schedules. Often their design ideas will be implemented in several enterprises at once. These research institutes do, however, attempt to determine the customer's wishes for new product features and to incorporate those features into their new product designs. Furthermore, as USSR firms now have more wholesale orders from large customers, they are beginning to get more direct customer feedback.

In both countries, new product introduction was affected by government edicts, though more strongly so in the Soviet Union. Government regulations on emissions were a primary motivator for the introduction of AmTruck's 1.5C engine, as they were for SovTruck's K90 carburetor. Nearly all of the new products introduced in our Soviet cases were part of a central plan of product improvement. The Soviets have also found that punishment (a 15% penalty payment) for continued production of old products has encouraged firms to introduce new products, as in the SovElectric case of AIR. In this regard, the government represents the customer. In the United States, economic penalties are levied on firms by the market.

In both countries, continuous improvement represents a major element of product change. And in both countries, continuous improvement is often "bottom up"—initiated by the lower levels in response to tighter targets on manufacturing and product use performance. These improvements tend to be relatively minor changes that are later approved by engineers or higher management; they also tend to be more numerous and rapid (1–4 years) than radical product changes (5–7 years). However, radical product changes initiated from above typically accounted for the larger percentage of new product investment.

It is important to note that since these companies all manufacture relatively mature products, many of their changes were really product extensions. Only SovTruck was introducing a truly "new" product—diesel engines—that required substantial investment and was managed centrally. Such large-scale, high-profile new product introductions as that may take place separately from existing manufacturing facilities.

Unlike these examples, AmTruck introduced its 1.5C engine (considered a class 1 product change, the highest possible major product change) into the existing organizations with the use of multiple and overlapping teams of marketing, design, and production specialists. This reflects a trend in US corporations to incorporate changes into the existing organization by breaking down barriers and promoting lateral linkages.

In general, when faced with the difficult task of introducing a new product, Soviet enterprises have less maneuverability than the typical US firm. This is partially due to the segmentation and separation of the many decisions under different institutes and agencies (i.e., one ministry demands the product change, another institute designs it, a third purchases the new equipment, a fourth sets prices, and so on). In SovElectric's case, the price for its new product was not under its control, and the equipment used for manufacturing was not chosen by the institute that designed the new product.

PART

III

Comparative Decision-Making Patterns

Chapter 10

Managerial Patterns: Differences and Commonalities

It is time to pull together the evidence collected in this research and make some general observations about Soviet and American managerial practices, in particular about the ways decisions are made. In Chapters 6 through 9 we have focused, one at a time, on four decision issues that every organization must deal with. Although those four issues are of interest to managers planning US–USSR joint ventures, many Soviet practices may be subject to fairly rapid change under perestroika. In addition, the ground rules for operating joint ventures in the USSR are different from the ground rules for operating state enterprises. So in this chapter we will move beyond these four discrete issues to draw out of the evidence the patterns of behavior that have a more timeless quality. We will see the four issues as examples of decision practices, as presented in Part I, that are more deeply rooted in tradition and theory, the kinds of practices Soviet and US managers will, without even explicit awareness, carry along as they shift from working in a conventional organization to working in the new joint ventures. Managers must become aware of taken-for-granted ways of doing things if a newly formed management team is to manage any joint venture effectively.

What is the nature of the patterns to be identified in this chapter? Stated quite simply, a managerial pattern is a management practice or behavior that is used over and over again by different people. We will report on these patterned behaviors, drawing on the decision examples presented in the last four chapters. Beyond this, we will highlight the differences and similarities in the patterns observed in the two countries. Perhaps we should say that we will emphasize the differences, because it is knowing the differences that will most benefit joint venture management. These differences require understanding, adaptation, and adjustment in forming an effective joint management team. We stress at the outset, however, that we did find many commonalities—certainly many more than we can report here. It is our impression that managers from both countries tend to assume that there exist greater differences and fewer commonalities than we in fact found. To highlight this observation, it is worth noting some of the common attitudes that we found each side to hold about the other.

Prevalent Thinking

Given the history of adversarial relations between the two countries and the lack of exchange, the existence of certain stereotypes is not at all surprising. Prevalent American assumptions seem to go as follows:

1. The two systems are mutually exclusive.
2. The Soviets know little about management. It follows that we have nothing to learn from them about the subject. They are basically trying with very limited success to apply Western management methods in order to cope with three perennial problems of their system—shortage of inputs, detailed planning and control from the central government, and lack of performance motivation among individuals.
3. Western management methods and techniques have proven vastly superior to those of the Soviets; therefore we have a lot to contribute toward the success of modernization of the Soviet economy.
4. Decision making in local enterprises is dominated by the politics of the Communist party.
5. The dual aim of perestroika—to increase centralization and democratization—is conflicting and therefore impossible.
6. Ordinary Soviet citizens are intimidated and afraid of stating their honest opinions.

Prevalent Soviet thinking about American management could be summarized as follows:

1. American managers operate like economic robots driving aggressively over human values to maximize short-term profits.
2. American managers are given an entirely free hand by the government to run their firms as they see fit.
3. American managers have a vast store of specialized and rather miraculous management techniques that Soviets can quickly adopt to improve performance.
4. American enterprises are not limited in the resources they can bring to bear.
5. Joint ventures provide a way to tap into the US resources of both techniques and capital.

Our study has revealed that these prevalent assumptions from both sides are at best half truths; at worst they are dangerous. We trust that what has been reported already has gone a long way to correct the biases. Further, we want our readers to recognize what managers in both systems have in common. Like managers in all major industrial systems, they work in large bureaucratic organizations that are striving to cope with the common denominators of technology, people, and limited resources. These facts of organizational life cut across differences of ownership and ideology.

Commonalities and Differences: Decision-Making Mechanisms

The statements we will be making about patterns are made in an affirmative manner, but they should be seen as hypotheses based on our limited data from eight field sites. Obviously they need to be tested further, especially in view of the fact that the two management systems are so different. We emphasize also that the differences can be attributed mainly to differences in the two systems and not to any innate differences in individuals. Our statements simply represent the best generalizations we can draw at present from our limited evidence. The comparisons that follow are organized in terms of the different kinds of decision-making mechanisms spelled out in the section on US theory in Chapter 4, and by a set of basic managerial practices.

THE USE OF HIERARCHY IN DECISION MAKING

*In making decisions and resolving conflict, Soviet managers rely more on the hierarchy than US managers do.

Since hierarchy is universally used to achieve coordination in an organization, it is not surprising that the Soviets make extensive use of it. For example, when conflicts arose in SovTruck's introduction of the sandblasting machine (Chapter 8) or in SovElectric's purchase of the Eastern European automatic rotor line, decisions were sent up through the enterprise hierarchy and then at times to the ministry to resolve differences and problems. In contrast, when AmTruck's purchase of the Tekcontrol machine ran into difficulties, the plant managers worked together to reach a solution. US managers use the hierarchy less because, as spelled out in Chapter 3, the pace and complexity of business in recent years has led to increased reliance on lateral and network decision methods. This was especially true at AmTruck. In general, US managers push the decentralization of decision making to the level closest to the needed information and the implementation. This is not true in the USSR, although under perestroika the centralism of the system is being moderated by the introduction of democratic mechanisms.

*Soviet managers reconcile the apparent paradox built into their key management concept of centralized leadership/grass-roots democracy by a signaled alternation of these methods.

We observed the alternation of the two sides of CL/GD in particular around managerial elections and in the development of the annual plan. In the United States, we saw some of this process in what has been called top-down–bottom-up planning. In the Soviet elections we saw this back-and-forth action during the preparation of a slate of candidates, as well as in the final two steps of conducting the election and confirming the choice by higher authority. By this process the selected STU leader was doubly legitimated and thereby doubly strong. Americans are inclined to think that the paradox of CL/GD is impossible to solve, a sham, because they imagine a simultaneous solution. It needs to be emphasized that it is by alternating the action that the paradox is solved.

*Soviet managers are expected to provide strong directive leadership in carrying out policy decisions. This is less true for US managers.

By being clear and assertive—perhaps even inspiring—in leading their subordinates, Soviet managers are being consistent with the centralist aspect of centralized leadership/grass-roots democracy (CL/GD). To do otherwise would in all likelihood be seen as weakness. It is not unusual for Soviet managers to raise their voices with subordinates to clarify and stress what is wanted.

*Soviet managers take their official responsibilities very seriously and are extremely cautious about involving themselves in affairs for which others are officially responsible. This is less true for US managers.

The care Soviet managers take regarding the responsibilities of themselves and others probably stems from a history of severe sanctions for failing to meet responsibilities. Even more basically, the STU system teaches managers to take their own carefully defined responsibilities seriously and not to meddle with those of others. They expect strong negative reactions in response to any incursions into the responsibilities of others and would be expected to guard their own turf in a similar way.

*Soviet managers make greater use of official mechanisms for resolving decision conflicts than do US managers.

Regular provision is made in Soviet management systems for referring disputes to standing committees such as technical councils and to ad hoc commissions created by social organizations. In addition, disputes are often referred to third parties such as arbitration bodies. These mechanisms are used to justify making and paying claims and to absolve individuals of responsibility. Such mechanisms are less frequently used in the United States.

*Soviet managers make more frequent direct contact with subordinates and superiors two or more levels from them in the hierarchy. US managers tend to avoid much direct contact with subordinates more than one level away so as not to disrupt the chain of command.

As a traditional part of the STU system, Soviet managers feel comfortable skipping the chain of command and involving themselves in on-the-spot problems. Soviet plant managers see it as part of their duty to make several plant tours daily and to pick up work-oriented conversations with people at any level. While such actions were also observed in the United States, they were rare.

*The Soviet management system legitimates subordinates from all lower levels having direct access to STU leaders. This is less true of US managers.

One custom we observed was the posting of office hours when any employee or any member of an employee's family could talk with the manager. On plant tours it was customary for employees to initiate a conversation with a senior. This direct access is considered a right of all employees. Employees on duty may even call managers at home if a production problem needs to be solved without delay. While it is not unusual for a US manager to announce an open-door policy, such direct access was much less frequently observed. US managers may sometimes consult with groups of workers on issues that affect them, but they do not do this consistently.

*Soviet managers are more involved in the after-work-hours lives of their employees than are US managers, and Soviet employees expect this. This is much less true in the United States.

This practice probably results from the legally required extensive involvement of Soviet state enterprises in such matters as worker housing, medical care, day care for infants, vacation and recreation facilities, and the procurement of hard-to-get food and consumer products. For example, on the evening of the SovTruck soccer team's game, nearly all managers and workers left the plant to attend. Many of the managers returned to work after the game was over. Though this meant working late into the night, the managers explained that they were expected to attend this important company function.

*Soviet managers use the party and the union organizations to help secure commitment to goals and, at times, to help with human resource development. US managers have no point of comparison.

This practice was observed several times in the Soviet plants. As we saw in Chapter 9, when SovTruck needed help installing equipment for the K90 carburetor, the union helped recruit workers from other areas. And when the new work flow required canceling the second shift, the party helped explain the new schedule to those workers who were inconvenienced by it. However, although the managers view such involvement as a definite help to them in carrying out the work of the plant, they caution against its frequent use.

*Over the years, the Soviets' use of a centralized hierarchy and a directive management style has tended to generate resentment and weakened worker commitment. The emphasis of perestroika on renewing the democratic aspects of CL/GD is beginning to address this problem.

Our interviews with managers and members of the workers' councils convinced us that these democratic mechanisms were being taken seriously. It is still too soon, however, to say how far and how fast these and other democratic mechanisms are swinging the work force from an attitude of alienation and apathy to one of mutual commitment.

*Soviet managers expect to clear management candidates with the social organizations in terms of social acceptability before elections and confirmations proceed. US managers have no point of comparison.

*Soviet managers make a great deal of use of informal contact to facilitate their work, and this is less frequently done in the United States.

The rigidity of the formal system and the constant shortages of needed inputs create the need for Soviet managers to cultivate their outside and their inside personal contacts and friendships even more than US managers, and they are prepared to trade favors to expedite the work.

THE USE OF GROUPS IN HIERARCHICAL DECISION MAKING

*Groups are used more in the USSR than in the United States as a permanent official part of the hierarchical decision process.

The clearest example of group involvement is the role of the council of the workers' collective in the annual planning process, which is an application of the democratic aspect of CL/GD. The plan is not official until the council has approved it. Moreover, this right of the council can be used by the director general of an enterprise to reopen negotiations with the ministry for more favorable terms. The council must also elect STU leaders before the leaders can be officially confirmed by higher authorities. So the council both prepares and makes decisions. The employees' council has its own internal hierarchy with its elected chairman and deputy chairman and elected councils at the shop, plant, and enterprise levels. All members of an STU, including managers, vote to elect council members. Scientific and technical councils also play an important role in investment and innovation policy, and the *khozraschet* commission is used as an adviser on economic and financial problems. The councils are part of the management system and operate differently from the social organizations, the party, the union, Komsomol, and other special groups such as those representing veterans, women, the elderly, and environmental activists. Among these groups the party is especially active in influencing managerial selection and reward, the union in matters of working conditions, rewards and sanctions of workers, and the Komsomol in issues concerning young people. As we saw in the overview of USSR hiring and firing practices, a certifying committee ascertains managers' qualifications. In Soviet capital investment and new product decisions, the technical committee plays a key role, recommending and rejecting expenditures and products. In the United States, on the other hand, the extensive use of committees in the decision process is apt to be seen as a sign of weak management.

*Managers and employees are more likely to identify strongly with their structural task unit (STU) than Americans are likely to identify with their organizational units.

Soviet employees expect their STU leader to represent their interests with higher authorities, and STU leaders expect personal loyalty in return. Soviet individuals gain some security from the protection of their STU. This difference is probably due also to the extensive set of social programs provided by the Soviet enterprises.

*Face-to-face work groups are used more in the USSR than in the United States as the focal unit for productive effort and responsibility.

These groups provide the backbone of the STU system. The use of brigades as a work unit at the bottom of the organization has a long history; this tradition is now being reinforced under perestroika. While there are different forms of brigades, the usual approach is to give a work group a clear-cut, complete task and enter into a quasi-contract to pay the group a lump sum for a specified volume of acceptable output. The group decides how to allocate earned payments that exceed the base wage. This approach bears some similarity to the use of semiautonomous work groups we found in use at AmTruck.

*Soviet managers tend to utilize short daily meetings to conduct affairs with their subordinates. US managers tend to utilize longer weekly meetings with their subordinates.

The meetings conducted by the Soviets are more formal than those we saw in the United States. There is a regular agenda, and a ritual is observed. Participants sit around a rectangular table with the STU leader at the head and others along the sides in descending rank. Representatives of the party and the union, if present, sit back from the table but near the head. The atmosphere is serious; joking is a privilege reserved for the STU leader, who uses it sparingly. There is usually a round of standard reports from each subordinate and then a discussion of any problem areas; the leader dominates the discussion. US meetings tend to be less structured, with an emphasis on open collaborative problem solving and frequent use of round tables and seating that does not reflect rank. (For an elaboration of these practices, see the plant managers' daily schedules in Chapter 5, as well as the USSR section of Chapter 6.)

*Soviet managers make a clearer distinction than do US managers between meetings convened to problem-solve and brainstorm in an exploratory mode and meetings held to execute an action plan by issuing directives to subordinates.

We saw this practice of running two types of meetings as another example of the alternation of the democratic and the centralist approach to resolve the paradox built into the CL/GD system.

*Soviet managers make considerably more use of plantwide meetings than do US managers.

Plantwide meetings are usually used in the USSR to explain the production plan and to appeal for some form of special effort.

*Soviet managers have some limited experience with work in cross-functional project teams when the team coordinator is named by their STU leader.

We saw such teams used when the coordinator was a deputy director from the enterprise staff appointed by the director general and the members were drawn from the lower plant staff, but we were not able to judge their effectiveness.

*Managers in both countries expect strict punctuality at appointments and meetings. In the USSR this applies to superiors as well as to subordinates and peers.

THE USE OF RULES IN DECISION MAKING

*Soviet managers rely more heavily on rules and regulations to achieve integration than do US managers.

The heavy reliance on rules in the USSR is undoubtedly a result of the long reliance on central planning. Many aspects of work at the plant level are governed by rules that have the effect of laws. Chapter 6 elaborated the formal planning process, including the requisite signatures and documents, which culminates in a formal plan that is a legal requirement for the enterprise. Similarly, in SovTruck's new-product introduction process, the instructions (*predpisanje*) are managed centrally and documented carefully along the way. These rules originate from the level of sector ministries or higher. While we observed the use of rules at US sites, it was much less frequent. Rules are a useful way of coordinating action, but they clearly add rigidity that slows down innovation and the adjustment to changing circumstances.

*Soviet managers are more likely than US managers to stick carefully to the rules. This is true even though Soviet managers are ingenious about manipulating the rules to serve their purposes.

Soviets pride themselves in getting things done in spite of the rules and without breaking them.

THE USE OF PLANS IN DECISION MAKING

*Soviet and US mangers rely very heavily on plans to integrate their affairs.

In both countries, planning is a major activity that requires a substantial percentage of management time. The bargaining process is similar in terms of the negotiations that go on between echelons. Of course, in the USSR planning for a plant comes from the ministry, while in the United States it moves up to corporate headquarters. This is a big difference.

*US control and accounting systems used for planning and reporting are more flexibly tailored for management needs, whereas those systems in the USSR are centrally designed, primarily for auditing purposes.

US managers make more use of special situation reports, interim plan reports, and contingency plans.

*Managers in both countries usually try to moderate the performance expectations received from higher authorities.

This is especially true in the USSR and is likely a residual of their history of strong sanctions for missing plan targets.

*US managers expect and are given more flexibility in adjusting plans to changing market circumstances, whereas Soviet managers expect more rigidity.

We saw examples of reopening annual plans in both countries. Some flexibility is possible in both systems, albeit through different methods and to different degrees. AmElectric's plan changed frequently based on incoming market information, and AmTruck utilized a rolling forecast in which numbers were tracked and adjusted monthly. In contrast, the SovTruck motor plant's actual plan changed only once, after the plant economist proved to superiors that the plant's wage fund was underfunded. Despite its efforts to get plan targets reduced or product mix changed, SovElectric's Plant W found its targets unchanged by the ministry. (See Chapter 6.)

THE USE OF DIRECT LATERAL CONTACTS
FOR DECISION MAKING

*US managers make greater use of direct lateral contacts as a legitimate way to make decisions than do Soviet managers.

This difference may be one of the more important ones. Decisions in the United States are regularly made by direct lateral contact among peers at all levels of the firm's hierarchy. They are made within the context of the overall blessing of their shared superior (the common boss) in the interests of getting faster, more economical, and more responsive decision making. Soviet managers seem conditioned to avoid such decision making when it entails crossing STU boundaries; instead, they go up the hierarchy to their common boss for every decision. Soviet managers do, however, use lateral grapevine contacts—if they have an informal relationship—to develop predecision consensus.

*A higher proportion of US managers directly handle relationships with outside groups: customers, suppliers, regulators, and so forth.

Contacts with outsiders help inform US managers of market and other environmental requirements, and this information enables rapid adaptation. The outside contacts are often facilitated by direct computer linkages. Soviet managers are more likely to cultivate informal outside contacts to help develop a predecision consensus.

*US managers are more accustomed to working with blurred and overlapping responsibilities and are therefore willing to concern themselves with issues for which others have primary responsibility but in which they also have a stake.

This history of ambiguity means that US managers are more comfortable with the more frequent reorganizations observed in American firms. It also means they have a great deal more flexibility in processing information in the most expedient manner.

THE USE OF LATERAL CROSS-FUNCTIONAL TEAMS
IN DECISION MAKING

*US managers more frequently employ temporary groups (task forces) whose members are selected from different units and different levels for their special ability to contribute to the particular decision at issue. Soviets use more permanent institutionalized councils, such as the technical council.

In the United States, task-force groups were observed working on new product development, capital equipment projects, and managerial selection. AmTruck's hiring and firing process was team based, and these teams included workers from various areas that might be affected by the hiring or firing decision. New-product introduction processes in both US companies were run by lateral groups composed of engineers, marketers, production staff, financial staff, purchasing staff, and others. These groups are intended to avoid overloading higher authorities and to bring more relevant information to the decision.

*US managers have experience working in cross-functional task forces when leadership is provided by one of their peers, as well as when it comes from a higher level.

We observed US managers not only working in task forces with peer leadership, but also switching leaders on their own initiative as different aspects of the shared task became salient.

Commonalities and Differences: Managerial Practices

MANAGERIAL PRACTICES: TIME

*Soviet managers take more time to deliberate over important decisions than do US managers, but STU leaders do make daily operating decisions very quickly.

It appears that major Soviet decision making moves through the usual pattern revealed in the three-step sequence: the leader poses the issue; the appropriate group deliberates and reaches a group conclusion; the leader considers the group conclusion, makes the decision, and quickly moves on with the necessary operating or implementing decisions. The contrasting fast-slow-fast pace of decision making showed up in the daily rounds of plant managers and in the regular management meetings.

*Managers in both countries work long hours.

We were not able to see any meaningful difference in this regard. Soviet managers say, "The eight-hour day means eight to eight."

*As long as the output plan is fulfilled, Soviet managers do not see time as a cost. US managers consistently see time as a cost factor and regularly search for ways to reduce the time taken to complete an action and to conserve their own time.

*Soviet managers tend to avoid commitments to firm deadlines to reduce the consequences of nonfulfillment. This seems to be less true in the United States.

*At comparable ranks (such as plant manager), US managers seem to spend more time on longer-term issues than do Soviet managers.

The US managers have more ways of delegating operational details that free them to work on future business issues than we observed among Soviet managers, who are much more preoccupied with daily operating chores and hurdles.

MANAGERIAL PRACTICES: COMMUNICATIONS

*For communications, US managers rely more on informal written memoranda and telephone conversations, while Soviet managers rely more on face-to-face encounters.

*Managers in both countries are in transition in learning to use more participative management methods effectively.

In the United States, AmTruck has had more experience in using participative management than AmElectric. This method, while relatively new in both Soviet enterprises, is currently being used extensively as an official part of the system.

*Soviet managers are more reserved about sharing enterprise information with outsiders than are US managers.

Soviet managers made a clear distinction between members of their STU and outsiders. They did not share information with outsiders without a clear explicit instruction. In other words, they rarely volunteer information.

MANAGERIAL PRACTICES: RISKS AND POWER

*Soviet managers are more cautious about taking risks and assuming specific obligations for achieving results than are US managers.

Again, this is probably a result of their history of sanctions. Also, we found that lower levels of management in the United States were able and willing to take on the risk of new projects and proposals. For example, a $5-million investment in AmElectric's flexible machining division was initiated and managed at the plant level. AmTruck's investment cam lobe mill was initiated and managed by a plant engineer. In the Soviet Union, many equipment purchases and product changes were decided on by headquarters and the ministries. For example, SovElectric's Eastern European automatic rotor line (Chapter 8) was ordered by the technical institute of the ministry; SovTruck's diesel engine program was driven by central authorities (Chapter 6); SovElectric's AIR engine introduction was mandated by the State Committee for Science and Technology (Chapter 9).

*Managers in both countries avoid using raw power to resolve conflict, preferring compromise, problem solving, or avoidance.

Managers in both countries go to great lengths to avoid the use of power. It damages the other's sense of self-respect and honor and can lead to lasting ill will.

*Soviet subordinates expect their managers to tell them what to do but not how to do it. In the United States, it is more customary to explain the how as well as the what.

When Soviet employees are told how to do a task, they may take it as an insult to their intelligence and especially to their right to take responsibility for their own job. To tell Soviets how to proceed before they have a chance to deliberate is to omit the second and third phases of the Soviet system of decision making presented in Chapter 4. It risks aborting the decision process and making implementation unlikely. This attitude is seen in the United States more exclusively with professionals and technicians.

*Soviet STU managers have both a right and a responsibility to inform the next-higher STU leader immediately regarding situations in which they feel they do not have adequate resources to fulfill their part of the plan. This also seems true of US managers, but it is not as clear a part of the system.

This, too, is part of the STU system. As all responsibilities are borne by the leader, he or she absolutely needs to be informed of a problem when it arises because only the leader has the authority to make decisions regarding its solution.

*Soviet managers are adept at overcoming unexpected obstacles. They are ingenious at finding solutions once problems have arisen. They can deal with hardship.

As explained in Chapter 4, the Soviet management system grants managers a great deal of discretion in deciding how to fulfill assigned tasks. Ingeniously, patiently, and persistently each manager in his or her own way tackled obstacle after obstacle, usually associated with shortages. For example, when SovTruck introduced a more fuel-efficient carburetor, full production was delayed because the rubber supplier did not provide a new gasket. The plant developed a "detour" assembly process that enabled them to begin production of the new carburetor in limited numbers.

MANAGERIAL PRACTICES: GOALS AND VALUES

*Soviet managers by far put their greatest emphasis on fulfilling the output plan. US managers put their greatest emphasis on meeting the profit goal.

For the Soviet managers this emphasis was apparent as they frequently checked throughout each day the output results for which they were responsible. Although on a much less frequent basis, the US managers kept very close track of costs and profits.

*Soviet managers are likely to see the problem of shortages of supply as their greatest constraint, while the greatest constraint for US managers is apt to be profitable sales. Both sets of managers are apt to see securing qualified people as their second-greatest problem.

This difference was very clear. The US managers had learned to be customer oriented, and the Soviet managers were trained to be oriented to their supply problems. Shortages were a constant. This supply issue is reflected in the fact that Soviet managers prefer to source components from their own enterprise, while US managers display a preference for buy over make.

*Soviet managers are accustomed to coping with plant undercapacity, wherein a single disruption spreads into a production crisis. This means that they have had to develop their skills as troubleshooters. US managers are more experienced with overcapacity and a corresponding need for cost control.

When a problem becomes acute, Soviet managers have been known to deliberately let it develop into a crisis because a crisis is more likely to mobilize an effective response by authorities who have the power and the resources necessary to solve it.

*US managers believe it is important to have every member identify with the goals of the total organization, and they work to achieve this. Soviet managers seem less concerned with goal identification and rely more on individual bonuses and piece rates to motivate managers and workers.

MANAGERIAL PRACTICES: PERSONNEL

*Soviet managers are more likely to have their entire career in one industry than are US managers.

Soviet managers practice some mobility among firms in their industry but to a much lesser degree than US managers. In Soviet firms there is a formal practice of spending a standard amount of time gaining experience at a lower level before one becomes a candidate for promotion to the next higher level. In the United States, the time it takes to move up to a higher level seems to be longer than in the USSR.

*Managers in both countries are generally familiar with bonus schemes that can add significantly to their base salaries, and they do shape their actions to increase these rewards.

As perestroika takes hold, Soviet managers are becoming increasingly aware of their opportunity to enhance their rewards and sense of achievement through their own judgment and effort.

*Rewards tend to be weighted toward fringe benefits in the USSR and toward cash in the United States.

Shortages of goods and services in the USSR have rendered fringe benefits such as housing and other consumer goods more valuable than cash.

*When goals are not met, Soviet managers use sanctions in the forms of cuts in bonus and fringe benefits, demotion, and public criticism. US managers in similar circumstances withhold normal pay raises and use private reprimands. In both countries, dismissal of managers is used in extreme cases.

*Soviet managers are more inclined to use sanctions to correct problems, whereas US managers are more inclined to use rewards.

We see two themes running through the points of differences and commonalities. First is the pervasive influence of shortages in the USSR as against excess capacity in the United States. The behavior of Soviet managers has been conditioned for many years by the persistence of shortages as a central problem. American managers are accustomed to being so constantly concerned with customers that it is difficult for them to imagine as strong a pressure coming from the supply side of the firm. One way to clarify the point is for Americans to imagine their purchasing officer switching roles and power with their head of marketing: that is the condition managers in the Soviet Union take for granted. In the USSR the director general expects to spend a significant amount of time on supply problems, even as in the United States the general manager expects to spend significant time with key customers.

The second summary point is the pervasive influence of the STU and CL/GD system in contrast to the chain-of-command approach. We researchers have been struck with how many points of difference between the two systems can be explained by some aspect of these hierarchical theories. This fact makes it clear that if US managers thoroughly comprehend STU and CL/GD, they will have mastered many of the key aspects of the Soviet managerial culture. Soviet managers, on the other hand, need to understand that US managers are accustomed to using a chain-of-command approach to decision relationships. They expect to communicate up and down the hierarchy one step at a time. The freedom for direct contact between STU leaders and subordinates at any level will initially strike US leaders as hazardous and unnatural. The Soviet manager needs also to realize that US managers have learned to make decisions directly with their peers in other units within the broad context of the agreed-upon plan or budget. These direct lateral relations, one-on-one or in a task group, will initially strike Soviet managers as hazardous and unnatural.

Soviet managers will also find it strange that US managers are accustomed to *requesting* their subordinates to follow instructions rather than ordering them to do so. US managers, on the other hand, do not expect to have to stand for election as well as be appointed by higher authority. In effect, they do not have as strong a foundation for their authority as the Soviet system provides its managers. The distinctive management system of each country has evolved a different way of handling both the vertical and the horizontal relations in the organization. Awareness of this difference is a fundamental step toward working out some mutually acceptable guidelines for the successful operation of any future joint ventures. Addressing this issue is the theme of the final chapter.

Chapter 11

Trends and Conclusions

In Chapter 10 we examined differences and similarities in management practices in the United States and the USSR. The value of such comparisons is that they highlight basic characteristics that need to be taken into account in the operation of any Soviet-American joint venture. They help us understand how our partners traditionally do things, and at the same time they help us sharpen our awareness of how we do things ourselves.

Another way of looking at a management system is with a focus on change. Identifying trends helps us anticipate the future. It helps us see the direction in which things are moving. Part of what we looked for in our study was evidence of change in each country's management practices. After we have both comparisons and trends in hand, we will conclude by discussing the implications of our findings for the operation of joint ventures.

Trends in Management Practice

TRENDS IN THE USSR

Trends in management practices in the USSR can be summarized around the word *perestroika,* or restructuring. Manifestations of the economic part of this reform movement were apparent at the operating level in all the sites we studied. We cannot sufficiently emphasize how fundamental and all-encompassing this process of change is. All elements of the process of conducting economic transactions are being radically altered. While a number of elements have already been changed, many other changes are awaiting implementation. It is unrealistic, of course, to expect that once reforms have been announced, Soviet stores will quickly fill up with a full range of consumer goods at affordable prices. Reforms of the magnitude envisaged by perestroika cannot be implemented with a stroke of the pen; it will take many years for them to be realized. After discussing this issue with many Soviet citizens, we find that the Soviets are more realistic about the time required for basic change than most Western commentators are. If the trends we observed at the factory level are carried through on a widespread and consistent basis, they should, by all economic logic, lead to significant improvements.

Managers of joint ventures between US and USSR enterprises will want to pay special attention to elements of perestroika reform that are directly relevant to the management of enterprises. One is the system of self-financing, along with the corresponding gradual shift from complete reliance on state orders to the use of direct wholesale trade relations. If fully implemented, this will entail a radical decentralization of the economic system. It involves nothing less than the shift from a single monopolistic ministry as the corporate headquarters for an entire industrial sector, to some dozens of competing enterprises comprising that sector. It also represents a general restructuring of industry, a shift from large enterprises only to a mix of large and small enterprises competing with one another within a framework of reduced state guidance. This trend is beginning to make managers at both SovElectric and SovTruck feel more responsible for their own destiny. An example in our study was the setting up of certain brigades as independent suppliers in a cooperative legal form. These infant enterprises were acting as subcontractors and at times leased their parent's facilities for off-hour production.

As a by-product of self-financing, Soviet managers are developing an increased cost consciousness. Under the traditional central planning system, enterprises had learned to negotiate production targets that were relatively easy to meet. This fact, in combination with price controls, meant that managers did not need to worry too much about costs. If losses occurred, it was rather customary for them to be covered by grants from higher authorities. Under perestroika, incentives are gradually shifting. In the one site we studied that had elected to use the riskier form of self-financing (model 2), managers were beginning to see that it was to the advantage of their firm and themselves to focus their effort on restraining costs of all kinds. As a result, we saw them flattening their structures and shopping for more cost-effective capital equipment.

A number of democratizing mechanisms are being introduced as part of perestroika. The principal examples are institutionalizing the rights of the new employees' collective councils and the election—as well as the selection—of structural task unit (STU) leaders. These mechanisms constitute an important step toward engaging and renewing the interest and support of rank-and-file employees in the tasks of an enterprise. In both SovTruck and SovElectric we observed that these mechanisms are having definite impacts on management practice. At our field research sites, people at all levels are taking democratization very seriously. Managers are using these new mechanisms as a regular part of their decision process. We were frankly surprised at the speed with which these aspects of reform were being implemented. We concluded that these democratic elements were renewing a latent element of Soviet culture, the tradition of communal work discussed in Chapter 2.

An additional perestroika element we saw being introduced was the establishment of direct supplier-industrial customer relations. This is the start of a wholesale trade system planned largely to supplant the use of state orders. The swing in this direction is just starting to influence management decision practice. We saw, for example, some evidence of managers, having obtained the opportunity to bargain for better prices with the ministry, paying more attention to their customers' requirements in terms of product design, quality, and delivery. Even though both Soviet enterprises had some years of experience in meeting the more demanding requirements of export customers, they are motivated to be even more responsive to these demands now that they have their own free currency accounts and can deal with foreign customers on a direct basis. We saw the same process of customer orientation developing with their few direct domestic customers. Continued progress in the direction of direct wholesale trade is clearly dependent on implementation of the government's plans for general price reform and further reduction of state orders.

Perestroika supports the development of new kinds of foreign economic linkages. The current emphasis is primarily on joint ventures with Western partners. Enactment of the new joint venture law itself and the subsequent startup of numerous joint ventures with foreign partners provide concrete evidence of this trend. The directors general of both enterprises we studied talked to us of their active search for ways to find mutually attractive joint ventures with foreign partners. We believe that this interest may have been one of the reasons they agreed to host our research work.

The trends we have been discussing are early steps toward the complete economic reform visualized by perestroika. Nevertheless, they are significant steps. They indicate that perestroika is under way at the factory level. The managers we talked to are generally trying to understand perestroika. Its aims make sense to them. Managers were willing, by and large, to change their thinking and behavior in pace with changes in the larger system. They were willing to move to direct wholesale trade contracts as the level of state orders was cut back to free up production capacity. They were willing to move to the riskier model-2 form of self-financing when facts indicated their enterprises had a reasonable chance of meeting profit goals. They were quickly learning the new economic thinking and its implications for their action and well-being. They were learning about customer requirements for higher quality and on-time delivery. The amount of change they were being asked to accommodate was awesome, and the resulting stresses and strains were apparent. Given the scope of the changes, their rate of implementation was impressive. While commitment to change varied from individual to individual, we observed no real resistance to change at the factory level. We see this as an important finding with clear, positive implications for the success of joint ventures.

TRENDS IN THE UNITED STATES

A considerable amount of information is available about general trends in management practices in the United States. While these new approaches are evolving in response to economic conditions rather than governmental directives, they in fact amount to a restructuring, US style. We will review some of the trends that were evident at our AmTruck and AmElectric research sites.

AmTruck and especially AmElectric have been significantly reducing levels of employment and increasing the number of components they purchase from outside sources. In this process the divisions we studied are becoming more focused, reflecting a general US trend away from large, highly integrated and/or diversified firms toward smaller, more focused enterprises. In the 1980s, many large firms have become smaller in terms of employment. To cite one indicator, the Forbes 800 largest US firms employed 23 million people in 1979 and only 20.6 million people in 1986, even though total employment rose during that period. This persistent unprecedented drop in relative employment in large firms is taking the form not only of attrition and out-sourcing, but—perhaps more interestingly —of divestments and spinoffs. Divestments and leveraged buyouts often are initiated either in anticipation of, or subsequent to, hostile takeovers. Divestment followed approximately 60% of the hostile takeovers of 1985 and 1986.[1]

Both of the US enterprises we studied are using lateral networking in innovative ways to reduce their costs and response time. The practice of lateral networking has been spreading in firms throughout the United States

1. Bhide, Amarnath, "The Causes and Consequences of Hostile Takeovers," Dissertation, Harvard Business School, 1987.

as they trim the size of staff departments and the numbers of echelons in their hierarchies. In an effort to improve competitive stance, firm after firm has been reducing overhead costs by becoming "flat and lean." Through this process, the span of control of executives is widening. Coordination is increasingly achieved by the use of various lateral integration methods. The need for faster, more innovative responses to changing markets and technologies has fostered the use of mechanisms such as task forces, cross-functional teams, and matrix systems. The boundaries between functional departments are becoming permeable in the interest of shortening the time required between product design and manufacturing and sales.

Another general trend in US industry is toward participative management. In the past, as shown in Chapter 3, tensions and conflicts between management and labor in both union and nonunion enterprises have been costly. With today's global competition, these costs often are no longer tolerable. New arrangements are being developed. Mutual commitment and collaboration between management and labor are taking the place of what were formerly adversarial relationships. Both AmElectric and AmTruck use participative management methods. Many firms, including AmTruck, are even making structural changes by setting up semiautonomous work groups (not totally unlike Soviet labor brigades) that perform an entire step in the production process. The labor group assumes responsibility not only for output volume, but also for quality control, safety, supplies, scheduling, process improvements, machine maintenance, training, and—at times— hiring, discipline, and even leader selection. Such groups can achieve significant overhead savings as well as improve direct labor productivity. Firms often follow up such changes with new kinds of compensation arrangements—various forms of gainsharing and pay for group performance. Many firms are also setting up elected worker councils for the purpose of involving rank-and-file personnel in planning with managers. This bottom-up process contributes to greater mutual commitment and generates useful ideas from all levels of the organization.

AmElectric and AmTruck are moving from arm's-length commercial relationships with supplier firms into relationships with more of a partnership nature. This reflects a trend in the United States. As firms from the raw-material end of the value-added chain to the final retailer face stiffer competition, managers are realizing that every unit of the chain needs to be an effective, profitable performer: the entire chain can be no stronger than its weakest link. This awareness has focused attention on ways to reduce costs and improve performance at every step. It has led industrial customers to trim their list of suppliers to a select group who can be depended on for on-time, high-quality deliveries. Relationships are entered into on a long-term basis with the exchange of many kinds of mutual help. Partners in the supply chain join in efforts to reduce inventories, achieve zero defects and on-time deliveries, coordinate designs, and reduce costs both by anticipating fluctuations in orders and by minimizing transport expenses. The development of lasting wholesale trade relations calls for an extensive exchange of information about orders and business plans, an exchange often facilitated by direct computer linkages. Through these processes, trust is gradually built up so that business partners will honor commitments and avoid taking advantage of temporary opportunities to exploit the others' weaknesses. We saw evidence that both AmTruck and AmElectric were actively moving their relationships with suppliers and customers in this direction.

A conspicuous trend in restructuring US industry is the increased use of joint ventures as a vehicle for doing business internationally. These strategic alliances have been evolving in many fields during the eighties, often in response to changing national industrial policies. US firms entered into some 2,000 of these alliances in Europe during the 1980s. General Motors offers an especially interesting example. In 1966, GM stated in its annual report that "Unified ownership for coordinated policy control of all of our operations throughout the world is essential for our effective performance as a worldwide corporation." Twenty years later, GM had created joint ventures and other cooperative arrangements with numerous firms around the world. In Japan alone, these tie-ups linked GM with Toyota, Isuzu, Suzuki, Nissan, Hitachi, Fanuc, and many smaller firms. All these arrangements represent a dramatic change from the firm's traditional policy of vertical integration. Both US firms we researched for this project are involved in foreign joint ventures. In fact, while we were doing our research at AmElectric, it entered into a major joint venture arrangement with a leading European firm. AmTruck has several similar arrangements in place in Europe and Asia.

The simple listing of these trends in the United States and the USSR reveals some surprising similarities in how the two countries are restructuring. Even though it is true that the process had a very different starting point in each country and has proceeded longer and further in the United States than in the USSR, similarities in the direction of movement are evident. In both countries the trends can be given roughly the same labels: smaller, focused enterprises; flatter, network organizations; mutual commitment work forces; supplier partnerships; and strategic foreign alliances. Trends in both countries represent an effort to come to terms with the realities of an increasingly competitive global economy, sophisticated information technology, and a better educated, more demanding work force.

Conclusions of the Study for Joint Ventures

With both comparisons and trends in focus, we can turn now to the implications of our research for operating US–USSR joint ventures. Our analysis of implications will assume that both partners have sensible strategic reasons for working with each other and that both partners see potential profits to be shared from the value that can be added by the combination of their resources and skills. All successful joint ventures must be built upon a foundation of complementary long-term interests. This foundation alone, however, is not sufficient to assure the success of a US–USSR joint venture. Success will also depend on the creation of an effective organization, one composed of managers drawn from both cultures who are committed to work together and integrate the essential elements of the two management systems. The creation of such an integrated organization cannot be taken for granted. The process of building it will be the focus of our conclusions.

Our study reveals that the United States and the Soviet Union have distinct management systems that have evolved from their own traditions, values, and priorities. It would be all too easy to blur these differences and brush over their importance. Joint venture managers will need to work at recognizing and understanding the differences. The differences can become real only when they are seen in comparative terms: one needs enhanced insights into one's own system as well as into that of one's partner. Beyond simply *recognizing* differences, joint venture managers will need to *respect* the differences. Respect in this instance does not mean automatic endorsement: it means comprehending the reasons and rationale behind the management practices. It means understanding the strengths and weaknesses of the practices. Joint venture managers will need to "go to school" on each other's management system.

To be successful, joint ventures will need to integrate elements from both management systems. It makes no sense to propose that a joint venture should be run entirely by Soviet methods or entirely by American methods. On the other hand, a successful joint venture cannot be a random mixture of US and Soviet practices. What is clearly needed is careful, selective integration of elements from both systems. Accomplishing this represents the key challenge to the effective operation of all joint ventures between US and USSR enterprises. We suggest two guidelines to address this issue.

1. If management practices on a given issue are contradictory, recognize that even though both may have merit, one approach needs to be chosen over the other to achieve consistency. The choice should logically favor the

"homeland" partner on whose turf the venture is located and who in all likelihood will supply the majority of employees.
2. If management practices on a given issue are complementary, look for ways to utilize the strength of both systems.

The application of these guidelines can be demonstrated by drawing examples from major differences we have already identified.

We have shown that managers in the two systems use different ground rules to manage hierarchies. In the USSR these ground rules are latent in the STU system; in the United States, in the chain-of-command system. To simplify the differences, the chain-of-command system expects managers to pass messages and instructions up and down the command ladder one step at a time. The STU system provides for direct communication, up or down, between an STU leader and any STU members at any level, in effect bypassing intervening levels of managers. Each system mirrors the other's strengths and weaknesses. The strength of the STU system is that it fosters personal loyalty, commitment, and clarity of communication among leaders and followers at all levels. Its weakness is that there is the potential, if great care is not taken, for different STU leaders to communicate conflicting instructions to subordinates and for the interests of smaller STUs to be given priority over the interests of the enterprise. The US system's strength is that it better ensures that conflicting instructions are not given to subordinates. Its weakness is that a gap can easily develop between the top and bottom of the hierarchy, with the top leader isolated from followers and followers alienated from the vision of the top leader. In the chain-of-command system, special effort has to be exerted to avoid this hazard.

Each of these hierarchical systems works. However, they are basically contradictory systems. It is hard to imagine both working effectively in a single organization. Managers using chain-of-command could well feel bypassed and violated by a superior using STU methods. The STU leader could well experience the chain-of-command superior as indifferent and uncommitted. This would be especially true if the partners failed to recognize the latent differences and assumed they were both playing by the same hierarchical rules.

On this issue we suggest that a choice of hierarchical systems must be made. Either could work, but since in most projected joint ventures the USSR enterprise will be the homeland partner, we suggest that American joint venture managers consciously choose to learn and practice the STU system. American managers will need to learn to exercise their right to communicate directly with subordinates at every level. This presents an obvious challenge to American managers, but their Soviet colleagues, aware of the need, can help by serving as on-the-job coaches.

To move to another important difference, we found that Soviet managers, who have to deal routinely with commands from above and chronic supply shortages, have developed special expertise in procurement of inputs and resources for their enterprises. We also found that US managers, working in an arena of intense competition and limited demand, have developed special expertise in marketing and sales. These are important and dramatic differences, but in this instance they are clearly complementary. Successful US–USSR joint ventures will need expertise and skills in terms of both procurement and marketing. In comparison to Soviet managers, US managers would be babes-in-the-woods regarding procurement in the Soviet Union. In regard to international marketing, the opposite would probably be true. Clearly, a solution lies in fully utilizing the special expertise of each partner for the common good.

We have seen evidence that each country's management system employs a special kind of decision process that is relatively unfamiliar to the other. In the US system we are referring to the use of lateral networking; in the Soviet system, to the use of centralized leadership/grass-roots democracy. Both systems have special strengths that must be reviewed and assessed in terms of whether or not they are complementary.

The US system of lateral networking has evolved a set of procedures to facilitate making decisions directly between functional units in an enterprise (design, manufacturing, marketing, and so forth) and also directly between these units and suppliers and customers. We have described these methods as network decision making and partnership supplier relations. These methods have emerged in US practice in response to increased competitive pressure and increased complexity of decision making. They serve to expedite, economize, and upgrade the decision process. They bring a firm closer to its customers and suppliers. They also lessen dependence on the hierarchical decision system, relieving upper management from operational issues to reserve its strength for strategic issues. These methods, which are in use at both the US firms we studied, represent the latest wave of organizational development in the United States. If integrated with other practices, we believe they should strengthen joint ventures by helping them meet high standards of efficiency and innovation.

The special decision-making method that the Soviets practice is, of course, CL/GD. Like the STU system, this element is deeply embedded in the Russian manager's culture. Its democratic side offers the clear advantage of helping to achieve a well-considered decision with full commitment to back it up. What may not be so clear, but probably is equally valuable, is that its centralized side offers the power of clear, strong leadership and the mechanism for disciplined execution. This strength of leadership, a virtue frequently missing in current US practice, can be utilized only if it is balanced by the democratic phase. The Soviets are ingenious in resolving the apparent paradox built into CL/GD by clearly alternating the two phases. These alternating centralized and decentralized phases are separated in time, and the switches from one phase to the other are signaled by social rituals. Each phase is an inseparable part of an integrated whole; if either is ignored or exaggerated, the whole decision process is weakened. This system offers real advantages for a US–USSR joint venture.

We see no major obstacle to a joint venture's using both decision-making methods on a concurrent basis. Any organization profits from a decision system that effectively pulls the top and bottom of an organization together as a coordinated team. The CL/GD system offers this strength. Any organization can also use a decision system that makes possible direct coordination between functional units and between those units and suppliers and customers. Networking offers this strength. To sum it up, Soviet decision practices (CL/GD) can strengthen the vertical aspects of decision making, and networking can strengthen the horizonal aspects.

Fitting these two decision systems into a harmonious single system will be a challenge, but we see no insurmountable obstacles to its accomplishment. What will be involved is essentially a learning process. US joint venture managers will need to learn to allow time for each phase of the decision process to run its course and to shift cleanly and gracefully from one stage to the next. They must learn to act with decisive authority in the centralized phase, and in the democratic phase they must learn to work constructively with employees' councils whether or not the councils are actually mandated. Implementing network decision methods and supplier partnerships in joint ventures will require accommodations on the part of Soviet partners. Soviet managers must learn to work directly with other STUs without consulting their common boss. As we noted earlier, Soviet managers traditionally do not share their problems with members of other STUs. This ingrained habit will need to be modified to achieve the kind of lateral openness that is necessary for networking to function properly. We saw encouraging evidence that some Soviet managers are beginning to use network and partnership methods. They are starting to set up task forces and conduct direct wholesale trade relations. In many instances the use of networking methods in joint ventures will speed up changes that are already under way.

To repeat, we see no unmanageable obstacle to integrating both decision-making systems in a single joint venture. To the contrary, we see a potential for real added strength in a careful combination of these two approaches.

The three examples of handling differences discussed here demonstrate potential ways of integrating features of both management systems into a single joint-venture system. Similar efforts will undoubtedly have to be made in other aspects of the managing process. Integrating solutions will vary depending on characteristics of the industry, market, and technology involved. Partners in each joint venture will need to make joint decisions about integration on a case-by-case basis. We have outlined an approach to this integration process. It addresses the issue of understanding and handling contradictory practices, and it points out the potential of complementary practices.

Our research team's experience suggests additional ideas for joint ventures and some reasons for cautious optimism. In many respects, our team project provided a microcosm of some of the challenges of a joint business venture. Jointly we had to accomplish a specific task; we worked with specific objectives, methodologies, and constraints to which we had jointly agreed. We found that not everything could be worked out in advance. Often we had to proceed on trust and learn by working together on a concrete task. Our study provided us with fresh insights not only into the systems of our colleagues, but also into our own systems as we began to see them mirrored from the other's perspective. Finally, we had the greatest success as a team when both sides brought a desire for learning to the relationship, as well as a desire for teaching. While both drives were needed, things worked better when the desire for learning dominated.

Our analysis has highlighted the distinctive features of each country's management system and the possibilities for the creative combination of differences, but we do want to remind our readers that both systems also have a great deal in common. Managers in both systems have learned to manage in large bureaucratic organizations; they have had to deal with the shared realities of managing people and technologies with limited resources. These common aspects of organizational life cut across differences of ownership and ideology. In fact, one important insight from our research is that the gap between our two theories is greater than the gap between our practices.

In summary, we believe there are sound reasons for optimism about the potential for success of US–USSR joint ventures. This optimism is based primarily on the fact that opportunities now exist for negotiating joint ventures that meet the long-run strategic interests of both parties. It is also based on our findings about management practices in the two countries. We have learned that understanding and integration are the keys to success. The challenges are manageable, the rewards can be substantial, and there is much at stake.

PART IV

Appendices

Appendix A

A Description of Soviet Laws and Policies on Joint Ventures

Definition and Policies

Foreign economic relations are making a tangible and increasing contribution to the development of the Soviet economy and to the nation's wider involvement in the international division of labor. There is now practically no industrial sector that has been left out of the sphere of foreign economic relations. Soviet international trade policy is now aimed at moving from the exchange of goods to more comprehensive and effective forms of cooperation such as joint ventures. This new approach to international economic relations is reflected in Article XIX of the Law on the Soviet State Enterprise of June 30, 1987. Article XIX determines that the foreign economic activities of the Soviet enterprise are to be an important component in its overall economic performance. All Soviet enterprises have the right to establish joint ventures directly with foreign partners.

Joint ventures are enterprises that can be established abroad and/or on the territory of the USSR. The joint venture is a joint activity in the area of manufacturing or services on the basis of united ownership and joint management of manufacturing and sales, as well as division of the profits and risks. Decree No. 49 of the USSR Council of Ministers, dated January 13, 1987, as amended and supplemented by Decree No. 1074 of September 17, 1987 and Decree No. 51 of December 2, 1988, stipulates the conditions for the creation and operation of joint ventures in the USSR. Joint ventures thus occupy a special place in the Soviet economy. Together with industrial, scientific, and technical cooperation, joint ventures are considered to be a major channel for developing direct economic ties between Soviet enterprises and firms from capitalist and developing countries.

301

AIMS OF JOINT VENTURES

The Soviet decrees stipulate that the following objectives should be obtained by joint ventures in the USSR:

- Attain more fully national aims in a number of industrial products, raw materials, foodstuffs, and consumer products of high quality.
- Infuse the Soviet economy with the best in foreign technologies and management, as well as with additional financial resources.
- Further develop the country's exports.
- Reduce imports.

CONDITIONS

The following are some of the main conditions established:

1. According to Instruction No. 224 of the USSR Ministry of Finance of November 24, 1987, joint ventures can engage in all fields of economic activities stipulated in their official registration. Instruction No. 224 contains all the regulations concerning the procedure of registering joint ventures with Soviet authorities.
2. The joint venture is not included in the Soviet system of centralized planning (Gosplan).
3. The ministry or department in control of a given sector of the economy does not have the legal or economic right to involve itself in the commercial dealings of joint ventures.
4. Profitability is a basic condition of the functioning of the joint venture enterprise.
5. Joint ventures must be self-sufficient in free currency.
6. The state does not assume responsibility for providing inputs to, and/or for absorbing outputs of, the joint venture.
7. Insofar as the joint venture enterprise interacts with sectors of the Soviet economy for the sale of its goods or services to the domestic market and for obtaining inputs from Soviet suppliers, it is subject to Soviet law.
8. The joint venture decides by itself the questions of input procurement, import-export operations, technology, and machinery and equipment within the constraint of its economic and free-currency self-sufficiency.
9. The Decree of December 2, 1988 grants to Soviet enterprises and cooperatives broader rights in the decision process of the establishment of a joint venture and stipulates that Western partners can hold majority ownership; they can have equal power in company decisions; and they can name their general manager or chairman of the board. It further stipulates that joint ventures no longer need permission from Soviet authorities to hire and fire, and that they can make incentive payments to Soviet employees as

they see fit. Other clauses decrease import duties and taxes, diminish the involvement of government bureaucracies in the approval of the establishment of joint ventures, and permit foreign employees of joint ventures to pay their housing and other costs of services in rubles. Joint ventures may also have direct communication links with foreign countries.

AREAS OF JOINT VENTURE ACTION

The areas of joint venture activity given priority by current Soviet economic policies are the following: machine building, oil and gas refining, the manufacture of computer hardware and other high-tech industries, agribusiness, public health, and high-quality consumer goods. Moreover, Soviet approving agencies give priority to joint ventures with the highest technology for the product they will produce, for contemporary Western methods of organization and management, and for exportability of their product to international markets. By late 1989 1,106 joint ventures with Western partners had been established in the Soviet Union, 116 of which were with American companies. Hundreds of other joint venture proposals are now in various stages of the negotiation process.

ESTABLISHING A JOINT VENTURE

A joint venture is to be established according to the following sequence of steps:

1. *The search for alternative suitable interested partners.*   At the present stage of economic reform, the search for suitable partners is one of the most important issues in the creation of a joint venture. It is crucial that both sides examine a number of possibilities, creating alternative choices.
2. *Choice of partners and preliminary discussions with partners and their Soviet superior agency.*   Special care must be given to identifying the *authorized* superior agency.
3. *Letter of intent.*   Preparation and signature of a letter of intent with the partners and approved by the Soviet partners' superior agency.
4. *Joint preparation of the feasibility study and negotiation of the terms of the charter (founding documents) of the joint venture.*   Both the feasibility study and the charter are obligatory for a joint venture to be approved. The charter is the most important guide for the activities of the enterprise and for managerial decision making; it is also the principle governing relations between partners. As there is no corporate law in the USSR yet, the charter of the joint venture, as approved by the Soviet authorities, constitutes the basis for the law applicable to the venture partners. Although So-

viet civil law applies to joint ventures, the Law on the Soviet State Enterprise is not directly applicable to them. Therefore the charter can stipulate that all disputes between partners will be settled by a court of arbitration sitting either in the Soviet Union or in any other country on which the partners agree.

5. *Submission of the feasibility study and the charter by the Soviet partners to their superior authority for approval.*

6. *Registration of the joint venture by the Department of State Revenues and Taxes of the Soviet Ministry of Finance.* After registration with the Ministry of Finance, the joint venture is recognized as a legal Soviet entity and can start operating.

The Managerial Structure of the Joint Venture

According to Soviet law, the managerial bodies of a joint venture are the board of directors, management, and a review committee. The structure of management varies depending on the activity of each joint venture and on the policy of its partners.

The highest body of the joint venture is the board of directors, which can consist of up to seven members. All members of the board are appointed by the partners. The chair of the board can be either Soviet or Western, but either the chair of the board or the chief executive officer must be Soviet. Each partner has the right to remove its representatives at its own discretion at any time and replace them with new ones after informing the other partners. The charter should stipulate the length of notice a partner must give the other partner before changing its representatives.

One of the board's principal responsibilities is decision making. The decision-making procedure must be the one outlined in the charter. The board of directors should meet quarterly or semiannually to address the following basic issues of the enterprise:

- Changes in the charter
- Substantial changes in the assets
- Changes in the shares of partners
- Increasing capital
- Approval of the annual balance sheet and profit-and-loss statement
- Use and dispersal of after-tax profits
- Personnel evaluation

Management is appointed by the board of directors. The structure of managerial functions must be designed to meet the particular needs of the enterprise. The board receives and approves reports from the chief executive officer and approves managerial personnel hired.

The Joint Venture's Assets and Financing

There are no limits on the size of the joint venture's assets, but joint ventures are required to keep a liquidity reserve of at least 25% of their assets. This reserve can be drawn on for unanticipated working capital needs, but has to be restored. The partners agree on the kinds and amounts of assets needed as well as on the value of one another's contributions of assets to the joint venture. Soviet laws stipulate a minimum depreciation rate for assets, but shorter depreciation periods can be established in the joint venture charter. The law also stipulates that funds for research and development (before taxes) and funds for employee incentives and social problems (after taxes) should be set aside before calculating profits. The books must be kept according to relevant Soviet legislation, either in rubles or in foreign currency. The charter and the board of directors establish the arrangements for net profit distribution and the reinvestment policy of the joint venture. A number of Soviet banks provide credits for joint ventures in the Soviet Union. Credits are granted in rubles and/or in free currency on the basis of internationally accepted criteria for financing.

Inputs and Outputs of the Joint Venture

While state enterprises in the Soviet Union are supplied with inputs by a state-controlled industrywide system, joint ventures are free to select their raw material inputs from the Soviet market or from abroad, independently of the state plan. The same is true for the procurement of machines and equipment. Furthermore, know-how and technology can constitute an input. However, the charter of the joint venture should clearly stipulate the obligations and rights of the joint venture to receive Soviet inputs and to supply outputs, and the methods to be used for calculating the prices of inputs from and outputs to the Soviet economy. Essentially, prices should correspond as closely as possible to those of the international market.

Unless otherwise stipulated in the charter, inputs and outputs of joint ventures from and to the Soviet market will be settled in rubles. Joint ventures are free to import inputs from abroad, provided that the necessary free currency derives from the joint venture's own funds. Import duties for imports of foreign goods by joint ventures will be assessed, although import duty exemptions for special cases are foreseen in the legislation and should be mentioned in the charter.

Decision Making about Joint Enterprise Personnel

The personnel of the joint venture are made up of Soviet and foreign citizens, and the remuneration and benefits as well as working conditions of Soviet employees are decided by joint venture management. But joint ventures can agree to different conditions for the remuneration of foreign personnel.

Appendix B

Aspects of Forming Joint Ventures in the USSR

Comments for the Western Investor

Soviet government reforms in the area of foreign economic relations have opened a wide range of new opportunities for business with the West. Today's Soviet attitude is one of pragmatic willingness to expand areas of activity and develop new structures for the country's involvement in the international marketplace.[1] In fact, within the context of this radical change of attitudes, perhaps the most spectacular step away from the policy of economic autarchy is the institutionalization of industrial cooperation with the West.

By fostering the establishment of joint ventures between Soviet and foreign partners on Soviet soil, the Soviet government has opened to Western companies a major route for long-term access to the huge Soviet market and its resources. The Soviet economy's basic strengths—abundant raw materials, a well-educated labor force, and above all, a huge market—form a sound foundation for joint ventures. Although current transitions in the Soviet system will make it initially difficult for Western companies to assess risks and identify levels of return on their investments, the number of joint ventures in the Soviet Union with Western partners had well exceeded 1,000 by the end of 1989. Thus an altogether new marketplace is emerging for American companies large and small.

The Western company that enters a joint venture with the Soviet Union will have three main expectations:

- To obtain access to the otherwise sealed Soviet market.
- To make a secure and profitable investment.

1. Gorbachev, M., Speech to UN General Assembly, November 1988. "The existence of any 'closed' societies is hardly possible today. That is why we need a radical revision of views on the sum total of the problems of international cooperation as the most essential component of universal security." Reported in *Pravda,* November 16, 1988.

• To receive its profits in free currency.

The avenue of joint venture offers the Soviet partner a number of advantages. In addition to profits, it can obtain direct access to advanced techniques and Western markets. Moreover, it can circumvent some of the bureaucratic procedures of the Soviet planned economy.

While this book focuses on the operating dynamics of US–USSR joint ventures, we believe that specific information on the establishment of such ventures will be useful to American managers who are contemplating business partnerships with Soviet firms.

Important Startup Issues

AMBIGUITY OF SOVIET JOINT VENTURE DECREES

Although the original USSR joint venture decree has been twice amended for the purpose of clarifying terminology, many ambiguities remain. Attachment B is a glossary of some joint venture terms that have been worked out between Soviet and Western experts. Explaining their terminology, however, does not entirely explicate the decrees. According to Kay Hober, a scholar of US–USSR joint ventures,

> Generally speaking, these decrees lack the specificity that Western lawyers are accustomed to in the laws and regulations, but on the other hand provide a flexible framework for negotiations. When the decrees were published, this vagueness was criticized to a certain degree by Western companies. It should be pointed out, however, that flexibility and vagueness may be two sides of the same coin. In fact, the flexibility provided enables Western partners to influence the joint venture to a very high degree.[2]

While ambiguity allows flexibility, it also demands close attention and special care.

Decree No. 49 of the USSR Council of Ministers dated January 13, 1987 specifies under paragraph II-8 that the foundation documents of the joint venture shall consist of the joint venture agreement and the joint venture statute, which we will refer to as "the charter." In open concert with each other, American and Soviet partners should exploit flexibility to the fullest by clarifying in the charter only those points that absolutely need clarification, thus reserving the option to interpret rules as problems or opportuni-

2. Hober, Kay, "Negotiating Joint Ventures in the Soviet Union," *International Financial Law Review*, October 1988, p. NR 4.

ties arise in the operation of the joint venture. The American partner should, however, clarify essential points before entering into a joint venture agreement. Whereas contracts among Western firms need not spell out minute details and foresee every possible eventuality, contracts with the Soviets must do exactly that on essential points.

LOCATING THE APPROPRIATE SOVIET PARTNER

With certain limitations, nearly all Soviet state enterprises and cooperatives are entitled to deal directly in international trade and establish joint ventures with foreign partners. The decree of the Soviet Council of Ministers of March 7, 1989, "Measures Concerning the State of Foreign Economic Activities," which was followed by Regulations by the State Foreign Economic Commission on March 20 on "Foreign Trade Licensing System" provides for licenses and controls connected with the establishment of joint ventures, with the import and export activities of joint venture enterprises in the USSR, and with the Soviet countertrade goods to earn the convertible currencies needed by joint ventures. By enhancing direct access and increasing the number of alternative choices,[3] this reform poses a great challenge to the American company in search of a suitable Soviet partner. Selecting the optimal enterprise is often as difficult as it is critical. Fortunately, a number of qualified American and Soviet organizations stand prepared to assist the effort. (See Attachment A for a listing of them.) We recommend selecting at least two qualified Soviet partners and initiating parallel negotiations in an attempt to secure the best arrangement.

THE DOCUMENTS

To finalize a joint venture with a foreign partner, a Soviet enterprise must negotiate and sign six sets of documents:

1. The protocol of intent. This document, signed by both or all prospective partners, declares the parties' intention to negotiate a specific joint venture. It states the objective of the joint venture and includes secrecy clauses to protect the technical rights of the partners. The protocol of intent is not legally binding.
2. Negotiations memoranda. This set of protocols reports the progress that is made in negotiating the joint venture, clarifying the goals and expecta-

3. The deputy chairman of the Soviet Chamber of Commerce and Industry, W. Jefremov, declared in April 1989 that under the new regulations, the number of Soviet enterprises directly involved in foreign economic relations will soon rise from 400 to 22,000. This represents all Soviet republics.

tions of each party. Here the Soviet partner offers the necessary reasons and arguments to obtain clearance from its superior authority.

3. The feasibility study. Working together to assess the feasibility of a proposed joint venture and prepare this document will enable Soviet and Western partners to evaluate one another's assumptions, expectations, and criteria for success.

4. The joint venture agreement. This document evolves from the previous three and should include clarification of every aspect of the partners' relationship in the establishment, management, and development of the joint enterprise.

5. The charter. This is the document that will become the law that governs the activities of the joint venture. Therefore, the charter must address explicitly the aims, activities, and management process of the joint venture.

6. The registration. All Soviet-foreign joint ventures must be registered with the Department of State Revenues and Taxes of the Soviet Ministry of Finance. This registration, described in detail in Regulation No. 224 of the USSR Ministry of Finance of November 24, 1987, indicates that the establishment of the joint venture is officially recognized by the Soviet government, which grants the venture an official registration number. The joint venture is now a separate legal entity, and an official announcement to that effect should be made in the press.

MAIN ISSUES TO BE NEGOTIATED

Getting convertible currency.   For Western companies, the governing constraint in doing business with the Soviets is their lack of freely convertible currency.[4] During negotiations, therefore, the American partner should prepare realistic and flexible plans to help create and secure for the joint venture the convertible currency required by the Soviets to pay for their inputs. An interesting recent development is the implementation of foreign currency auctions by the State Bank, the bank for foreign economic activity, and the Soviet State Planning Committee. It is still uncertain, however, whether joint ventures will be allowed to participate as sellers and buyers at these auctions. In another recent development, 19 Soviet banks and foreign trade organizations have established a company, SovFintreid, which for a fee will convert rubles belonging to joint ventures and other Soviet enterprises to free currency.[5] SovFintreid's international commercial transactions are often complex. Six basic paths to convertible currency may be followed individually or in combination:

---

4. Aganbegyan, Abel, a senior Soviet economist, suggested recently that a second Soviet currency could be created, this one convertible in limited quantities, backed by the nation's gold and foreign currency reserves. *The Wall Street Journal,* May 2, 1989, p. A3.
5. Convertible currency needed by the joint venture.

1. The joint venture produces goods that it can partially or totally export from the Soviet Union in return for free currency.

2. The joint venture produces goods or services that can be sold for free currency to tourists and Western residents of the USSR.

3. If the venture will produce on Soviet soil an important product that was previously imported, the Soviet partner assumes in the joint venture agreement responsibility for arranging at least partial payment in free currency.

4. The venture can enter into a financial consortium with other Western firms that will swap free currency for rubles.

5. The rubles earned by the joint venture can be used to purchase Soviet goods or services, which in turn can be resold in Western markets for currency. This is countertrade. The March 7, 1989 decree as supplemented by the regulations of March 14, 1989 (see point D of Attachment C, part I) provides controls and limitations of Soviet products that can be used by joint ventures for this purpose. (Creative countertrade ideas can sometime be worked out. The Pepsico-Norwegian-Soviet deal that gets the money for Pepsi Cola out of the USSR in the form of used Soviet submarines bought by the Norwegians who pay the free currency to Pepsico is an excellent example of the type of imaginative solutions available.)

6. The investment can be located in an economic zone. In mid-1989 the Soviets were drafting legislation to create throughout the USSR special economic zones[6] that will deal in some form of convertible currency backed by Soviet gold. The zones will not have customs duties and will be freely accessible to foreign investors who may own up to 100% of the investment. Two prospective zones have been singled out already: one near the Finnish border and another in the far eastern part of the country. A district near Odessa is among other areas under consideration for special economic zones.

Prices of inputs/outputs.   A major goal of perestroika is the gradual deregulation of the Soviet economy; eventually state planning will be limited to strategic issues.[7] Within this general policy, the Soviet government has announced preparation of a comprehensive price reform designed to increase the influence of supply and demand on prices. But to avoid negative consumer reaction to abrupt price increases that will likely result during the early stages of retail price deregulation, the reform has been postponed. Meanwhile, prices of consumer products have been targeted for stabilization through stricter "administrative controls" in an attempt to restrain inflation. Thus most prices continue to be determined by the government. Furthermore, judging by the Laws for Private Cooperatives and the Soviet State Enterprise, and by the resolution of the USSR Council of

6. *The Wall Street Journal,* May 2, 1989, p. A3.
7. See p. 3 of the address of Dr. Ivan D. Ivanov, vice chairman, State Foreign Economic Commission of the Soviet Union, to the Committee of the ICC and the Chambers of Commerce and Socialist Countries for the Development of East/West Trade and Economic Cooperation on December 14, 1988.

Ministers of February 1989, "On Measures to Eliminate Shortcomings in the Existing Practice of Price Formation,"[8] the attitude of the Soviet government toward the price-defining mechanism of the future is mixed. On the one hand, demand will be allowed to play a decisive role; but on the other, unclarified factors such as the "social responsibility of the enterprise" will be influential. Here are some examples:

> The enterprise is responsible for the strict observance of price discipline and must prevent the overstating of prices. Profits obtained in an unwarranted manner by the enterprise as a result of violations of state price discipline ... are subject to withdrawal into the [state] budget.[9]

and

> Mandatory ceiling prices are to be set at the stage of designing new products. ... The USSR State Standards Committee has been instructed to step up supervision ... over the correct establishment and application of prices ... to increase the responsibility of executives in the service sphere for the strict observance of state price discipline. ... Cooperatives should be guided by the maximum amounts of price markups for acquisitions as established by the USSR State Prices Committee. ... creating for this purpose a uniform, nationwide system of monitoring prices.[10]

Ambiguous pricing laws and regulations—as well as a lack of clarity about which ones apply to joint ventures—cannot be interpreted as freedom of a venture to establish prices for its goods or services. Therefore it is imperative that the Western company include suitable mechanisms for establishing and changing prices in its agreement with the Soviet partners; otherwise it may find itself locked into a position of loss after the agreement has been finalized. Because it is difficult to devise formulas that predict discrepancies between ruble prices of inputs and administratively fixed prices for output with sufficient accuracy, long-term contracts with Soviet wholesale customers of joint venture enterprises must provide for automatic readjustment procedures that absorb input price fluctuations.

Ambiguous Soviet laws and regulations.   It is essential to clarify a profusion of ambiguous regulations and resolutions issued by the Soviet government and determine their relevance to the proposed joint venture. Here are a few examples along with some questions a Western partner might ask:

8. *Pravda*, February 4, 1989, pp. 1–2.
9. The Law on the Soviet State Enterprise, Article XVII.6.
10. "On Measures to Eliminate Shortcomings in the Existing Practice of Price Formation," *Current Digest of the Soviet Press*, 41, 5 (1989), p. 10.

1. The State Foreign Economic Commission was recently given the right to revoke export-import privileges of enterprises that carry on "unscrupulous competition or activities that damage the State's interests." Exactly what constitutes "unscrupulous competition" and "activities that damage the state's interest"? What is the procedure by which a joint venture can defend itself against such penalties?

2. The USSR Council of Ministers called on "all Soviet enterprises" to form "volunteer trade associations" to "eliminate unwarranted competition between Soviet exporters." Does this apply to joint ventures? What constitutes "warranted" and "unwarranted" competition? What happens if a joint venture, through modern technology, know-how, and organization, achieves lower production cost than its Soviet competitors and decides to pass the savings along to its clients? Is this "unwarranted competition"?

3. It has been announced that in 1990 a new Soviet customs tariff and a draft law on foreign trade will be introduced.[11] How will these developments affect the joint venture?

Financing.   There is an increasing number of sources of government and private financing available for Western and Soviet investors that should be contacted by the joint venture partners before the capital that needs to be invested by the joint venture partners themselves is estimated. Due to considerable credit lines recently opened by a number of Western European countries to be utilized for investments from these countries in the USSR, financing is now available to investors with preferential conditions.

Soviet and Western banks are actively engaging in joint venture financing. The USSR Bank of Foreign Economic Relations is opening a representative office in New York. The International Moscow Bank is a joint venture established in Moscow in 1989 with a capital of 100 million convertible rubles.[12] Its participants are three Soviet banks, which together own 40% of the capital, and five large Western European banks, which each own 12%. Vnesheconombank now offers financing of joint ventures in the USSR, and about 70% of its lending activity is expected to be in convertible currencies. Other sources of funds are becoming increasingly available; for example, promoters of closed-end funds are reported to be interested in setting up a $100-million private fund to finance US–Soviet joint ventures mainly in tourism, consumer goods, and technology.[13] Western banks are developing innovative approaches in the financing of investments in the USSR, linking repayment with the ability of the investments to earn the convertible currency in time to meet debt service.

11. Source: *The Soviet Observer,* January 26, 1989. Taken from *Ekononicheskaia Gazeta,* 51, 1988. On customs changes, *Izvestia,* November 15, 1988. The issue of whether new regulations can affect negatively the rights that have been approved in the foundation documents of existing joint ventures needs to be explicitly clarified.
12. *East-West Bulletin,* May 31, 1989, p. 4.
13. Ibid., p. 7.

Investment protection.   One of the first models of protection of Western investments in the Soviet Union is the Belgo-Soviet agreement on "mutual promotion and protection of investments," which contains a number of provisions.

1. Protected are all of the following: buildings, installations, equipment, and other material values; financial property, including shares and other forms of participation and related dues; rights related to any service having an economic value; intellectual property rights such as patents, trade, and origin marks, commercial names, designs, models, copyrights, technical processes, and know-how.

2. The term *investments* refers also to indirect investments carried out by an investor. The term *revenue* refers to profits, dividends, interest, advances on copyright and licenses, commissions, and payments for assistance or technical services.

3. Each contracting party guarantees to apply the "most-favored-nation" clause to assess import duties on machinery and equipment imported by investors of the other contracting party.

4. If disputes between joint venture partners cannot be settled within six months, the investors may turn to ad hoc arbitrage under the regulations of the United Nations Commission for International Trade Law.

5. The Belgo-Soviet agreement contains a provision on the avoidance of double taxation. However, some have criticized it for failing to cut the tax rates enough.[14]

Although the Soviet joint venture decrees explicitly legislate protection of the investment of foreign partners, some Western countries have found it expedient to enter mutual investment promotion and protection treaties with the USSR. Finland, Belgium, and England have concluded such agreements. The treaty with Germany has been initialed, and agreements with other Western countries are expected to follow. While there is some lack of precision, especially concerning compensation in the case of nationalization, the treaty with Belgium stipulates that compensation shall correspond to the real value of the investment on the eve of the day in which expropriation or nationalization was made public.[15]

Protecting the dollar value of the investment.   The ruble at today's official exchange rate of roughly $1.60 is grossly overvalued. The Soviets have already announced that a substantial internal ruble devaluation will be made in 1990. As price reform is instituted and the Soviet economy is gradually geared toward convertibility of the ruble, it should be expected that more devaluations will follow. While Soviet labor and other Soviet input-intensive joint ventures exporting to the West stand to benefit from devalu-

14. *East/West No. 452,* February 28, 1989, pp. 12–14.
15. Ibid., pp. 12–13.

ations, it is imperative for the Soviet authorities to give the American partner of a joint venture the opportunity to hedge against the drop in the ruble's dollar value. Investments should be protected by obtaining the license to sell rubles to the Soviet Vnesheconombank (Bank of Foreign Economic Relations) at negotiated exchange rates to cover both long- and short-term obligations. There are indications that the Soviets are prepared to accept such an arrangement.[16]

The shortage of Soviet inputs. The American company should obtain for the joint venture an a priori license and guaranteed convertible currency allotment enabling it to import from abroad any input that the Soviet suppliers are unable to deliver in the necessary quantity and quality at the time agreed. The chronic imbalance between supply and demand and the shortages that invariably ensue make this license essential. Because Soviet state enterprises have begun to lease out their facilities and more cooperatives stand ready to contract their services, shortages may become somewhat less problematic in the future.

A definition of the joint venture's "social functions." Article 13 of the Law on the Soviet State Enterprise of June 30, 1987 addresses "the social development of the labor collective." The article specifies the responsibilities of Soviet enterprises to provide "accelerated development of the material base of the social sphere and the creation of conditions for healthy everyday life and recreation for employees and their families." Such "conditions" include residential buildings, children's institutions, camps, and other facilities. Soviet enterprises take these responsibilities very seriously. During a recent two-year period, for example, an increasing number of enterprises invested part of their funds in cooperation with farms in exchange for a guaranteed supply of fruits and vegetables and other food items for their work force.[17] Since these activities can absorb substantial outlays by the enterprise, and since the decrees on joint ventures do not specify the extent to which the requirements affect joint ventures, negotiating and stipulating social obligations in the joint venture charter are essential.

Valuation of joint venture partner contributions. Evaluating each partner's tangible and intangible contributions to the joint venture capital can lead to long, frustrating negotiations. Each partner may tend to undervalue the other's contributions and overvalue its own. While the Soviets have tried to alleviate this problem,[18] their decrees do not cover all possibilities. If venture partners cannot agree, it is expedient to agree to appoint impartial third parties to value contributions.

Applicable law. At this time there is no corporate law in the Soviet

16. *BusinessWeek,* February 27, 1989, p. 54.
17. *Pravda,* May 12, 1989, p. 2.
18. See point IIG of Attachment C.

Union. Decrees No. 49, 1074, and 1405 constitute the primary legislation for joint ventures; they are supplemented by a number of decisions, instructions, and acts issued by ministries and governmental agencies (see Attachment C). However, no specific legal structure for joint ventures has been provided, and the degree to which Soviet civil law and the Law on the Soviet State Enterprise apply is not clear. Neither is whether—or on what issues—a joint venture can sue a Soviet government agency. The degree of applicability of the Law on the Soviet State Enterprise[19] is especially important to clarify. In this respect, our study raises a number of crucial questions: Will the joint venture enterprise have a workers collective? If so, how will its functions in the joint venture be reconciled to those of the board of directors? How will its input to the decision process of the enterprise be channeled? In what issues will the collective and/or its council have a voice? Will subordinates vote for leaders of production structural task units in the joint venture enterprise? If so, up to what level of the enterprise hierarchy? What will be the institutional role of the social organizations that are active in Soviet state enterprises—the party, the union, the Komsomol, the veterans, and others? Will representatives of those social organizations have offices in joint venture factories? Will they be entitled to attend management meetings as they do in Soviet state enterprises? Will they have a voice in the decision-making process? While our research in Soviet plants has indicated that joint ventures stand to gain a lot by using these organizations, their legal status and roles in the joint venture decision making need to be clarified.

Unclear also are some important points concerning the applicable law on relations between Soviet and foreign partners, joint ventures and foreign parties, and joint ventures and Soviet authorities.[20] Clarification of the applicable law is of utmost importance. The services of qualified legal experts in both countries are available to American companies; their counsel should be sought on every possible detail.

Arbitration.   A number of joint venture contracts stipulate that particular foreign laws be applied to their mutual relations. Frequently specified are portions of Swedish law that address disputes between partners. Joint venture partners may agree to arbitration in Stockholm, under the Uncitral Arbitration Rules.[21]

19. See Attachment C.
20. *The ICC Guide to Joint Ventures in the USSR,* International Chamber of Commerce, 1988, pp. 25–32 offers a general analysis of the issues involved. A special joint Soviet/ICC task force has been set up recently to elaborate and suggest a suitable Soviet corporate law.
21. "This [Uncitral] is an agreement between the American Arbitration Association and the USSR Chamber of Commerce and Industry to the effect that these two institutions recommend to their respective members to insert the optional clause into their agreements. It is important to note that use of the optional clause is always dependent on the agreement of the parties." Hober, Kay, "Negotiating

Items for unanimous decision by joint venture governing bodies.   Although most Western companies have found their Soviet partners open, flexible, and cooperative in negotiating joint venture agreements, it is important to stipulate in the charter what key issues will be decided unanimously by the joint venture board of directors. The ICC's *Guide to Joint Ventures in the USSR* offers a list of these points, which we include at the end of this appendix as Attachment D.

Exact meaning of English and Russian contract terms.   Because there may be no words in one (or either) language for the specific business terms required, creative thinking in translation is essential. All translations should be checked carefully by disinterested third parties to ensure that the terms and their usage express the exact intention of both parties.

This overview of major areas that require clarification at the negotiations stage is far from exhaustive. Not discussed here are issues pertaining to financing, tax exemptions, avoidance of double taxation, differences between Soviet and Western accounting systems for establishing the base on which profit will be calculated, shortage of accommodations for Western employees and other conditions of employment of Soviet and foreign personnel, establishment of affiliates, clarification of mortgaging procedures, access to international markets for financing, insurance, treatment of gains and losses in exchange rates, handling of foreign currency operations, transport, protection of know-how, allocation of specific responsibilities between the partners, limits of inspection and audits, legal status of foreign nationals employed by the joint venture, settlement of labor disputes, and termination and liquidation of the joint venture. All these areas are subject to some degree of ambiguity in the Soviet decrees. Therefore partners must reach agreement on specific points and spell out relevant clauses in the charter of each joint venture.

Sources Helpful to US Companies in Joint Venture Startup

For the American firm about to enter a joint venture with a Soviet enterprise, several government agencies as well as some private nonprofit groups can help clear the path often at little or no cost.

The US Department of Commerce provides several services. In the United States, its International Trade Administration has a Soviet division that offers policy guidance, current analysis on economic and regulatory developments, Soviet trade contacts, and other information.

In Moscow, the Commerce Department's US Commercial Office [USCO] offers up-to-the-minute briefings on US–Soviet commercial relations, as well as on specific markets. USCO staff can identify appropriate Soviet contacts and arrange meetings with them. In addition, the office provides temporary meeting space, audiovisual and simultaneous translation equipment, telex and photocopying services, and a commercial library; the staff can locate temporary secretaries and translators as well. USCO also arranges trade shows in Moscow and invites the appropriate Soviet officials and purchasing agents to attend.

Beyond USCO, several Soviet government ministries, consulting concerns, and trading companies also foster Western-Soviet joint ventures. American managers may find liaisons with these organizations a necessity. In the past, for example, most Soviet enterprises sold only to a single client—the state Foreign Trade Organization—so most newly independent factories have neither the experience nor the internal personnel to deal with foreign companies. They are not accustomed, say, to arranging for visits, fielding questions about Soviet markets, or handling issues related to the establishment of joint ventures. Soviet and US agencies, public, cooperative, and private, can bridge those gaps (see Attachment A).

In June 1988, our Soviet partner for this project, the All-Union Institute of Foreign Economic Relations under the State Commission for Foreign Economic Relations of the Council of Ministers of the USSR, published a book for business people and managers, entitled *USSR: New Business Opportunities.* The book has been produced by a team of leading Soviet economists and members of relevant Soviet authorities in the area of international economic relations. It includes materials about Soviet economic reforms, the foreign economic relations of the USSR, and Soviet legislation related to joint ventures on Soviet territory. It also includes general information for the Western business person in Moscow, as well as excerpts from normative legal acts governing Soviet foreign economic relations.[22]

In 1986, on the initiative of the USSR Chamber of Commerce and Industry, a joint task force with the International Chamber of Commerce was set up to study the legal and administrative framework of joint ventures in the Soviet Union. On the basis of the group's work, the International Chamber of Commerce published in 1988 a *Guide to Joint Ventures in the USSR.* A second edition, incorporating all changes and recent relevant developments, will be published early in 1990. Researched and compiled by Soviet

22. The book is available from Vneshtorgizdat, 1 Fadeyev Street, Moscow 125047, USSR; telex, 411238.

and Western experts and members of the task force, the guide addresses basic steps, the legal framework, and operational and financial issues; it includes practical advice to Western companies on matters connected with the establishment of joint ventures in the Soviet Union.[23]

23. The guide is available from the International Chamber of Commerce, 38 Cours Albert 1er, 75008, Paris, France; telephone, 45-62-34-56; telex, 650770.

Attachment A

SOURCES HELPFUL TO US COMPANIES FOR THE ESTABLISHMENT OF JOINT VENTURES IN THE SOVIET UNION

A. *United States Government Agencies*

US Department of Commerce
Washington, DC 20230

General number	(202) 377-2000
Soviet export counseling	(202) 377-3181
Soviet market assessments and policy	(202) 377-4655
Export services licensing	(202) 377-4811
Dumping and duty investigations	(202) 277-5497

The US Commerce Department's Bureau of Export Administration will counsel companies considering joint ventures in the USSR to advise them whether proposals conform to US export control policy.

US Commercial Office [USCO]
15 Ulitsa Chaykovskogo
Moscow, USSR

Phone	225-48-48
	225-46-60
Telex	413205

B. *Soviet Ministries, Consulting and Trading Organizations*

Joint Venture Department
USSR Ministry of Foreign Economic Relations
32/34 Smolenskaya Sennaya Place
SU-12200 Moscow, USSR

USSR Trade Representation
2001 Connecticut Avenue NW
Washington, DC 20008

Phone	(202) 232-5988

Amtorg Trading Corporation
750 Third Avenue
New York, NY 10017
Phone   (212) 972-1220
Telex   147185

V/O Vnesheconomservice
6 Kuibyscheva Street
Moscow, 103 684 USSR
Phone   925-93-45
Telex   411-126

(This is a company created by the Soviet Chamber of Commerce and Industry to provide services connected with the establishment of joint ventures to Soviet and foreign companies.)

C. *Examples of joint ventures providing services for the establishment and operation of joint ventures in the USSR.* A number of Soviet and Western companies and joint ventures either have been or are being established to provide assistance to Western companies investigating the Soviet market for opportunities to negotiate, set up, and operate joint ventures. The USCO office in Moscow provides specific relevant information to inquiring US companies. Other services are offered by the following agencies:

1. International Moscow Bank (see p. 313)
2. SovFintreid (see p. 310)
3. San Francisco/Moscow Teleport. This direct computer communications link between the United States and the USSR was established in January 1989. A personal computer user in either country may dial a local telephone number that is connected via network to a computer at the San Francisco/Moscow Teleport. The call is relayed via satellite to the Staten Island Teleport, a satellite communications earth station. Users in the Soviet Union can be connected to a Moscow-based computer that is linked directly to the San Francisco computer. The Soviet computer is maintained by the Institute of Automated Systems in Moscow.
4. Under an agreement concluded in April 1989 by the USSR Ministry of Communications and the US Postal Service, an electronic mail link began operating between Moscow and twelve American cities; this link will enable addressees to receive mail either the day it is sent or the day following.
5. Sona Ventures Limited. This is a Soviet-Canadian joint venture established by the prestigious Institute of USA and Canada and the USSR Academy of Sciences. Its staff consists of former leading employees of

Soviet ministries and trade organizations as well as Soviet lawyers and other professionals.

6. An interactive trade communications network linking Soviet and Western enterprises to be operated as a joint venture by International Trade and Communications, Inc. of Philadelphia and several Soviet partners will enable participants to exchange information on types of products available and all terms of sale including countertrade alternatives. The system will feature an electronic-mail bulletin board, announcements, and access to data on exchange rates, news, and directories. Among the Soviet partners of the joint venture are the USSR Ministry of Communications, Tass, and the Soviet Chamber of Commerce and Industry.

7. Mosrent. This Soviet-Swiss joint venture based in Moscow will rent cars to joint venturers and other convertible-currency-paying clients.

8. A Soviet Joint Venture Management Association has been established in Moscow and is available to answer questions about the establishment and operation of joint ventures in the USSR.

9. Inpred. Owned by the Soviet Chamber of Commerce, this organization offers services connected with all phases of joint venture establishment.

    12 Krasnopresnenskaya Nab.
    Moscow, USSR
    Phone   256-63-03
    Telex   411486 SOVIN SU

10. Interfact (for dealing with Soviet private cooperatives)
    Khoroshovskoe Shosse 41
    SU-123308 Moscow, USSR
    Phone   125-14-85
                                                       195-10-93
    Telex   413560

D. *Private Nonprofit Agencies*

US–USSR Trade and Economic Council
805 Third Avenue
New York, NY 10022
Phone   (212) 243-5740

US–USSR Trade and Economic Council
3 Naberezhnaya Schevchenko
SU-121248 Moscow, USSR
Phone   243-54-70
Telex   413212

American Committee on US–Soviet Relations
109 Eleventh Street SE
Washington, DC 20003
Phone   (202) 546-1700

East-West Committee, International Chamber of Commerce
38, Cours Albert 1ᵉʳ
F-75008 Paris, France
Phone   45-623456
Telex   6500770

E.   *Ongoing Sources for Soviet Foreign Trade Information*

United Nations Economic Commission for Europe (ECE)
  Palais des Nations
  1211 GENEVA 10
  Switzerland
  Cable   UNATIONS GENEVE
  Telex   289696
  Telephone   (41 22) 346011, 334000, 332000, 331000
  Telefax   (41 22) 339879

Business International Index (a print index to publications of
Business International S.A.)
  12-14 Chemin Rien
  1208 Geneva Switzerland
  Phone   (41 22) 475355
  Telex   422669
  Fax   (41 22) 478118

ECOTASS (weekly periodical)
  Pergamon Press, Inc.
  Maxwell House, Fairview Park
  Elmsford, NY 10523
  Phone   (914) 592-7700

FBIS (Foreign Broadcast Information Service)
  US Department of Commerce
  National Technical Information Service
  5285 Port Royal Road
  Springfield, VA 22161
  Phone   (703) 487-4630

Foreign Trade (monthly publication)
  Ministry of Foreign Trade
  32/24 Smolenskaya Sennaya
  SU-12200 Moscow, USSR

Interflo: An East-West Trade News Monitor (periodical)
Paul Surovell, editor and publisher
P.O. Box 42
Maplewood, NJ 07040
Phone   (201) 763-9493

Journal of the US–USSR Trade and Economic Council (bimonthly periodical)
New York phone   (212) 644-4550
Moscow phone   243-54-70

PlanEcon Report: Developments in the Economies of the
Soviet Union and Eastern Europe
Washington, DC 20036
Phone   (202) 898-0471

East-West (fortnightly bulletin)
10 Boulevard St. Lazare
B-1210 Brussels, Belgium
Phone   (02) 218-4349
Telex   21 108 EUROPE

Sovscan
FYI Information Resources
735 Eighth Street SE
Washington, DC 20002
Phone   (202) 544-2394

Attachment B

GLOSSARY OF SOVIET TERMS USED IN CONNECTION WITH JOINT VENTURES*

Attachment: Seizure of assets in the possession of the defendant or the interests of the defendant in the possession of a third party.

Confiscation: Seizure of personal chattels by the state. No indemnity or compensation may be granted. Applied as a punishment for criminal offenses when ordered by a Soviet court or for infringing customs regulations.

Cost accounting: That branch of accounting that deals with methods and systems of compiling and analyzing costs in selling and manufacturing, classifying, summarizing, recording, reporting, and allocating current or predicted costs.

Feasibility study: A technical, economic, and commercial base for an investment decision on an industrial project. It should describe a project of a defined production capacity at a selected location using a particular technology in relation to specific materials at identified costs yielding a defined return on investment.

Foreign partner: A business entity of any nationality other than a Soviet (or other CMEA member country) legal entity.

Foundation documents: The set of documents necessary for the establishment and operation of a joint venture

*From *Guide to Joint Ventures in the USSR,* International Chamber of Commerce, 38, Cours Albert 1er, 75008, Paris; telephone, 45-62-34-56; telex, 650770.

	as between the partners and vis-à-vis third parties.
Freely convertible currency:	A currency that can be freely exchanged by a national of one country into the currency of any country he or she chooses.
Joint venture:	A legal entity in the nature of a partnership engaged in the joint execution of a particular transaction for mutual profit. It requires a community of interests in the performance of the subject matter, a right to direct the policy, and a duty to share in both profits and losses.
Liquidation:	Settling the financial affairs of a company by the discharge of liabilities and the realization of assets.
Requisition:	Expropriation of personal property by the state against fair compensation. Documents must be issued by the requisitioning body on the basis of which a claim is fixed with the ministry concerned.
Self-administration:	The practical management and direction of the corporation by its owners.
Self-financing:	A joint venture must finance its operations from its own gains and credit and not from public sources.
State enterprise:	Similar to a government corporation, it is organized by ministries and receives allocations of property from the state. A charter defines its powers and must be registered with the financial agencies of government. Enterprises must keep strict corporate accounts and submit profit-and-loss statements to auditing agencies.
Termination:	Legally ending a contract without it being broken by either side.

Attachment C

LIST OF DECREES AND GOVERNMENTAL DECISIONS PERTAINING TO JOINT VENTURES WITH FOREIGN ENTERPRISES IN THE SOVIET UNION*

I. Decrees

A. Decree of the USSR Council of Ministers on the Establishment in the Territory of the USSR and Operation of Joint Ventures with the Participation of Soviet Organizations and Firms from Capitalist and Developing Countries (January 13, 1987), No. 49, as amended by Decree No. 385 dated May 6, 1989. "Concerning Amending and Treating as Null and Void Some Decisions of the Soviet Government on Aspects of Foreign Economic Activities to Decree No. 49 dated 13 January 1987."

B. Decree of the CPSU Central Committee and the USSR Council of Ministers on Additional Measures to Improve the Country's External Economic Activity in the New Conditions of Economic Management (September 17, 1987), No. 1074.

C. Decree of the USSR Council of Ministers on Various Measures of Foreign Economic Relations of State Companies, Cooperatives, and other Organizations (December 2, 1988), No. 1405.

D. Decree of the USSR Council of Ministers No. 203 of March 7, 1989 "On Measures Concerning State Regulation of Foreign Economic Activities." This text is complemented by an annex dated March 14, 1989 entitled "Order of Registration of Enterprises, Amalgamations, Production Cooperatives and Other Organizations Engaged in Export-Import Operations"; a joint venture must register with the Ministry of Foreign Economic Relations if it wishes to carry out export and import operations. This is a separate registration procedure from the one that must be made with the USSR Ministry of Finance.

E. Decree of the USSR Council of Ministers No. 238 dated March 21, 1989 entitled "On the General Trade Agreement between the Soviet Foreign Economic Consortium and the American Trade Consortium."

F. Decree of the Presidium of the USSR Supreme Soviet No. 10402-XI dated May 10, 1989, amending Decree No. 6362-XI dated January 13, 1987 regulating taxation of joint ventures.

G. Decree of the USSR Council of Ministers No. 253 dated March 17, 1989 "On Measures to Streamline Insurance Activities."

---

*The texts of some of these decrees can be found in the ICC's *Guide to Joint Ventures in the USSR;* others can be found in *USSR: New Business Opportunities,* available from Vneshtorgizdat, 1 Fadeyev Street, Moscow 125047, USSR; telex, 411238.

II. Regulations and Instructions of Various Soviet Authorities Concerning Joint Ventures*

A. Regulations on Registration of Joint Ventures, International Amalgamation and Organizations Established in the USSR Territory with the Participation of Soviet and Foreign Firms and Management Bodies of the USSR Ministry of Finance (November 1987), No. 224.

B. Accounting and Bookkeeping of Joint Ventures, International Amalgamation and Organizations Established in the USSR Territory by the Ministry of Finance Central Board of Statistics (February 27, 1987), No. 53/13-09.

C. Regulations on Taxation of Joint Ventures by the Ministry of Finance (May 4, 1987), No. 124, as amended by Ministry of Finance Instruction No. 226 (November 30, 1987) and Model Reimbursement Forms.

D. Instruction No. 74, "Supplies of Materials and Equipment to Joint Ventures Established in the USSR Territory with the Participation of Other Countries and Foreign Firms and Marketing of Their Products" by the State Committee for Supplies (June 4, 1987). This instruction was amended on November 4, 1987.

E. Instructions "On the Procedures Governing the Insurance of the Assets and Interests of Joint Ventures" of June 5, 1987 issued by the USSR Ministry of Finance, No. 45-15-1.

F. A Procedure for Crediting and Settlement of Accounts of Joint Ventures, International Amalgamations and Organizations of the USSR and Other CMEA Member Countries as Well as of Joint Ventures between Soviet Organizations and Firms from Capitalist and Developing Countries, approved by the USSR State Bank and the USSR Vneshtorgbank (September 22, 1987).

G. "Procedures of Assessing the Land, Natural Resources, Buildings, and Structures Forming Part of the Soviet Partners' Contribution to the Authorized Capital of Joint Ventures, or Leased to Joint Ventures for Temporary Use" issued by the USSR Committee on Prices, dated February 14, 1988.

H. Regulations of August 8, 1989 "On the Order of Drawing Up Annual Accounting Reports by Joint Ventures in the USSR" issued by the Ministry of Finance of the USSR No. 91 and by the USSR State Committee on Statistics No. 8-07.

III. Laws with Sections of Relevance to Joint Ventures

A. USSR Law on the Soviet State Enterprise, June 30, 1987.

B. USSR Law on Cooperatives, May 26, 1988.

---

*A number of additional relevant decrees, regulations, and instructions are presently being prepared, and are expected to be issued shortly. The new legislation will deal with such issues as property, taxes, leasing of land and national resources, the uses of land, the rights of Soviet republics on land, national resources, the Continental Shelf, rights of foreign and Soviet enterprises, reformation and creation of new forms of cooperatives, and free economic zones.

Attachment D

CHECKLIST OF CERTAIN KEY ITEMS

The following items are recommended for unanimous decision by governing bodies of joint ventures of which more than 50% of the equity is owned by Soviet partners.*

- Determine the joint venture's general policy (including the profit target) and decide on the annual budgets, the long-term plan, the investment plans, changes in the range of products, the research and development budget, and other plans, as well as on the measures resulting from deviations from the budget with respect to established plans.
- Amendment or reorganization of the charter.
- Any capital reduction or capital increase.
- Any change in ownership.
- Any change in percentage of ownership.
- Merger with another juridical person.
- Transfer of the principal business or of all or part of the assets.
- Decision to change the purpose of the joint venture.
- Undertakings that change the structure of the company substantially—e.g., establishment, acquisition, transfer, and dissolution of affiliated companies or branch offices.
- Dissolution or liquidation of the joint venture.
- Election and compensation of the director general and other members of the directorate and/or management, as well as auditors (however, dismissal or transfer upon request of any party).
- Regulations for the directorate.
- Approval of the balance sheet and of the net annual profit.
- Establishment of reserve and other funds.
- Nondistribution of all or part of the net annual profit.
- Approval of changes in the organization of the joint venture and of the number of workers to be employed, as well as the transfer or dismissal of senior staff.
- Purchase, acquisition, lease, or disposal of any immovable property.
- Contracts between the joint venture and any of the partners and/or members of the board, directorate, or management.
- Conclusion of agreements with the trade union.
- Acquisition and disposal of patents, trademarks, and industrial property

---

*From the ICC's *Guide to Joint Ventures in the USSR*. The guide is available from the International Chamber of Commerce, 38 Cours Albert 1er, 75008, Paris, France; telephone, 45-62-34-56; telex, 650770.

and/or know-how; acquisition and/or license grant for patents, trademarks, industrial property rights, and/or know-how.

- Conclusion, alteration, or termination of agreements (e.g., agency agreements).
- Taking loans with a value of more than _____ or exceeding _____ per annum or with a period exceeding three years (amount and currency to be indicated in each individual agreement).
- Granting loans with a value of more than _____ or with a period exceeding one year (amount and currency to be indicated in each agreement).
- Taking over or granting financial commitments or similar liabilities of more than _____ (amount and currency to be indicated in each agreement).
- All transactions in excess of a specified amount.
- Any other resolution of an important or extraordinary nature; for example, initiation of legal procedures, conclusion of compromises, and amicable settlements with a value of more than _____ (amount and currency to be indicated in each agreement).
- Any other items as provided for in bylaws or in the articles of association to be unanimously resolved by the board.

Glossary of Soviet Terms

Autonomous plant within the enterprise: A plant included in the enterprise which, however, has its own bank account and operates as a profit center.

Collective agreement: A written agreement between the labor union and the enterprise management regarding rights and responsibilities of both parties.

Collectivism: The value placed on working together (versus individualism).

Collegiate: A function performed by a collective-advisory (consulting body) within the organization.

Commonness: The Russian value of belonging, affiliation with a larger group of people.

Concentration of lands: A period of Russian history (14–16 centuries) when Moscow grand dukes annexed other Russian dukes' estates by purchase or military force.

Consolidated plan for development of science and technology: The special part of the enterprise plan devoted to new product and technology development.

Council of People's Deputies: Elected organ to administer territorial units from the state down to the village through republic, district, city, region, town, and so forth.

Council of the worker collective: A council elected by the enterprise's worker collective to participate directly in a number of management decisions of the enterprise.

Democratic centralism: Theoretical principle of management used to organize decision making within political and industrial organizations, based on the combination of the centralization of power at the top with active grass-roots participation from the bottom.

Democratism: Style of management based on the principles and ideas of democracy (versus totalitarianism).

Democratization: The move from proclaimed democracy to real democracy in political and economic life.

Election of village authorities: By open voting of all members of the village council such appointments are made.

Enterprise results: The results of the enterprise's activity compared to its targets.

Enterprise sales: The amount of money received by the enterprise for the product it has delivered to distributors' warehouses or to customers.

Enterprise union committee: Elected organ for managing union organization at the enterprise; consists of chairman, deputies, and union members; creates commissions to work with the collective and management on issues such as working conditions, women, children, recreation, conflicts, and so forth.

Exchange between the cities and the villages: Exchange of products between industrial and agricultural production units.

Experimental model: The prototype of a new product built to conduct testing.

Full economic accountability and self-financing (*khozraschet*):   The system of enterprise management within a centralized planned economy. It is based on the rule that an enterprise may spend only the money that it earns.

Functional bureaucracy: The fulfillment of the function for which a manager is responsible, at the expense of fulfilling other functions if necessary.

Funds: Part of the profit set aside in special enterprise accounts for specific purposes (product development, wage and salary bonuses, social programs, or benefits).

Glasnost: The Russian word means that everyone may speak out, write and express his or her opinion about every aspect of social and political life. In the West it is sometimes rendered as "openness."

Goskomtsen: The USSR state committee for pricing, a governmental body that calculates, fixes, and controls prices.

Gosplan: The USSR state planning committee, a governmental body that develops and monitors planning targets for the national economy.

Gosstandart: The USSR state committee for quality and standards—the primary government body that establishes technical standards for products and production processes.

Internal contradictions: Contradictions based on internal policy; for example, contradictions between a plan and the market's demand.

Kollectivnost: The principle of decision making by the whole collective of an organization.

Marxism/Leninism: An ideology based primarily on the works of Karl Marx, Frederich Engels, and Lenin; it is the official ideology of the CPSU and Soviet society.

Material incentive fund: Part of the enterprise's profit that is set aside for bonus payments and money awards to its employees, including managers. It is separate from the wage and salary fund. The size of the material incentive fund depends on the enterprise fulfilling the plan and meeting quality and delivery targets.

Mutual aid in the commune: For example, if somebody's house burns down, all members of the commune are best obliged to help build a new one.

Net income: Total sales less costs.

Objective laws of societal development: Non-manmade requirements for building human society; generally, each historical period has its own.

Obschina-volost: *Obschina* is a Russian term for the peasant commune; *volost* is the nineteenth-century Russian name for a territorial unit; combined, they represent a part of country administration.

One-man leadership: An organizational form wherein the leader of the organization bears complete responsibility for the organization and makes all final decisions.

Overseeing agency: The directly superior authority. For example, the ministry is the overseeing agency of the enterprise.

Party organization (of the enterprise): A group consisting of enterprise employees, including managers, who are members of the CPSU; it is headed by a party secretary and committee elected by the members.

Perestroika: The Russian word for today's policy of radical political and economic changes in Soviet society (the literal English translation is "reconstruction" or "restructuring"—from the foundations to the roof of a house).

Price as an accounting function: Prices are used to measure enterprise targets or assignments and to serve as a stimulus for efficiency, not as indicators of the actual cost of goods and services or of an equilibrium between demand and supply.

Production collective: The cooperative unit of the enterprise.

Radical management reform: The part of perestroika that enables and motivates enterprise managers to assume responsibility for the financial viability of their enterprises; it has been accompanied by nationwide decentralization in industry, agriculture, and regional development.

Relational bureaucracy: The bureaucratic behavior wherein the manager tries to please the boss by all available means, and neglects the opinions of colleagues, subordinates, or the public.

Rural council (*sel'ski soviet*):   The elected administrative body or organ in the village; consists of a chairman, deputies, and support staff if necessary.

Scientific production association: An organizational unit in high-tech production, combining R&D activity and production under "one roof." The SPA has a status similar to that of an enterprise.

Self-criticism: Publicly admitting mistakes in a meeting or in the press. It is done by organizations as well as individuals.

Social and political unification of the country: A goal based on the theory that people are not to be divided into exploiters and exploited; therefore there is only one political party—the CPSU.

Social insurance: The enterprise sets up a special fund to provide pensions and compensation for illness, accidents, and fatalities.

Social investment: An enterprise's investment from profit in a social program such as a kindergarten for the workers' children.

Social justice: Equal work for equal pay; fair remuneration for effort; a citizen's right to have living space, a job, sufficient food, medical benefits, child care, and so forth.

Socialist economy: A national economy where the basic means of production are property of the state.

Socialist self-management: Self-management in a socialist society may occur when the subject and object of management are the same.

Societal ownership of the means of production: Wherein the basic means of production (land, plants, roads, equipment, raw materials, and so forth) are the property of the state.

Stable economic guidelines: Ministries set long-range (usually five-year) production targets or limits for enterprises and plants.

State plan for economic and social development: A special document developed by the USSR State Planning Committee that describes the five-year goals and targets for the national economy, broken down in one-year periods.

State representation of all people: The government expresses the interests of all the people. The government runs the state; therefore, the state represents all the people.

Syndicated enterprise: An enterprise that is a part of an association of enterprises; the association is a form of business organization.

Traditional pricing mechanism: The method has two major features: the centrally established price and the final price, which is the sum of the costs of the product.

Union: The trade union organization at the enterprise, consisting of enterprise employees (including managers) who are members of the same trade union. It is headed by a chairman and a committee or bureau, all of whom are elected by the membership.

Wholesale trade: Under perestroika products are sold and bought by the enterprises directly, not through a government supply office.

Wide latitude: The freedom of shops to decide to whom, when, how much, and what incentives to pay workers.

Worker collective: A unit composed of all the employees in an enterprise.

Worker control of the distribution of products: An early form of worker participation in enterprise management practiced after the revolution but before the nationalization of production.

About the Authors

Eugene Brakov is the director general of Zil, the Soviet automobile manufacturer. He joined the firm in 1956 after graduating from the Moscow Technical College. He left the firm to work at the Research Institute of the Automobile Industry and rejoined it in 1959. In 1971, Brakov graduated from the Moscow Auto Production Institute. He is a candidate to the Central Committee of the CPSU and a deputy of the Moscow Soviet.

Igor Faminsky graduated from Moscow State University in 1958 with a Ph.D. in international economics. He joined the faculty of the university and served as an academic deputy dean of the Department of Economics and, since 1986 as a full professor. In October of that year, he was appointed director of the USSR Institute for External Economic Affairs. He has published extensively in the Soviet and foreign scientific press on economics. He is a member of many Soviet scientific councils, editorial boards, and public societies, including the All-Union Public Economic Society where he is chairman of the international economics section.

Paul R. Lawrence is the Wallace Brett Donham Professor of Organizational Behavior at the Harvard Business School where he has been on the faculty since 1950. He is the author or co-author of 22 books and numerous articles on organizational change, organizational structure, and human resource management. A recent study with Davis Dyer, *Renewing American Industry*, addresses the issue of US competitiveness.

Alexander Naumov is an associate professor of economics at Moscow State University. He graduated from the university in 1976 with a Ph.D. in management. He is the author of *Organizing Management Improvement in Capitalist Countries* (1980) and more than 25 articles and chapters for edited volumes. Professor Naumov was a Sloan Fellow at MIT in 1975–1976, a research scholar at SUNY, Albany, in 1977, and a UN staff member in New York City from 1979 to 1985. In

337

addition, he was executive secretary to the Institute for External Economic Affairs in Moscow in 1987–1988.

Vitale Ozira is a senior research fellow at the Research Institute for External Economic Affairs. He received his M.A. in economics (1959) and a Ph.D. in management (1965) from Moscow State University. He attended the International Teachers Program at the Harvard Business School; he was a lecturer, then dean and chairman of the Management Development Department at the Soviet Institute of National Economy from 1970 to 1981. He then became a research officer in the Management Training Section of the International Labour Office in Geneva for the period 1981–1985. He is the author of over 50 articles in the fields of management development and consulting.

Sheila Puffer is an assistant professor of human resource management at the College of Business Administration, Northeastern University. She received her Ph.D. in business administration from the University of California at Berkeley. In 1979–1980, she studied management in Moscow and graduated from the Plekhanov Institute of the National Economy.

Charalambos A. Vlachoutsicos, a Greek businessman, received his M.B.A. from the Harvard Business School. Since 1956 he has been engaged in trade with the Soviet Union and other socialist countries. He is chairman of the East-West Committee of the Hellenic chapter of the International Chamber of Commerce; a member of the joint Soviet–ICC task force on joint ventures in the USSR. He is also a fellow of the Russian Research Center at Harvard University and a research fellow at the Harvard Business School. He has published articles and papers on subjects relating to East–West trade.

Elise Walton is a Ph.D. candidate at the organizational behavior program at Harvard University. She has a B.A. from Bowdoin College and an M.A. in organizational psychology from Columbia University. She has worked with numerous US firms and with firms in Yugoslavia.

Selected Bibliography

Aganbegyan, Abel. *The Economic Challenge of Perestroika.* Bloomington: Indiana University Press, 1988.

Andrle, Vladimir. *Managerial Power in the Soviet Union.* Lexington, MA: Lexington Books, 1976.

Armstrong, John. "Sources of Administrative Behavior: Some Soviet and Western European Comparisons," *The American Political Science Review* 59 (September 1965), pp. 651–653.

Badaracco, Joseph, Jr. "Changing Forms of the Corporation," in John R. Meyer and James M. Gustafson (eds.), *The U.S. Business Corporation: An Institution in Transition.* Cambridge, MA: Ballinger, 1988.

Baldwin, Corliss. "Strategic Capital Budgeting: The Case of New Product Introduction." Working paper, Harvard Business School, January 1988.

Ball, Alan. *Russia's Last Capitalists: The Nepmen 1921–1929.* Berkeley: University of California Press, 1987.

Baranson, J. "Ideology versus Innovation in Soviet Industry," *World Economics* (March 1987), pp. 85–96.

Barnard, Chester. *Functions of the Executive.* Cambridge, MA: Harvard University Press, 1946.

Beissinger, Mark. *Scientific Management, Socialist Discipline, and Soviet Power.* Cambridge, MA: Harvard University Press, 1988.

Berliner, Joseph. *Factory and Manager in the USSR.* Cambridge, MA: Harvard University Press, 1957.

———. *The Innovation Decision in Soviet Industry.* Cambridge, MA: MIT Press, 1976.

———. "Soviet Management from Stalin to Gorbachev: A Comparison of the Harvard Project and SIP Interviews." Working paper 203, Brandeis University Department of Economics, 1988.

Bhide, Amarnath. "The Causes and Consequences of Hostile Takeovers." Dissertation, Harvard Business School, 1987.

Billington, James. *The Icon and the Axe.* New York: Vintage Books, 1970.

Bornstein, Morris (ed.). *The Soviet Economy: Continuity and Change.* Boulder, CO: Westview Press, 1981.

Bower, J. *Managing the Resource Allocation Process.* Boston: Division of Research, Harvard Business School, 1970.

Burns, T., and A. Stalker. *The Management of Innovation.* London: Tavistock Press, 1973.

Bushnell, John. "Peasants in Uniform: The Tsarist Army as a Peasant Society," *Journal of Social History* (Summer 1980), pp. 565–576.

Conyngham, William. *The Modernization of Soviet Industrial Management.* Cambridge: Cambridge University Press, 1982.

Cyert, Richard, and James March. *A Behavioral Theory of the Firm.* Englewood Cliffs, NJ: Prentice-Hall, 1963.

Davis, Stanley, and Paul Lawrence. *Matrix.* Reading, MA: Addison-Wesley, 1977.

de Pauw, John. *Soviet/American Trade Negotiations.* New York: Praeger, 1979.

Egiazaryan, G. A. (ed.). *Radical Reform of Business (or economic) Management.* Moscow: Ekonomika, 1988.

Eklof, Ben. *Russian Peasant Schools: Officialdom, Village Culture, and Popular Pedagogy.* Berkeley: University of California Press, 1986.

Engelgardt, A. N. *From the Village: 12 Letters, 1872–1887.* Moscow: Mysl, 1987.

Ericson, Richard E. "The New Enterprise Law." *Harriman Institute Forum,* vol. 1, no. 2 (February 1988), pp. 1–8.

Faminsky, I. P. *USSR New Business Opportunities.* Moscow: Vneshtorgizdat, 1988.

Feonova, L. A., et al. *Organization and Techniques of the Foreign Trade of the USSR.* Moscow: I.M.O., 1974.

Galbraith, J. *Designing Complex Organizations.* Reading, MA: Addison-Wesley, 1973.

Galuska, P., W. D. Marbach, R. Brady, B. Javetski, and G. Schares. "Soviet Technology," *BusinessWeek* (November 7, 1988), pp. 68–78.

Gorbachev, Mikhail. "Political Review of the Twenty-seventh Congress." Speech, February 25, 1986.

———. *Perestroika: New Thinking for Our Country and the World.* New York: Harper & Row, 1987.

———. Review of the Seventy Years of the Socialistic Evolution. Speech, Fall 1987.

Graham, L. R. "Gorbachev's great experiment," *Issues in Science and Technology* (Winter 1988), pp. 23–32.

Granick, David. *Management of the Industrial Firm in the USSR: A Study in Soviet Economics Planning.* New York: Columbia University Press, 1955.

———. *The Red Executive: A Study of the Organization Man in Russian Industry.* New York: Doubleday, 1960.

———. *Managerial Comparisons of Four Developed Countries: France, Britain, U.S. and Russia.* Cambridge, MA: MIT Press, 1972.

Gustafson, Thane. *Soviet Negotiating Strategy: The East/West Pipeline Deal.* Santa Monica, CA: Rand Corporation, 1985.

Hanson, P. "The economics of research and development, some East–West comparisons," *European Economic Review* 32 (1988), pp. 604–610.

Hofman, Erik. "Changing Soviet Perspectives on Leadership and Administration," in Stephen Cohen (ed.), *The Soviet Union since Stalin.* Bloomington: Indiana University Press, 1980, pp. 71–82.

Hopps, Eric. "Peasants and Politics," *The Journal of Peasant Studies,* vol. 1, no. 1 (1973), pp. 3–22.

Hough, Jerry. *Opening Up the Soviet Economy.* Washington, DC: The Brookings Institution, 1988.

International Chamber of Commerce and USSR Chamber of Commerce and Industry, *Guide to Joint Ventures in the USSR.* Paris: ICC Publishing S.A., 1988.

Johnston, Russell, and Paul Lawrence. "Beyond Vertical Integration—The Rise of the Value-Adding Partnership," *Harvard Business Review* (July–August 1988), pp. 94–101.

Klyuchevskiy, Vasily O. *Works in 9 Volumes. Vol. I Russian History.* Moscow: Mysl, 1987.

Kozlov, I. M. *Collegiality and One-Man Management in Soviet State Administration.* Moscow: State Legal Press, 1956.

Kuromiya, Hiroaki. "Edinonachalie and the Soviet Industrial Manager 1928–1937," *Soviet Studies* (April 1984), pp. 185–204.

Larson, E. W., and D. H. Gobeli. "Organizing for product development projects," *Journal of Product Innovation Management* 5 (1988) pp. 180–190.

Lawrence, P., and D. Dyer. *Renewing American Industry.* New York: Free Press, 1983.

Lawrence, P., and J. Lorsch. *Organization and Environment.* Boston: Division of Research, Harvard Business School, 1967.

Lenin, V. I. *Complete Collection of Works.* Moscow: Politizdat, 1968.

Lindblom, Charles. *The Intelligence of Democracy.* New York: Free Press, 1965.

Linnemann, H., J. P. Pronk, and J. Tinbergen. "Convergence of Economic Systems in East and West," in Morry Bornstein and D. Fusfeld (eds.), *The Soviet Economy.* Homewood, IL: Irwin, 1970.

March, James, and Johan Olsen. *Ambiguity and Choice in Organization.* Bergen, Norway: Universitetsforlaget, 1976.

March, James, and Herbert Simon. *Organizations.* New York: John Wiley, 1958.

Matosich, A. J., and B. Matosich. "Machine building: Perestroika's sputtering engine," *Soviet Economy* 4 (1988), pp. 144–176.

Milner, B., V. Rapoport, and L. Yvenko. *Design of Management Systems in USSR Industry: A Systems Approach.* Dordecht, The Netherlands: D. Reidel, 1987.

Mosley, Philip. "Some Soviet Techniques of Negotiation," in R. Dennett and J. Johnson (eds.), *Negotiating with the Russians.* Boston: World Peace Foundation, 1951.

Naylor, T. H. "The reeducation of soviet management," *Across the Board* (February 1988), pp. 28–37.

"Negotiating Joint Ventures in the Soviet Union," *International Financial Law Review* (November 1988), pp. 34–38.

"On Radical Reform for Managing the Economy." Collection of documents. Moscow: Politizdat, 1988.

Pfeffer, Jeffrey, and Gerald Salancik. *The External Control of Organizations.* New York: Harper & Row, 1978.

Piskotin, M. I. *Socialism and State Management,* 2d ed. Moscow: Nauka, 1988.

Popov, G. Kh. *Effective Management,* 2d ed. Moscow: Ekonomika, 1985.

Protopopov, V. A., ed. *Managing the Socialist Economy.* 3d ed. Moscow: Moshovskiy Rahochiiy, 1986.

Quinn, James Brian. *Strategies for Change: Logical Instrumentalism.* Homewood, IL: Irwin, 1980.

Ragzievnkij, A. I. *Centralization and Independence.* Moscow: Ekonomika, 1987.

Richman, Barry. *Soviet Management: With Significant American Comparisons.* Englewood Cliffs, NJ: Prentice-Hall, 1965.

Safronova, I. P. *One-Man Management and Collegiality in the Socialist Industrial Enterprise.* Kiev, 1978.

Schroeder, G. E. "Organizations and hierarchies: the perennial search for solution," *Comparative Economic Studies* 29 [4] (1988), pp. 7–28.

Shorina, E. V. *Collegiality and One-Man Management in Soviet Administration.* Moscow, 1959.

Simon, Herbert. *Administrative Behavior.* New York: Free Press, 1976.

Sloss, Leon, and M. Scott Davis. *A Game for High Stakes: Lessons Learned in Negotiating with the Soviet Union.* Cambridge, MA: Ballinger, 1986.

Smith, Adam. *The Wealth of Nations.* New York: Modern Library, 1937.

Solovev, S. M. *Works in 18 Books.* Moscow: Mysl, 1988.

Sutton, Antony C. *Western Technology and Soviet Economic Development 1917–1930.* Stanford, CA: Hoover Institution, 1968.

Therrien, L., and P. Finch. "Mr. Rust Belt," *BusinessWeek* (October 17, 1988), pp. 72–83.

Thompson, James. *Organizations in Action.* New York: McGraw-Hill, 1967.

Turner, Frederick. *The Frontier in American History.* Huntington, NY: Krieger, 1976.

Vikhanskiiy, O. S. *Historical Experience of the USSR National Economy Management System Development, Part One: Forming the Fundamentals of the Management System.* Moscow: Moscow State University, 1988.

Vlachoutsicos, Charalambos. "Where the Ruble Stops in Soviet Foreign Trade," *Harvard Business Review* (September–October 1986), pp. 67–79.

———. "How Small to Mid-Sized Firms Can Profit from Perestroika." Working paper 89-025, Harvard Business School, 1988.

———. "What Business with the Soviets? Current Soviet Priorities and Business Opportunities for American Companies beyond the Sphere of Strategic High Technology." *Columbia Journal of World Business* 23 (Summer 1988), pp. 67–79.

Waller, Michael. *Democratic Centralism: An Historical Commentary.* New York: St. Martin's, 1981.

Weber, Max. *The Protestant Ethic and the Spirit of Capitalism.* New York: Scribner's, 1930.

Zelenevskiiy, Yan. *Organizing the Labor Collective.* Moscow: Progress, 1971.

Index

343